AGING AND WORK IN THE 21ST CENTURY

Aging and Work in the 21st Century, Second Edition reviews, summarizes, and integrates existing literature from various disciplines with regard to aging and work, but with a focus on recent advances in the field. Chapter authors, all leading experts within their respective areas, provide recommendations for future research, practice, and/or public policy. Fully revised and updated, the second edition takes up many of the same critical topics addressed in the first edition, and incorporates 18 new authors across the volume and three brand new chapters on recruitment and retention, legal issues, and global issues in work and aging.

The intended audience is advanced undergraduate and graduate students, as well as researchers in the disciplines of industrial and organizational psychology, developmental psychology, gerontology, sociology, economics, and social work. Older worker advocate organizations, such as AARP, will also take an interest in this edited book.

Kenneth S. Shultz is a Professor of Psychology and Director of the Master of Science in I/O Psychology program at California State University, San Bernardino, USA.

Gary A. Adams is Professor of Management and Director of the Master of Science in Human Resources program at Marquette University, USA.

Series in Applied Psychology
Series Editors
Jeanette N. Cleveland
Colorado State University
Kevin R. Murphy
Landy Litigation and Colorado State University

Edwin A. Fleishman, Founding Series Editor (1987–2010)

Bridging both academic and applied interests, the Applied Psychology Series offers publications that emphasize state-of-the-art research and its application to important issues of human behavior in a variety of societal settings. To date, more than 50 books in various fields of applied psychology have been published in this series.

Human Error
Cause, Prediction, and Reduction
John W. Senders and Neville P. Moray

Psychology in Organizations
Integrating Science and Practice
Kevin R. Murphy and Frank E. Saal

Patterns of Life History
The Ecology of Human Individuality
Michael D. Mumford, Garnett Stokes, and William A. Owens

Work Motivation
Uwe E. Kleinbeck, Hans-Henning Quast, Henk Thierry, and Hartmut Häcker

Teamwork and the Bottom Line
Groups Make a Difference
Ned Rosen

Aging and Work in the 21st Century
Second Edition
Edited by Kenneth S. Shultz and Gary A. Adams

AGING AND WORK IN THE 21ST CENTURY

Second Edition

Edited by
Kenneth S. Shultz and
Gary A. Adams

Routledge
Taylor & Francis Group

NEW YORK AND LONDON

Second edition published 2019
by Routledge
711 Third Avenue, New York, NY 10017

and by Routledge
2 Park Square, Milton Park, Abingdon, Oxon, OX14 4RN

Routledge is an imprint of the Taylor & Francis Group, an informa business

© 2019 Taylor & Francis

The right of Kenneth S. Shultz and Gary A. Adams to be identified as authors of this work has been asserted by them in accordance with sections 77 and 78 of the Copyright, Designs and Patents Act 1988.

All rights reserved. No part of this book may be reprinted or reproduced or utilized in any form or by any electronic, mechanical, or other means, now known or hereafter invented, including photocopying and recording, or in any information storage or retrieval system, without permission in writing from the publishers.

Trademark notice: Product or corporate names may be trademarks or registered trademarks, and are used only for identification and explanation without intent to infringe.

First edition published by Lawrence Erlbaum Associates 2007

Library of Congress Cataloging-in-Publication Data
A catalog record has been requested for this book

ISBN: 978-1-138-05274-1 (hbk)
ISBN: 978-1-138-05276-5 (pbk)
ISBN: 978-1-315-16760-2 (ebk)

Typeset in Bembo
by Wearset Ltd, Boldon, Tyne and Wear

For my endlessly supportive family – Deb, Benjamin, Amanda, Socks, and Roxy – KSS

For Ben and Will, my two wonderful wonderful sons – GAA

CONTENTS

Notes on Contributors ix
Series Foreword xv
Preface xvii

1 Introduction and Overview 1
   Gary A. Adams and Kenneth S. Shultz

2 Recruiting and Retaining Older Employees: Planning, Designing, Implementing, and Evaluating Programs 13
   Mary Anne Taylor

3 Diversity Issues for an Aging Workforce: A Lifespan Intersectionality Approach 34
   Jennica Webster, Christian Thoroughgood, and Katina Sawyer

4 An Expanded View of Age Bias in the Workplace 59
   Lisa M. Finkelstein, Elizabeth A. Hanrahan, and Courtney L. Thomas

5 Legal Issues and the Aging Workforce 102
   E. Patrick McDermott and Caren B. Goldberg

6 Employee Age and Performance in Organizations 123
   Jerry W. Hedge and Walter C. Borman

7 Age(ing) and Work Attitudes   146
   Janet L. Barnes-Farrell, Gretchen A. Petery,
   Jeanette N. Cleveland, and Russell A. Matthews

8 Employee Development and Training Issues Related to
   the Aging Workplace   171
   Deborah A. Olson and Debora Jeske

9 Career Embeddedness and Career Crafting among
   Older Workers   191
   Daniel C. Feldman and Kenneth S. Shultz

10 Aging and Occupational Health   213
   Yisheng Peng, Steve M. Jex, and Mo Wang

11 Age and Technology for Work   234
   Neil Charness and Sara J. Czaja

12 Age and Work–Family Issues   255
   Reed J. Bramble, Emma K. Duerk, and Boris B. Baltes

13 Retirement from Three Perspectives: Individuals,
   Organizations, and Society   273
   Minseo Kim and Terry A. Beehr

14 Global Issues in Work, Aging, and Retirement   292
   Cort W. Rudolph, Justin Marcus, and Hannes Zacher

Name Index   *325*
Subject Index   *330*

CONTRIBUTORS

Editors

Gary A. Adams, PhD, is Professor of Management and Director of the Master of Science in Human Resources program in the College of Business at Marquette University. He received his PhD from Central Michigan University. Dr Adams has taught a variety of courses including those in the areas of organizational behavior and human resources management, as well as research methods, multivariate statistics, and occupational stress. In addition to his teaching, Dr Adams also enjoys conducting research and consulting to business organizations. His research interests include older workers and occupational health. He has made professional presentations at national conferences such as those sponsored by the American Psychological Association, the Society for Industrial and Organizational Psychology and the Academy of Management. He has published two books, several book chapters, and a number of articles in journals such as *Personnel Psychology*, *Journal of Applied Psychology*, *Journal of Occupational Health Psychology*, *Journal of Organizational Behavior*, and *American Psychologist*.

Kenneth S. Shultz, PhD, is a Professor in the Psychology Department at California State University, San Bernardino. His degree is in industrial and organizational psychology from Wayne State University in Detroit, Michigan. He also completed postdoctoral work as a National Institute on Aging Postdoctoral Fellow in gerontology at the Andrus Gerontology Center at the University of Southern California. He has more than 50 publications (including a dozen book chapters and several encyclopedia entries) and more than 100 presentations on a variety of topics, most recently focusing on aging workforce and retirement issues. He also has three other co-authored books: *Measurement*

Theory in Action: Case Studies and Exercises (2nd edition) and *Mid and Late Career Issues: An Integrative Perspective*, both published by Routledge, and *Happy Retirement: The Psychology of Reinvention*, published by DK Publishing.

Contributing Authors

Gary A. Adams, PhD, is a Professor at Marquette University where he directs the Master of Science in Human Resources Management program. He has published two books, several book chapters, and a number of articles in peer-reviewed journals on topics related to aging, diversity, and occupational stress.

Boris B. Baltes, PhD, is a Professor and Chair of the Department of Psychology at Wayne State University. His research interests include age and workplace issues, and work–family balance. He is well-known for his meta-analysis contributions, including those on flexible work weeks, perceptions of older workers, and psychological climate perceptions.

Janet L. Barnes-Farrell, PhD, is Professor of Psychological Sciences at the University of Connecticut and a Fellow of the Society for Industrial and Organizational Psychology. She has been conducting research on issues related to our aging workforce for over three decades; her work includes publications and presentations on the workplace concerns of older workers on topics ranging from age discrimination to retirement decision processes.

Terry A. Beehr, PhD, is a Professor in the I/O Psychology affiliated with the PhD program at Central Michigan University. His research interests include organizational psychology, retirement, occupational stress, and leadership.

Walter C. Borman, PhD, is a Professor of Psychology at the University of South Florida. He has written more than 350 books, book chapters, articles, technical reports, and conference papers in the areas of performance measurement, personnel selection, assessment, and the aging workforce.

Reed J. Bramble, MA, is a doctoral candidate of I-O Psychology and Institute of Gerontology fellow at Wayne State University. He has contributed to several book chapters and publications pertaining to the aging workforce, particularly centering on age-related changes in attitudes, motivation, and values.

Neil Charness, PhD, is the William G. Chase Professor of Psychology and Director of the Institute for Successful Longevity at Florida State University. He has published over 200 articles, book chapters, and technical reports, and three co-authored books. His research focuses on aging and technology use.

Jeanette N. Cleveland, PhD, is Professor of I-O Psychology at Colorado State University. She is an elected Fellow of SIOP (Division 14 of APA) and the American Psychological Association. Her books include, *Performance Appraisal and Management*, *Understanding Performance Appraisal: Social, Organizational and Goal Perspectives*, and *Women and Men in Organizations: Sex and Gender Issues*.

Sara J. Czaja, PhD, is a Leonard M. Miller Professor of Psychiatry and Behavioral Sciences, and also the Director of the Center on Aging at the University of Miami Miller School of Medicine and the Director of the Center on Research and Education for Aging and Technology Enhancement (CREATE).

Emma K. Duerk, MA, is a doctoral student of I-O Psychology at Wayne State University. Her primary research interests focus on the role of caregiving responsibilities in the work–family domain. She is also interested in studying the experiences of minority individuals in the workforce, such as those of elderly individuals, pregnant women, and child-free individuals.

Daniel C. Feldman, PhD, is the Synovus Chair of Leadership Emeritus and the former Senior Associate Dean at the University of Georgia. He has authored seven books and 200 articles on career development and his research has been featured in the *Wall Street Journal*, *Business Week*, and other major media outlets.

Lisa M. Finkelstein, PhD, is a Professor of Industrial/Organizational Psychology at Northern Illinois University. Her research contributions are primarily in age stereotyping, meta-stereotyping, and discrimination, generation myth debunking, stigma in the workplace, mentoring relationships and behaviors, high potential identification, and humor at work. She serves on several editorial boards and is a Fellow of SIOP.

Caren B. Goldberg, PhD, is an Associate Professor at Bowie State University, whose research focuses on diversity and sexual harassment. Her work has been published in a variety of Management and Women's Studies journals. She is currently serving as Treasurer of the Gender and Diversity in Organizations Division of the Academy of Management and is on the editorial boards of several journals. Dr Goldberg has also testified in over a dozen employment law matters.

Elizabeth A. Hanrahan, MA, is a doctoral candidate at Northern Illinois University. Her research centers on stereotypes in the workplace and high potential programs. She is also a consultant for Vaya Group, a talent management consultancy.

Jerry W. Hedge, PhD, is the Senior Program Director for Workforce and Organizational Effectiveness at RTI International. He has published four books, and numerous book chapters, journal articles, and technical reports on topics such as performance measurement, the aging workforce, program evaluation, and technology acceptance.

Debora Jeske, PhD, is a Work and Organizational Psychologist in the School of Applied Psychology at University College Cork, Ireland. She has published in a number of areas, including work psychology and HRM. Her research focuses mainly on the use and influence of technology in the workplace.

Steve M. Jex, PhD, is currently Professor of Psychology at the University of Central Florida where he directs the PhD program in I/O Psychology. His research focuses primarily on occupational stress, employee health, and retirement decision making.

Minseo Kim, PhD, earned her PhD from Central Michigan University with a major in Industrial and Organizational Psychology. Her research interests include occupational stress, leadership, motivation, careers, job crafting, and employee well-being.

Justin Marcus, PhD, is an Assistant Professor in the College of Administrative Sciences and Economics at Koç University in Istanbul, Turkey. He has authored a number of book chapters and articles in peer-reviewed journals, such as *The Gerontologist*, focusing on topics related to older workers, and cross-cultural organizational behavior.

Russell A. Matthews, PhD, is the Miller Professor of Management and Associate Professor in the Department of Management in The Culverhouse College of Commerce at the University of Alabama. His research focuses on employee attitudes, health, safety, and well-being. He has published extensively in various journals, including *Journal of Applied Psychology Journal of Organizational Behavior*, and *Journal of Occupational Health Psychology*.

E. Patrick McDermott, PhD, JD, is a Professor of Management and Legal Studies at the Franklin P. Perdue School of Business and Director of Research and Evaluation at the Center for Conflict Resolution at Salisbury University. He has written a book and numerous law review and peer reviewed journal articles on workplace conflict and legal issues. He litigates labor and employment law cases in state and federal court.

Deborah A. Olson, PhD, is a Professor of Leadership and Management at the University of La Verne. She has published books, book chapters and journal articles in the areas of mid/late careers, leadership development, and human resource management.

Yisheng Peng, PhD, is an Assistant Professor at Hofstra University where he works in the Applied Organizational Psychology program. His research mainly focuses on aging and employee health, emotional aging, workplace mistreatment, bridge employment, and eldercare issues.

Gretchen A. Petery, PhD, is currently a post-doctoral research fellow at the Centre for Transformative Work Design at the University of Western Australia. Her research takes an occupational health psychology perspective and revolves around aging workers, specifically examining issues such as age discrimination, alternative measures of age, and health and well-being.

Cort W. Rudolph, PhD, is an Assistant Professor of Industrial & Organizational Psychology at Saint Louis University. He received his BA from DePaul University, and his MA and PhD from Wayne State University. Dr Rudolph's research focuses on a range of issues related to the aging workforce, including the application of lifespan theoretical perspectives, career development, successful aging, proactivity, wellbeing, and ageism.

Katina Sawyer, PhD, is an Assistant Professor at Villanova University, within the Graduate Programs in Human Resource Development. She has published several book chapters and a number of articles in peer-reviewed journals on topics related to work–family balance, diversity, and leadership.

Kenneth S. Shultz, PhD, teaches in the Psychology Department at California State University, San Bernardino. He has published over 50 articles and a dozen book chapters, primarily on aging and work. In addition, he has also published three books on aging, work, and retirement, and one on psychometrics.

Mary Anne Taylor, PhD, is a Professor of Industrial/Organizational Psychology at Clemson University. She has published book chapters and articles in the areas of recruiting and retaining older employees, and on retirement adjustment. She also has field experience in these areas.

Courtney L. Thomas, BS, is a doctoral candidate in I/O psychology at Northern Illinois University. Her research centers on person perception and discrimination processes related to a variety of social categories, including age, in a workplace setting.

Christian Thoroughgood, PhD, is an Assistant Professor at Villanova University in the Graduate Programs in Human Resource Development. He has published a number of peer-reviewed journal articles and book chapters. His research focuses on leadership, workplace diversity, co-worker envy, and mindfulness in organizations.

Mo Wang, PhD, is the Lanzillotti-McKethan Eminent Scholar Chair at the Warrington College of Business at the University of Florida. He has published more than 100 peer-reviewed journal articles and his research has been featured on the BBC, NPR, in the *Wall Street Journal*, and other major media outlets.

Jennica Webster, PhD, is an Associate Professor in the Management Department at Marquette University. Her research interests center on occupational health and well-being with an emphasis on gender, diversity, and underrepresented groups. She has published several book chapters and peer-reviewed articles in these areas.

Hannes Zacher, PhD, is Full Professor of work and organizational psychology at Leipzig University, Germany. He received his PhD from the University of Giessen. In his research program, he investigates successful aging at work, career development, proactive behavior, occupational well-being, and the work–nonwork interface.

SERIES FOREWORD

The goal of the Applied Psychology Series is to create books that exemplify the use of scientific research, theory and findings to help solve real problems in organizations and society. Shultz and Adams' *Aging and Work in the 21st Century, Second Edition* is an example of this approach. The first edition of this book, published in 2007, quickly became established as the go-to reference for research on virtually every aspect of the relationships between age and work and the experiences of older workers. Research in this field is rapidly growing and advancing our knowledge on a number of topics. This new edition examines a wide range of issues that the aging of the workforce brings to the fore.

The current edition includes 14 chapters dealing with issues including stereotypes and discrimination, aging and health, work–family challenges of older workers, age and job performance. Every chapter is either new or substantially revised. The 2019 edition includes new information on topics such as the recruitment and retention of older workers, intersectionality of age and other diversity factors that might lead to differential treatment in the workplace, advances in our understanding of age bias, legal protections for older workers, age and job performance, age and work attitudes, age and employee development, career change, occupational health, coping with technological change, work–family challenges faced by older workers, retirement, and cross-cultural perspectives on aging.

The chapters in this volume are thorough, thought-provoking, and cover a broad range of important, current or emerging workplace issues. Like the first edition, *Aging and Work in the 21st Century, Second Edition* is likely to become an essential resource for both researchers and practitioners that will have an impact on future research questions as well as on the application of science-based practice.

Shultz and Adams' first edition was an important addition to this series, and we are thrilled to add *Aging and Work in the 21st Century, Second Edition* to the Applied Psychology Series. This book accomplishes the goals that exemplify the Series, bringing together the best scholarship, and new and emerging ideas to address problems that are becoming increasingly important in the workplace.

Kevin R. Murphy
Jeanette N. Cleveland

PREFACE

Population aging is a global phenomenon that is bringing with it an aging of the workforce for nearly every country in the world. Given the sheer size of this phenomenon and the centrality of work to people's lives and livelihoods, as well the importance of the workforce to organizations and the economy, researchers, organizational decision-makers, those interested in public policy, and even the general public have shown an increased interest in better understanding issues associated with an aging workforce. Our contention is that a better understanding of this topic requires a comprehensive review of the theoretical and empirical literature with an eye toward identifying both recommendations for applied practice and future research needs. Thus, we set out to do just that in this updated and expanded 2nd edition of *Aging and Work in the 21st Century*. We bring together the top scholars in the various areas of aging and work to provide chapters that review and summarize their respective areas. See Chapter 1 for a quick overview of the remaining chapters in this edited book.

Approach

Rather than adopt a particular theoretical or disciplinary approach, the authors of each chapter focus on a specific topic related to aging and work, integrating theory and the various interdisciplinary literatures as appropriate, related to that given topic. Additionally, the issues involving aging and work revolve around not only the individual worker, but also the employing organizations and society in general. Therefore, each chapter addresses and incorporates material relevant to each of these major constituents. While the chapter authors describe what we do know and offer practical suggestions to address the issues that are identified, they also highlight some as yet unanswered questions and directions for future research. Many of the authors also provide cases, exercises, or examples, in order to more fully illustrate the issues discussed in their chapter. We hope that inclusion of these additional materials in the chapters will help the reader gain an even better appreciation of the issues related to aging and work espoused in each chapter.

Audience

The primary audience for this book is advanced undergraduate and graduate students, as well as scholars in both academic and applied settings. The disciplines of industrial and organizational psychology, developmental psychology, gerontology, sociology, economics, and social work (that study aging work force issues) serve as the primary audience. However, while the book is intended primarily as a reference text for students and scholars, organizational decision makers, public policy makers, and older worker advocates (e.g., AARP) will also have a keen interest in the various topics discussed in this book.

What's New to the Second Edition

The first edition of *Aging and Work in the 21st Century* was published in 2007 by Lawrence Erlbaum (now part of Taylor & Francis). Its major aims were to review, summarize, and integrate the extant literature on a wide variety of issues related to aging and work. At that time, we noted the importance of the progressive aging of the baby boomers to some of the most critical issues related to work. Among these were topics such as the importance of aging to job performance, work-related attitudes, technology, careers, and occupational health, to name a few.

The impact of the aging workforce for all of these topics remains as relevant today as it was some dozen years ago. However, in the decade plus since the first edition was published there have been significant advances in the literature. Both the quantity and quality of research on aging and work has increased exponentially. It is now common to see articles on aging and work published in leading journals and new journals aimed specifically at publishing research on the aging workforce have been established (e.g., the new Oxford University Press journal – *Work, Aging and Retirement*). Key concepts such as the meaning of age itself have evolved from a simple count of years into concepts such as subjective age, social age, and age identity. The notion of aging has evolved from a focus on growing older to encompass concepts such as successful aging and productive aging. In addition, the nature of work, bridge employment, and retirement have all also continued to evolve in the last decade. The economic downturn and "great recession" that started right after the publication of the first edition had important effects on older workers, those who were retired or planning to retire, as well as public and private retirement funding mechanisms.

Continued advances in the area of technology and the use of automation have had important implications for the aging workforce, as have changing social norms and values around such topics as diversity and inclusion.

All of these developments suggested it was time to prepare a revised and updated second edition of *Aging and Work in the 21st Century*. Thus, the primary aim of the book is again to review, summarize, and integrate the extant literature on a wide variety of issues related to aging and work, but with a focus on recent advances in the field. We believe this updated and expanded edited text will have a profound influence on the next generation of students, scholars, organizational decision makers, and public policy professionals.

In terms of what's new, the second edition of the book includes three brand new chapters by leading authors in their respective areas. These include new chapters on the Recruitment and Retention of Older Workers; Legal Issues and the Aging Workforce; and Global Issues in Work and Aging. In addition, six of the existing chapters have new lead authors and more than a dozen of the authors in total are new to this edition of the book. Of course, all the chapters include the most up-to-date research and theorizing on their respective areas of aging and work in the 21st century.

Acknowledgments

We would like to thank numerous individuals who provided assistance in various phases of the development and completion of this book. First, we thank Jan Cleveland and Kevin Murphy, the Applied Psychology Series Editors for encouraging us and providing the impetus for working on a second edition of this edited book. We are, of course, first and foremost indebted to the authors who agreed to write chapters for this edited volume and are appreciative of their timeliness in submitting drafts and the final versions of their chapters. Most chapter authors also provided a friendly peer review of at least one other chapter in this book. Thus, this book would obviously not be possible without their fine work. Thanks also go out to those who reviewed the prospectus for this book and/or the final manuscript, providing helpful suggestions for improvement. Our colleagues Eric Dunleavy, Jackie James, Leslie Hammer, Ariane Froidevaux, and Kène Henkens also provided reviews of various chapters in this work. We thank them for their keen insights and suggestions for improvements of the various chapters. Last, but certainly not least, we thank our respective families and friends for their support and encouragement as we completed this book.

Kenneth S. Shultz
Gary A. Adams

1
INTRODUCTION AND OVERVIEW

Gary A. Adams and Kenneth S. Shultz

In the current chapter we seek to set the stage for those that follow. We begin by introducing both population aging and labor force participation as the key trends that lead to an aging workforce. Then we discuss current projections surrounding labor force participation rates of older workers and the impact of these on the size and composition of the workforce. Following this, we describe how the text unfolds and we highlight some of the key findings and issues raised by each chapter. In doing so, we provide the reader with a broad view of aging and work in the 21st century and a sense of the interconnectedness of the topics covered.

The Aging Population

The world's population was gradually aging over the second half of the last century and it will continue to do so at an accelerating rate well into the 21st century (United Nations, 2017). Between 1950 and 2000 the median age of the population worldwide increased from 24 years old to 27 years old, and it is projected to increase rapidly through 2050 when it will reach 37 years old. In more developed countries the median age has already risen quickly – from 29 years old in 1950 to 37 years old in 2000, and it is projected to reach 45 years old by 2050. In less developed countries those ages have increased from 21 years old in 1950 to 24 years old in 2000, and to 35 years old by 2050 (projected). Both the absolute increase in the age of the population and the rate at which population aging is occurring is unprecedented in recorded history (United Nations, 2017).

The key driver of population aging is a pattern of fertility and mortality rates that occur over time, generally referred to as demographic transition (Thompson, 1929). As nations and societies develop, they experience decreasing fertility rates (births) and decreasing mortality rates (deaths). This pattern occurs as the result of improvements in health, education, and socioeconomic status, as well as increased economic opportunity that accompany development. A fertility rate of 2.1 births per woman is necessary to stabilize a population. This is the replacement rate. Decreasing fertility rates reduce the number of young people in subsequent cohorts. As the fertility rate approaches and falls below the replacement rate, the number of young people in subsequent age cohorts drops precipitously and they become fewer in number than the number of older people in the population. Decreasing mortality has the effect of leaving more people alive to reach older ages and also by extending the number of years in old age that they will live. The combination of successively smaller numbers of younger people and larger, longer-living numbers of older people results in population aging.

These aging trends are well underway worldwide. The global fertility rate has dropped from 4.5 live births per woman in the 1970–1975 timeframe to 2.5 in 2010–2015 and it is expected to decline to 2.4 by 2025–2030 (United Nations, 2015). Further, nearly half of the world's population lives in countries with near or below replacement rate fertility levels. These include all of Europe, North America, and almost all of Asia, as well as Latin America and the Caribbean. With regard to mortality declines, the average life expectancy around the world in 1950 was 47 years old, but by 2000 that number had risen to 65 years old and it is projected to reach 76 years old by 2050. These trends result in a larger older population. As He, Goodkind, and Kowal (2015) report, between 2015 and 2050 the number of people in the world over the age of 65 is projected to increase from 617.1 million to 1.6 billion. In terms of their share of the world's total population, while people over the age of 65 accounted for 8.5 percent of the world's 7.2 billion people, it is expected that they will account for 16.7 percent of the world's 9.3 billion people by 2050. Over this same period the number of young people (under the age of 19) will remain relatively unchanged and the share of the world's population held by those in the prime working years (ages 20–64) will decrease slightly. Although there are differences across countries in the rate at which the demographic transition process is proceeding, every country in the world is affected by it.

For specific countries, such as the US, demographic transition and immigration influence the size and age distribution of the population. Figure 1.1 presents age and sex population 'pyramids' for the United States in 1950, 2000, and 2050 (projected). Looking across the three time periods, several trends are evident. First, the overall size of the population will grow over the course of the three time periods, but the growth will occur more slowly between 2000 and 2050. It should be noted that more than half of that growth is expected as a result of immigrants (who tend to be younger) coming to the country. Second, in 1950, most of the population were in their 20s and 30s and there were progressively fewer people in each of the older age groups above them. Third, the largest sized age group in

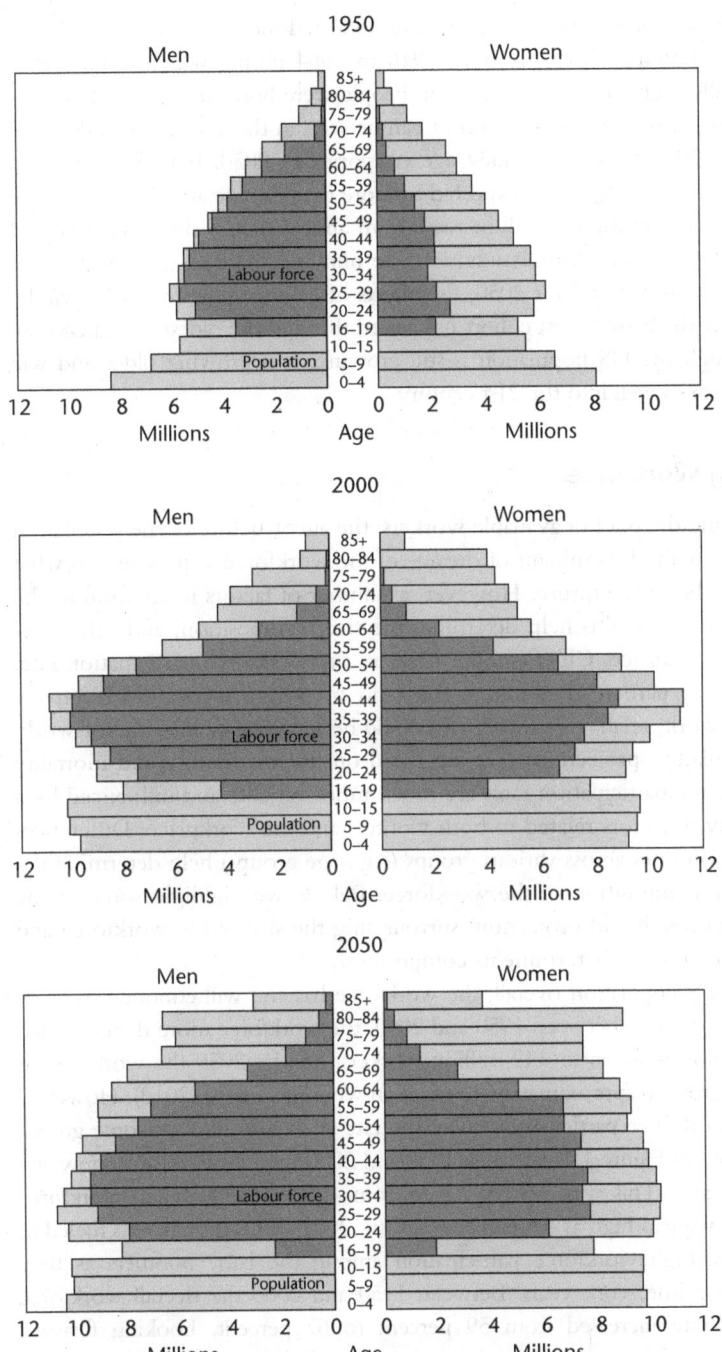

FIGURE 1.1 US population/labor force pyramid by gender.

1950 was in the youngest age category. This reflected the start of the post-World War II baby boom – that time from 1946 to 1964 during which fertility rates were generally high and some 80 million people were born in the US. The progressive aging of the baby boom cohort can be seen in the very large middle age categories in 2000 and in the oldest age categories by 2050. Between 2000 and 2050 those over the age 65 are expected to more than double and the average age of the population in the US will increase from approximately 35 to 41 years old (United Nations, 2017). Importantly, as these numbers indicate, and can be seen in the population pyramid for 2050, the effects of demographic transition will be felt even after the baby boom cohort has passed through the oldest age categories. Thus, although the US population is still growing, it is growing older and will continue to do so well into the 21st century.

The Aging Workforce

By establishing the pool of available workers, the age structure of the population overall is the main determinant of the age of the workforce at present and what it is likely to be in the future. However, a number of factors in addition to the population structure also help determine the size, composition, and other features of the workforce. Chief among these are the workforce participation rate. The workforce participation rate is the ratio of people working, or actively looking for work, relative to those who could be working or looking for work. Unlike population projections that are based on known fertility and mortality rates, workforce participation rates are much more variable and influenced by a broader array of factors related to both workers and the workplace. Differences in participation rates across various groups (e.g., age groups) help determine the demographic composition of the workforce. Below, we highlight some of the key historical trends and projections surrounding the size of the workforce and participation rates that determine its composition.

Like the US population overall, the workforce has and will continue to grow over time. In the US, between 1950 and 2000, the workforce more than doubled from 62 million workers to 142 million workers, and by 2050 the workforce is expected to grow to approximately 200 million workers (Toossi, 2012). However, changes in workforce participation affect the rate at which the workforce grows. As can be seen in Figure 1.1, between 1950 and 2000 the US workforce grew at a considerable rate. This was especially true from 1960 to 1980 when workforce growth rates were as high as 2.6 percent (Toossi, 2012). This growth was fueled in large part by high workforce participation among the baby boomers as they entered their prime work years. Between 1950 and 2000 the overall workforce participation rate increased from 59 percent to 67 percent. Looking forward however, the workforce participation rate is expected to decrease to 58 percent by 2050. As a result, the workforce is expected to grow older and at a much slower pace (<1 percent) than in previous decades (Toossi, 2012).

Differences in workforce participation rates across age groups help determine the age composition of the workforce. Based on data from the Bureau of Labor Statistics (Toossi, 2016; Toossi & Torpey, 2017) for most of the second half of the last century workforce participation by younger and prime working age workers had increased. For example, in 1950, participation among those age 16–24 and 25–54 was 60 percent and 66 percent respectively. By the 1990s those numbers had climbed to 67 percent and 84 percent. At that same time workforce participation among those over the age of 55 declined from 43 percent to 30 percent. Since that time these trends have seen a complete reversal. Workforce participation among younger workers has decreased, and especially so for workers age 16–24 (down to 55 percent), while workforce participation among older workers has increased (up to 40 percent). Looking to 2050, the growth of the workforce among those 24–54 years old is expected to remain relatively flat and, for those who are 16–24, it is actually expected to decline. However, during this same time those over the age of 55 will be the fastest growing age group and this is especially true for those over the age of 65. As a result, those over the age of 55, who accounted for 13 percent of the workforce in 2000, are expected to make up 24 percent of the workforce by 2050.

One factor underlying increased workforce participation among older workers has been the transformation that has taken place around the concept of retirement (Shultz & Wang, 2011). Beginning around 1950, retirement generally came to be viewed as a period of leisure that followed labor force exit after a lifetime of work (Feldman, 1994) and increasingly earlier retirement ages became common (at least among men). However, by the 1990s that trend toward earlier retirement ages had come to an end (Cahill, Giandrea, & Quinn, 2006) and for many older workers retirement characterized as a period of nonwork leisure also changed. Retirement began to involve various forms of work referred to as bridge employment (Shultz, 2003, Beehr & Bennett, 2015), which may involve continuing full-time or part-time work with the same or different employers, in the same or different career field, self-employment (Wang, Adams, Beehr, & Shultz, 2009) and 'unretirement' – returning to work after having been retired (Cahill, Giandrea, & Quinn, 2013). Concerns regarding personal finances, changes to public and private pension systems, better health and education, and changes in work that make it less physically demanding along with a desire to remain active and engaged have all increased the number of workers engaging in bridge employment and unretirement. This period of employment among older workers has already become important and common enough to be conceptualized as a late life career stage (Wang et al., 2009; Wang, Olson, & Shultz, 2013). Research suggests that these trends surrounding increased levels of bridge employment and unretirement are likely to continue with estimates suggesting that between 53 percent (Collinson, 2017) and 79 percent (Greenwald, Copeland, & VanDerhei, 2017) of current workers indicate that they plan to work during their retirement years. In summary, there are more older workers and they are staying in the workforce longer than before.

Workforce participation rates also affect the composition of the aging workforce in terms of sex and racial/ethnic diversity. Owing to changing social and cultural norms, legal protections, and economic conditions, women have increased their participation in the work force considerably over the past half century. Again, as can be seen in Figure 1.1, in 1950 only about one-third of women participated in paid work, but by 2000 that percentage had doubled. During that same time, men's workforce participation rate declined from over 86 percent in 1950 to just under 75 percent in 2000. These changes in workforce participation rates had the effect of changing the composition of the workforce such that women constitute a more equal share of the workforce relative to men. As these women grow older, they are likely to continue to participate in the workforce. In fact, workforce participation among women over the age of 65 has doubled since 2000 (Toossi & Morisi, 2017) and this group is expected to have the largest percentage increase in workforce participation of any age group in the coming decades (Bureau of Labor Statistics, March, 2017).

Regarding racial and ethnic diversity, as the population of the US has become more diverse, so too has the workforce. Although presently concentrated at younger ages relative to non-Hispanic whites, people with diverse backgrounds will also grow older during the 21st century. For example, while the share of the population over the age of 65 will increase, it is projected that between 2010 and 2050 this increase will be especially pronounced among racial and ethnic groups other than non-Hispanic whites (Colby & Ortman, 2014). With regard to the workforce, approximately 78 percent of the workforce is currently made up of non-Hispanic whites (Bureau of Labor Statistics, November, 2017). However, workforce participation rates among, for example Hispanics (65.9 percent) are higher than they are for non-Hispanic whites (62.8 percent; Bureau of Labor Statistics, September, 2016). Taken together, an increase in the number of people with diverse racial and ethnic backgrounds in the population combined with higher workforce participation rates suggests that these groups will expand their share of the aging workforce considerably in the future.

Overview to the Book

The dramatic, accelerating, and inevitable demographic shifts happening worldwide, in both the general population and workforce, as outlined above, necessitates a renewed look at the aging workforce in the 21st century. The implications of these shifts for a wide variety of issues, from human resources practices of hiring and retention, to training, to increasing the levels of work engagement of workers as they age, will be dramatic. Thus, we now outline and overview the key issues discussed in each of the subsequent chapters in this revised and updated edition of *Aging and Work in the 21st Century*.

In one of the several new chapters in this edition of the book, Chapter 2 by Mary Anne Taylor examines programs and practices aimed at recruiting and retaining older workers. She begins by describing how the aging workforce is contributing to the growing mismatch between the supply of skills in the labor pool and the demand for skills on the part of organizations. She then adopts a talent management perspective, which emphasizes the importance of maximizing outcomes for both workers and organizations, to recommend a four-step process that involves (1) planning, (2) designing, (3) implementing, and (4) evaluating programs for recruiting and retaining older workers. For each of these steps she identifies the issues that must be considered and reviews the research surrounding them. She also calls for a greater recognition of the heterogeneity among aging workers on the part of both researchers and practitioners interested in attracting and retaining older workers in the workforce.

In Chapter 3, Jennica Webster, Christian Thoroughgood, and Katina Sawyer, in another chapter new to this edition, on the topic of diversity, address some of the most important issues regarding heterogeneity among older workers. In their chapter, Webster, Thoroughgood, and Sawyer develop a lifespan intersectionality approach to the topic of diversity among aging workers. From a lifespan perspective, they call attention the cumulative effects of lifelong experiences of classic, overt, and modern forms of discrimination (e.g., microaggressions) on the part of workers from diverse backgrounds that impact them differently as those workers age. They use the intersectionality perspective to examine stereotypes associated with age in combination with stereotypes associated with other diverse identities. More specifically they examine how stereotypes of older workers might combine with stereotypes about visible stigmatized identities including gender and race/ethnicity, as well as 'invisible' stigmatized identities such as sexual orientation and gender identity. Recognizing that age can combine with these other stigmatized social identities to doubly or triply stigmatize older workers allows for a more nuanced approach to the experience of aging and work that can lead to better research on aging workers and practical solutions to the issues that they confront.

Continuing on the theme of stereotypes, Chapter 4 by Lisa Finkelstein, Elizabeth Hanrahan, and Courtney Thomas provides an expanded and in-depth review of age-related bias. Adopting the tripartite view, which describes attitudes in terms of cognition, affect, and behavior, they provide a state of the art review of the theoretical and empirical research on age-related bias. In doing so they describe the motives, mechanisms, contextual boundary conditions, and outcomes of age bias. Importantly, they also answer the question, what can be done about it? They offer suggestions for individuals, organizations and society. One important outcome of age bias these authors describe is discrimination in employment decisions. In the US and elsewhere there are legal protections intended to prevent discrimination against older workers when it comes to employment decisions.

In Chapter 5, another chapter that is new to this edition, E. Patrick McDermott and Caren Goldberg provide a review of these legal protections with a focus on the Age Discrimination in Employment Act (ADEA). They describe the types of discrimination charges that can be brought, the standards of proof needed, as well as the barriers to successfully litigating those charges. They also discuss a number of changes to the law and judicial rulings that have, unfortunately, eroded the protection of older workers. Looking forward, they call attention to emerging issues such as the growing "gig economy," rapidly advancing technology, and the use of social media for recruiting and screening of applicants, that all have implications for potential age bias and discrimination.

The next two chapters deal with aging and two of the most central variables of concern for both researchers and practitioners alike. These are employee performance and work-related attitudes. In Chapter 6, two authors new to this edition, Jerry Hedge and Walter Borman provide an update on the research regarding the relationship between age and performance at work. They begin by identifying the various and evolving ways in which age has been conceptualized in addition to chronological age (e.g., functional age, perceived age, relative age). They then describe research linking age to multiple dimensions of work-related performance. These include task performance, citizenship behavior, counterproductive behavior, adaptive performance, and technology performance. Conceiving of work performance broadly, they also discuss age in relation to emerging constructs such as employability, work ability, and sustainability.

In Chapter 7 on age and work attitudes, Janet Barnes-Farrell, Gretchen Petery, Jeanette Cleveland, and Russell Matthews discuss contemporary theory and research relating age to work attitudes. They too take a broad view of the research domain and consider attitudes such as global and facet job satisfaction, involvement, along with attitudes about change and development. Next, they turn their attention to motivation and motives including motivation to engage in training and development. Importantly, they not only discuss how age relates to attitudes, but also provide theoretical insights for why it does. Both chapters highlight the need for the development of human resource management practices that meet the needs of aging workers and organizations.

The discussion of job performance and work attitudes provided in the preceding chapters leads nicely to the next two chapters, which address aging related to training and development, and older workers' careers. In Chapter 8, Deborah Olson and Debora Jeske (another pair of authors new to this edition), review theory, research, and practice surrounding aging with regard to training and development. They dispel many of the inaccurate stereotypes and 'misguided' beliefs managers and aging workers themselves hold about the value of investment in training and development for aging workers and the willingness and ability of aging workers to undertake it. For example, they review research indicating that learning motivation remains relatively constant over the life course. Beyond examining traditional training activity, they also call particular attention to informal learning and job crafting as important developmental actions taken by aging workers; however, they also note that such workers are often not given these opportunities. They call attention to the importance of entrepreneurship for organizations and the contributions older workers can make in terms of creativity and innovation. Olson and Jeske recommend more intergenerational contact (e.g., through reverse mentoring) to help overcome biases and the development of inclusive and supportive training and development environments.

Next, Daniel Feldman and Ken Shultz's Chapter 9 addresses the topic of career change among older workers. In their chapter they describe the individual, job, and organizational-level factors that influence the decision of those over the age of 50 to change careers. Similar to the notion of job embeddedness, they describe the construct of career embeddedness. Career embeddedness refers to a multidimensional construct that is composed of a collection of variables that tend to tie individuals to their career. The construct of career embeddedness furthers our understanding of career change by moving our attention from strictly time-based variables (e.g., age, organizational tenure) to the underlying mechanisms for which these other variables tend to serve as proxies (e.g., involvement, personal investment, and maintaining important relationships). Then they introduce a new construct called career crafting and describe it as the ways in which workers can customize their careers. Like job crafting, it too has cognitive, task, and relational components that allow workers to tailor their careers in order to meet their career goals. This notion of career crafting holds considerable promise for helping to explain sustainable and successful careers well in to old age as well as the individual and contextual factors that facilitate or undermine those careers.

Chapter 10 by Yisheng Peng, Steve Jex, and Mo Wang tackles the issue of age and occupational health. These authors begin by reviewing the various perspectives on health and settle on the idea that health is a state of physical, psychological, and social wellbeing. In doing so, they move away from the narrow focus on physical health and the absence of disease. They then review the physical and cognitive changes that come with increasing age and their relationship to this expanded view of occupational health. They offer a number of suggestions for improving the health and wellbeing of aging workers. Among others, these include job redesign, job crafting, safety training, and health promotions programs. They also offer a number of suggestions for future research, such as those aimed at identifying those factors that may make aging workers more resilient to poor occupational health than younger workers.

Perhaps the single biggest factor that has brought about changes in the basic nature of work itself is the accelerated use of technology, particularly computer technology. Recognizing this, and the unique issues it presents to an aging workforce, Neil Charness and Sara Czaja, describe the age-related changes in attention, perception, cognitive, and psychomotor abilities that influence the use of technology in their update to Chapter 11. An important conclusion in their chapter is that aging workers are both willing and able to use technology, but there are steps that can be taken to enhance this willingness and ability. Accordingly, they provide a series of recommendations for the design of training programs and the computer software that are aimed at increasing aging workers' effective use of technology.

In the first edition of this book it may have seemed odd to have a chapter on aging and work/family issues. As pointed out in that first edition however, the basic issue of balancing the competing demands of the two most influential spheres of adult life is no less salient for aging workers than it is for younger workers. The amount of research investigating and examining aging and the interface between work and family has grown considerably in the last decade since the publication of the first edition of this book. Therefore, Reed Bramble, Emma Duerk, and Boris B. Baltes review, in Chapter 12, the research in this area and note some of the different priorities and demands faced by older, as opposed to younger, workers. They also discuss differences in coping strategies and resources that aging workers use to meet both work and nonwork demands. They then focus on the issue of eldercare; an issue increasingly salient to many older workers. They describe three theories of aging and work to help explain why balancing work and nonwork would be of particular importance to aging workers. The chapter concludes with a number of recommendations for practices that can help aging workers balance work and family (e.g., flexible schedules and telework) and suggestions for future research.

Chapter 13 by Minseo Kim and Terry Beehr addresses the topic of retirement. These authors point out that while at one time retirement meant an end to involvement in paid work, this is no longer the case for many retirees. They again organize their review by examining the predictors and outcomes of retirement at three levels: (1) individual and family, (2) organizational, and (3) societal, but focus on research published since the first edition. They also discuss bridge employment and volunteer work. In doing so, they provide a coherent and comprehensive review of what is known about the topic of retirement, and identify some important, yet unanswered, questions. A key takeaway point is that retirement in the 21st century is already very different than in the past and it is likely to continue to change well into the future.

As noted at the outset of this chapter, workforce aging is a global phenomenon affecting countries around the world. Therefore, in the final chapter (Chapter 14), which is also new to this edition, Cort Rudolph, Justin Marcus, and Hannes Zacher highlight many of the issues associated with aging and work from an international and cross-cultural perspective. They begin by discussing the lifespan perspective and its recognition that aging is influenced by social, cultural, and historical contexts. They examine cross-national demographic trends and their implications for health, healthcare, and retirements. With the lifespan perspective and demographics shifts providing the backdrop, they then touch on a range of issues associated with aging and work but from a decidedly cross-national and cross-cultural vantage point. Their review uncovers many of the important similarities and differences in aging and work around the world. They discuss and provide policy recommendations for countries, work organizations, and non-government organizations (NGOs), while offering poignant suggestions for future research.

Taken together, the various chapters included in this revised and updated 2nd edition of *Aging and Work in the 21st Century* provide a comprehensive and contemporary summary and integration of the literature on aging and work. They identify gaps in the existing knowledge base and offer recommendations to address those gaps. They also make substantive suggestions for public policy and organizational decision-makers to consider as they confront the issues associated with managing an aging workforce. In doing so, the chapters that comprise this updated and revised text tell us not only where we have already been, but also provide a comprehensive roadmap useful for charting a course into the domain of aging and work in the 21st century.

References

Beehr, T. A., & Bennett, M. M. (2015). Working after retirement: Features of bridge employment and research directions. *Work, Aging and Retirement, 1*, 112–128.

Bureau of Labor Statistics. (September, 2016). Labor force characteristics by race and ethnicity, 2015. BLS Reports, Report 1062. Washington, DC: U.S. Department of Labor, Bureau of Labor Statistics. www.bls.gov/opub/reports/race-and-ethnicity/2015/home.htm.

Bureau of Labor Statistics. (March, 2017) *Women at work*. Washington, DC: U.S. Department of Labor, Bureau of Labor Statistics. www.bls.gov/spotlight/2017/women-at-work/pdf/women-at-work.pdf.

Bureau of Labor Statistics. (November, 2017). *Projections of the labor force, 2016–26*. Washington, DC: U.S. Department of Labor, Bureau of Labor Statistics. www.bls.gov/careeroutlook/2017/article/projections-laborforce.htm.

Cahill, K. E., Giandrea, M. D., & Quinn, J. F. (2006). Are traditional retirements a thing of the past? New evidence on retirement patterns and bridge jobs. *Business Perspectives, 18*, 26.

Cahill, K. E., Giandrea, M. D., & Quinn, J. F. (2013). Retirement patterns and the macroeconomy, 1992–2010: The prevalence and determinants of bridge jobs, phased retirement, and reentry among three recent cohorts of older Americans. *The Gerontologist, 55*, 384–403.

Colby, S., & Ortman, J. (2014). Projections of the size and composition of the U.S. population: 2014 to 2060. *Current Population Reports, P25–1143*. U.S. Census Bureau, Washington, DC.

Collinson, C. (2017). *Wishful thinking or within reach? 3 generations prepare for retirement*. Los Angeles, CA: Transamerica Center for Retirement Studies.

Feldman, D. C. (1994). The decision to retire early: A review and conceptualization. *Academy of Management Review, 19*, 285–311.

Greenwald, L., Copeland, C., & VanDerhei, J. (2017). The 2017 retirement confidence survey: Many workers lack retirement confidence and feel stressed about retirement preparations. EBRI Issue Brief, no. 431 Washington, DC: Employee Benefit Research Institute.

He, W., Goodkind, D., & Kowal, P. (2015). U.S. Census Bureau, International Population Reports, P95/16–1. *An aging world: 2015*. Washington, DC: U.S. Government Publishing Office.

Shultz, K. S. (2003). Bridge employment: Work after retirement. In G. A. Adams & T. A. Beehr (Eds.), *Retirement: Reasons, processes, and results* (pp. 214–241). New York: Springer.

Shultz, K. S., & Wang, M. (2011). Psychological perspectives on the changing nature of retirement. *American Psychologist, 66*, 170.

Thompson, W. S. (1929). Population. *American Journal of Sociology, 34*, 959–975.

Toossi, M. (2012). Projections of the labor force to 2050: A visual essay. *Monthly Labor Review, 135*, 3–16.

Toossi, M. (2016). *BLS spotlight on statistics: A look at the future of the U.S. labor force to 2060*. Washington, DC: U.S. Department of Labor, Bureau of Labor Statistics.

Toossi, M., & Morisi, T. (2017, July). *BLS spotlight on statistics: Women in the workforce before, during, and after the great recession*. Washington, DC: U.S. Department of Labor, Bureau of Labor Statistics.

Toossi, M., & Torpey, E. (2017, May). *Older workers: Labor force trends and career options, Career outlook*. Washington, DC: U.S. Department of Labor, Bureau of Labor Statistics.

United Nations, Department of Economic and Social Affairs, Population Division. (2017). *World population prospects: The 2017 revision*. https://esa.un.org/unpd/wpp/.

United Nations, Department of Economic and Social Affairs, Population Division. (2015). *World fertility patterns 2015 – Data booklet* (ST/ESA/SER.A/370).

Wang, M., Adams, G. A., Beehr, T. A., & Shultz, K. S. (2009). Bridge employment and retirement: Issues: Opportunities during the latter part of one's career. In S. G. Baugh and S. E. Sullivan (Eds.), *Maintaining focus, energy, and options over the life span* (pp. 135–162). Charlotte, NC: IAP – Information Age Publishing.

Wang, M., Olson, D. A., & Shultz, K. S. (2013). *Mid and late career issues: An integrative perspective*. New York: Routledge.

2

RECRUITING AND RETAINING OLDER EMPLOYEES

Planning, Designing, Implementing, and Evaluating Programs

Mary Anne Taylor

As noted by several chapter authors in this book, shifts in demographics have created a unique configuration of potential employees in today's labor force, with a projected 19.8 percent increase in the representation of those 55 and older from 2014–2024. Coupled with a modest 3.9 percent labor force increase in those 25–54 years of age and a projected 13.1 percent decrease in labor force representation of those 16–24 years old, older individuals are likely to become a significant consideration in workforce planning (BLS, 2015a). Further examination of these projections suggests that the greatest proportion of jobs that will be created during the period are skilled in terms of technical and educational prerequisites. Forecasters believe that the fastest growing occupations will be within the healthcare support, healthcare practitioner, and technical occupations. These occupations alone are expected to characterize 25 percent of new jobs in the 2014–2024 time period. Furthermore, as one might expect, most of the fastest growing occupations require some level of postsecondary education even for entry level jobs (BLS, 2015a).

The combination of the wave of retirement-eligible employees coupled with a lower supply of skilled younger workers emphasizes the need for workforce planning. Consideration of typical peak retirement times for the Baby Boomer demographic, born from 1946–1964, suggests that attention to the effective recruitment and retention of skilled workers will become increasingly important in the coming decade. The leading cusp of the Baby Boomer cohort was eligible for early receipt of Social Security benefits at age 62 in 2008, and by 2024, the cohort will be 60–78 years old (BLS, 2015b). Many will have the option to leave the workforce and may do so unless motivated to stay by properly designed incentive systems.

Current labor force participation rates suggest that there is substantial interest in continued employment, with 40 percent of those 55 and older working or seeking work in 2014 (Toossi & Torpey, 2017). This participation in the workforce, according to Toossi and Torpey, is expected to increase through 2024, particularly for those 65 and older. In fact, this segment of the labor force is expected to increase more by 2024 than any other age segment. Given the total impact of shifts in demographics, the increase in the need for educated and technically skilled workers, and the interest in continued work among some of the older employee population, this is prime time for employers to plan, design, execute and evaluate effective ways to meet shifting labor force demands.

In the current review, workforce planning is presented as the initial step in recruitment and retention, with an emphasis on identification of jobs that may be disproportionately influenced by the exit of the older demographic. The second step is the design phase, which incorporates a consideration of the characteristics of successful recruitment and retention programs. The third phase is implementation, which considers the climate for acceptance of recruitment and retention by both the firm and the older worker. The fourth and final stage is the evaluation of the effectiveness of the intervention (see Figure 2.1). The applied and academic implications of the research reviewed in each phase are discussed in the final segments.

Stage One. Workforce Planning and Talent Management

Workforce planning can encompass a variety of techniques, ranging from system-wide HR software that incorporates incentive systems and forecasting data (Aral, Brynjolfsson, & Wu, 2012) to a more individualized assessment of an employee's talents and the fit of those talents with existing needs of the firm (Schuler, 2014). The latter approach incorporates principles from talent management and provides a useful framework for examining how companies may deal with upcoming retirement increases and labor force shortages (Minton-Eversole, 2012).

A talent management perspective applied to recruitment and retention presumes that one should target older individuals who have critical abilities and high performance levels that are key in meeting organizational goals (Mehdiabadi & Li, 2016). A general overview of the steps involved in talent management as applied to the planning stage of recruitment and retention reveals that this approach may prove helpful in designing programs that meet an organization's needs while maximizing the fit between the potential employee and critical jobs. The perspective taken in the current model is consistent with the philosophy of talent management noted by Church and Silzer (2016), who point out that I/O psychologists should seek to maximize the companies' outcomes along with those of the worker. Thus, their perspective on talent management frames it as a social system that should mutually benefit employers and employees.

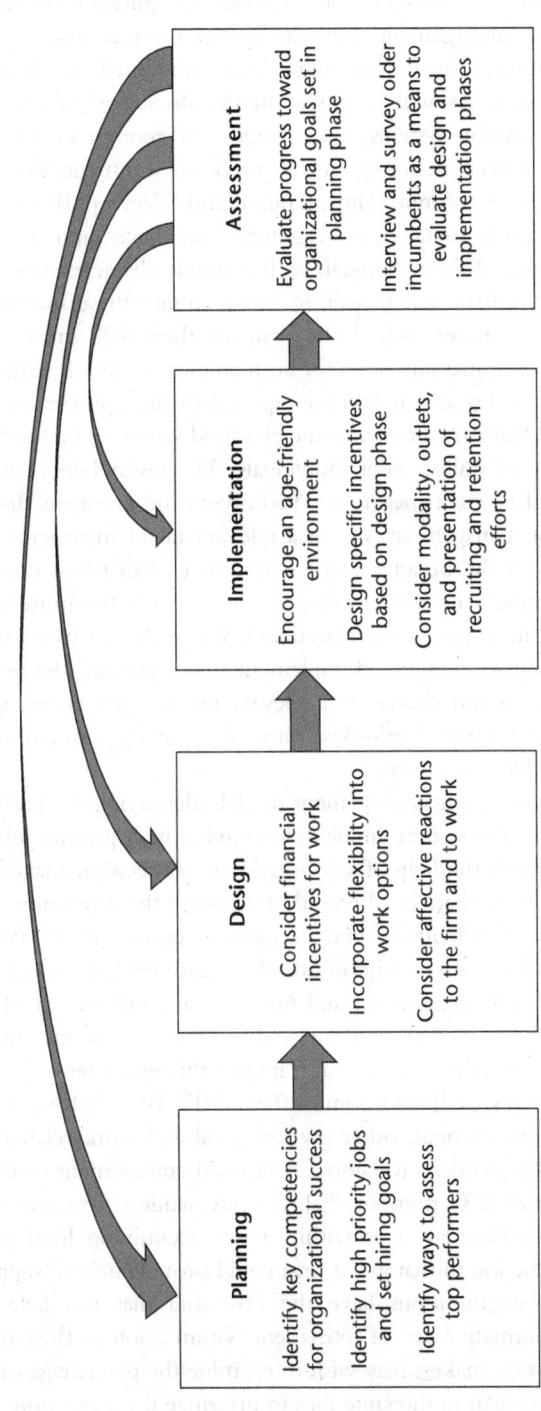

FIGURE 2.1 A four-stage model of recruiting and retaining older employees.

Social system considerations are not emphasized in purely economic models of human resource management, but are critical for retaining or recruiting skilled older employees or retirees who have substantial freedom in their employment decisions. As will be noted in the discussion of the design of recruitment and retention systems, older employees' interest in continuing or returning to work reflects responsiveness to work environments that take their psychosocial needs into account. Thus, Church and Silzer's (2016) socially oriented systems approach to talent management may have high utility in this setting. Since targeting those individuals with desirable characteristics is a central consideration for the firm and recruiting and retaining these individuals may provide a work environment where they can use their skills more effectively, this approach may optimize outcomes for both employees and the organization.

While research in this area is typically applied to high potential individuals on a "fast track," talent management principles hold when applied to the retention or recruitment of skilled older individuals. The researchers recommend a four-stage model of talent management: Identifying the problems that need to be solved by talent management; use of a relevant talent management model; considering factors in the broader social system as part of talent management; and finally, promoting a normative perspective in which the mutual needs of the company and the employee are considered. While the last two steps will be discussed in the program design and implementation segments, the first steps of problem identification and choice of a relevant talent management model are potentially important, often overlooked dimensions of recruitment and retention programs for older employees.

The first step in the talent management model, identifying the problems that need to be solved by the system, involves identifying high priority jobs that are central in the firm with the help of key organizational decision-makers. Within these key jobs, the immediate need would be to target those positions that have a sizable proportion of individuals who are nearing retirement age. Peak retirement ages are related to early receipt of Social Security benefits, which for Baby Boomers is 62 for early retirement, and 66 or 67 for full receipt of benefits. Other factors, such as spousal retirement dates, unforeseen life events, and incentives for delayed retirement may also impact this retirement age and labor force participation rates for Baby Boomers (Lee, 2017, BLS, 2015c). And as will be seen in the design segment, other psychological and work-related employment factors may lead workers to choose continued employment or to strongly oppose it (c.f., Davies & Cartwright, 2011). Thus, while a firm may use 62 or 66–67 to estimate retirement ages within a job, examining local norms for retirement within the job in that given firm could provide helpful supplemental information. Most organizations have the HR data that can help decision makers assess the normative age of retirement within a job in their firm. Furthermore, HR decision makers may wish to examine the percentage of younger or early-career individuals in the same jobs to prioritize those positions that may have the largest employment gaps because of upcoming retirements coupled with a lower supply of younger workers.

The next step involves identification of top performers within those targeted jobs that hold desirable skills. Such skills may be aligned with the strategy and goals of the business (Paese, 2010). Church, Rotolo, Ginther and Levine's (2015) approach to identification of "high potential" individuals within a talent management framework may readily be applied to the identification of older employees that have valuable KSAOs that the firm wishes to retain. Specifically, Church et al. suggest that corporate executives and other subject matter experts should identify critical competencies that feed into potential or performance in key jobs. In addition, they may identify the range and optimal percentage of workers with those talents that are desired in the company.

Other tactical questions that are recommended at this point involve the ability of the firm to assess these skills, and the relevancy and recency of performance data that exists as indicators of these skills. Thus, performance information may be used to target individuals for recruitment and retention. If adequate performance data do not exist, the firm may want to invest in ways to assess performance before moving forward to other recruitment or retention efforts. Alternatively, of course, organizations may choose to develop more widespread recruiting and retention efforts that cover a broad range of occupations. However, examining retirement trends within jobs as discussed above may help an organization plan for upcoming workforce needs. So this talent management based approach to workforce planning may yield information that allows practitioners to design effective tailored recruiting and retention programs. This should serve as a competitive advantage for companies pursuing limited labor within a shifting pool of employees.

The second phase in successful recruitment and retention in the current model involves the design of programs. Consistent with the philosophy of considering both organizational and potential employee needs, this review will include a discussion of both perspectives.

Stage Two. Designing the Program

The underlying philosophy of this discussion of program design is consistent with Wang and Wanberg's (2017) assertion that retirement can be viewed as a career development stage, emphasizing the positive career potential for retirees and old workers. Other researchers reinforce this idea, citing that more educated workers and wealthier individuals may even prefer continued full-time work over bridge employment or full retirement, with some of these individuals choosing an "encore" career of their own crafting (Boveda & Metz, 2016). Griffin, Hesketh and Loh (2012) suggest that individuals' ideas of post-retirement work are predicted by their own estimates of their remaining years, with those expecting longer lifespans showing increased interest in returning to work and more interest in delaying retirement. Thus, current research calls for career counseling that continues throughout the work life of individuals and actively incorporates and develops older employees. Implications of adopting this perspective include a consideration of those factors that are valued by older skilled employees and the ability of the organization to reasonably accommodate these preferences.

Design of Recruitment and Retention Programs

Research on bridge employment over the last decade reveals a significant shift in our understanding of the factors that increase retirees' or older employees' interest in continued employment past traditional retirement age. The literature encompasses variables including the fundamentals of health and finances, and affect toward the employing firm such as job stress and organizational commitment. While some psychological variables such as generativity and achievement striving have been incorporated into the literature, these do not emerge as strong and consistent predictors of work at later ages, perhaps because these needs can so easily be satisfied outside work. That being said, there is a preference for engaging work among most individuals and this will be considered in the design of appealing work options in the implementation phase.

While health is a significant and consistent predictor of post-retirement adjustment, retirement decisions, and intentions to continue work (c.f., Beehr, 2014; Shultz, Morton, & Weckerle, 1998; Wohrmann, Deller, & Wang, 2014), a full treatment of this variable is beyond the scope of the current review. Of course, organizations may invest in valued health and wellness programs throughout an employee's career to maximize their physical well-being in late-career stages. This ability to work, as noted by Beehr, is a primary determinant of workforce participation at older ages.

In addition to these personal and organizational factors, Beehr (2014) suggests that other dimensions of employment also deserve attention. These include whether the work is the same or different as the former job (career or non-career work, respectively), whether post-retirement employment is immediate or delayed, steady or intermittent, and self or other employed. Although research in the latter three topics is somewhat limited, adequate literature exists to incorporate an examination of the choice of career or non-career work. As one might expect, choice of returning to the same or different organizations often depends on reactions to one's occupation, their employing organization, and the amount of stress in their job. Thus, the choice of career versus non-career work will be discussed throughout this segment.

The first variable that is central in the design of recruitment and retention programs is financial incentives for work. We turn from a discussion of this factor to a discussion of affective reactions to different aspects of work and to the organization and note implications for design of programs.

Personal Finances as a Moderator of the Design of Recruitment and Retention Programs

The current economic environment may increase the proportion of individuals who choose to work past traditional retirement ages. A change from defined benefits to defined contributions plans for employees, decreases in personal savings, and policy changes in Social Security benefits may all incentivize workers to stay in the workforce longer, whether through phased retirement, bridge employment, or self-employment (Quinn & Cahill, 2016). In fact, researchers suggest that economics may be a primary consideration in the decision to delay retirement for individuals and for older couples making joint decisions (Beehr, 2014; Lee, 2017).

Financial concerns are a consistent predictor of the choice to return or continue work in some form rather than retire fully (Wang, Zhan, Liu, & Shultz, 2008; Weckerle & Shultz, 1999; Zhan, Wang & Yao, 2013). As a methodological note, subjective perceptions of financial comfort may be more predictive of interest in retirement or work options than objective measures. Although there are rare exceptions to this trend (Boveda & Metz, 2016) self-reported subjective measures of financial comfort are inversely related to a preference to continue work or to choose some form of employment. There is little cause to believe that the significance of finances as an incentive to delay retirement or to choose part-time work will decrease in the coming decades. In fact, if the trends outlined by Quinn and Cahill continue, the importance of finances may increase.

While few current employees or retirees would be expected to ignore monetary incentives for work, those who are under financial stress may be particularly sensitive to financial aspects of retention and recruitment programs so it is particularly important to emphasize those benefits of continued work to these potential workers. These financial benefits encompass not only the salary associated with the job, but could extend to other benefits as well. For instance, health benefits may make part time options more appealing to some potential employees, as will be discussed in the implementation segment.

While research on the interactive effects of personal finances with other characteristics of work is relatively new, an increasing body of research suggests that joint consideration of finances and other variables may inform the design of bridge employment options for specific occupations. From a psychological perspective, financial well-being is important in that it may moderate the ability of factors such as affective reactions to the firm to predict decisions to take bridge employment (Zhan, Wang & Yao, 2013). The individual who is under financial stress may be more influenced by monetary gain from continued or bridge employment than by the nature of the work itself. Furthermore, those who are less financially prepared for retirement are more likely to choose bridge employment options regardless of the level of their social anxiety regarding retirement

(Mariappanadar, 2013). Overall, this suggests that financial comfort allows an individual to consider and weigh psychological factors such as affective reactions to the firm and to retirement when considering continued employment. Those who are not financially prepared may prioritize monetary needs over other psychological comfort-based needs.

In the next steps, we review information on the general dimensions of work that are most appealing to those considering post-retirement work or continued employment. These general findings will be extended to specific interventions in the third implementation phase.

Flexibility of Work

One of the most consistent predictors of the attractiveness of bridge employment in general is flexibility of the work (Nobahar, Ahmadi, Alhani, & Khoshknab, 2015; Rau & Adams, 2005). Consistent with the prior discussion, this may be most important for those who are financially stable, since those who are more anxious about post-retirement finances may be more comfortable with more predictable and extensive work opportunities. For those who are more financially comfortable, flexibility of work may be associated with greater freedom in pursuing other valued leisure and social activities after retirement. In fact, in one study, social approval of work options by ones' family and friends was a significant predictor of post-retirement career intentions (Wohrmann, Deller, & Wang, 2014), suggesting that there may be a social/leisure basis underlying preferences for flexibility.

For those workers who are not primarily motivated by finances, offering flexibility may be key in their decision to continue or return to employment. Further research is needed to explore the dimensions of flexibility (hours, days, fixed versus variable) that specifically impact work interest among this demographic. Again, Beehr's (2014) dimensions of the type of post-retirement work (immediate versus delayed, intermittent versus steady) provide guidance here, as well as Mariappanadar's (2013) distinction between formal and more rigid arrangements (part-time employment, job sharing) versus more casual arrangements such as contract-based work.

Affective Reactions to Work, the Firm, and the Job

A significant predictor of interest in bridge employment/continued work, particularly within the same firm, involves affective reactions to the employing organization and the existing job. In one remarkable study, 25 percent of respondents had the lowest possible score in terms of willingness to work in their current job past traditional retirement age, and 38 percent expressed a desire to retire five or more years earlier than their actual planned date (Davies & Cartwright, 2011). While one would hope that most organizational decision-makers would not find themselves in this dire recruitment and retention situation, organizational decision-makers should have a realistic appraisal of commitment to the firm and appreciate the potential power of workers' psychological attachment and attractiveness of work as determinants of delayed retirement.

In contrast, affective reactions to the firm or company itself are not generally a strong predictor of the decision to fully retire (Schmidt & Lee, 2008). Many researchers have noted that workers can simultaneously enjoy their work at a company and look forward to retirement. As noted earlier, such affective reactions to the firm may be more important to those who have more financial flexibility in their decision to accept or reject continued employment (Zhan, Wang, & Yao, 2013). As one might expect, organizational commitment does seem to predict interest in working in a bridge employment capacity within the same firm as opposed to work in a different firm (Jones & McIntosh, 2010). This suggests that organizations that wish to successfully compete for older workers need to invest in them in terms of expressing the value of older workers and treating them with respect and regard.

Differentiating between the impact of commitment to a firm and commitment to an occupation is important in the design of attractive work options. As contrasted with organizational commitment, occupational or job commitment focuses on embeddedness in a type of work, not necessarily linked to a specific firm. Occupational or job commitment and being in a job that is intrinsically motivating is associated with continuing the same type of work, although not necessarily within that same firm (Gobeski & Beehr, 2009; Jones & McIntosh, 2010; Schmidt & Lee, 2008). Thus, employers should not mistake involvement in the work itself with a lasting commitment to their firm. Instead, identifying dimensions of work that are most rewarding to desirable employees and designing bridge employment options that allow the worker to continue those rewarding aspects of the job can be an effective way to retain their skills and knowledge.

Other emotionally laden reactions to work may also serve to shift retirement intentions. Lower work stress has been associated with a preference for bridge employment (Nobahar, Ahmadi, Alhani, & Khoshknab, 2015; Wang, Zhan, Liu, & Shultz, 2008). Conversely, jobs that have high demands, low decision authority, and low recognition and those that produce low job satisfaction are associated with higher odds of exit among older employees (Carr et al., 2016; Oakman & Wells, 2013). Similarly, job strain is associated with choosing post-retirement work options outside of the originally employing firm (Gobeski & Beehr, 2009). A rare exception was found in work by Bennett, Beehr, and Lepisto (2016) who found that distress predicted staying in full-time rather than bridge work. The authors surmised that this may have been because bridge employment would add more uncertainty to an already stressful situation. This explanation seems likely given that role overload, measured in this same study, was indeed related to a preference for bridge employment over full time employment. Again, this suggests that assessing the greatest stressors of the job from the perspective of potential post-retirement employees may provide critical data for design of more appealing work options.

It should be noted that creation of bridge employment options that offer fulfilling, less stressful and intrinsically rewarding work does not necessarily increase the attraction of work over retirement given that, for those in good health with adequate income, retirement has its own social and leisure oriented charms. Generativity and status and achievement-oriented strivings, while significant for some participants (cf., Zhan, Wang & Shi, 2015) can be satisfied by other post retirement options such as volunteering and thus may not serve as robust motivators to return to work or to prolong work. Furthermore, those who are highly educated and financially stable may be more likely to choose self-employment than returning to a traditional job setting so firms may be competing with the former/current employee's preference to set up their own work environment (Boveda & Metz, 2016; van Solinge, 2014). However, the breadth of research suggesting that aversive work and unpleasant work environments may push a worker out of the job suggests that those interested in recruitment and retention of older workers should view enriched work options as a necessary yet insufficient condition for workers to consider continued employment or return to the firm.

Stage Three. Implementation: Tailoring the Recruitment and Retention Program to the Organization

As noted in the prior segment, key characteristics of effective recruiting and retention programs include financial incentives, flexibility of work options, and the creation of a work environment where older workers feel valued and the work is intrinsically rewarding, particularly for skilled workers. In this segment, we examine best practices as a way to move from a general understanding of factors that serve as barriers or facilitators in program design to actual implementation of programs.

Consideration of Age Bias in the Firm

As noted in the introduction to this chapter, some initial assessment of the organization's climate and readiness for change underlies successful interventions. A sensitive and important part of this assessment, which may take more time to discover is the presence or absence of age bias. The climate for retaining or hiring older employees is key in their interest in staying at a firm and requires an investigation of this issue. In a recent meta-analysis, age bias was significantly related to age discrimination in selection, suggesting that it is still a force in the ability of older employees to continue their work life as desired (Jones et al.,

2017). Age stereotypes are not uniformly negative but are mixed and include beliefs that older workers are work oriented, efficient and logical yet self-centered (Crumpacker & Crumpacker, 2007). The most negative beliefs regarding older workers include that they are less flexible and productive, not entitled to paid employment and that they even block employment opportunities for younger workers (Pritchard & Whiting, 2014; Wood, Wilkinson & Harcourt, 2008). However, a positive finding in this area is that perceptions of competence may increase with positive exposure to older workers, so integration of competent older employees into the firm may weaken ageist beliefs and gradually contribute to a better climate for change (Fasbender & Wang, 2017).

It seems likely that age bias along with other age-linked factors would also impede the ability of older workers to migrate into a range of occupations. In fact, data show that employment options start to narrow as a function of age. The quality of employment options narrows in the late 50s for men with less education and in the early 60s for women and more educated men (Rutledge, Sass & Ramos-Mercado, 2017). While these barriers are often discussed and sometimes emphasized in the public media, they are seldom part of the media released by firms. Instead, firms may publicize general policies that are intended to provide equity to all employees. Despite this positive focus, older potential employees seem well aware of the threat of potential age bias in their employment options (Kroon, van Selm, Hoeven & Vliegenthart, 2017), and most firms do not have targeted policies that benefit older workers (Martin, Dymock, Billett, & Johnson, 2014).

Age-friendly policies may set an organization apart from other firms and may help to change ageist behaviors over time. Martin et al. (2014) call for more emphasis on age-relevant policies within organizational communications. Research by Rau and Adams (2005) on EEOC policies that emphasize mature workers' rights suggests that while such policies may be most effective in impacting organizational attraction when coupled with other desirable aspects of bridge employment, such as flexibility, the mention of such age-supportive policies hold promise for increasing the interest of older workers in employment opportunities.

In sum, providing opportunities for competent older workers to positively interact with decision-makers on a more frequent basis and having age-friendly policies in place are two simple attempts to enhance the quality of the work environment for potential older recruits and those interested in staying at work longer. An age-friendly climate may be a prerequisite for the success of interventions designed to enhance the interest of older employees.

In the next segment, innovative ways to provide the financial incentives valued by older employees and retirees are discussed, along with creative ways to provide flexible and engaging work. Finally, we summarize the importance of a supportive social climate in designing an environment that engages workers and fosters the commitment that is associated with more organizational attachment.

Financial Incentives for Workforce Participation

As noted in the earlier segment on design, compensation for work is an important incentive for both retirees considering workforce re-entry and those who are considering bridge or partial retirement (cf., Beehr, 2014). While pay is of course a primary consideration for potential older employees, other financial incentives may be equally desirable. As outlined by Paullin (2014) in a SHRM report, these incentives may include health care for part time workers, group discounts on drugs, group rate long-term care or life insurance rates, supplemental insurance to cover Medicare gaps, and other benefit programs. According to the author of this report, these options are likely to be valued by those who are weighing the costs and benefits of retirement.

Again, there is a need for more research in this area. Basic information on the types of financial incentives that are preferred and why, would help firms design more effective incentive systems.

Flexibility of Work Options

A second primary consideration in the successful implementation of recruitment and retention programs is to build flexibility into work options. Specific ways to accomplish this goal include traditional and relatively fixed part-time or voluntary work, working for 1000 hours/year without pension penalties, a flexible work option around a core work period, non-traditional part-time work (e.g., one week on and one week off), phased retirement where the worker gradually exits the workforce, job sharing, and seasonal work (SHRM, 2016). These and other options are contemporary ways to recruit and retain valued workers who either cannot or choose to not work full time. However, the factors that would determine an individual's attraction to these options are not fully understood. We also need to know more about the burden placed on firms in the administration of these options and the financial options discussed in order to understand which programs may be most realistic from an organizational decision maker's perspective.

The Importance of Engaging Work

As noted in the design segment, older workers, particularly those in skilled and relatively high income professions, are likely to be most enticed by enriched work that engages their skills without the high level of stress or demands that they may have found in their former positions. A variety of techniques simultaneously provide this type of opportunity for older workers while contributing to the organization's need to share the knowledge that may be lost when Baby Boomers retire.

A variety of mentoring practices embody this shared goal of providing stimulating work while preserving the experience and knowledge that exits when older workers retire. Mentoring and coaching programs are often viewed as the most effective way to transfer both explicit knowledge related to job content and tacit knowledge such as how to network within the firm and information on corporate culture to younger workers (Calo, 2008). Specific mentoring policies that may be utilized by firms include short-term mentoring sessions, periodic mentoring sessions (e.g., once every 4–6 months for short sessions), open mentoring plans that are conducted as needed, and weekly or monthly coaching sessions (Dopson et al., 2017). These authors note that the logistics of planning and coordinating these sessions may be lessened using technology to provide virtual meetings between mentees and mentors and using simple phone calls or audio meetings to supplement face-to-face meetings.

Research that investigates the relative interest of potential older employees in these and other non-traditional work assignments is needed. We also need to understand if these programs are more effective when they are initiated while the employee is still within the firm, rather than using these programs as a recruitment device. Instituting the plans while older workers are still in the firm, as part- of full-time employment or phased retirement, may be one way to build investment in mentoring programs. In addition, flexibility is key when designing mentoring programs. We need to understand what level of commitment to mentoring programs seems reasonable to older individuals, particularly when they have left the firm.

Social Considerations in the Work Environment

Given the significance of organizational and work environments as potential determinants of interest in work among Baby Boomers, understanding characteristics that are particularly valued by older workers is an important goal. Respect, open communication, creativity, recognition, pay/benefits for a job well done as well as an appreciation of knowledge management are values held in high regard for older workers and may enhance interest and commitment to firms (Carver & Candela, 2008; Kontoghiorghes, 2016). A change from the high-pressure nature of professional work is associated with engagement not only for older workers but for workers of most ages. For those older employees who are in high demand work, supervisor support, and opportunities to learn and develop are associated with engagement, particularly as their personal resources and confidence decrease (Matz-Costa, 2016).

This emphasis on the importance of the social environment of work to older employees has been echoed by other researchers who note the criticality of intrinsically engaging work and a positive social work climate (Twenge, Campbell, Hoffman & Lance, 2010; Westerman & Yamamura, 2007). It should be noted that this type of environment should benefit workers of all ages.

In summary, a variety of creative ways to meet the needs of older employees are available to provide the financial, social, and work-oriented aspects of employment that are valued by them. In the next segment, a brief discussion of the modality of implementation is given. Methods for reaching the intended demographic of older employees or retirees is explored.

Reaching the Audience: The Importance of Communication Modality

Regarding the best means of reaching the intended audience for recruitment and retention, Paullin (2014) provides an excellent list of recommendations for practitioners and for researchers alike. When reaching out to potential older employees within the firm as part of retention efforts, she suggests including workers on messaging, job postings and applications and ensuring that the job descriptions are inclusive in terms of age. Recall that work by Rau and Adams (2005) suggested that advertisements that explicitly encourage senior employees through discussion of age-related EEOC incentives engaged their interest in applying for jobs under certain conditions.

In terms of sources for recruiting, community colleges, which often target older individuals for training, may allow recruiters the chance to reach a broad audience of engaged potential employees. Similarly, Paullin (2014) notes that there are many partners that match employees and employers. In addition, posting in age-friendly outlets, such as in AARP's Life Reimagined for Work Program, targets older individuals. And finally, a range of communication techniques are recommended in addition to those noted above, ranging from print outlets and magazines to seminars and career fairs.

Research on internet-based recruiting is mixed. While those older individuals with little experience with computer technology may be less responsive to online recruitment and retention ads, those with experience are likely to be comfortable with this mode of advertising (Niemela-Nyrhinen, 2007). However, overall, older individuals are less likely than younger ones to be familiar with such types of technology. Use of computer technology is associated with several cognitive and motivational factors, including computer self-efficacy (Czaja et al, 2006). Experience with computers is likely to be quite varied, with those in lower paid jobs less likely to have the opportunity to interact with technology. Thus, firms should not ignore internet-based recruiting, yet not rely solely on it to recruit older individuals.

Finally, recruiters should be aware of the nature of the materials that they use to express interest in older potential employees. Often, these materials may feature only younger workers. Having positive images of older individuals in the company literature is likely to be perceived as inclusive by older workers given findings in marketing research (Robinson & Umphery, 2006). Thus, effective recruiting and retention involves a consideration of proper outlets, proper modality and proper presentation of information (Taylor, Shultz & Doverspike, 2005).

In the final segment, we briefly examine evaluation of recruitment and retention efforts.

Stage Four. Evaluation of Recruitment and Retention Efforts

A variety of techniques may be drawn from the Industrial/Organizational literature to evaluate the success of recruiting and retention for older workers. In keeping with the talent management approach discussed earlier, a definition of "success" may be generated in conjunction with organizational decision makers to ensure that they encompass corporate goals. These are typically performance-based measures and numerical recruitment goals. If the workforce planning goals initially discussed in this chapter are well-specified, assessment of progress toward those goals will be facilitated, as will revision of the goals as needed.

A more psychologically based assessment may depend on affective reactions from recruited or retained older employees. Simply surveying or interviewing individuals on their reactions to each stage of the experience, from recruitment to their current job environment, can provide helpful feedback for revising and revisiting recruitment and retention efforts. In addition, surveying older employees to discover how they found out about opportunities and the reason they applied to the firm may increase efficiency of recruiting and retention efforts. As noted earlier, older employees are a valuable resource for contributing to the design of each of these phases in recruitment and retention.

Thus, the dimensions of success may be traditional measures such as attainment of a given number of workers with certain valued competencies, performance ratings or indices for those recruited and retained, and affect toward the firm and the work. Additional insight into the success of a program may include assessing transfer of knowledge, a core theme in hiring older workers. This information might be gathered from mentored individuals who benefit from the guidance of older individuals. Data collection may range from surveys and exit interviews to informal interviews with older employees. Feedback from employees may be used not only to evaluate existing recruitment and retention efforts but to strengthen them.

Directions for Future Research

Planning

For academics, many questions may arise regarding the relative effectiveness of talent management-based programs as compared with more general recruiting or retention programs. While identifying high performers that are currently in the firm or have recently left the firm is desirable when maximizing productivity, talent management researchers have noted that the lack of anonymity involved in the process of inadvertently labelling other unchosen workers as "B level" may be demoralizing (Church et al., 2015). The anonymity of the process of identifying talented workers is a topic of ongoing debate in I/O psychology.

Design and Implementation

An interesting question for researchers involves three or the four relatively under-investigated dimensions of post-retirement work noted by Beehr (2014): Immediate or delayed, steady or intermittent, and self- or other-employed. We know very little about the timing of post-retirement work decisions and the factors that spur an individual into the job search. Similarly, preferences for particular forms of intermittent or steady work are not well-understood in terms of the personal factors that drive these decisions or in terms of the organization's ability to offer and maintain these work options. And finally, work on encore jobs, or self-employed jobs, is a growing area of interest characterized by engaging but limited research (cf., van Solinge, 2014).

We also know little about the underlying basis of the preference for flexible work. Which factors external to the work environment drive the preference for fewer hours, fewer assignments, or short term assignments? Are leisure pursuits and social pursuits key in this decision, and would incorporating these factors into the organization's culture encourage the entry of more desirable workers? A more detailed understanding of the specific underlying dimensions of flexibility that are most appealing to skilled and financially stable older employees would aid design of recruitment and retention efforts.

More research is also needed to understand how employers may redesign post-retirement or bridge work options to make them appealing to individuals. In lieu of the ability to redesign work, more research is needed to investigate whether there are buffers that can help individuals deal with the unpleasant aspects of post-retirement work options such as increased supervisor support or increased pay. While these areas have been well-developed in I/O psychology, it is not clear whether research regarding typical buffers for stress and research on the aspects of work that typically increase commitment are applicable to the recruitment and retention of older workers. Again, financially stable, late-career potential employees may be unique from a psychological perspective, and it is unclear whether truisms regarding work redesign and worker commitment and well-being apply to their situation.

There are also unanswered questions related to perceived workforce ageism and support of older workers. Which aspects of work itself and the social environment produce the highest levels of attraction and engagement for older employees? While eliminating stressors focuses on negative aspects of work, equal attention to the specific dimensions valued by workers at this point in their career would be helpful in design and implementation of programs. More involvement of older employees in this part of the design and implementation process may increase their own engagement with work and provide a work environment well-suited for recruitment and retention.

While findings suggest that older workers are attuned to the presence of potential bias in their firm, more research is needed to understand the particular cues that are most important in their evaluation of bias. Whether the cues are based on broad age-related policies, on opportunities for continued development, on social recognition or on more informal social interaction, we need to understand how older individuals form their ideas regarding bias. In this way, we can make more effective recommendations for the design of a supportive and respectful environment for workers of all ages.

Finally, there is limited information on how older individuals respond to recruitment and retention efforts as determined by who provides the information, how it is presented, and the nature of the recruitment materials. Even in marketing, there is less research on Baby Boomer behavior and preferences than one might expect. This is a promising area for research and one that would help us reach out to older prospective employees more effectively.

Implications for Practice

Planning

A joint survey of AARP and the Society for Human Resource Management found that 71 percent of corporate respondents indicated that their company has not conducted any strategic workforce assessment to analyze upcoming issues associated with the exit of retirees, and 60 percent have not identified their workforce needs in the coming five years (Minton-Eversole, 2012). Further research suggests that organizations can be fit into a typology based on their reactions to upcoming retirements (Lee, Zikic, Noh & Sargent, 2017). Gatekeepers simply maintain existing policies and track retirement, Improvisers are aware of shifts based on retirements but may recruit individuals back into the firm only when they realize there is a need for their skills. In both cases, the organization is more reactive than proactive where the consequences of retirement are concerned. In contrast, companies deemed Orchestrators examine overall workforce demographics and proactively gather information on workforce demographics and needs of potential retirees inside the firm. In contrast to the first two categories, an awareness of upcoming changes in demographics is coupled with planning in the form of recruitment and retention policies and monitoring internal shifts in firm demographics. Finally, in firms labelled Partners, there is a more comprehensive and individualized emphasis on ways to engage older workers in passing on their knowledge while ensuring that these workers feel that they belong in the company. The latter is consistent with Church et al.'s (2015) recommendation to look at recruiting and retention as part of a larger social system within the firm, since investing in workers while they are in the organization may encourage them to consider staying with the firm.

A fruitful area for further research would be to identify the aspects of an organization's culture which leads the firm to deal with retirement shifts in more passive or active ways, and to identify more proactive and more sophisticated strategies for meeting the demands of the workforce changes associated with retirement. Assessment of interventions intended to increase the involvement of key decision makers in workforce planning would provide helpful information for theorists and practitioners alike.

Design and Implementation

There are clear practical implications for the design of recruitment and retention programs based on the research reviewed. Specifically, while design of intrinsically and socially rewarding bridge employment options would be viewed more favorably by most individuals targeted by recruitment and retention techniques, these variables may have the greatest impact on the bridge/continued employment decisions for those who are financially stable. One may hypothesize that similar relationships hold for other work characteristics such as the stress level in the job and the flexibility of the work. Therefore, when recruiting skilled workers who may have little need to continue employment for financial gain, designing enriched and appealing work options is particularly important. Ethically, one would hope that the organization would strive to create a positive work environment regardless of financial need of workers, since this may enhance commitment to the firm and associated OCBs, as well as employee well-being.

Summary

The field of recruitment and retention of older employees is rapidly developing. However, many questions remain about the applicability of traditional models to this specific demographic. Based on the reviewed information, we need models tailored to the heterogeneous groups of senior employees in order to fully understand their needs and their responsiveness to the economic, social and organizational aspects of recruitment and retention programs.

References

Aral, S., Brynjolfsson, E., & Wu, L. (2012). Three-way complementaries: Performance pay, human resource analytics, and information technology. *Management Science, 58,* 5, 913–931.

Beehr, T. A. (2014). To retire or not to retire: That is not the question. *Journal of Organizational Behavior, 35,* 1093–1108.

Bennett, M. M., Beehr, T. A., & Lepisto, L. R. (2016). A longitudinal study of work after retirement: Examining predictors of bridge employment, continued career employment, and retirement. *The International Journal of Aging and Human Development, 83*(3), 228–255.

Boveda, I., & Metz, A. J. (2016). Predicting end-of-career transitions for Baby Boomers nearing retirement age. *The Career Development Quarterly, June, 64,* 153–168.

Bureau of Labor Statistics. (2015a, December 8). *Employment projections: 2014–2025 summary*. Retrieved from www.bls.gov/news.release/pdf/ecopro.pd.

Bureau of Labor Statistics. (2015b, December). *Monthly Labor Review*. Labor force projections to 2024: The labor force is growing, but slowly. Retrieved from www.bls.gov/opub/mlr/2015/article/labor-force-projections-to-2024.htm.

Bureau of Labor Statistics. (2015c, October). Civilian labor force participation rates by age, gender, race and ethnicity. Employment projections. Retrieved from www.bls.gov/emp/ep_table_303.htm.

Calo, T. J. (2008). Talent management in the era of the aging workforce: The critical role of knowledge transfer. *Public Personnel Management, 37*(4), 403–416.

Carr, E., Hagger-Johnson, G., Head, J., Shelton, N., Stafford, M. Stansfeld, S., & Zaninotto, P. (2016). Working conditions as predictors of retirement intentions and exit from paid employment: A 10-year follow-up of the English Longitudinal Study of Ageing. *European Journal of Ageing, 13*, 39–48.

Carver, L., & Candela, L. (2008). Attaining organizational commitment across different generations of nurses. *Journal of Nursing Management, 16*, 984–991.

Church, A., & Silzer, R. (2016). Are we on the same wavelength? Four steps for moving from talent signals to valid talent management applications. *Industrial and Organizational Psychology: Perspectives on Science and Practice, 9*, 645–654.

Church, A. H., Rotolo, C. T., Ginther, N. M., & Levine, R. (2015). How are top companies designing and managing their high-potential programs? A follow-up talent management benchmark study. *Consulting Psychology Journal: Practice and Research. 67*(1), 17–47.

Crumpacker, M., & Crumpacker, J. M. (2007). Succession planning and generational stereotypes: Should HR consider age-based values and attitudes a relevant factor or a passing fad? *Public Personnel Management, 36*(4), 349–369.

Czaja, S. J., Charness, N., Fisk, A. D., Hertzog, C., Nair, S. N., Rogers, W. A., & Sharit, J. (2006). Factors predicting the use of technology: Findings from the center for research and education on aging and technology enhancement (create). *Psychology and Aging, 21*, 333–352. Doi:10.1037/0882-7974.21.2.333.

Davies, E., & Cartwright, S. (2011). Psychological and psychosocial predictors of attitudes to working past normal retirement age. *Employee Relations, 33*(3), 249–268.

Dopson, S. A., Griffey, S., Ghiya, N., Laird, S., Cyphart, A., & Iskander, J. (2017). Structured mentoring for workforce engagement and professional development in public health settings. *Health Promotion Practice, 18*(3), 327–331.

Fasbender, U., & Wang, M. (2017). Intergenerational contact and hiring decisions about older workers. *Journal of Managerial Psychology, 32*(3), 210–224.

Gobeski, K. T., & Beehr, T. A. (2009). How retirees work: Predictors of different types of bridge employment. *Journal of Organizational Behavior, 30*, 401–425.

Griffin, B., Hesketh, B., & Loh, V. (2012). The influence of subjective life expectancy on retirement transition and planning: A longitudinal study. *Journal of Vocational Behavior, 81*, 129–137.

Jones, D. A., & McIntosh, B. R. (2010). Organizational and occupational commitment in relation to bridge employment and retirement intentions. *Journal of Vocational Behavior, 77*, 280–303.

Jones, K. P., Sabat, I. E., King, E. B., Ahmad, A., McCausland, T. C., & Chen, T. (2017). Isms and schisms: A meta-analysis of the prejudice-discrimination relationship across racism, sexism, and ageism. *Journal of Organizational Behavior, 38*, 1076–1110.

Kontoghiorghes, C. (2016). Linking high performance organizational culture and talent management: Satisfaction/motivation and organizational commitment as mediators. *The International Journal of Human Resource Management, 27*(16), 1833–1853.

Kroon, A. C., van Selm, M. ter Hoeven, C., & Vliegenthart, R. (2017). Age at work. *Journalism Studies, 18*(9), 1167–1186.

Lee, A. (2017). Late career job loss and retirement behavior of couples. *Research on Aging, 39*(1), 7–28.

Lee, M. D., Zikic, J., Noh, S.-C., & Sargent, L. (2017). Human resource approaches to retirement: Gatekeeping, improvising, orchestrating and partnering. *Human Resource Management, 56*(3), 455–477.

Mariappanadar, S. (2013). Do retirement anxieties determine bridge employment preference? A study among pre-retirees in the Australian construction industry. *Personnel Review, 42*(2), 176–204.

Martin, G., Dymock, D., Billett, S., & Johnson, G. (2014). In the name of meritocracy: Managers' perceptions of policies and practices for training older workers. *Ageing & Society, 34*, 992–1018.

Matz-Costa, C. (2016). Understanding factors that promote or impede subjective well-being at work. *Best Practices in Mental Health, 12*(2), 43–63.

Mehdiabadi, A. H., & Li, J. (2016). Understanding talent development and implications for Human Resource Development: An integrative literature review. *Human Resource Development Review, 15*(3), 263–294.

Minton-Eversole, T. (2012, April 9). *Concerns grow over workforce retirements and skills gaps*. Alexandria, VA: Society for Human Resource Management.

Niemela-Nyrhinen, J. (2007). Baby boomer consumers and technology: Shooting down stereotypes. *Journal of Consumer Marketing, 24*(5), 305–312.

Nobahar, M., Ahmadi, F., Alhani, F., & Khoshknab, M. F. (2015). Work or retirement: Exploration of the experiences of Iranian retired nurses. *Work, 51*, 807–816.

Oakman, J., & Wells, Y. (2013). Retirement intentions: What is the role of push factors in predicting retirement intentions? *Ageing and Society, 33*, 988–1008.

Paullin, C. (2014). The aging workforce: Leveraging the talents of mature employees. SHRM. Retrieved from: www.shrm.org/hr-today/trends-and-forecasting/special-reports-and-expert-views/Documents/Aging-Workforce-Talents-Mature-Employees.pdf.

Paese, M. J. (2010). The role of assessment in succession management. In J. C. Scott and D. H. Reynolds (Eds.), *Handbook of workplace assessment* (pp. 465–494). San Francisco: Jossey Bass.

Pritchard, K., & Whiting, R. (2014). Baby Boomers and the lost generation: On the discursive construction of generations at work. *Organization Studies, 25*(11), 1605–1626.

Quinn, J. F., & Cahill, K. E. (2016). The new world of retirement income security in America. *American Psychologist, 71*, 321–333.

Rau, B. L., & Adams, G. A. (2005). Attracting retirees to apply: Desired organizational characteristics of bridge employment. *Journal of Organizational Behavior, 26*, 649–660.

Robinson, T., & Umphery, D. (2006). First and third person perceptions of images of older people in advertising: An inter-generational evaluation. *International Journal of Aging and Human Development, 62*(2), 159–173.

Rutledge, M. S., Sass, S. A., & Ramos-Mercado, J. D. (2017). How does occupational access for older workers differ by education? *Journal of Labor Research, 38*, 283–305.

Schmidt, J. A., & Lee, K. (2008). Voluntary retirement and organizational turnover intentions: The differential associations with work and non-work commitment constructs. *Journal of Business Psychology, 22*, 297–309.

Schuler, R. S. (2014). The 5-C framework for managing talent. *Organizational Dynamics*, *44*, 47–56.

Shultz, K. S., & Wang, M. (2011). Psychological perspectives on the changing nature of retirement. *American Psychologist*, *66*, 170–179.

Shultz, K. S., Morton, K. R., & Weckerle, J. R. (1998). The influence of push and pull factors on voluntary and involuntary early retirees' retirement decision and adjustment. *Journal of Vocational Behavior*, *53*, 45–57.

Social Security Administration. (2008). *Early or late retirement*. Retrieved from www.ssa.gov/oact/quickcalc/early_late.html.

Society of Human Resource Management (2016). *Employing Older Workers*. Retrieved from www.shrm.org/resourcesandtools/tools-and-samples/toolkits/pages/employingolderworkers.aspx.

Taylor, M. A., Shultz, K., & Doverspike, D. (2005). Academic perspectives on recruiting and retaining talented older workers. In P. T. Beatty & R. M. S. Visser (Eds.), *Thriving on an aging workforce: Strategies for organizational and systemic change* (pp. 43–50). Melbourne, Fl: Krieger Publishing.

Toossi, M., & Torpey, E. (2017, May). Older workers: Labor force trends and career options. *Career Outlook*. Washington, DC: U.S. Department of Labor, Bureau of Labor Statistics.

Twenge, J. M., Campbell, S. M., Hoffman, B. J., & Lance, C. E. (2010). Generational differences in work values: Leisure and extrinsic values increasing, social and intrinsic values decreasing. *Journal of Management*, *36*(5), 1117–1142.

van Solinge, H. (2014). Who opts for self-employment after retirement? A longitudinal study in the Netherlands. *European Journal of Aging*, *11*, 261–272.

Wang, M., & Wanberg, C. R. (2017). 100 Years of applied psychology research on individual careers: From career management to retirement. *Journal of Applied Psychology*, *102*(3), 546–563.

Wang, M., Zhan, Y., Liu, S., & Shultz, K. (2008). Antecedents of bridge employment: A longitudinal investigation. *Journal of Applied Psychology*, *93*(4), 818–830.

Weckerle, J. R., & Shultz, K. S. (1999). Influences on the bridge employment decision among older USA workers. *Journal of Occupational and Organizational Psychology*, *72*, 317–329.

Westerman, J. W., & Yamamura, J. H. (2007). Generational preferences for work environment fit: Effects on employee outcomes. *Career Development International*, *12*(2), 150–161.

Wohrmann, A. M., Deller, J., & Wang, M. (2014). A mixed-method approach to post-retirement career planning. *Journal of Vocational Behavior*, *84*, 307–317.

Wood, G., Wilkinson, A., & Harcourt, M. (2008). Age discrimination and working life: Perspectives and contestations – A review of the contemporary literature. *International Journal of Management Review*, *10*(4), 425–442.

Zhan, Y., Wang, M., & Yao, X. (2013). Domain specific effects of commitment on bridge employment decisions: The moderating role of economic stress. *European Journal of Work and Organizational Psychology*, *22*(3), 362–375.

Zhan, Y., Wang, M., & Shi, J. (2015). Retirees' motivational orientations and bridge employment: Testing the moderating role of gender. *Journal of Applied Psychology*, *100*(5), 1319–1331.

3
DIVERSITY ISSUES FOR AN AGING WORKFORCE

A Lifespan Intersectionality Approach

Jennica Webster, Christian Thoroughgood, and Katina Sawyer

With the dramatic increases in life expectancy and the general movement toward healthier lifestyles, human beings are living longer than they ever have been before. In the United States, for example, it is projected that by 2030 there will be roughly 72.1 million older people (officially denoted as 65 years and over), more than twice as many as in 2000 (Administration on Aging, 2014). Consequently, today's modern workforce is growing more diverse in terms of age. Indeed, by 2020, five different generations are expected to be working alongside one another (Robbins & Judge, 2010). Because age carries with it a certain social stigma in Western societies, including a widespread view of older people as frail, weak, and grumpy (Kulik, 2014), it is perhaps not surprising that this older population of workers are susceptible to various negative work outcomes relative to younger employees. Compounding this problem, older workers may carry other pre-existing stigmas, including, among others, those related to gender, race, ethnicity, mental illness, or physical disability, all of which may intersect with the unique stigma acquired with age. As such, the aging nature of today's workforce places pressure on management scholars and practitioners to better understand and address issues related to age-related stereotypes and prejudice in organizations.

The stigma literature underscores that individuals may carry a wide range of visible (e.g., race, sex, obesity, physical disability) and invisible (e.g., sexual orientation, gender identity, physical disease, mental illness) stigmas. Based on Goffman's (1963) seminal work, a "stigma" reflects a personal characteristic that is perceived to be socially undesirable, or deviant, within a given social context. Stigmas devalue and discredit one's social identity in the eyes of other people by reducing one "from a whole and usual person to a tainted, discounted one" (Crocker, Major, & Steele, 1998; Goffman, 1963, p. 3). These "marks" become associated with negative stereotypes, which tend to be widely espoused in a social system and which creates a basis for excluding and marginalizing those who possess (or who are thought to possess) them (Major & O'Brien, 2005). As individuals with preexisting stigmas grow older, these stigmas, whether visible or invisible, intersect with the unique stigma acquired as an older person. Within the workplace, this intersection of age and other stigmatized identities therefore may combine to jointly shape the experiences of employees across the lifespan.

In this chapter, we review the relevant literature pertaining to various stigmatized identities and their intersections with age. In each case, we will briefly describe cross-classified demographics in order to provide a sense of its scope. We then describe the conditions that render an identity more salient, the likely stereotypes that are activated in such situations, and the effects of these situations on the work experiences of those possessing a given identity. Unfortunately, even a cursory glance of the literature suggests that many of these experiences are likely to be negative. Yet, societal perceptions of identity groups do change and are malleable within organizations. Indeed many organizations have adopted policies and practices aimed at reducing these negative experiences by promoting greater inclusion. It is also true that those with stigmatized identities display remarkable levels of resilience in the face of these negative experiences. With this in mind, we review some of the organizational and individual factors that may mitigate the negative combined effects of being an older worker with a pre-existing stigma. We conclude by discussing practical recommendations for employers who seek to promote inclusivity using an intersectional lens. In the following sections, we first provide a theoretical background on stigma and minority stress, intersectional identities, and lifespan development to provide a conceptual foundation for our discussion.

Stigma Theory

To explain further the process of stigmatization, Goffman (1963) argued that stigma creates an assumption in social perceivers that a person who possesses a given stigma is, in essence, less than human. This assumption, in turn, provides a foundation for various forms of discrimination that, according to Goffman, effectively reduce such an individual's life chances. Goffman (1963) specifically noted that, "We construct a stigma theory, an ideology to explain his [or her] inferiority … [and] impute a wide range of imperfections" (p. 14). This public perception of one's stigma, in turn, tends to permeate all other possible characteristics, qualities, or features of a person. Stigmas also vary along a series of dimensions (Jones et al., 1984). For example, some stigmas are concealable (e.g., sexual orientation, mental illness, criminal record), while others are not (e.g., race, physical disability). Some may be seen as controllable (e.g., obesity, drug addiction), while others are viewed as uncontrollable and are thus attributed less blame (e.g., physical deformity, cancer). Further, some stigmas vary in their course – or the extent to which they become more prominent over time (e.g., degenerative disorders such as multiple sclerosis and Alzheimer's disease) – while others vary in their disruptiveness to social interactions (e.g., stuttering, seizures). In terms of aging, this stigma may be classified as non-concealable and non-controllable, progressing over the life course, and potentially disruptive to social interactions later in life, especially if individuals develop degenerative diseases that undermine their cognitive functioning.

Intersectionality

Based on the seminal work of Crenshaw (1989, 1991), intersectionality refers to the ways in which multiple aspects of identity combine and interact with one another to form qualitatively different meanings and social experiences (Warner, 2008). From this perspective, social identity structures do not reflect independent axes of demographic categories, but rather interlocking matrices of privilege and oppression (Gopaldas, 2013). For example, according to theories of intersectionality, the social experiences of African American women are qualitatively different from the experiences of African American men (or Caucasian women) due to the intersection between the two subordinate identities of being Black and female. With respect to the workplace, for example, recent research suggests Black female leaders may be reacted to differently from White female and Black male leaders due to differences in how social perceivers ascribe meaning to dominant behavior based on a leader's multiple group membership (Livingston, Rosette, & Washington, 2012; Rosette & Livingston, 2012).

While earlier definitions of intersectionality emphasized intersections between race, gender, and class, newer definitions expand the concept of intersectionality to include all possible social classifications, including sexual orientation, gender identity, mental health status, religion, height, weight, attractiveness, and age, among others. What this means is that a given person's social identity and related life experiences can only be viewed and understood within the context of the multiplicity of social advantages and disadvantages they possess (Gopaldas, 2013). In the workplace, employees may also possess various minority and majority statuses at the same time. These statuses are, in turn, often tied to organizational hierarchies, whereby employees may hold positions of both dominance and subordination at once (Kollen, 2014). Below, we highlight the importance of taking an intersectional perspective when examining how those with existing stigmas may be perceived and reacted to differently over the course of their careers as they slowly age and take on stigmatizing traits associated with this identity category.

Lifespan Theories

In examining the intersection of aging with existing stigmas on employees' work experiences, a consideration of within-person changes over time is necessary.

As such, we broadly discuss lifespan theories below given that they are well-suited to explaining such changes. Indeed, lifespan approaches have been used to explain various topics related to work and aging, such as motivation (Kanfer & Ackerman, 2004), retirement (Wang, 2007), job design (Truxillo, Cadiz, Rineer, Zaniboni, & Fraccaroli, 2012), and leadership (Walter & Scheibe, 2013).

According to lifespan theorists, human development represents a fluid, continuous process whereby individual and contextual factors interact with one another to produce significant inter-individual variation over time. As such, a lifespan perspective requires a recognition of individuals' unique developmental trajectories (i.e., individual differences in developmental pathways) over time. In a review of the literature, Rudolph (2016) summarized several core tenets underlying existing perspectives on human development. First, development is a lifelong process and thus no age or period is more or less important. Thus, in order to understand aging at work, an equal focus must be placed on understanding how individuals develop from their initial entry to their final exit (i.e., retirement). Second, development is marked by both gains and losses, growth and decline, such that an understanding of aging at work cannot ignore how these gains and losses interactively contribute to individuals' unique developmental trajectories. Third, development is multidirectional, suggesting pluralism in trajectories of developmental change. Finally, development is a dynamic, within-person process that does not take place within a vacuum, but rather is influenced by various contextual factors, including historical, cultural, and organizational factors. Relatedly, Rudolph and Zacher (2017) expanded on these ideas within the context of generations in the workplace, arguing that generations are better understood from a contextualized lifespan perspective that accounts for contemporary time period and history-graded developmental influences on individuals' attitudes, values, beliefs, motives, and behavior at work.

From this perspective, it should be recognized that aging may have differential impacts on the work experiences of employees with existing stigmas, given individual differences (e.g., personality, cognitive abilities), prior history (e.g., parenting, experiences in childhood and young adulthood), and organizational factors (e.g., coworker support). In sum, a lifespan view provides a richer, more nuanced perspective on how intersections of aging and stigmas, whether invisible or visible, may shape people's work lives.

Stereotypes of Older Workers

Stereotypes are generalized beliefs ascribed to a particular group about their assumed characteristics or traits (Fiske & Neuberg, 1990), and thus age-based stereotypes are ascribed to people based on their age (Finkelstein, King, & Voyles, 2015). Although Finkelstein et al. (in the current volume) provide a detailed review of research in this area, our intention is to highlight parts of this research that are relevant to our focus, which is to help understand the dynamic and compounding effects of age stereotyping with that of other diversity categories over the lifespan.

Studied rather extensively, research has found that older workers face a number of age stereotypes in the workplace. Posthuma and Guerrero's (2013) recent work helped classify age stereotypes as varying across two dimensions, (1) polarity, and (2) veracity, where polarity reflects the degree to which the content of the stereotype favorably (vs. unfavorably) depicts the group, and veracity represents the degree to which the stereotype is empirically supported (true vs. false). Reviews of the age stereotype research (e.g., Finkelstein, Ryan, & King, 2013; Ng & Feldman, 2012; Posthuma & Campion, 2009; Posthuma, Wagstaff, & Campion, 2012) suggest that among the common stereotypes of older workers with negative polarity are the beliefs that older workers are poorer performers, less motivated, less willing and able to learn, and more resistant to change compared with younger workers. Among the stereotypes with positive polarity are the beliefs that older workers are more dependable, experienced, committed, and less likely to quit their jobs compared with younger workers. With regard to the veracity of these stereotypes, an abundance of empirical evidence has refuted nearly all of the negative stereotypes while many of the positive stereotypes have been supported. For example, in a series of meta-analyses, Ng and Feldman (2008, 2009, 2010, 2012) showed that, while age is largely unrelated to task performance, it is positively related to organizational citizenship behavior and negatively related to counterproductive behavior, absence, and turnover (Ng & Feldman, 2008, 2009). They also found that older workers had more positive task-, people- and organization-based attitudes at work (Ng & Feldman, 2010), and no evidence supported the stereotypes that older workers are less motivated or more resistant to change compared with younger workers (Ng & Feldman 2012).

Despite considerable disconfirming evidence, negative stereotypes of older workers persist and have negative effects on those workers. A growing body of work has begun to relate these negative stereotypes to discrimination against older workers (Chiu, Chan, Snape, & Redman, 2001; Fasbender & Wang, 2017). For example, older workers are evaluated more negatively than younger workers more generally, and with regard to advancement, selection, and performance appraisals (Bal, Reiss, Rudolph & Baltes, 2011; Gordon & Arvey, 2004). Beyond the possibility for discrimination, working in an environment where one may be aware of others holding negative stereotypes can also have negative effects on older workers via the process of meta-stereotypes and stereotype threat. Indeed, there is a large body of research that has shown the deleterious effects of stereotype threat on the performance of other stigmatized groups such as ethnic minorities (Walton, Murphy, & Ryan, 2015), and evidence for its negative effects on older workers is beginning to accumulate (Lamont, Swift, & Abrams, 2015; Oliveira & Cabral-Cardoso, 2017). Below, we will discuss the intersection of age and three categories of diversity including gender, race/ethnicity, and LGBT identities.

Social Categories of Diversity and Their Intersection with Age

Gender

Over half a century ago, women began entering the workforce in large numbers. Currently women make up 57 percent of the United States labor force and are staying in the workplace longer than ever before (US Department of Labor, Women's Bureau, 2016). In 2016, labor force participation rates for women between the ages of 55 and 64 was 58 percent, while it was 70 percent for men, but by 2024 participation rates are projected to increase to 63 percent for women and stagnate for men (US Department of Labor, Women's Bureau, 2016). Thus, the gender gap in labor force participation rates for older workers is narrowing and especially so at older ages. Although participation rates for older workers are becoming increasingly equal, the work experiences of men and women are substantially different. Many occupations in the labor market continue to be segregated by gender where female-dominated occupations tend to have less prestige and status compared with male-dominated occupations (Cha, 2013). Women also tend to be concentrated in lower-level positions, and have difficulty reaching senior leadership roles (Catalyst, 2016a; Haveman & Beresford, 2011). Ultimately, this horizontal and vertical segregation of men and women in the labor market has contributed to pay disparity where women are still paid less than men (Catalyst, 2016b). The traditional division of labor between men and women across work and nonwork roles also helps to create differences in the work experiences of women and men. Women still bear the brunt of household duties in child rearing and, as a result more, often have a discontinuous work history (Abele & Spurk, 2011). At older ages, women are also more likely to take on caring for elderly parents (Aumann, Gajinsky, Sakai, Brown, & Bond, 2010).

One of the most well-reasoned and supported explanations for these differences in work experiences lies in the differing gender norms and expectations for the roles men and women inhabit. According to social role theory (Eagly, 1987; Eagly, Wood, & Diekman, 2000) gender stereotypes stem from these traditional social roles as well as power inequalities between men and women. Gender stereotypes are descriptive and prescriptive such that they reflect the beliefs about how women and men behave and set expectations for how they *should* behave (Burgess & Borgida, 1999; Eagly, 1987). For men, they are ascribed as having more achievement-oriented traits, often characterized as being more agentic, aggressive, forceful, and ambitious, whereas for women, they are viewed as having more service-oriented traits, such as being more communal, interpersonally sensitive, warm, nurturing, and deferential (Prentice & Carranza, 2002; Eagly, 1987). These stereotypes are problematic insofar as they are often inaccurate, and when one violates the stereotypes associated with one's gender this can be met with backlash in the form of negative social and economic consequences (Rudman & Phelan, 2008). These stereotypes are also problematic when they are misaligned with stereotypes regarding specific work roles. This lack of fit (Heilman, 1983) or incongruity (Eagly & Karau, 2002) between gender role and work role stereotypes can often lead to bias and discrimination. This misalignment and its effects are exemplified by the 'think manager–think male' phenomenon (Schein, 1973) which has received considerable support in the literature (Heilman, 2001; Schein, Mueller, Lituchy, & Liu, 1996).

Viewed from the perspective of intersectionality, gender role stereotypes can jointly interact with stereotypes associated with other social identities to produce unique consequences for those who are subjected to them. This is sometimes referred to as double or multiple jeopardy if more than one set of negative stereotypes are combined (Dowd & Bengtson, 1978). One early example of double jeopardy is the double standard of aging (Sontag, 1972), which suggested that as women age they are judged more negatively in terms of being old, less attractive and less valuable than men who are seen as being distinguished, well off and of higher status. Recent research on this model suggests that not all evaluations of aging women are necessarily more negative (Kite, Stockdale, Whitley, & Johnson, 2005) and we speculate that not all stereotypes of aging men are positive (e.g., that men are confronted with a loss of the agentic stereotype as they become older). Rather, it is likely that the degree to which negative evaluations of women and men occur depends on the context (e.g., work versus nonwork domain; Kornadt, Voss, & Rothermund, 2013).

Based on this more general literature, we would argue that the extent to which stereotypes operate within the workplace to produce differential negative consequences for older men and women also depends on context, and more specifically, the degree to which the joint stereotypes of multiple identities are more or less incongruent with the specific work situation. For example, some occupations are gender stereotyped as more male (e.g., construction), whereas others are age stereotyped as more youthful (e.g., information technology). Clearly these varying workplace contexts are likely to activate, or render specific stereotypes, more salient, and in turn, produce different effects on outcomes for older men and women. Research is beginning to emerge that shows the effects of jointly ascribed gender and age stereotypes and how they differentially influence ratings of adaptive performance (DeArmond et al., 2006) and, importantly, hiring decisions (Ruggs, Hebl, Walker, & Fa-Kaji., 2014) and leadership potential (Hirschfeld & Thomas, 2011). Taking a lifespan perspective, a long history of disadvantage in the workplace, owing in large part to gender role stereotypes that limit women's earnings and advancement, has translated into lower lifetime wealth for women overall (Ruel & Hauser, 2013). This, combined with the additional burden of stereotypes regarding age that impact hiring and advancement decisions for older workers, amount to a cumulative and continuing disadvantage for women into old age and retirement.

Race/Ethnicity

There has been a considerable increase in racial and ethnic diversity among older adults in the workforce. Currently, White workers make up the highest percentage of the US labor force (80 percent), but this population is expected to grow at a much slower rate than in previous decades. Owing to higher birth, labor force participation, and international migration rates of other racial and ethnic groups (Toossi, 2012, 2016), it is projected that by 2039 people of color will make up the majority of the labor force (Wilson, 2016). The Hispanic and Asian populations are expected to have the highest growth rate compared with all other racial and ethnic groups (Toossi, 2012). The experiences of racial and ethnic minorities in the workforce has been considerably different from that of the White majority. Racial and ethnic minorities have long experienced the manifestations of prejudice. Before major changes were made to legal and regulatory oversight and societal norms, overt acts of discrimination were quite pervasive and even sanctioned in US organizations. These acts had a direct effect on the types of occupations, work-roles, and work-related experiences of racial and ethnic minorities. Yet, more recently, this more overt form of discrimination has been at least partially replaced with more insidious and covert forms of discrimination (Cortina, 2008). Generally, more subtle forms of discrimination have been referred to as micro-aggressions and include experiences such as neglect, ostracism, and incivility (Rowe, 1990; Van Laer & Janssens, 2011). Studies have shown that the impact of such prejudice and discrimination can be significant and damaging to the target's physical, psychological, and work-related well-being (e.g., Deitch et al., 2003).

The overt and subtle discrimination that racial and ethnic minorities face often stem from societal stereotypes that shape the perceptions, interpretations, and judgements people have of different groups (Dovidio, Gaertner, & Kawakami, 2010). As mentioned above, the stereotypes ascribed to particular groups are derived from the social roles they inhabit. Commonly-held stereotypes ascribed to White and Asian Americans are smart, hardworking, and ambitious (Hurh & Kim, 1989), where Asian Americans are seen as the 'model minority' (Gilbert, Carr-Ruffino, Ivancevich, & Lownes-Jackson, 2003). Hispanics and African Americans, however, are believed to be lazy, ignorant, and less determined (Dixon & Rosenbaum, 2004). Other studies have found that African Americans are characterized as having more negative traits (e.g., incompetent and confrontational) than Hispanics (e.g., hardworking and loyal; Heilman, Block, & Lucas, 1992; Kirschenman & Neckerman, 1991). The stereotypes and discrimination that many racial and ethnic minority groups face in the workplace has hindered the advancement of these groups in the workplace. Indeed, the data show that minorities face a steep climb to reach top leadership positions. In January 2016 there were only five Black CEOs working in Fortune 500 companies (McGirt, 2016). Another recent estimate found that, in Fortune 500 companies, 72 percent of corporate leadership roles are held by Whites, followed by Asians at 21 percent, Latino/a's at 2 percent, and African Americans at 0.6 percent (Jones, 2017). One reason for this is the incongruence between stereotypes of the successful manager and stereotypes of African American and Hispanic managers. Chung-Herrera and Lankau (2005) examined the congruence between perceptions of a successful manager prototype and ratings of racioethnic managerial stereotypes and found that White and Asian American manager stereotypes were most similar to the prototype of a successful manager whereas African American and Hispanic manager stereotypes were most dissimilar. Others have examined racial and gender identities, leadership style (dominance vs. communal) and effectiveness and found that Black men and White women leaders were rated more negatively when they used a dominant style of leadership, while Black women and White men did not face the same consequence (Livingston, Rosette, & Washington, 2012). This finding however, has been more of the exception than the rule. Other research has shown that Black women leaders are often judged more harshly for making mistakes in science-based occupations (Williams, Phillips, & Hall, 2014), and under conditions of organizational failure (Rosette & Livingston, 2012). These results suggest that Black women are held to higher standards than others who only violate one leadership prototype stereotype (i.e., Black men or White women).

Although somewhat mixed, the research regarding the effects of racial identity and gender suggest that the consequences of co-occurring stereotypes varies substantially across individuals doubly stigmatized by their group memberships. The addition of age to create multiply stigmatized individuals subject to compounded (race × gender × age) stereotypes adds an additional layer of complexity. The process of combining multiple stereotypes may occur in several ways. In some instances, stereotypes may combine in an additive fashion. The combination of negative stereotypes associated with membership in two or more groups may simply sum to produce even stronger negative stereotypes that lead to a truly multiple disadvantage. However, the simple sum of stereotypes may be inadequate when the stereotypes of multiple group memberships are not uniformly positive or negative. In this case, one possibility is that certain stereotypes will be weighted more heavily (or that they will be discounted) to either positive, negative, or no effect. For example, older people tend to be perceived as low in competence and high in warmth, while African Americans tend to be perceived similarly low in competence but low in warmth (Fiske, Cuddy & Glick, 2007). When combined it may be that older African Americans will be perceived as higher in warmth but still low in competence. Some evidence for this comes from Kang and Chasteen (2009) who found that the effect of negative stereotypes of African American men was 'buffered' when presented in combination with older age. Of course, other combinations of stereotypes may interact in such a way as to exacerbate their negative effects. Still another possibility is that stereotypes associated with multiple stigmatized group memberships may be synthesized to create an emergent category that is altogether unique (Kang & Bodenhausen, 2015). The 'cognitive calculus' by which stereotypes of individuals with membership in two or more stigmatized groups are combined is poorly understood and likely depends on individual differences among the perceivers (e.g., implicit attitudes) and characteristics of the work environment (e.g., occupation, level in hierarchy) that render some stereotypes more salient (Marcus & Fritzsche, 2015). What is clear, however, is that racial minorities fare poorer in the workplace over the course of their work lives and that translates into cumulative disadvantage at older ages in terms of poorer health (Brown, 2016), wealth and retirement savings (McKernan, Ratcliffe, Steuerle, & Zhang, 2013).

Sexual Orientation and Gender Identity

Gender and race represent two visible characteristics that carry with them negative stereotypes and stigma. As the workforce has grown more diverse, a number of 'hidden' or potentially concealable stigmatized characteristics have become increasingly acknowledged. Chief among these are sexual and gender minority identities such as those who are lesbian, gay, bisexual, and transgender (LGBT). Based on population estimates, it is reported that 2.7 million older adults aged 50 and older, or 2.4 percent of older adults in the US, identity as LGBT, and it is projected that by 2060 this number will double to over five million (Fredriksen-Goldsen & Kim, 2017). Others have suggested that 1.75 to four million older adults aged 60 and older identify as LGBT (Administration on Aging, 2014).

However, these estimates are likely rather conservative given that studies have found that some report being attracted to or have engaged in sexual activities with others of the same sex but do not identify as a sexual or gender minority (Copen, Chandra, & Febo-Vazquez, 2016), while others identify as LGBT but decide to conceal their identity given the negative social stigma it carries (King, Mohr, Peddie, Jones, & Kendra, 2014). The decision to disclose or conceal is driven by multiple factors. One factor to conceal stems from the fear of discrimination, which is justified given that as many as 80 percent of LGB people have faced some form of harassment throughout their life (Katz-Wise & Hyde, 2012), and an estimated 56 percent of LGB employees who have disclosed at work report at least one form of employment discrimination because of their sexual orientation (Sears & Mallory, 2011). For those employees who identify as transgender, a Williams Institute report found that 15 to 57 percent of transgender employees reported experiencing discrimination at work, 6 to 60 percent reported being unemployed, and 22 to 64 percent of those working earned less than $25,000 per year (Badgett, Lau, Sears, & Ho, 2007). Others have reported as many as 90 percent of transgender employees have experienced harassment, mistreatment, or discrimination at work, where 47 percent reported being either fired, not hired, or denied a promotion due to their transgender identity (Grant et al., 2010). A recent study further found that experiences of transgender discrimination at work were associated with emotional exhaustion, and that this relation was explained by heightened levels of non-abnormal paranoid cognition (Thoroughgood, Sawyer, & Webster, in press). While these are the experiences of those who decide to disclose their LGBT identity, those who conceal their identity are not spared from negative effects. For example, research shows that those who conceal their LGBT identities experience heightened levels of fear about being found out and/or deciding how, when, and where to disclose (Clair, Beatty, MacLean, 2005; King, Reilly, & Hebl, 2008; Ragins, Singh, & Cornwell, 2007). Thus, those with a concealable stigmatized identity face a double-edged sword.

Societal attitudes and stereotypes are the primary cause of the types of discriminatory behaviors faced by LGBT people. Commonly held negative stereotypes of LGBT individuals include "... HIV positive, sexual predators, man-hating, swishy, butch, confused, sick, or other such stereotypes" (Lucksted, 2004, p. 31). For gay and lesbians specifically, Kite and Deaux (1987) proposed the implicit inversion hypothesis, which argued that people hold the belief that gays and lesbians violate traditional gender roles and are expected to possess characteristics of the opposite gender. This hypothesis has been supported by empirical studies showing that gay men are perceived as more feminine/less masculine, and lesbian women are perceived as less feminine/more masculine compared with their heterosexual counterparts (Blashill & Powlishta, 2009). It should also be noted that there is considerable heterogeneity in the stereotypes and attitudes that people have about specific sexual or gender minority identities. That is, people can have somewhat different stereotypes and attitudes toward lesbian women than they do toward gay men, or between gay men and bisexual or transgender people from both outside and even within the LGBT community. For example, negative stereotypes of those who identify as transgender are more negative than those who identify as lesbian, gay or bisexual (Norton & Herek, 2013), and there have been calls to study these groups separately (Sawyer, Thoroughgood, & Webster, 2016). While not wanting to obscure differences across LGBT identities nor confound these groups, a complete discussion across all possible LGBT identities cross-classified by race, gender, and age is beyond the scope of this chapter.

Societal beliefs of LGBT-based stereotypes can have detrimental effects for LGBT employees when the content of those stereotypes does not fit with the characteristics of a particular occupation or work role they may want to hold. In a recent study, Liberman and Golom (2015) reported that the prototype of a successful manager was most similar to heterosexual men and women managers, and most dissimilar to the profile of a gay male manager. Interestingly, however, lesbian women managers were viewed as having a moderate fit with the successful manager prototype. Thus, gay men may be more in danger of work-related discrimination than lesbian women due to the perceived mismatch between gay-related stereotypes and that of the successful manager prototype. Another study, examining perceptions of transgender leaders, found that participants rated leaders who revealed a transgender identity lower in effectiveness and likability than cisgender leaders (Adams & Webster, 2017).

Like the intersection of gender and race, the inclusion of sexual or gender minority identity as it too intersects with age creates a number of different stereotypes that may compete with or complement each other. For example, people hold stereotypes that sexuality among older people is either 'distasteful' or that older people are simply asexual (Dixon, 2012). On the one hand, the extent to which the 'distasteful' stereotype combines with the stereotype of LGBT people as 'sick' could combine to produce stronger negative effects at the intersection of age *and* sexual/gender minority status. On the other hand, it could be that the asexual stereotypes of old people tempers the effect of the stereotype of LGBT people as promiscuous. This type of finding would be consistent with research showing that counter-stereotypes may buffer the effects of negative stereotypes and increase liking of lesbian women and gay men (Cohen, Hall & Tuttle, 2009; Pedulla, 2014). Similar to the intersection age with other diversity group characteristics, the process by which multiple stereotypes become combined is poorly understood and likely influenced by individual differences among the perceivers and organizational/occupational context. Regardless of the process that produces it, however, considerable evidence indicates that a lifetime of overt discrimination (owing in part to a lack of legal protections) and more covert discrimination (i.e., in the form or micro-aggressions) as well as the stress associated with identity management and disclosure can have a negative impact on the wellbeing of LGBT at older ages. Substantial evidence finds that compared with heterosexual people, LGBT people have poorer physical health and mental health outcomes at older ages (Fredriksen-Goldsen, Kim et al., 2013). Considering the intersection of race and LGB at older ages, several studies find that among older LGB adults, both African American and Hispanic people reported higher instances of lifetime discrimination, lower socioeconomic status, and social support which, in turn, led to lower mental health (Kim & Fredriksen-Goldsen, 2016; Kim, Jen, & Fredriksen-Goldsen, 2016). Similarly, Bostwick, Boyd, Hughes, West, and McCabe (2014) found that among LGB adults, sexual minority discrimination in combination with racial/ethnic and gender discrimination were related to mental health disorders. The few studies examining older transgender individuals found that their mental and physical health risks were significantly more detrimental than those of the LGB participants (Fredriksen-Goldsen, Cook-Daniels et al., 2013). Interestingly, some research reports that compared younger with older adults, the relationship between lifetime discrimination and physical and mental health was strongest among those who were over 80 years old (Fredriksen-Goldsen, Kim, Shiu, Goldsen, & Emlet, 2015). The authors suggest that one reason for this may be differences in the sociopolitical context in which their participants came of age.

Indeed, social and political attitudes surrounding LGBT people have been changing rapidly and it may be the case that older workers (who came of age when their LGBT identity was considered a mental illness and even illegal) experienced and were impacted by LGBT stereotypes differently than current and future workers.

Directions for Future Research

As alluded to above, research that examines the intersections of age with other potentially stigmatized statuses is rare. Intersectionality (Crenshaw, 1989) is important to study because it gives researchers a more accurate view of how various identity categories operate in tandem, giving a more accurate and nuanced perspective on how individuals are perceived overall. Thus, future researchers should certainly examine how holding multiple minority identity statuses, in conjunction with age, might affect perceptions of others at work and beyond. Further, while very little intersectional research examining the impact of age exists in the literature, even smaller amounts of research exist that study the actual perspectives of those who experience stigma stemming from age. Being able to better understand the lived experiences of those who hold multiple stigmatized identities, in combination with age, will allow researchers to truly make space for the voices of those suffering from age-related and other stigmas to "shine." Qualitative work may be particularly important in laying the foundation for strong theoretical frameworks that expand our understanding of how intersectionality operates for those who face stigma related to age.

Specifically, within the literature, two approaches to intersectionality exist: the additive approach and the multiplicative approach. The additive approach suggests that holding a greater number of minority statuses will result in increasingly negative outcomes (Cole, 2009; Purdie-Vaughns & Eibach, 2008). Contrastingly, the multiplicative approach suggests that holding a greater number of minority statuses will likely result in different outcomes, but that they might not always make outcomes "worse" (Hancock, 2007; King, Reilly, & Hebl, 2008; McCall, 2005). Given the small amount of intersectional work conducted on age, we believe that researchers would benefit from understanding how age might compound the impact of other minority identities or change the meaning of these identities, across contexts. For example, in a workplace consisting mostly of young, white males, an older, Black woman may stand out significantly from her peers, making her more likely to suffer negative outcomes. However, being an older, Black woman may also make her so distinctive from her peers that they don't perceive her as a "threat." Thus, the likelihood that she might face negative consequences may actually decrease as the number of minority statuses she holds increases.

As another example, an older person who also has a physical disability may be viewed more negatively at work, if stereotypes about being older and being physically disabled both hold negative connotations regarding a lack of ability to perform the job properly. However, if individuals view having physical disabilities and being older as normative in combination (i.e., people are more likely to suffer physically as they age), it may be the case that being older decreases negative perceptions related to disability status, compared with those that might be faced by someone younger with a physical disability. Therefore, future researchers should attempt to tease apart the effects that age might have in combination with other identities, not to determine who has it "worse," but rather to understand how different combinations of age and other identities might uniquely impact the work experiences and attitudes of employees across the lifespan.

Future Directions for Practice

As discussed above, age is an impactful identity that can intersect meaningfully with other identity categories to create unique experiences and outcomes that occur throughout the lives of working individuals. We will now turn to the ways in which organizations and individuals can alleviate stigma associated with age, in order to create more diverse and inclusive workplaces for employees across the lifespan. Because it is always preferable to resolve stigma at the source, we will first outline how organizations can create more inclusive workplaces. However, because individuals do not always have job mobility and may have a lot of vested costs in organizations that they have been with for some time, it is also important to think about how individuals might buffer some of the negative impacts associated with age-related stigma at work. We will start by discussing organizational-level solutions for alleviating age discrimination at work and then move into discussing individual-level strategies for combating negative age-related perceptions that may be encountered in the workplace.

Organizational-Level Solutions

While organizations may resort to solving the effects age of stereotyping, including age-related discrimination and harassment by relying on formal organizational policies, research suggests that having inclusive and fair policies are just the starting point. For example, a recent meta-analysis demonstrated that, within a LGBT population, supportive workplace relationships were more strongly related to workplace attitudes and strain, and inclusive climates were more strongly related to perceived discrimination and disclosure (Webster, Adams, Maranto, Sawyer, & Thoroughgood, in press). Thus, organizations can not just rest on having good policies "on the books." Having a climate that is in alignment with these policies is also important in shaping the workplace experiences of stigmatized employees. Of course, policies can protect employees from discrimination and provide peace of mind when employees are attempting to navigate potentially hostile work environments. But, proactively achieving inclusivity is not the same as avoiding discriminatory events. Companies must strive to be actively age inclusive, as well as inclusive in other areas of diversity (in addition to being forward thinking with regard to the law), to truly create positive working environments for employees across age ranges and with diverse, intersectional identities.

To achieve inclusivity at work, recent research has outlined some steps that are useful for achieving equity from the top down. For example, work that has been conducted in transgender populations suggests that instituting diversity training, which includes specific information about the population at hand (in this case, various age categories), as well as ensuring that inclusivity is consistent across organizational functions (legal, marketing, HR, etc.) (Sawyer & Thoroughgood, 2017), can drive perceptions of stigma and climate overall. Across age groups, this means that age-related stereotypes, and the ways in which they may intersect with the stereotypes of other diversity categories should be addressed in diversity trainings, and relevant research that highlights similarities between dominant and non-dominant groups should be reviewed. Further, creating consistency in age inclusivity across organizational functions requires organizational leaders to be trained on all areas of inclusivity, so that decisions are not made which contradict the organization's messaging overall. For example, while employees may feel their co-workers are generally well-versed in a particular type of inclusivity, a marketing campaign that presents elderly women as being unattractive or that stereotypes racial minority youth may fly in the face of these broader efforts toward decreasing age-related, and intersectional stereotypes at work.

Further, prior research has demonstrated that contact with employees who are stigmatized can help to decrease stereotypes associated with that particular group (Allport, 1954; Amir, 1969). However, as described above, age stereotypes may vary according to other intersectional identities one holds. Thus, contact alone may not be enough to capture all of the nuances associated with truly understanding the lived experiences of those with intersectional stigmas that include age – contact may have to happen under optimal conditions in order for change to occur. In a review of the literature on the contact hypothesis, Pettigrew (1998) described four cognitive, affective, and behavioral mechanisms by which contact may lead to understanding of and support for out-group members. These four components may be particularly useful in determining how to create a positive work environment for employees across the lifespan.

First, learning new information about out-groups may reduce stereotyping and increase positive attitudes toward out-group members (Pettigrew, 1998). This is especially likely if new information is inconsistent with existing stereotypes, out-group members are perceived as prototypical for their group (i.e., they are not seen as outliers when stereotypes are counteracted), and if contact is frequent (Rothbart & John, 1985). Thus, organizations may want to facilitate intergroup contact that is specifically oriented toward the goal of better understanding the perspective of employees from different age groups and with other intersecting, non-dominant identities. As mentioned above, this could occur through diversity training, or it could occur through diverse, cross-age group mentoring pairs or networking events. Any event that allows for sharing of information that might be stereotype inconsistent may be useful for achieving this goal. Second, by being civil toward out-group members in order to fulfil one's duty to be a good team member, one's attitudes may change (Pettigrew, 1998). Cognitive dissonance theory suggests individuals revise their attitudes to align with their behaviors (Aronson & Patnoe, 1997). As such, because working toward common team goals requires a certain degree of civility, more inclusive attitudes may result from greater contact and collaboration with team members from perceived out-groups. Thus, organizations should also attempt to create diverse, cross-age teams when possible, to enhance perceptions of similarity (working toward a common goal) as opposed to difference (being from various age or other demographic groups).

Third, emotional ties may be strengthened as a result of intergroup contact (Pettigrew, 1998), such that empathy increases as a function of enhanced contact with out-group members (Batson, 1987, 1991; Batson et al., 1989; Batson, Early, & Salvarani, 1997). Because empathy has been found to increase prosocial behaviors (Eisenberg & Miller, 1987; Batson, 1987, 1991; Batson et al., 1989, 1997), enhanced contact with out-group members may promote sympathy toward such individuals and, in turn, support for them by in-group members. Finally, these more inclusive, empathetic attitudes may generalize to other out-group members not known specifically by the target individual (Pettigrew, 1998). Thus, in-group members may become involved in broader efforts to promote workplace equality as a result of contact with out-group members. Such individuals may be more likely to pledge public support to potential victims of discrimination, in all of their intersections, thereby conveying to out-group members that they are valued despite their broader perceptions of discrimination.

Overall, organizations should focus on creating environments in which age, and the intersections of age and other stigmatized identities, are not ignored, but rather celebrated and highlighted – with the goal of breaking down stereotypes, highlighting similarities, and encouraging empathy and productive collaboration across diverse groups of employees. In fact, research shows that being accepted for one's authentic self by co-workers is a key predictor of job attitudes (Martinez, Sawyer, Thoroughgood, Ruggs, & Smith, 2017). Thus, achieving inclusivity may help to improve the attitudes and work lives of those who promulgate stigma, as well as those who might experience it.

Individual-Level Factors

Again, while it is the goal to ensure that workplaces are inclusive and individuals do not need to combat stigma on their own, this does not accurately describe the current state of affairs. Thus, individuals may need to leverage specific strategies that might allow them to cope with potential stigma, should it arise. Fortunately, diverse, older populations have been demonstrated to be quite resilient in the face of hardships (Averett, Yoon, & Jenkins, 2016; Hall & Fine, 2005; Jones & Nystrom, 2002). Interestingly, those with intersectional stigmatized identities in addition to age may fare even better than their non-stigmatized counterparts in some respects (Butler, 2004). For example, they may have developed skills that help them to cope when faced with prejudice and bias due to their identities, and have already located a support system of friends, colleagues, and family who have helped them to overcome difficult situations in the past (Butler, 2004). Thus, while age-related stigma is challenging, diverse aging employees may be able to draw on past stigmatizing experiences to better respond to and cope with current or ongoing stigmatization.

Prior research has also documented specific ways in which those with a stigmatized identity may be more resilient. One recommendation is to identify and leverage those positive relationships (family, friends, co-workers) that can help those facing intersectional age-related stigmas (Follins, Walker, & Lewis, 2014). For example, individuals could become more involved in groups within the local community in which they feel safe, or continue to remain engaged in leisure activities despite being busy with many life responsibilities (perhaps for younger workers) or constrained by loss of friends or family (perhaps for older workers). These activities may already be commonplace within diverse aging populations, given that prior research has demonstrated that 91 percent of LGBT older adults engage in weekly leisure and wellness activities, while 82 percent engage in moderate physical activities (Fredriksen-Goldsen, 2016). This is particularly important for older workers, given that group ties enhance cognitive health as individuals age (Haslam, Cruwys, Milne, Kan, & Haslam, 2016).

Further, positive attitudes toward oneself and the life cycle overall, may predict positive outcomes for diverse employees in various life stages, as they grow and change. For example, self-efficacy has been demonstrated to create resilience in stigmatized populations (Follins, Walker, & Lewis, 2014). Thus, engaging in activities at work and at home which help to drive mastery and pride in one's work can be useful in developing a buffer for those most likely to encounter stigmatizing experiences. Additionally, in a review of the literature on positive psychology and aging (Vahia, Chattillion, Kavirajan, & Depp, 2011), resilience, optimism, self-efficacy, and positive attitudes toward aging were outlined as key indicators of successful growth across the lifespan. Similarly, in a study of aging transgender individuals, agency, nurturing the spiritual self, and self-acceptance were all found to relate to resilience in the face of aging

(McFadden, Frankowski, Flick, & Witten, 2013). Thus, examining ways in which these resilience factors might be enhanced within diverse aging populations could help to create psychological reserves that might be drawn upon when stigmatizing events occur. In a recent study on transgender employees, mindfulness was shown to buffer the negative effects of perceived discrimination (Thoroughgood, Sawyer, & Webster, in press). Older workers experiencing stigma may be able to train themselves to effectively separate themselves from the stigmatizing views of others and to focus and draw on prior resources (past experiences with stigma, support networks), in order to overcome the negative consequences associated with intersectional age-related bias at work.

Conclusion

Overall, age and other diverse identities can intersect to create unique and meaningful employment experiences across the lifespan. In an increasingly diverse population, with regard to age, as well as gender, race/ethnicity, and sexual orientation it is important to understand the implications of age for employees who may hold other non-dominant identities. Stereotypes that exist at the interstices of age, race, gender, and sexual orientation can accumulate and exacerbate over the lifespan. Thus, it is important that workplaces, and society more broadly, create inclusive spaces for individuals at every age, and within every diverse group. In this way, we can strive to be the generation that creates a more fair and just world for future generations to come.

References

Abele, A. E., & Spurk, D. (2011). The dual impact of gender and the influence of timing of parenthood on men's and women's career development: Longitudinal findings. *International Journal of Behavioral Development, 35*, 225–232.

Adams, G. A., & Webster, J. R. (2017). When leaders are not who they appear: The effects of leader disclosure of a concealable stigma on follower reactions. *Journal of Applied Social Psychology, 47*, 649–664.

Administration on Aging (2014). *A profile of older Americans 2014.* US Department of Health and Human Services. Retrieved from www.acl.gov/sites/default/files/Aging%20and%20Disability%20in%20America/2014-Profile.pdf.

Allport, G. W. (1954). *The nature of prejudice.* Reading, MA: Addison-Wesley.

Amir, Y. (1969). Contact hypothesis in ethnic relations. *Psychological Bulletin, 71*, 319.

Aronson, E., & Patnoe, S. (1997). *The jigsaw classroom.* New York: Longman.

Aumann, K., Gajinsky, E., Sakai, K., Brown, M., & Bond, J. T. (2010). *The elder care case study: Everyday realities and wishes for change.* New York: Families and Work Institute.

Averett, P., Yoon, I., & Jenkins, C. L. (2013). Older lesbian experiences of homophobia and ageism. *Journal of Social Service Research, 29*, 3–15.

Badgett, M. V., Lau, H., Sears, B., & Ho, D. (2007). *Bias in the workplace: Consistent evidence of sexual orientation and gender identity discrimination.* Los Angeles: The Williams Institute, University of California.

Bal, A. C., Reiss, A. E. B., Rudolph, C. W., & Baltes, B. B. (2011). Examining positive and negative perceptions of older workers: A meta-analysis. *The Journals of Gerontology Series B: Psychological Sciences and Social Sciences, 66*, 687–698.

Batson, C. D. (1987). Prosocial motivation: Is it ever truly altruistic? *Advances in Experimental Social Psychology, 20*, 65–122.

Batson, C. D. (1991). *The altruism question: Towards a social-psychological answer*. Hillsdale, NJ: Erlbaum.

Batson, C. D., Batson, J. G., Griffitt, C. A., Barrientos, S., Brandt, J. R., Sprengelmeyer, P., & Bayly, M. J. (1989). Negative-state relief and the empathy – altruism hypothesis. *Journal of Personality and Social Psychology, 56*, 922.

Batson, C. D., Early, S., & Salvarani, G. (1997). Perspective taking: Imagining how another feels versus imaging how you would feel. *Personality and Social Psychology Bulletin, 23*, 751–758.

Blashill, A. J., & Powlishta, K. K. (2009). Gay stereotypes: The use of sexual orientation as a cue for gender-related attributes. *Sex Roles, 61*, 783–793.

Bostwick, W. B., Boyd, C. J., Hughes, T. L., West, B. T., & McCabe, S. E. (2014). Discrimination and mental health among lesbian, gay, and bisexual adults in the United States. *American Journal of Orthopsychiatry, 84*, 35.

Brown, T. H. (2016). Diverging fortunes: Racial/ethnic inequality in wealth trajectories in middle and late life. *Race and Social Problems, 1*, 29–41.

Burgess, D., & Borgida, E. (1999). Who women are, who women should be: Descriptive and prescriptive gender stereotyping in sex discrimination. *Psychology, Public Policy, and Law, 5*, 665–692.

Butler, J. (2004). *Undoing gender*. Demark: Psychology Press.

Catalyst (2016a). *Catalyst quick take: Women's earnings and income*. New York: Catalyst.

Catalyst (2016b). *2015 Catalyst census: Women and men board directors*. New York: Catalyst.

Cha, Y. (2013). Overwork and the persistence of gender segregation in occupations. *Gender and Society, 27*, 158–184.

Chiu, W., Chan, A. W., Snape, E., & Redman, T. (2001). Age stereotypes and discriminatory attitudes towards older workers: An East–West comparison. *Human Relations, 54*, 629–661.

Chung-Herrera, B. G., & Lankau, M. J. (2005). Are we there yet? An assessment of fit between stereotypes of minority managers and the successful-manager prototype. *Journal of Applied Social Psychology, 35*, 2029–2056.

Clair, J. A., Beatty, J. E., & MacLean, T. L. (2005). Out of sight but not out of mind: Managing invisible social identities in the workplace. *Academy of Management Review, 30*, 78–95.

Cohen, T. R., Hall, D. L., & Tuttle, J. (2009). Attitudes toward stereotypical versus counter-stereotypical gay men and lesbians. *Journal of Sex Research, 46*, 274–281.

Cole, E. R. (2009). Intersectionality and research in psychology. *American Psychologist, 64*, 170–180.

Copen, C. E., Chandra, A., & Febo-Vazquez, I. (2016). Sexual behavior, sexual attraction, and sexual orientation among adults aged 18–44 in the United States: Data from the 2011–2013 National Survey of Family Growth. *National Health Statistics Reports, 88*, 1–14.

Cortina, L. M. (2008). Unseen injustice: Incivility as modern discrimination in organizations. *Academy of Management Review, 33*, 55–75.

Crenshaw, K. (1989). Demarginalizing the intersection of race and sex: A black feminist critique of antidiscrimination doctrine, feminist theory and antiracist politics. *University of Chicago Legal Forum*, 139–167.

Crenshaw, K. (1991). Mapping the margins: Intersectionality, identity, politics, and violence against women of color. *Stanford Law Review, 43*, 1241–1299.

Crocker, J., Major, B., & Steele, C. (1998). Social stigma. In D. T. Gilbert, S. T. Fiske, & G. Lindzey (Eds.), *The handbook of social psychology* (pp. 504–553). New York: McGraw-Hill.

DeArmond, S., Tye, M., Chen, P. Y., Krauss, A., Rogers, D. A., & Sintek, E. (2006). Age and gender stereotypes: New challenges in a changing workplace and workforce. *Journal of Applied Social Psychology, 36*, 2184–2214.

Deitch, E. A., Barsky, A., Butz, R. M., Chan, S., Brief, A. P., & Bradley, J. C. (2003). Subtle yet significant: The existence and impact of everyday racial discrimination in the workplace. *Human Relations, 56*, 1299–1324.

Dixon, J. (2012). Communicating (St)ageism: Exploring stereotypes of age and sexuality in the workplace. *Research on Aging, 34*, 654–669.

Dixon, J. C., & Rosenbaum, M. S. (2004). Nice to know you? Testing contact, cultural, and group threat theories of anti-Black and anti-Hispanic stereotypes. *Social Science Quarterly, 85*, 257–280.

Dovidio, J. F., Gaertner, S. L., & Kawakami, K. (2010). Racism. In J. F. Dovidio, M. Hewstone, P. Glick, & V. M. Esses (Eds.), *Handbook of prejudice, stereotyping, and discrimination* (pp. 312–327). Thousand Oaks, CA: Sage.

Dowd, J. J., & Bengtson, V. L. (1978). Aging in minority populations: An examination of the double jeopardy hypothesis. *Journal of Gerontology, 33*, 427–436.

Eagly, A. H. (1987). *Sex differences in social behavior: A social role interpretation.* Hillsdale, NJ: Lawrence Erlbaum.

Eagly, A. H., & Karau, S. J. (2002). Role congruity theory of prejudice toward female leaders. *Psychological Bulletin, 108*, 233–256.

Eagly, A. H., Wood, W., & Diekman, A. B. (2000). Social role theory of sex differences and similarities: A current appraisal. In T. Eckes, & H. M. Trautner (Eds.), *The developmental social psychology of gender* (pp. 123–174). Mahwah, NJ: Lawrence Erlbaum.

Eisenberg, N., & Miller, P. A. (1987). The relation of empathy to prosocial and related behaviors. *Psychological Bulletin, 101*, 91.

Fasbender, U., & Wang, M. (2017). Negative attitudes toward older workers and hiring decisions: Testing the moderating role of decision makers core self-evaluations. *Frontiers in Psychology, 7*, 1–10.

Finkelstein, L. M., King, E. B., & Voyles, E. C. (2015). Age metastereotyping and cross-age workplace interactions: A meta view of age stereotypes at work. *Work, Aging and Retirement, 1*, 26–40.

Finkelstein, L. M., Ryan, K. M., & King, E. B. (2013). What do the young (old) people think of me? Content and accuracy of age-based metastereotypes. *European Journal of Work and Organizational Psychology, 22*, 633–657.

Fiske, S. T., & Neuberg, S. L. (1990). A continuum of impression formation, from category-based to individuating processes: Influences of information and motivation on attention and interpretation. *Advances in Experimental Social Psychology, 23*, 1–74.

Fiske, S. T., Cuddy, A. J., & Glick, P. (2007). Universal dimensions of social cognition: Warmth and competence. *Trends in Cognitive Sciences, 11*, 77–83.

Follins, L. D., Walker, J. N. J., & Lewis, M. K. (2014). Resilience in Black lesbian, gay, bisexual, and transgender individuals: A critical review of the literature. *Journal of Gay & Lesbian Mental Health, 18*, 190–212.

Fredriksen-Goldsen, K. I. (2016). The future of LGBT+ aging: A blueprint for action in services, policies, and research. *Generations, 40*, 6–15.

Fredriksen-Goldsen, K. I., & Kim, H. J. (2017). The science of conducting research with LGBT older adults – An introduction to Aging with Pride: National Health, Aging, Sexuality and Gender Study. *The Gerontologist, 57*, 1–14.

Fredriksen-Goldsen, K. I., Cook-Daniels, L., Kim, H. J., Erosheva, E. A., Emlet, C. A., Hoy-Ellis, C. P., … & Muraco, A. (2013). Physical and mental health of transgender older adults: An at-risk and underserved population. *The Gerontologist, 54*, 488–500.

Fredriksen-Goldsen, K. I., Kim, H. J., Barkan, S. E., Muraco, A., & Hoy-Ellis, C. P. (2013). Health disparities among lesbian, gay, and bisexual older adults: Results from a population-based study. *American Journal of Public Health, 103*, 1802–1809.

Fredriksen-Goldsen, K. I., Kim, H. J., Shiu, C., Goldsen, J., & Emlet, C. (2015). Successful aging among LGBT older adults: Physical and mental health-related quality of life by age group. *The Gerontologist, 55*, 154–168.

Gilbert, J., Carr-Ruffino, N., Ivancevich, J. M., & Lownes-Jackson, M. (2003). An empirical examination of inter-ethnic stereotypes: Comparing Asian American and African American employees. *Public Personnel Management, 32*, 251–266.

Goffman, E. (1963). *Stigma: Notes on a spoiled identity.* Traverse City, MI: Jenkins Publishing Group.

Gopaldas, A. (2013). Intersectionality 101. *Journal of Public Policy and Marketing, 32*, 90–94.

Gordon, R. A., & Arvey, R. D. (2004). Age bias in laboratory and field settings: A meta-analytic investigation. *Journal of Applied Social Psychology, 34*, 468–492.

Grant, J. M., Mottet, L. A., Tanis, J., Harrison, L., Herman, J., & Keisling, M. (2010). *National transgender discrimination survey report on health and health care.* National Center for Transgender Equality and the National Gay and Lesbian Task Force.

Hall, R. L., & Fine, M. (2005). The stories we tell: The lives and friendship of two older Black lesbians. *Psychology of Women Quarterly, 29*, 177–187.

Hancock, A. (2007). Examining intersectionality as a research paradigm: Multiplication doesn't equal quick addition, *Perspectives on Politics, 5*, 63–79.

Haslam, C., Cruwys, T., Milne, M., Kan, C. H., & Haslam, S. A. (2016). Group ties protect cognitive health by promoting social identification and social support. *Journal of Aging and Health, 28*, 244–266.

Haveman, H. A., & Beresford, L. S. (2011). If you're so smart, why aren't you the boss? Explaining the persistent vertical gender gap in management. *Annals of the American Academy of Political and Social Science, 639*, 114–130.

Heilman, M. E. (1983). Sex bias in work settings: The lack of fit model. *Research in Organizational Behavior, 5*, 269–298.

Heilman, M. E. (2001). Description and prescription: How gender stereotypes prevent women's ascent up the organizational ladder. *Journal of Social Issues, 57*, 657–674.

Heilman, M. E., Block, C. J., & Lucas, J. A. (1992). Presumed incompetent? Stigmatization and affirmative action efforts. *Journal of Applied Psychology, 77*, 536.

Hirschfeld, R. R., & Thomas, C. H. (2011). Age and gender based role incongruence: Implications for knowledge mastery and observed leadership potential among personnel in a leadership development program. *Personnel Psychology, 54*, 661–692.

Hurh, W. M., & Kim, K. C. (1989). The "success" image of Asian Americans: Its validity, and its practical and theoretical implications. *Ethnic and Racial Studies, 12*, 512–538.

Jones, E. E., Farina, A., Hastorf, A. H., Markus, H., Miller, D. T., & Scott, R. A. (1984). *Social stigma: The psychology of marked relationships.* New York: Freeman.

Jones, S. (2017, June). White men account for 72% of corporate leadership at 16 of the Fortune 500 companies. *Fortune Magazine.* Retrieved from http://fortune.com/2017/06/09/white-men-senior-executives-fortune-500-companies-diversity-data/.

Jones, T. C., & Nystrom, N. M. (2002). Looking back ... looking forward: Addressing the lives of lesbians 55 and older. *Journal of Women and Aging, 14*, 59–76.

Kanfer, R., & Ackerman, P. L. (2004). Aging, adult development, and work motivation. *The Academy of Management Review, 29*, 440–458.

Kang, S. K., & Bodenhausen, G. V. (2015). Multiple identities in social perception and interaction: Challenges and opportunities. *Annual Review of Psychology, 66*, 547–574.

Kang, S. K., & Chasteen, A. L. (2009). Beyond the double-jeopardy hypothesis: Assessing emotion on the faces of multiply-categorizable targets of prejudice. *Journal of Experimental Social Psychology, 45*, 1281–1285.

Katz-Wise, S. L., & Hyde, J. S. (2012). Victimization experiences of lesbian, gay, and bisexual individuals: A meta-analysis. *Journal of Sex Research, 49*, 142–167.

Kim, H., & Fredriksen-Goldsen, K. (2016). Disparities in mental health quality of life between Hispanic and non-Hispanic White LGB midlife and older adults and the influence of lifetime discrimination, social connectedness, socioeconomic status, and perceived stress. *Research on Aging, 39*, 991–1012.

Kim, H., Jen, S., & Fredriksen-Goldsen, K. (2016). Health differences among African American, Hispanic, and White LGBT older adults. *The Gerontologist, 56*, 653–653.

King, E. B., Mohr, J. J., Peddie, C. I., Jones, K. P., & Kendra, M. (2014). Predictors of identity management: An exploratory experience-sampling study of lesbian, gay, and bisexual workers. *Journal of Management, 43*, 476–502.

King, E. B., Reilly, C., & Hebl, M. (2008). The best of times, the worst of times: Exploring dual perspectives of "coming out" in the workplace. *Group & Organization Management, 33*, 566–601.

Kirschenman, J., & Neckerman, K. M. (1991). "We'd love to hire them, but ...": The meaning of race for employers. *The Urban Underclass, 203*, 203–232.

Kite, M. E., & Deaux, K. (1987). Gender belief systems: Homosexuality and the implicit inversion theory. *Psychology of Women Quarterly, 11*, 83–96.

Kite, M. E., Stockdale, G. D., Whitley, B. E., & Johnson, B. T. (2005). Attitudes towards younger and older adults: An updated meta-analytic review. *Journal of Social Issues, 61*, 241–266.

Kollen, T. (2014). A review of minority stress related to employees' demographics and the development of an intersectional framework for their coping strategies in the workplace. In *The role of demographics in occupational stress and well being* (pp. 41–82). Bingley, UK: Emerald Publishing Group.

Kornadt, A. E., Voss, P., & Rothermund, K. (2013). Multiple standards of aging: Gender specific age stereotypes in different life domains. *European Journal of Ageing, 10*, 335–344.

Kulik, C. T. (2014). Working below and above the line: The research-practice gap in diversity management. *Human Resource Management, 24*, 129–144.

Lamont, R. A, Swift, H. J., Abrams, D. (2015). A review and meta-analysis of age-based stereotype threat: Negative stereotypes, not facts, do the damage. *Psychology of Aging, 30*, 180–193.

Liberman, B. E., & Golom, F. D. (2015). Think manager, think male? Heterosexuals' stereotypes of gay and lesbian managers. *Equality, Diversity, and Inclusion: An International Journal, 34*, 566–578.

Livingston, R. W., Rosette, A. S., & Washington, E. F. (2012). Can an agentic Black woman get ahead? The impact of race and interpersonal dominance on perceptions of female leaders. *Psychological Science, 23*, 354–358.

Lucksted, A. (2004). Lesbian, gay, bisexual, and transgender people receiving services in the public mental health system: Raising issues. *Journal of Gay and Lesbian Psychotherapy, 8*, 25–42.

Major, B., & O'Brien, L. T. (2005). System-justifying beliefs and psychological well-being: The roles of group status and identity. *Society for Personality and Social Psychology*, *31*, 1718–1729.

Marcus, J., & Fritzsche, B. A. (2015). One size doesn't fit all: Toward a theory on the intersectional salience of ageism at work. *Organizational Psychology Review*, *5*, 168–188.

Martinez, L. R., Sawyer, K. B., Thoroughgood, C. N., Ruggs, E. N., & Smith, N. A. (2017). The importance of being "me": The relation between authentic identity expression and transgender employees' work-related attitudes and experiences. *Journal of Applied Psychology*, *102*, 215–226.

McCall, L. (2005). The complexity of intersectionality. *Signs*, *30*, 1771–1800.

McGirt, E. (2016, January). Why race and culture matter in the c-suite. *Fortune Magazine*. Retrieved from http://fortune.com/black-executives-men-c-suite/.

McFadden, S. H., Frankowski, S., Flick, H., & Witten, T. M. (2013). Resilience and multiple stigmatized identities: Lessons from transgender persons' reflections on aging. In J. D. Sinnott (Ed.), *Positive psychology: Advances in understanding adult motivation* (pp. 247–267). New York: Springer.

McKernan, S. M., Ratcliffe, C., Steuerle, C. E., & Zhang, S. (2013). *Less than equal: Racial disparities in wealth accumulation*. Washington, DC: Urban Institute.

Ng, T. W., & Feldman, D. C. (2008). The relationship of age to ten dimensions of job performance. *Journal of Applied Psychology*, *93*, 392–423.

Ng, T. W., & Feldman, D. C. (2009). How broadly does education contribute to job performance? *Personnel Psychology*, *62*, 89–134.

Ng, T. W., & Feldman, D. C. (2010). The relationships of age with job attitudes: A meta-analysis. *Personnel Psychology*, *63*, 677–718.

Ng, T. W., & Feldman, D. C. (2012). Evaluating six common stereotypes about older workers with meta-analytical data. *Personnel Psychology*, *65*, 821–858.

Norton, A. T., & Herek, G. M. (2013). Heterosexuals' attitudes toward transgender people: Findings from a national probability sample of US adults. *Sex Roles*, *68*, 1–16.

Oliveira, E., & Cabral-Cardoso, C. (2017). Older workers representation and age-based stereotype threats in the workplace. *Journal of Managerial Psychology*, *32*, 254–268.

Pedulla, D. S. (2014). The positive consequences of negative stereotypes: Race, sexual orientation, and the job application process. *Social Psychology Quarterly*, *77*, 75–94.

Pettigrew, T. F. (1998). Intergroup contact theory. *Annual Review of Psychology*, *49*, 65–85.

Posthuma, R. A., & Campion, M. A. (2009). Age stereotypes in the workplace: Common stereotypes, moderators, and future research directions. *Journal of Management*, *35*, 158–188.

Posthuma, R. A., & Guerrero, L. (2013). Age stereotypes in the workplace: Multidimensionality, cross-cultural applications, and directions for future research. In J. Field, R. J. Burke, & C. L. Cooper (Eds.), *The SAGE handbook of aging, work and society* (pp. 250–265). Thousand Oaks, CA: Sage.

Posthuma, R. A., Wagstaff, M. F., & Campion, M. A. (2012). Age stereotypes and workplace age discrimination. In W. C. Borman & J. W. Hedge (Eds.), *The Oxford handbook of work and aging* (pp. 298–312). New York: Oxford University Press.

Prentice, D. A., & Carranza, E. (2002). What women and men should be, shouldn't be, are allowed to be, and don't have to be: The contents of prescriptive gender stereotypes. *Psychology of Women Quarterly*, *26*, 269–281.

Purdie-Vaughns, V., & Eibach, R. P. (2008). Intersectional invisibility: The distinct advantages and disadvantages of multiple subordinate-group identities. *Sex Roles*, *59*, 377–391.

Ragins, B. R., Singh, R., & Cornwell, J. M. (2007). Making the invisible visible: Fear and disclosure of sexual orientation at work. *Journal of Applied Psychology, 92*, 1103–1118.

Robbins, S. P., & Judge, T. A. (2010). *Organizational Behavior* (14th ed.). Upper Saddle River, NJ: Prentice Hall.

Rosette, A. S., & Livingston, R. W. (2012). Failure is not an option for Black women: Effects of organizational performance on leaders with single versus dual-subordinate identities. *Journal of Experimental Social Psychology, 48*, 1162–1167.

Rothbart, M., & John, O. P. (1985). Social categorization and behavioral episodes: A cognitive analysis of the effects of intergroup contact. *Journal of Social Issues, 41*, 81–104.

Rowe, M. P. (1990). Barriers to equality: The power of subtle discrimination to maintain unequal opportunity. *Employee Responsibilities and Rights Journal, 3*, 153–163.

Rudman, L. A., Phelan, J. E. (2008). Backlash effects for disconfirming gender stereotypes in organizations. *Research in Organizational Behavior, 28*, 61–79.

Rudolph, C. W. (2016). Lifespan developmental perspectives on working: A literature review of motivational theories. *Work, Aging, and Retirement, 2*, 130–158.

Rudolph, C. W., & Zacher, H. (2017). Considering generations from a lifespan developmental perspective. *Work, Aging and Retirement, 3*, 113–129.

Ruel, E., & Hauser, R. M. (2013). Explaining the gender wealth gap. *Demography, 50*, 1155–1176.

Ruggs, E. N., Hebl, M. R., Walker, S. S., & Fa-Kaji, N. (2014). Selection biases that emerge when age meets gender. *Journal of Managerial Psychology, 29*, 1028–1043.

Sawyer, K., & Thoroughgood, C. (2017). Gender non-conformity and the modern workplace. *Organizational Dynamics, 46*, 1–8.

Sawyer, K., Thoroughgood, C., & Webster, J. R. (2016). Beyond the gender binary: Achieving a more complete understanding of transgender workplace experiences. In T. Kollen (Ed.), *Sexual orientation and transgender issues in organizations – Global perspectives on LBGT workforce diversity* (pp. 21–42). New York: Springer.

Sears, B., & Mallory, C. (2011). *Documented evidence of employment discrimination and its effects on LGBT people*. Los Angeles, CA: The Williams Institute, UCLA School of Law.

Schein, V. E. (1973). The relationship between sex-role stereotypes and requisite management characteristics. *Journal of Applied Psychology, 57*, 95–100.

Schein, V. E., Mueller, R., Lituchy, T., & Liu, J. (1996). Think manager – think male: A global phenomenon? *Journal of Organizational Behavior, 17*, 33–41.

Sontag, S. (1972). The double standard of aging. *Saturday Review, 55*, 29–38.

Thoroughgood, C., Sawyer, K., & Webster, J. (in press). What lies beneath: How paranoid cognition explains the relations between transgender employees' perceptions of discrimination at work and their job attitudes and wellbeing. *Journal of Vocational Behavior*.

Toossi, M. (2012). Labor force projections to 2020: A more slowly growing workforce. *Monthly Labor Review*, 3–64.

Toossi, M. (2016). *BLS spotlight on statistics: A look at the future of the U.S. labor force to 2060*. Washington, DC: U.S. Department of Labor, Bureau of Labor Statistics.

Truxillo, D. M., Cadiz, D. M., Rineer, J. R., Zaniboni, S., & Fraccaroli, F. (2012). A lifespan perspective on job design: Fitting the job and the worker to promote job satisfaction, engagement, and performance. *Organizational Psychology Review, 2*, 340–360.

US Department of Labor, Women's Bureau (2016). Latest annual data. Retrieved from www.dol.gov/wb/stats/NEWSTATS/latest.htm#one.

Vahia, I. V., Chattillion, E., Kavirajan, H., & Depp, C. A. (2011). Psychological protective factors across the lifespan: Implications for psychiatry. *Psychiatric Clinics of North America, 34*, 231–248.

Van Laer, K., & Janssens, M. (2011). Ethnic minority professionals' experiences with subtle discrimination in the workplace. *Human Relations, 64,* 1203–1227.

Walter, F., & Scheibe, S. (2013). A literature review and emotion-based model of age and leadership: New directions for the trait approach. *The Leadership Quarterly, 24,* 882–901.

Walton, G. M., Murphy, M. C., & Ryan, A. M. (2015). Stereotype threat in organizations: Implications for equity and performance. *The Annual Review of Organizational Psychology and Organizational Behavior, 2,* 523–550.

Wang, M. (2007). Profiling retirees in the retirement transition and adjustment process: Examining the longitudinal change patterns of retirees' psychology well-being. *Journal of Applied Psychology, 92,* 455–474.

Warner, L. R. (2008). A best practices guide to intersectional approaches in psychological research. *Sex Roles, 59,* 454–463.

Webster, J. R., Adams, G. A., Maranto, C. L., Sawyer, K., & Thoroughgood, C. (in press). Workplace contextual supports for LGBT employees: A review, meta-analysis, and agenda for future research. *Human Resource Management.*

Williams, J. C., Phillips, K. W., & Hall, E. V. (2014). *Double jeopardy? Gender bias against women in science.* Technical report. University of California, Hastings College of the Law.

Wilson, V. (2016). *People of color will be a majority of American working class in 2032.* Washington, DC: Economic Policy Institute.

4

AN EXPANDED VIEW OF AGE BIAS IN THE WORKPLACE

Lisa M. Finkelstein, Elizabeth A. Hanrahan, and Courtney L. Thomas

A Tale

Craig sighed in frustration as his computer froze again when he tried to use the new software IT had installed on his desktop over the weekend. A new IT manager, Alex, had been hired recently and was making a lot of upgrades. Since he couldn't send an email to Alex, Craig took the stairs up to the IT department. Upon entering, he observed a young nerdy guy speaking to an older woman. Directing his attention toward the young man, Craig said, "Hi, Craig Smith from accounting. It seems like my computer is having some issues with the new software you've installed on it. You must be Alex, the new IT manager; nice to meet you."

Craig reached out to shake the young man's hand when the woman said, "Actually, I'm Alex. This is my intern, Brian. Why don't I swing by your office in a few minutes to troubleshoot?" Craig tried to hide his surprise as the older woman reached out to shake his hand.

We ask you, the reader: Is this a tale of age bias in the workplace?

Our Purpose

Our purpose is to tackle the issue of age bias against older workers from a broad perspective, acknowledging the complex nature of bias. It has been encouraging to see earlier laments (Finkelstein, Burke, & Raju, 1995) of methodological drawbacks, scattered focus of issues, and lack of attention to theory being tackled. Reviews have appeared with greater frequency, updating where the research stands on major issues, and providing more helpful conceptual frameworks for understanding age discrimination (e.g., Bal, Reis, Rudolph, & Baltes, 2011; Posthuma & Campion, 2009; Truxillo, Finkelstein, Pytlovany, & Jenkins, 2017). This is exciting, but also leaves us pondering: What can we add?

In the first edition of this chapter (Finkelstein & Farrell, 2007) we recognized that the workplace age bias literature could benefit from a wider lens that takes a broader look at advances in the literature on age bias in general (outside the workplace), and an even more panoramic lens considering newer approaches to studying bias in general. Our goal, then and now, was to use developments in these broader literatures to (a) provide some new insight to the work already done in age bias at work, and (b) point to avenues for future work that would be solidly grounded in theory. We organize our review around what we anticipate as key questions in the mind of the reader (Why? How? When/Where? Who? Then What? What can we do?).

Age Bias at Work: What Are We Talking About?

What *is* age bias, anyway? Does age bias mean stereotypes? Discrimination? Prejudice? The age bias in the workplace literature has not historically been precise about the meaning of age bias and the myriad forms it can take in the workplace. This solidified our resolve that a broader social-psychological perspective on bias could do us all some good.

Looking at this broader literature, one can see that the tripartite view of attitudes can provide a basic framework for tackling the complexity of the term bias (e.g., Bal et al., 2011; Fiske, 2004; Kite & Wagner, 2002). This view holds that there are three distinct components to an attitude, or an evaluation of a social object. There is a *cognitive* component, comprised of beliefs and expectancies about a social object due to group membership – this is where our stereotypes come into play. Age stereotypes have been the central focus of the workplace age bias research (e.g., Posthuma & Campion, 2009). There is an enumeration of negative stereotypes that people ascribe to older workers – e.g., absent-minded (Erber & Long, 2006); resistant to change (Chiu, Chan, Snape, & Redman, 2001); disinterest in technology (Büsch, Dahl, & Dittrich, 2009). However, some research has either found a lack of endorsement of negative stereotypes (e.g., Connor, Walsh, Litzelman, & Alvarez, 1978; Hassell & Perrewe, 1995; Weiss & Maurer, 2004) or endorsement of other positive stereotypes – e.g., Wise (Kogan & Shelton, 1960); experienced (Finkelstein, Higgins, & Clancy, 2000); and reliable (Bal et al., 2011). Thus, individuals perceive older workers in both positive and negative ways; however, the stereotypes held are not consistent across people and situations.

There is also a *behavioral* component to an attitude, describing our tendency to treat others in a particular manner due to their social category membership. Behavior toward people due solely to group membership and not to relevant individuating characteristics is unfair discrimination. Age discrimination at work has also been a key focus of workplace age bias research (cf. Gordon & Arvey, 2004), largely focusing on major decisions in a workplace context (e.g., selection, promotion, training opportunities). It should be noted that age stereotypes are quite often assumed (and occasionally shown) to be a precursor to age discrimination, but we see from bias work in general that the cognitive components and behavioral components of attitudes are often only modestly related (e.g., $r=0.16$; Dovidio, Brigham, Johnson, & Gaertner, 1996, as reported in Fiske, 2004). Limiting the explanation of discrimination to stereotyping alone could obscure our understanding of what we can do to reduce discrimination. Conversely, lack of age discrimination in employment-related decisions does not indicate that stereotypes are not insidiously operating in other ways in the course of everyday work life.

Third, there is an *affective* component of a biased attitude. This is the least consistently conceptualized and measured in the bias literature. To some, this affective component *is* the actual evaluative component. In other words, is the social object good or bad along a general or specific dimension? (Kite, Stockdale, Whitley, & Johnson, 2005). To others, the affective component is more indicative of actual feelings – negative "hot" emotions (e.g., disgust, hate) on the part of the bias holder. When we speak of prejudice, we may mean an overall evaluation encompassing our thoughts, feelings, and behavioral tendencies, or we may be homing in on affect (Fiske, 2004). This lack of consistency makes it difficult to determine if the literature is truly tackling this affective piece of the puzzle.

So, what *is* age bias at work? It can be some or all of these things – our thoughts and beliefs about older workers, our feelings and evaluations of older workers, and our treatment of older workers in big decisions and in everyday interactions. In Appendix 4.1, we classify which components of bias are being considered in the literature we reviewed. Before providing more details on this literature, we first consider some theoretical perspectives on bias that have informed our overview and outlook. Specifically, in the following section we introduce several theories that speak to the question of what might motivate our age biases. Following this, we describe the processes by which the components of bias may influence each other, and then index the conditions by which these processes might be tempered or enhanced.

Why Might We Hold Age Biases at Work? (The Motivators)

Fiske (2004) provides a meta-framework for classifying bias into two main categories: subtle and blatant. She asserts that most theories of bias can be considered through this lens, and that different core human motives drive different instances of bias. In Appendix 4.2 we use Fiske's framework to categorize several social-psychological theories of bias that either have been or potentially could be used to help us understand the underlying motives that may instigate age bias at work. Despite the encouraging fact that the age bias at work literature has grown significantly in the last decade, we maintain that it is still rare that researchers explicitly model the underlying motives for bias. Although a detailed discussion of these theoretical perspective is beyond the scope of this chapter, we demonstrate ways they could be integrated in the section below.

Fiske (2004) describes four core motives that underlie social bias. The first motive, understanding, reflects the idea that without malicious intent, people strive to make sense of the world through the use of schemas, expectancies, and categories. The second motive, belonging, refers to the idea that humans are driven to feel like part of a group and connected to others. Controlling is the third core motive that reflects our desire to have a sense of control over our lives and to avoid threat. The final core motive is enhancing self and refers to people's need to have a positive view of the self. These motives can lead to either a subtle, insidious type of bias, or a more blatant, recognized type of bias. Subtle biases are unlikely to be acknowledged by the bias holder, not merely out of social desirability but also out of true lack of awareness of their existence. A few researchers have considered similar motive constructs directly in relation to age bias. Snyder and Miene (1994) argued for an examination of the functions served by age-biased attitudes. Cheung, Kam, and Man-hung Ngan (2010) suggested that organizational motives (e.g., profit-making vs. social responsibility), and not just personal motives, may end up driving or reducing age biases. When we recognize that age bias at work can be driven by different forces in different people or groups of people, we are better positioned to tackle the problem from the source.

The core motive of *understanding* is bound to operate in many workplace circumstances. Given complex environments encouraging multitasking, people seek mental shortcuts to understanding others at work. Cognitive underpinnings for age bias at work have long been acknowledged, and certain contexts may prompt a heightened need for understanding. As the portrayals of competent and adaptive people in our society are not often old (e.g., Kroon, Van Selm, ter Hoeven, & Vliegenthart, 2016), we may not associate older people with the role of effective worker (Kite & Wagner, 2002). Moreover, research on the stereotype content model (Cuddy & Fiske, 2002) has found evidence that we tend to automatically categorize older people as warm but not competent; a lack of competence precludes a match to most work environments. The shifting standards model (Biernat, Manis, & Nelson, 1991) suggests that we may believe we are judging a person positively (an older person as quick), but due to our different group standards (quick "for her age"), our biases may ultimately impact a choice favoring younger individuals. This brings to light the ambivalence in our perceptions of older workers that might lead us to believe that we are truly unbiased. Additionally, Duguid and Thomas-Hunt (2015) warn that guilt resulting from recognizing that one may have implicit biases could result in a drive to attribute biased decisions to rational reasoning.

An organizational culture that induces a strong sense of organizational identity may satisfy the drive for *belonging*. If age, however, is homogeneous among a particular work group, it may be a salient feature upon which others are distinguished (e.g., Zenger & Lawrence, 1989). Lacking a sense of strong social belonging in other areas of life could prompt a stronger tie to a work-related group. Newer research (Duguid and Thomas-Hunt, 2015) suggests that descriptive norms for stereotyping that are sometimes emphasized as a means for reducing stereotyping (e.g., "stereotyping is a normal cognitive process – everyone holds stereotypes") ironically produce more, not less, stereotyping, presumably driven by needs to belong. Social identity theory and self-categorization theory (cf. Turner, 1985) have traditionally been applied to the age bias at work literature to explain preferences of one's own age group in ratings. However, we shall see that this finding has not been consistent, and this may be because (a) age is not a salient or important source of identity for everyone, and (b) other groups may satisfy belonging motives. The Cultural Anchors approach recently put forth by Marcus and Fritzche (2016) recognizes that the core and peripheral aspects of the larger culture can impact drives for identity, belonging, and following norms.

The need for control may become aroused in the workplace if a situation arose that was seen as somehow threatening. Realistic conflict theory (e.g., Bobo, 1983), for example, suggests that if there is a shortage of resources or limited opportunities in a situation, biases can result from an effort to gain control. North and Fiske (2015) describe how resource tensions between age groups can drive biases, not only at the individual level, but several levels higher as well.

A need for *self-enhancement* differs from the others in that it is personal in nature – it is not a tie to a group but rather a drive for a feeling of individual worth. Fiske (2004) notes that an immediate threat to one's self could increase derogation of different others. In terms of age bias at work, propping oneself up might involve emphasizing the benefits of youth. A compatible view is terror management theory (TMT; Martens, Goldenberg, & Greenberg, 2005). This perspective suggests that when mortality is made salient, people may try to distance themselves from older individuals and view them negatively (Wisdom, Connor, Hogan, & Callahan, 2014). Further, the strong fear component involved in TMT could motivate age bias manifested more in affect – dislike, disgust, and desired avoidance. TMT implicates the core motive of self-enhancement because mortality salience awakens a threat to the "continuity of the self" (Fiske, 2004, p. 443). Could it be that older workers awaken a threat to the "continuity of the *work* self," (e.g., retirement, obsolescence in productive society) eventually leading to bias?

What is the Process that it Takes? (The Mediators)

Now that we have considered motives that may *initiate* bias, we can address the *process* it takes in the workplace. Only with an understanding of the underlying causal mechanisms involved in producing age bias at work will we be fully prepared to reduce their likelihood.

The Use of Stereotypes to Explain Discrimination

As noted earlier, commonly held stereotypes about older workers are most often used to explain why there is age discrimination in the workplace (Posthuma & Campion, 2009; Shore & Goldberg, 2004). Given how often stereotypes are cited as an explanatory factor, surprisingly little research has made an empirical link connecting an endorsement of general stereotypes about older workers to behaviors or decisions toward a specific older worker. For example, Rosen and Jerdee's (1976b) study (replicated in 1977) illustrated that discrimination was found against older workers in scenarios created based on stereotypes regarding older workers' resistance to change, lack of creativity, slowness of judgment, among others. These studies, however, did not directly measure participants' endorsement of those beliefs. As such, they do not provide direct evidence of stereotype elicitation as a mediator explaining discrimination; rather, they imply that the reason one would make different decisions about an older worker and younger worker, while other non-age related variables are held constant, reflects differing ageist beliefs on the highlighted dimensions. Notably, Weiss and Maurer's (2004) replication of the study found discrimination evidence only in the resistance to change scenario.

Some studies have used qualitative methods to look for evidence of underlying stereotypes. For example, Finkelstein et al. (2000) coded open-ended responses to see if participants rating job applicants would justify their decisions about an older applicant using stereotypical beliefs. Age was more likely to be mentioned as a factor when a participant had made a decision about an older person versus a younger person. Common justifications were often related to the cost of an older worker, suggesting an economic-based stereotype. Experience came up more often as a positive justification for those who viewed an older applicant than for those viewing the younger applicant, although experience was held constant.

Chiu et al. (2001) directly measured the relationship between endorsement of adaptability/work effectiveness stereotypes and behavioral intentions regarding decisions on training, promotion, retention, co-working, and a preference for choosing an older worker over a younger worker. Adaptability stereotypes predicted these attitudes. Marcus, Fritzsche, Le, and Reeves (2016) found support for the endorsement of competence, warmth, and adaptability stereotypes (assessed with their new scale) to mediate the relationship between age and suitability for hire of applicants. Krings, Sczesny, and Kluge (2011) found evidence that endorsement of lower competence stereotypes for older workers mediated the age–interview intention relationship. In contrast to their expectations, they found that lower warmth ratings for older candidates also mediated this relationship, although in general older workers were endorsed as higher in warmth. This could be, as they suggest, a function of how the scenario-specific older worker may not have projected warmth as they were highly qualified. This also speaks to the more recent notion of prescriptive stereotype violations (North & Fiske, 2013), which is discussed in more detail later.

Perry (1994) fleshed out the idea of person-in-job prototypes, emphasizing that a decision about a person in a job may elicit a prototype that includes both central features and peripheral features. The importance of age in our ultimate decision is impacted by whether age is typically associated with the more central features of our person-in-job prototype. She did find supporting evidence for this process (Perry, 1994; Perry & Bourhis, 1998). Perry, Kulik, and Bourhis (1996) directly addressed the link between age stereotypes and discrimination in a simulated hiring context and found it to be moderated by other contextual factors, discussed in the following section. Thus, Perry's program of research points to a complex interplay between cognition and context.

A recent set of studies, one concerned with age, presents a fresh perspective to link competence stereotypes and selection, suggesting that decision makers focus on whether an applicant's competence will be instrumental to their own purposes. Lee, Pitesa, Thau, and Pillutla (2015) demonstrated that competence leads to perceptions of personal instrumentality, and subsequent favorability toward selection, when a person is seen in a cooperative position only; the opposite is found when we see a target as a competitor.

The Connection from Affect to Discrimination

Here we consider research that explains age-biased behavior at work through negative affect rather than through stereotypes. The line here is blurry as many stereotypes carry a negative connotation. For example, being thought of as resistant to change implies a negative evaluation, particularly in a situation that calls for change. Thus, it is important to distinguish this component of the tripartite view by considering work that has focused on affect or feelings about older people, or at a minimum has looked at evaluation (e.g., good/bad) in general.

Rupp, Vodanovich, and Credé (2005) first factor analyzed the Fraboni Scale of Ageism (Fabroni, Saltstone, & Hughes, 1990) to show evidence for these distinct components. Rupp and colleagues (2006) showed that individuals higher on the affective subscale of ageism were likely to assign more negative recommendations for an older person following poor performance. Thus, they found evidence of a connection between affect and behavior *and* between stereotypes and behavior.

Most of this work has been done outside the area of workplace research. Chasteen, Schwarz, and Park (2002) demonstrated the distinction between affect and stereotypes and acknowledged the potential of implicit bias. They found that individuals responded faster to stereotypically old traits following an old prime (stereotyping), but did *not* find faster responses when negative (vs. positive) traits followed an old prime. In fact, both older participants and younger participants seemed to show more positive affect toward elderly people than young people. They tied this into the stereotype content model, indicating that this commensurates with reactions to older people viewed as warm (such that we would like them) but not competent. They did not directly connect either affect or cognition to behaviors, however. Also, a line of work on subtypes of older people (e.g., Hummert 1990; Hummert, Garstka, & Shaner, 1997) has indicated that some subtypes are seen positively (e.g., grandmother), and others negatively (e.g., shrew/curmudgeon). Thus, it is not clear if primed with a more negative subtype that implicit affect would remain positive. An explicit consideration of subtyping in consideration of older workers appears in order. Is older worker itself a subtype that has not been acknowledged in the subtyping literature, or is this still too broad – are there many older worker subtypes that elicit different feelings, beliefs, and behaviors?

A recent study has purposefully sought to disentangle stereotypes, affect, and behavior. Iweins, Desmette, Yzerbyt, and Stinglhamber (2013) found that positive stereotypes about older workers predicted positive behaviors toward older co-workers as mediated through feelings of admiration. Their model supported a pattern consistent with this chain of events. However, as it was tested cross-sectionally, directionality is difficult to interpret.

Other Mediating Possibilities: Attributions and Self-Fulfilling Prophecies

Some researchers have considered whether differential decisions made between older workers and younger workers are due to different features of attributions made about these workers based on their behavior. For example, Connor and colleagues (Connor, Walsh, Litzelman, & Alvarez, 1978; Locke-Connor & Walsh, 1980) suggested that individuals might differentially attribute information about interview success or failure depending on the age of the applicant. Although not supported in the first study, their second study demonstrated that more stable and external attributions were made after witnessing an unsuccessful older interviewee. Dedrick and Dobbins (1991) found that internal attributions explained the finding that older workers were less likely to be recommended to training after an episode of poor performance than were younger workers. Rupp et al. (2006) also found mediation effects such that internal, stable, and global attributions explained the relationship between age and the choice of harsh consequences in light of poor performance. However, Erber and Long (2006) found that internal and stable attributions of slow and forgetful behavior ascribed to older workers compared to younger workers seemed to buffer them somewhat from negative consequences. Younger workers who acted slow and forgetful were thought to show less effort (not stable, but still internal), which led to the harshest consequences (in terms of promotion or raise decisions) when in a young-typed field (e-commerce). More work sorting out when internal and stable attributions for problematic behavior of older workers helps or hinders them is in order.

Another possibility for explaining the causal chain of why age discrimination may occur involves a more careful examination of dyadic processes in decision contexts. Decision makers, communication partners, and even contextual cues may trigger age metastereotypes in targets – beliefs about what they think others think about them because of their age group – which could produce a variety of reactions and behaviors, including stereotype threat (e.g., Finkelstein, King, & Voyles, 2015; Kulik, Perera, & Cregan, 2016; Lamont, Swift, & Abrams, 2015). Feeling threatened could possibly elicit distraction or defensive behaviors inappropriate to a situation, triggering negative behaviors from a partner who may be in a position to affect that person's outcomes. A related idea by McCann and Giles (2002) suggests that accommodations that people often use when speaking to older people could lead to a self-fulfilling prophecy where they could either adapt to an expected role in that type of interaction, or will be hindered in responding appropriately in a given work situation because of the way they are being talked to. This could reinforce the idea of lack of competence and even produce a heightened likelihood to accommodate inappropriately in the future (Nussbaum, Pitts, Huber, Krieger, & Ohs, 2005). The use of sophisticated dyadic methodology and experience sampling is in order to explore the veracity of these ideas.

When is it More Likely to Occur? (The Moderators)

Just as the *whys* of age bias are important in order to understand, to ultimately reduce it, so too are the *whens*. This can be of practical value to help us narrow our efforts to where they are needed most. We have organized the moderators into three broad categories: the context, the rater, and the target.

The Context

Here, the context refers to the situation in which an instance of age bias may occur at work. We take a look at context from very narrow factors (i.e., the decision context) to very broad factors (i.e., the national or cultural context).

The Decision Context

The amount of information about older workers that is available to a decision maker has received considerable attention (e.g., Avolio & Barrett, 1987; Finkelstein et al., 1995; Finkelstein & Burke, 1998; Gordon & Arvey, 2004; Kite et al., 2005; Lee & Clemons, 1985; Singer & Sewell, 1989; Vrugt & Schabracq, 1996). A cognitive approach suggests that when individuating information is provided about an older person, the perceiver may be less likely to rely on category-based processing and stereotypes. The perceiver is then more likely to individuate the older person, leading to bias reduction (Fiske & Neuberg, 1990).

Findings have been moderate and mixed. Kite et al.'s (2005) meta-analysis, which included work and nonwork studies, concluded that bias is reduced (but does not disappear) when more information is provided about a target. Finkelstein et al.'s (1995) meta-analysis found support only for particular types of decisions (e.g., potential for development). Gordon and Arvey's (2004) meta-analytic review found that providing a lot of information weakened bias, but providing little information was worse than none at all. The suggested explanation for this effect is that having age as the only information could alert individuals to the limited, and perhaps stereotypical, information they have to base their evaluation on. This then leads to even more negative effects.

Gordon and Arvey (2004) also indicate that field investigations, compared with lab investigations, tend to yield weaker age effects. This is further corroborated by Morgeson, Reider, Campion, and Bull (2008). One might logically assume that the lab setting artificially inflates effects. This infers that most real decision contexts have the appropriate amount of information available to raters, thus implying that the manipulation of information is an interesting academic issue, but not of real relevance. However, this perspective assumes that relevant information is indeed always present and attended to beyond any expectations the rater arrives with. Further, it doesn't consider any other motives beyond the understanding motive. For example, researchers have found support for social judgeability theory, which states that if people think they have some information for deciding against a target, *and* they feel they are entitled to judge, they become even more biased (e.g., Leyens, Yzerbyt, & Schadron, 1992). This feeling of entitlement can be driven by individual differences regarding need for control (Fiske, 2004). To truly understand if information about a target is likely to reduce bias, we must look more carefully into what is driving the decision maker.

Sometimes decision contexts call for a comparative decision among people, where older people are being considered in some way relative to younger people. Other times the older person is the sole focus of consideration. This has been addressed in the literature directly within primary studies (Lee & Clemons, 1985), or by meta-analysts who compared studies that used a comparative design (within-subjects; participants rate both old and young individuals) to an absolute design (between-subjects; participants rate either an old or young individual; Bal et al., 2011; Finkelstein et al, 1995; Gordon & Arvey, 2004; Kite et al., 2005). For example, Lee and Clemons (1985) found that an older worker was provided higher ratings for endorsing attending a conference when that worker was the only focus of consideration. When participants decided between a younger worker and older worker for a training program, the younger worker was favored. Finkelstein et al. (1995) suggested that age would be more salient in a comparison decision, and that salience could turn a rater's attention to age as a social category. While their meta-analysis found some support for this, there is also a compelling reason to expect the opposite effect. The salience of age produced by a comparison decision could alert individuals to the purpose of a study, and thus prompt socially desirable responding. This argument was supported by Gordon and Arvey's (2004) meta-analysis. However, the most updated meta-analysis (Bal et al., 2011), which includes lab studies and field studies, replicated the pattern of results found originally by Finkelstein et al. (1995), although only when selection decisions were being made. From a methodological standpoint, this emphasizes the large role that research design can play in determining conclusions about age bias at work.

Gordon and colleagues (Gordon, Rozelle, & Baxter, 1988, 1989) examined the accountability of the rater in a decision context. One might surmise that a situation where raters are accountable for their decision would lead them to carefully consider an individual and rely on biases less. However, accountability pressures can have the effect of making one more motivated toward a clear and organized impression, producing an over-reliance on stereotypes. Their studies provided evidence of raters finding younger applicants as more attractive, having more positive traits, and being more hirable than older applicants when these raters believed they would have to justify their decision to a group of personnel managers (i.e., accountable condition).

Perry et al. (1996) were the only researchers to directly manipulate cognitive busyness; this should be important if indeed the cognitive motives for bias are operating. Biased (age stereotype endorsing) raters were not less positive about older workers when they were cognitively busy, but were more positive about younger workers under that condition. Busy and unbiased raters tended to prefer the older applicant. The authors suggest that raters under high cognitive demand were relying on their positive stereotypes in making applicant ratings.

The Job Context

An earnest interest in the role of the job appeared in the 1980s (e.g., Cleveland & Landy, 1983; Cleveland, Festa, & Montgomery, 1988; Gordon & Arvey, 1986) as researchers successfully demonstrated that jobs could be age-typed. Perry and Finkelstein (1999) explained that a direct match could occur between an individual's age and the age type of a job, or an indirect match could occur where age would be associated with specific characteristics of a person, and these features would be matched to those needed for the job. Tying in other work on similarity-attraction theory (Shore & Goldberg, 2004), it is possible that a rater may not doubt the skills of an older worker, but might question an older worker's fit with younger people in a job context.

What leads a job to develop an age type? Lawrence (1988) has suggested that we develop age norms for the appropriate time in which we will transition through an organization, and these shared norms (developed in part through actual distributions of people in an organization, a notable tie-in with social role theory, discussed earlier) contribute to our age associations with particular jobs. Media portrayals underscore these age-typed job ideals (e.g., high-level jobs; van Selm & Van der Heijden, 2014). Shore, Cleveland, and Goldberg (2003) found evidence that employees older than their manager were seen as less promotable than those who were not. In addition, Cleveland, Festa, and Montgomery (1988) found that the age composition of the applicant pool had an impact on the age type of a particular position, such that a job was seen as *older* when there were more older people applying for it.

Age type could in some cases be associated with experience or status. If the word *Senior* is in the title of a position, a link could be made to a person with significant experience; the word *Assistant*, conversely, is likely to bring to mind a young person at the start of a career. In addition, jobs with technology language in their title (e.g., computer services) might associate quickly with a younger person (Perry & Finkelstein, 1999). Ruggs, Hebl, Walker, and Fa-Kaji (2014) recently found age bias in jobs requiring technology and those requiring physical effort; this, however, was further moderated by gender. However, as noted earlier, Erber and Long (2006) found that when it comes to judging someone's poor performance, younger people fared worse in an e-commerce (technology) position because of the violation of the expectation that young people are good at technology and attributions made toward lack of effort. Thus, the directional influence of job type might depend on the decision. Not all jobs are clearly categorizable; Finkelstein et al. (1995) were limited in their ability to clearly test this hypothesis meta-analytically as they didn't find that all jobs used in studies to look at different decisions could be clearly categorized. Perry and Bourhis (1998) suggested that job typing be considered more of a continuum than a dichotomy; consistent with their job-prototype matching theory, some jobs have age as more or less of a central feature, rather than an all-or-no feature. Perry and Parlamis (2005) also suggest that other contextual factors, such as rater characteristics, might obscure job type effects. We concur and also suggest that this factor may only be a consideration when age bias is driven by an understanding (cognitive) motive. Driven by other motives, people could ignore, or perhaps even distort, their perception of the context to satisfy their desire to avoid older workers.

The Organizational Context

Perry (e.g., Perry & Finkelstein, 1999; Perry & Parlamis, 2005) argued for scholars to consider macro-level, organizational features and their impact on age bias, perhaps through their impact on more proximal contextual factors and cognitive factors. Perry and Finkelstein (1999) offered a model of three organizational factors – structure, values, and technology – and how they could impact age typing of jobs, activation of age stereotypes of people and jobs, and ability for these matches to be used in decision-making. To our knowledge, this model has not been directly tested empirically. Chiu et al. (2001), however, examined several organizational factors, including sector (service vs. manufacturing/production), organizational size, and organizational ageism policy. Surprisingly, they found little impact of the organizational factors, with the exception of the presence of an ageism policy being positively related to beliefs that older people were adaptable. Remery, Henkens, Schippers, and Ekamper (2003) assessed organizational features that are considered in the interpretation of beliefs and policies toward older workers. Notably, those in organizations with more older workers actually had more negative opinions about them.

This later finding is further reflected in a recent and active program of work by Kunze, Boehm, and their colleagues (Boehm, Schröder, & Kunze, 2013; Kunze, Boehm, & Bruch, 2011, 2013; Kunze, Raes, & Bruch, 2015). These scholars use multilevel methodologies to look at the role that organizational age diversity plays in organizational performance outcomes. For example, Kunze et al. (2011) showed that age diversity at the firm level actually lowered firm performance outcomes through perceptions of an age discriminatory climate. They also demonstrated that diversity-friendly HR policies stressing inclusion, lower top management stereotypes, and lower member subjective age (Boehm et al. 2013, Kunze et al., 2015) reduce these consequences.

Lawrence (1988) showed that norms can develop in organizations regarding the ages seen as appropriate for different positions; these impact performance ratings. The content of age norms in any organization is likely determined in multiple ways. For example, a technology company permeated with messages of speed and change may harbor expectations that young people will start at or quickly rise to the top, and find any association with older age to be incompatible with their approach. This intersects with McCann and Giles' (2002) communication approach that stresses how language we use at work can have a substantial impact on the culture that develops around age. For example, if an expression such as "old timers" is part of acceptable discourse, it becomes a normative aspect of work life and impacts our age expectations. Further, motives for belonging may prompt in-group communication patterns that heighten distinctions among in-groups and out-groups; when age bias in a context is driven by these motives, the likelihood that these communication patterns abound increases. Riach and Kelly (2015) go as far as to use a vampire analogy to describe the language permeating organizations (e.g., "young blood," "regeneration") that are striving for survival (reflecting the controlling motive of threat avoidance).

The Cultural Context

The most macro of the contextual factors has received the least attention in the literature. Perry and Parlamis (2005) were the first to comprehensively consider the potential impact of country/culture on ageism at work. Several country-specific papers have now emerged with the goal of addressing their own age policy needs given the demographic climate, economic climate, and legal climate (cf., Abrams, Swift, Lamont, & Drury, 2015; Biggs, Phillipson, Money, & Leach, 2006; Poulston & Jenkins, 2013; Taylor & Walker, 1998).

The Age Discrimination in Employment Act (ADEA) in the US has made blatant ageism against those over 40 more difficult, but as we know ageism comes in many forms – some subtle – and our laws may just impact the form ageism takes. Cox and Barron (2012) demonstrated individual effects of stereotypes about an older target depending on the way anti-discrimination legislation is described, and depending on power-distance. As more countries begin to institute age discrimination laws, a valuable opportunity to longitudinally study the impact of forbidding blatant bias presents itself.

The status of older people in various cultures may have an impact on whether bias occurs against (or for) older workers. Chinese cultures, for example, have been known to be more respectful of older people (e.g., Levy & Langer, 1994). However, it is interesting to note that Cuddy, Norton, and Fiske (2005) found that the stereotype content model (older people are warm and incompetent) held up in such places as Hong Kong, South Korea, and Japan. Chiu et al. (2001) found similar levels of bias in the UK and Hong Kong. North and Fiske's (2015) recent cross-cultural meta-analysis sheds light on what may seem counterintuitive. Indeed, on average, Eastern countries demonstrate moderately more negative attitudes toward older people than do Western countries (with some exceptions). This appears to be mostly explained by rapid population aging and its effects on resources.

Marcus and Fritzche (2016) recently introduced a theoretical framework looking at whether multiple levels of culture and, more specifically, the factors of tightness-looseness and collectivism, should interact to temper or enhance all aspects of age bias we have discussed. North and Fiske (2015) uncovered an unexpected finding that individualism was related to more positive attitudes of older individuals than collectivism. Taken together, these new approaches highlight the complexities of culture and represent a much-needed step in the right direction.

The Rater

Age of Rater

Research has been mixed as to how rater age impacts age bias. In their meta-analysis, Finkelstein et al. (1995) found an in-group bias for young respondents only; old respondents showed no preference for younger workers or older workers. Chasteen and colleagues (2002) found that young adults are more negative than older adults on an explicit measure of attitudes toward older people, but found no rater age differences on the implicit measures. However, some recent studies have shown some evidence for an in-group bias among older raters. Henkens (2005), for example, found that older managers tend to hold more positive views of their older subordinates. With regard to training opportunities, older employees were more likely to be granted approval for involvement in a developmental opportunity if the HR individual evaluating the proposal was older (Lazazzara, Karpinska, & Henkens, 2013).

Finkelstein and Burke (1998) proposed that an in-group age bias would occur only when the rater identifies with his or her age group and when age is perceived as a salient category. Against their prediction, however, they found that among raters who highly identified with their age group, older raters viewed an older applicant as being *less* economically beneficial than a younger applicant. Similarly, Rauschenbach, Goritz, and Hertel (2012) found that older raters, compared with younger raters, viewed younger targets as more favorable. Shore et al. (2003) found older employees receiving lower performance ratings from older managers than younger ones. Research looking at age bias in general has shown an age favorability bias for young respondents in which they provide more positive ratings to older targets than to younger targets (e.g., Jackson & Sullivan, 1988; Linville, 1982). In Linville's (1982) study, older targets were preferred to younger targets by young individuals when positive information was provided. This seems to support her complexity–extremity theoretical framework, whereby more extreme (and favorable) ratings are given to out-group members than in-group members when positive information is provided.

In some studies, older raters have been shown to be generally more positive in their ratings regardless of target age. For example, older raters in the Jackson and Sullivan (1988) study held more positive stereotypes about targets overall. Bird and Fisher (1986) and Hassell and Perrewe (1995) both showed that older employees had more positive stereotypes regarding older employees than did younger employees. However, because in these latter two studies raters did not provide ratings of younger employees, it is unclear whether these results are a demonstration of in-group bias or of older workers being perceived as more positive overall.

Locke-Connor and Walsh (1980) first found that overall, middle-aged male raters had more negative expectations of older applicants than younger ones, suggesting that the relationship between rater age and overall favorability ratings may not be linear. A later meta-analysis covering studies on age bias in general (Kite et al., 2005) concurred that middle-aged respondents were most likely to favor younger targets over older targets. Terror management theory (TMT) may provide one potential explanation for this finding. For instance, young individuals who are highly anxious tend to report more negative stereotypes about older people (Wisdom et al., 2014). Additionally, middle-aged respondents on the verge of becoming 'old' may experience greater perceived threat, resulting in lower ratings for the older targets. However, recent work by

Finkelstein, Ryan, and King (2013) found that although the content of older worker stereotypes was somewhat different for middle-aged raters and younger raters, the middle-aged raters' stereotypes were generally more positive. It appears overall that the age of the rater often makes a difference, but the findings are so inconsistent that there is a need for carefully designed studies that could more clearly test competing theoretical positions.

Other Characteristics

Earlier research found that hourly employees held more positive stereotypes about older workers than did supervisors (Kirchner & Dunnette, 1954). Other research findings have shown that this effect depends on rater age (Bird & Fisher, 1986; Chiu et al., 2001; Hassell & Perrewe, 1995). For example, Hassell and Perrewe (1995) found that for hourly employees, but not for supervisors, older raters held more positive stereotypes about older workers than did younger raters. Chiu and colleagues (2001) similarly found that the positive relationship between respondent age and work effectiveness ratings were stronger for non-supervisors than for supervisors. Researchers have also looked at the difference between student respondents and managerial respondents. In their meta-analysis, Gordon and Arvey (2004) found that, in general, students were more negative than supervisors in their evaluations of older workers. Singer and Sewell (1989) compared a managerial sample with a student sample, finding that students preferred an older person for a high status job and managers preferred a younger person for a low status job. When exposed to positive information about older workers, however, the pattern was reversed; this suggests that conditions may moderate the impact of student status.

Rater demographics have also been examined. These have demonstrated, for example, that female respondents may have more positive beliefs about older workers (Chiu et al., 2001; Connor et al., 1978; Kalavar, 2001; Rosen & Jerdee, 1976a) and that Black students may hold more extreme age stereotypes (i.e., some larger differences in ratings between older workers and younger workers) than do White students (Crew, 1984). The author suggests that differences in educational achievement in his sample may have contributed to these differences, although this was not directly tested. While the findings described in this section demonstrate that characteristics of the rater do often influence age bias, the patterns are not always consistent.

The Target

We previously discussed the contextual effect of providing job relevant information versus not. Here, we consider the impact of the specific content of such information. In their meta-analysis, Kite et al. (2005) looked at the effect of the valence of information provided and found the greatest difference in ratings between younger targets and older targets, with lower ratings for older targets, when negative information was provided.

Triandis (1963) had personnel directors rate their likelihood of hiring job candidates and found an interaction between age and competence. Overall, the 30-year-old competent White male was most likely to be hired, while the 55-year-old competent African-American female was on the verge of being rejected (i.e., average rating just above the rejection cutoff). Competence does matter, however. Even the 30-year-old barely competent White applicant was rejected. Triandis' work was an early precursor toward a more recent recognition of intersectionality (Marcus & Fritzche, 2015; Ruggs et al., 2014) discussed in detail in another chapter of this book (see Chapter 3, this volume).

Haefner (1977) showed an interaction between age and competence such that age mattered less for a barely competent job applicant than for a highly competent applicant. For highly competent job candidates, the younger applicant was preferred to the older applicant. In contrast, Lee and Clemons (1985) found that more favorable decisions were made about an older worker than a younger worker when they were both presented as moderately competent.

Fusilier and Hitt (1983) instructed undergraduate participants to rate job applicants who varied on age and experience for an entry-level professional position. Older applicants with no experience were rated worst. If experience is considered a proxy for competence, this suggests that providing negative competence information is more detrimental for older applicants than for younger applicants. This ties in with findings described earlier, indicating that experience is a positive stereotype of old age. Others, however, have found no evidence that competence affects the degree to which age stereotyping occurs in the workplace (e.g., Locke-Connor & Walsh, 1980; Perry & Varney, 1978). Finally, Lee and colleagues (2015), as described in our mediators section, found that decision-makers may prefer a less competent candidate if they see them as competitors who would get in their way rather than cooperators who would be instrumental in accomplishing their goal. This deserves further exploration.

So Then What Happens? (The Consequences)

When updating this edition of the chapter, we noticed a major influx of new research looking not at the factors predicting age bias at work, but rather at the consequences of perceiving age stereotypes or age discrimination. This is different from consequences at an organizational level resulting from accusations of or prosecution for illegal age discrimination, which can have rather obvious consequences to the financial health, reputation, and morale of an organization. The studies we refer to here are about *perceptions* of being the target of age bias, and understandably so – people don't always have evidence that others actually are truly stereotyping, or that they are actually unfairly discriminating; often this is picked up on through cues in environment. Although this was not the intended focus of this chapter, we would be remiss to ignore this growing body of literature as it seems to comprise the majority of newer work, particularly over the last few years.

Earlier, we made brief mention about work on metastereotypes (what we think other age groups think of our age group) and stereotype threat (the fear we may confirm age stereotypes). Finkelstein et al. (2015) suggests that metastereotypes could lead to different reactions, including threat but also challenge or boost, depending on factors in the person and the situation. These reactions could in turn impact interactions with co-workers of different ages. Bal et al. (2015) found that Dutch taxi drivers who experienced negative age metastereotypes planned to retire earlier, explained in part by their differences in future time perspective. Lagacé, Charmarkeh, Tanguay, and Annick (2015) found that when older workers bought into negative stereotypes they were less likely to report competency using information technology, which was then related to social capital. A meta-analysis on stereotype threat found that older people reacting to stereotype threat had negative performance consequences in a variety of cognitive memory tasks (Lamont et al., 2015).

Perceived discrimination and perceived mistreatment have also seen a great uptick in attention. Perceived mistreatment refers to everyday interactions and perceptions of micro-injustices; perceived discrimination is an umbrella term that could include these smaller, insidious sleights, as well as actual loss of jobs, promotions, and opportunities. Many consequences have been examined in relation to these variables. For example, choice of when to retire (Bayl-Smith & Griffin, 2014; Zaniboni, 2015), job performance and engagement at work (Bayl-Smith & Griffin, 2014), concealment strategies in self-presentation (Berger, 2009), and a host of physical and mental health outcomes (Han & Richardson, 2015; Min, Park, Kim, & Min, 2014; Yuan, 2007). Effects throughout these studies are often moderated by other factors, such as age identification and personal resources. The Workplace Age Discrimination Scale has recently been developed to tap into the target's experience of overt and subtle discrimination (Marchiondo, Gonzales, & Ran, 2016).

What Can Be Done About It? (The Solutions)

This heading is admittedly optimistic and we don't claim to have all the answers; rather, we outline potential paths toward solutions. Stakeholders at multiple levels can and must play a role.

What Can the Bias Holder Do?

As we've seen, we need to distinguish unintentional biases from purposeful biases. Making oneself aware that some forms of bias are automatic can be a step toward reduction (Hummert, 1999; Levy & Banaji, 2002). Recognizing that bias could result from a generally respectable motive to understand one's complex environment may ease people's resistance to acknowledge the bias. Upon realization that automatic processes may be impeding fair treatment, bias holders could refocus their efforts to make decisions on a careful analysis of individual information (Cuddy & Fiske, 2002). For example, are you passing an older worker over for a training opportunity because they really aren't interested, or because you are assuming a 62 year old isn't interested? Even in one's everyday interactions with older people at work, people should take note of whether they are, for example, accommodating their conversation inappropriately (Nussbaum et al., 2005). Nussbaum and colleagues suggest that appropriate, individualized communication strategies can empower older people to respond appropriately, potentially breaking down stereotypes over time. Hagestad and Uhlenberg (2005) suggest all people practice mindfulness in their interactions at work; this is good advice wherever we are.

Some bias, however, is driven by complex motives, and even fears, that could be difficult to acknowledge, but may be key toward reducing bias based more in negative affect. Fear of death, obsolescence, or fading power/looks could result in an aversion to older individuals who serve as a reminder of these fears. If people made efforts to develop sources of esteem throughout their life that are in areas not vulnerable to age (Martens et al., 2005), this type of bias may be reduced.

It would be Pollyannaish, of course, to imagine that if only everyone took this to heart these problems would be solved. Implicit biases resist change. The idea that most people hold stereotypes – that it is a natural part of being human – may actually be working as a descriptive norm (Duguid & Thomas-Hunt, 2015) increasing, rather than reducing, their use. We must try to each take responsibility, but there are limits. Other stakeholders also have a role.

What Can the Older Worker Do?

Levy and Banaji (2002) have stated that older people are often not strong enough advocates against age bias. As we've seen throughout this review, they have been sometimes shown to hold negative attitudes about aging. An awareness among older people as to how they foster bonds *within* their age in-group (satisfying belongingness needs) may be telling. Could using terms such as "senior moments" with colleagues, for example, perpetuate and reinforce age stereotypes (Giles & Reid, 2005)?

Awareness that some age bias is automatic and results from cognitive shortcuts should encourage older workers to do their best to discourage easy categorization. For example, Perry (1994) suggested that older workers intentionally play up their characteristics that match the central features that are prototypic to a typical job-holder (e.g., expressed interests or skills). Finkelstein and colleagues' (2000, 2013) findings that experience stands out as a positive age stereotype suggests that playing up experiences relevant to those needed at a particular job would be beneficial. Focusing on the type and *relevance* of experience, rather than *years* of experience, may be more effective as years could call more attention to age and other associations thereof. We must encourage older workers, however, to heed the warnings inherent in North and Fiske's (2013) recent work showing that when older people violate prescriptive stereotypes (what older people *should* be like), they may face backlash from their younger counterparts. More work should be done to investigate how best one individuates oneself without wandering into this risky territory (Chasteen & Cary, 2015).

What Can an Organization Do?

It has been encouraging to see more organization-level approaches to combating age bias emerging over the last decade with mounting evidence that a positive age climate in an organization can make a difference to the social and business fabric of an organization (e.g., Bilinska, Wegge, & Kliegel, 2016; Boehm et al., 2013). Systematic and strategic HR practices have been implemented toward the goal of maximizing the productivity, health, and longevity of the workforce as they age; building a positive age diversity climate is a necessary element of such practices (e.g., Carden & Boyd, 2014). Organizations must monitor fairness perceptions of any age-specific practices, as there could be circumstances where the climate is negatively impacted (Iweins, Desmette, & Yzerbyt, 2012; Kulik et al., 2016).

People are motivated tacticians (Cuddy & Fiske, 2002), individuating others when they have the means and reasons to do so. The organization has a hand in this, with the power to create situations where non-rushed, well-informed decision making is encouraged (Perry, 1994). We have seen that accountability is a tricky thing (Gordon et al., 1988, 1989) as it can backfire and lead to more simplified processing. This should be examined in situations that mimic the quick-paced demands of organizational life – how can we strike a balance between those needs and effortful processing?

A promising avenue for reducing bias – and likely steeped in affect as well as cognition – is increased contact between people of all age groups at and outside of work; this concept is often referred to as intergenerational contact. Several researchers have shown that more exposure to older workers tends to be associated with more positive beliefs about them and desire to work with them (cf., Chiu et al., 2001; Hassell & Perrewe, 1995). From a sociological standpoint, Hagestad and Uhlenberg (2005) observe just how little inter-age contact we tend to have in our society, and how this segregation could be an important root of bias. However, just as mere contact with other types of groups (e.g., interracial) only tends to be successful under specific circumstances and backfires under others, so too with age (Iweins et al., 2013; Remery et al., 2003). It is crucial that sustained contact is consistently fostered in an organizational setting in ways that allow individuals to have the opportunity to forge friendships and positive affect, and allow for re-categorization of individual members of other age groups out of *age* as their distinguishing category and into others, such as common interests.

There have been some interesting lab interventions to reduce age bias that may provide ideas for an organization to adopt in the process of training or socialization. For example, Snyder and Miene (1994) found some evidence that exposure to a story of an individual who realized ways that they were biased and how they planned to change actually was helpful in some circumstances, given particular motives for the bias. Dasgupta and Greenwald (2001) found support for an intervention that appeared to reduce implicitly, but not explicitly, measured age bias. They exposed participants to photos of well-liked famous older people *and* commonly disliked famous younger people and found a reduction in implicit bias against the aged. A similar intervention in a training program at work could feasibly have similar effects. Truxillo, Cadiz, and Hammer (2015) recently provided a promising selection of intervention approaches, whereby systematic programs based on theory and research on aging and aimed toward positive change (including health, motivation, policy, and climate, to name a few) for older workers can be subject to systematic trial coupled with careful evaluation.

What Can a Country/Culture Do?

At a more macro level, age discrimination laws are important. Although the ADEA has certainly not rid the US of all age bias, blatant discrimination is more difficult and discouraged (though this may be more the case for termination than for hiring; see Lahey, 2006). Other countries without similar laws face direct discrimination as an accepted part of the culture. This is potentially disastrous not only because of lost opportunities for a growing population of older people (North & Fiske, 2015), but also for the attitudes that are perpetuated and renewed. Seeing advertisements blatantly targeting younger people, for example, is likely to be planting seeds very early on in a society that one's role as one ages is no longer that of productive worker (Kite et al., 2005; Lyon & Pollard, 1997). Walker (2005) notes a shift in policy in the EU from historical encouragement of early retirement toward a shift toward an "age management" policy to encourage healthy employability long term. Duncan (2008) provides examples of European programs for intergenerational solidarity.

Most cultures however, even those with age discrimination laws, are sending insidious messages about the worth of older people every day. Hagestad and Uhlenberg (2005) point out that even the very accepted tradition of sarcastic birthday cards have institutionalized ageism in our cultural humor. Having a sense of humor about aging may serve a valuable function on some level, but it could also be preventing us from questioning the age bias surrounding us daily. More public awareness of the myths versus realities of aging is imperative. Van Selm and Van der Heijden (2014) describe a proposal for a promising new national intervention in the Netherlands to help with such goals, using a systematic review and reframing of communications in Dutch organizations to decrease stereotypical messages and enhance messages of employability of older people.

What Next? (Future Research)

We have been delighted to see a continued uptick in sophisticated research attention to the issues of age bias at work. We have learned much, but there are many areas where additional efforts toward clarity are needed. We begin by highlighting some key directions we have noted throughout the chapter using our why, how, and when framework. We then emphasize some additional issues that were introduced in the first edition of this chapter but remain in need of attention: measurement, everyday interactions, and interventions.

The study of the underlying motives for age bias ("the whys") has the potential to produce a deeper understanding of both the insidious nature of age bias and of methods to reduce it. Trying to eliminate a bias that is driven by a motive of controlling, for example, with a solution that increases feelings of belonging is unlikely to be effective. We see the motives framework, and the host of theories categorized by it, as a guide for future theoretical and empirical work.

In addition to a focus on the initiation of bias, putting a focused lens on the underlying process ("the hows") and the connection among our affect, cognitions, and behaviors toward older workers is needed. As we mentioned, although some studies consider these processes together (Bal et al., 2011; Iweins et al., 2013; Rupp et al., 2005, 2006), it is rare. Moreover, research that acknowledges that bias often unfolds in the context of a dynamic and dyadic process is needed. Changing stereotypes and/or reducing the likelihood of their use, no easy feats in and of themselves, will not necessarily make people enjoy, seek out, and genuinely like older workers. Although it is a big ask, ambitious designs that (a) partition these three aspects of bias, (b) systematically examine the theoretical motivators we've advocated for in this chapter, and (c) consider the consequences to the well-being of the targets of perceived discrimination, meta-stereotypes, and felt dislike/disinterest, would make a significant impact in bringing the details of the process to light. Moreover, more frequent use of experience sampling methodologies, such as diary studies, could especially help with understanding the affective component of biases from the perspectives of both the bias holder and receiver.

Speaking of contexts ("the whens"), more work systematically recognizing the multiple levels of context – from the rater/decision maker, to the job, to the organization, to the country, will be very useful in allowing stakeholders to recognize or even modify conditions that may exacerbate bias. Although moderating conditions have received the most attention in the literature thus far, combinations at multiple levels would be welcome.

It is difficult to really understand older worker bias if we are in disagreement as to who older workers actually are. According to the ADEA, an older worker is over 40. We're betting many of our readers in their 40s (and possibly 50s, 60s, ...) do not think of themselves as older workers. Others might. There are several conceptualizations of age identity and subjective age (Barak, 1987; Kooij, De Lange, Jansen, & Dikkers, 2008; Martens et al., 2005; Pitt-Catsouphes, Matz-Costa, & Brown, 2011; Segers, Inceoglu, & Finkelstein, 2014) that differ in some dimensions but all come from the perspective that a sole focus on chronology is limiting our understanding of many aspects of aging. How much of a role the subjective age of older targets play in discouraging bias toward them is unclear; further, the particular dimension of subjective age (e.g., appearance? current life events?) is likely to garner different reactions. In addition, we have seen that it is possible that a younger subjective age, when manifesting as crossing into protected younger territory (by enjoying activities often stereotyped as belonging to a younger age group) may actually backfire (North & Fiske, 2013). We encourage researchers to carefully consider the characteristics of the older targets and younger targets that they present in experiments (in terms of their appearance, mannerisms, and content of self-presentation), through systematic measurement or control, and to observe in detail and account for these characteristics of targets in field research when possible.

The work literature's focus on personnel decisions (e.g., hiring, promotion, and training) is obviously necessary and important, but we would like to see more work looking beyond access discrimination to subtle, and even not-so-subtle, everyday treatment of older workers. An increased focus on communication (Finkelstein, 2015; McCann & Giles, 2002) and social networks will be a welcome expansion. The literature we briefly described on the consequences of perceived age bias (e.g., Bal et al., 2015; Zaniboni, 2015) makes it clear that many older workers have been the victims of mistreatment in their daily work lives but we know much less about the predictors of these types of more common biases than we do about those big, but more occasional, decisions.

Finally, while we came up with some research-based solutions in the prior section, we do not yet have enough evidence-based data to be confident they would work, and maybe there are others that would work better. Careful attention to the ultimate solutions to the problem of age bias at work needs intervention research (Truxillo et al. 2015) designed, executed, and evaluated with research-practice partnerships (Finkelstein, 2015) with a stake in these issues.

A Return to the Tale

We return now to the story that opened this chapter. So, is this a tale of age bias? In light of what we've reviewed, it is evident that age bias is a complex issue and is not always easy to detect. We leave you with some specific questions to guide an exploration of what is happening in the story. It may be useful to focus first on what type or types of bias may be occurring. Is there evidence of stereotyping? Prejudice? Unfair discrimination? If age bias is occurring, is it blatant or subtle? What core motives may be at work for Craig? What interventions might the individuals or organization try in an attempt to remedy such age bias?

Takeaway Points

- Age bias can have a lot of meanings – prejudice, stereotyping, and discrimination.
- Age bias at work is not solely a matter of access discrimination, but can include bias in everyday interactions as well.
- There may be many motives for being biased against older workers, many of which have been empirically under-tested.
- A complete understanding of age bias at work requires consideration of many potential mediators and moderators to clarify the process and context.
- Solutions will need to come from multiple levels, including the bias holder, the target, the organization, and the larger culture. The suggested solutions invite empirical scrutiny.
- Future research should use more complex methodologies and pay close attention to measurement; academic-practice research collaborations are needed.

References

Abrams, D., Swift, H. J., Lamont, R. A., & Drury, L. (2015). The barriers to and enablers of positive attitudes to ageing and older people, at the societal and individual level. Future of an ageing population: Evidence review. *Foresight*, Government Office for Science.

Avolio, B. J., & Barrett, G. V. (1987). Effects of age stereotyping in a simulated interview. *Psychology and Aging*, 2, 56–63. doi:10.1037/0882-7974.2.1.56.

Bal, A. C., Reiss, A. E., Rudolph, C. W., & Baltes, B. B. (2011). Examining positive and negative perceptions of older workers: A meta-analysis. *The Journals of Gerontology: Series B*, 66, 687–698. doi:10.1093/geronb/gbr056.

Bal, P. M., De Lange, A. H., Van der Heijden, B. I., Zacher, H., Oderkerk, F. A., & Otten, S. (2015). Young at heart, old at work? Relations between age, (meta-)stereotypes, self-categorization, and retirement attitudes. *Journal of Vocational Behavior*, 91, 35–45. doi:10.1016/j.jvb.2015.09.002.

Barak, B. (1987). Cognitive age: A new multidimensional approach to measuring age identity. *The International Journal of Aging and Human Development*, 25(2), 109–128. doi:10.2190/RR3M-VQT0-B9LL-GQDM.

Bayl-Smith, P. H., & Griffin, B. (2014). Age discrimination in the workplace: Identifying as a late career worker and its relationship with engagement and intended retirement age. *Journal of Applied Social Psychology*, 44, 588–599. doi:10.1111/jasp. 12251.

Berger, E. D. (2009). Managing age discrimination: An examination of the techniques used when seeking employment. *The Gerontologist*, 49, 317–332. doi:10.1093/geront/gnp031.

Biernat, M., Manis, M., & Nelson, T. E. (1991). Stereotypes and standards of judgment. *Journal of Personality and Social Psychology, 60*, 485–499. doi:10.1037/0022-3514.60.4.485.

Biggs, S., Phillipson, C., Money, A. M., & Leach, R. (2006). The age-shift: Observations on social policy, ageism and dynamics of the adult life course. *Journal of Social Work Practice, 20*, 239–250. doi:10.1080/02650530600931708.

Bilinska, P., Wegge, J., & Kliegel, M. (2016). Caring for the elderly but not for one's own old employees? *Journal of Personnel Psychology, 15*, 95–105. doi:10.1027/1866-888/a000144.

Bird, C. P., & Fisher, T. D. (1986). Thirty years later: Attitudes toward the employment of older workers. *Journal of Applied Psychology, 71*, 515–517. doi:10.1037/0021-9010.71.3.515.

Bobo, L. (1983). Whites' opposition to busing: Symbolic racism or realistic group conflict? *Journal of Personality and Social Psychology, 45*, 1196–1210. doi:10.1037/0022-3514.45.6.1196.

Boehm, S. A., Schröder, H., & Kunze, F. (2013). Comparative age management: Theoretical perspectives and practical implications. In J. Field, R. J. Burke, & C. L. Cooper (Eds.), *SAGE Handbook of aging, work and society* (pp. 211–237). Thousand Oaks, CA: SAGE.

Büsch, V., Dahl, S. A., & Dittrich, D. A. V. (2009). An empirical study of age discrimination in Norway and Germany. *Applied Economics, 41*, 633–651. doi:10.1080/00036840601007344.

Carden, L. L., & Boyd, R. O. (2014). Age discrimination in the workplace: Examining a model for prevention. *Southern Journal for Business and Ethics, 6*, 58–67.

Chasteen, A. L., & Cary, L. A. (2015). Age stereotypes and age stigma: Connections to research on subjective aging. *Annual Review of Gerontology and Geriatrics, 35*, 99–119.

Chasteen, A. L., Schwarz, N., & Park, D. C. (2002). The activation of aging stereotypes in younger and older adults. *The Journals of Gerontology: Series B: Psychological Sciences and Social Sciences, 57*, 540–547. doi:10.1093/geronb/57.6.P540.

Cheung, C. K., Kam, P. K., & Man-hung Ngan, R. M. H. (2010). Age discrimination in the labour market from the perspectives of employers and older workers. *International Social Work, 54*, 118–136. doi:10.177/0020872810372368.

Chiu, W. C. K., Chan, A. W., Snape, E., & Redman, T. (2001). Age stereotypes and discriminatory attitudes toward older workers: An East–West comparison. *Human Relations, 54*, 629–661. doi:10.1177/0018726701545004.

Cleveland, J. N., Festa, R. M., & Montgomery, L. (1988). Applicant pool composition and job perceptions: Impact on decisions regarding an older applicant. *Journal of Vocational Behavior, 32*, 112–125. doi:10.1016/0001-8791(88)90009-7.

Cleveland, J. N., & Landy, F. J. (1983). The effects of person and job stereotypes on two personnel decisions. *Journal of Applied Psychology, 68*, 609–619. doi:10.1037/0021-9010.68.4.609.

Connor, C. L., Walsh, P., Litzelman, D. K., & Alvarez, M. G. (1978). Evaluation of job applicants: The effects of age versus success. *Journal of Gerontology, 33*, 246–252. doi:10.1093/geronj/33.2.246.

Cox, C. B., & Barron. L. (2012). The effects of changing anti-discrimination legal standards on the evaluation of older workers. *Journal of Applied Social Psychology, 42*, 198–221. doi: 10.1111./j.1559-1816.2012.01040.x.

Crew, J. C. (1984). Age stereotypes as a function of race. *Academy of Management Journal, 27*, 431–435. doi:10.2307/255934.

Cuddy, A. J. C., & Fiske, S. T. (2002). Doddering but dear: Process, content, and function in stereotyping of older persons. In T. D. Nelson (Ed.), *Ageism: Stereotyping and prejudice against older persons* (pp. 3–26). Cambridge, MA: MIT Press.

Cuddy, A. J. C., Norton, M. I., & Fiske, S. T. (2005). This old stereotype: The pervasiveness and persistence of the elderly stereotype. *Journal of Social Issues, 61*, 267–286. doi:10.1111/j.1540-4560.2005.00405.x.

Dasgupta, N., & Greenwald, A. G. (2001). On the malleability of automatic attitudes: Combating automatic prejudice with images of admired and disliked individuals. *Journal of Personality and Social Psychology, 81*, 800–814. doi:10.1037/0022-3514.81.5.800.

Dedrick, E. J., & Dobbins, G. H. (1991). The influence of subordinate age on managerial actions: An attributional analysis. *Journal of Organizational Behavior, 12*, 367–377. doi:10.1002/job.4030120502.

Dovidio, J. F., Brigham, J. C., Johnson, B. T., & Gaertner, S. L. (1996). Stereotyping, prejudice, and discrimination: Another look. In C. N. Macrae, C. Stangor, & M. Hewstone (Eds.), *Stereotypes and stereotyping* (pp. 276–319). New York: The Guilford Press.

Duguid, M. M., & Thomas-Hunt, M. C. (2015). Condoning stereotyping? How awareness of stereotyping prevalence impacts expression of stereotypes. *Journal of Applied Psychology, 100*, 343–359. doi:10.1037/a0037908.

Duncan, C. (2008). The dangers and limitations of equality agendas as means for tackling old-age prejudice. *Aging & Society, 28*, 1133–1158. doi:10.1017/S0144686X08007496.

Erber, J. T., & Long, B. A. (2006). Perceptions of forgetful and slow employees: Does age matter? *The Journals of Gerontology Series B: Psychological Sciences and Social Sciences, 61*, 333–339. doi:10.1093/geronb/61.6.P333.

Fabroni, M., Saltstone, R., & Hughes, S. (1990). The Fabroni Scale of Ageism (FSA): An attempt at a more precise measure of ageism. *Canadian Journal on Aging, 91*, 56–66.

Finkelstein, L. M. (2015). Now that we know what ... how? In L. Finkelstein, D. Truxillo, F. Fraccaroli, and R. Kanfer (Eds.), *Facing the challenges of a multi-age workforce: A use-inspired approach.* (pp. 356–361). New York: Routledge.

Finkelstein, L. M., & Farrell, S. (2007). An expanded view of age bias in the workplace. In K. S. Shultz, & G. A. Adams (Eds.), *Aging and work in the 21st century* (pp. 73–108). Mahwah, NJ: Lawrence Erlbaum Associates.

Finkelstein, L. M., & Burke, M. J. (1998). Age stereotyping at work: The role of rater and contextual factors on evaluations of job applicants. *The Journal of General Psychology, 125*, 317–345. doi:10.1080/00221309809595341.

Finkelstein, L. M., Burke, M. J., & Raju, M. S. (1995). Age discrimination in simulated employment contexts: An integrative analysis. *Journal of Applied Psychology, 80*, 652–663. doi:10.1037/0021-9010.80.6.652.

Finkelstein, L. M., Higgins, K. D., & Clancy, L. M. (2000). Justifications for ratings of older and young job applicants: An exploratory content analysis. *Experimental Aging Research, 26*, 263–283. doi:10.1080/036107300404895.

Finkelstein, L. M., King, E. B., & Voyles, E. C. (2015). Age metastereotyping and cross-age workplace interactions: A meta view of age stereotypes at work. *Work, Aging, and Retirement, 1*, 26–40. doi:10.1093/workar/wau002.

Finkelstein, L. M., Ryan, K. M., & King, E. B. (2013). What do the young (old) people think of me? Content and accuracy of age-based metastereotypes. *European Journal of Work and Organizational Psychology, 22*, 633–657. doi:10/1080/1359432X.2012.673279.

Fiske, S. T. (2004). Stereotyping, prejudice, and discrimination: Social biases. In S. T. Fiske (Ed.), *Social beings: A core motives approach to social psychology* (pp. 397–457). Danvers, MA: John Wiley.

Fiske, S. T., & Neuberg, S. L. (1990). A continuum of impression formation, from category-based to individuating processes: Influences of information and motivation on attention and interpretation. *Advances in Experimental Social Psychology, 23,* 1–74. doi:10.1016/S0065-2601(08)60317-2.

Fusilier, M. R., & Hitt, M. A. (1983). Effects of age, race, sex, and employment experience on students' perceptions of job applications. *Perceptual and Motor Skills, 57,* 1127–1134. doi:10.2466/pms.1983.57.3f.1127.

Giles, H., & Reid, S. A. (2005). Ageism across the lifespan: Towards a self-categorization model of aging. *Journal of Social Issues, 61,* 389–404. doi:10.1111/j.1540-4560. 2005.00412.x.

Gordon, R. A., & Arvey, R. D. (1986). Perceived and actual ages of workers. *Journal of Vocational Behavior, 28,* 21–28. doi:10.1016/0001-8791(86)90036-9.

Gordon, R. A., & Arvey, R. D. (2004). Age bias in laboratory and field settings: A meta-analytic investigation. *Journal of Applied Social Psychology, 34,* 468–492. doi:10.1111/j.1559-1816.2004.tb02557.x.

Gordon, R. A., Rozelle, R. M., & Baxter, J. C. (1988). The effect of applicant age, job level, and accountability on the evaluation of job applicants. *Organizational Behavior and Human Decision Processes, 41,* 20–33. doi:10.1016/0749-5978(88)90044-1.

Gordon, R. A., Rozelle, R. M., & Baxter, J. C. (1989). The effect of applicant age, job level, and accountability on perceptions of female job applicants. *The Journal of Psychology, 123,* 59–68. doi:10.1080/00223980.1989.10542962.

Haefner, J. E. (1977). Race, age, sex, and competence as factors in employer selection of the disadvantaged. *Journal of Applied Psychology, 62,* 199–202. doi:10.1037/0021-9010. 62.2.199.

Hagestad, G. O., & Uhlenberg, P. (2005). The social separation of old and young: A root of ageism. *Journal of Social Issues, 61,* 343–360. doi:10.1111/j.1540-4560.2005.00409.x.

Han, J., & Richardson, V. E. (2015). The relationships among perceived discrimination, self-perceptions of aging, and depressive symptoms: A longitudinal examination of age discrimination. *Aging and Mental Health, 19,* 747–755. doi:10.1080/13607863. 2014.962007.

Hassell, B. L., & Perrewe, P. L. (1995). An examination of beliefs about older workers: Do stereotypes still exist? *Journal of Organizational Behavior, 16,* 457–468. doi:10.1002/ job.4030160506.

Henkens, C. J. I. M. (2005). Stereotyping older workers and retirement: The managers' point of view. *Canadian Journal of Aging, 24,* 353–366. doi:10.1353/cja.2006.0011.

Hummert, M. L. (1990). Multiple stereotypes of elderly and young adults: A comparison of structure and evaluations. *Psychology and Aging, 5,* 182–193. doi:10.1037/0882-7974. 5.2.182.

Hummert, M. L. (1999). A social cognitive perspective on age stereotypes. In T. M. Hess & F. Blanchard-Fields (Eds.), *Social cognition and aging* (pp. 175–196). San Diego, CA: Academic Press.

Hummert, M. L., Garstka, T. A., & Shaner, J. L. (1997). Stereotyping of older adults: The role of target facial cues and perceiver characteristics. *Psychology and Aging, 12,* 107–114. doi:10.1037/0882-7974.12.1.107.

Iweins, C., Desmette, D., & Yzerbyt, V. (2012). Ageism at work: What happens to older workers who benefit from preferential treatment? *Psychologica Belgica, 52,* 327–349. doi:10.5334.pb-52-4-327.

Iweins, C., Desmette, D., Yzerbyt, V., & Stinglhamber, F. (2013). Ageism at work: The impact of intergenerational contact and organizational multi-age perspective. *European Journal of Work and Organizational Psychology, 23,* 331–346. doi:10.1080/1359432X.20 12.748656.

Jackson, L. A., & Sullivan, L. A. (1988). Age stereotype disconfirming information and evaluations of old people. *The Journal of Social Psychology, 128*, 721–729. doi:10.1080/00224545.1988.9924552.

Kalavar, J. M. (2001). Examining ageism: Do male and female college students differ? *Educational Gerontology, 27*, 507–513. doi:10.1080/036012701316894199.

Kirchner, W. K., & Dunnette, M. D. (1954). Attitudes toward older workers. *Personnel Psychology, 7*, 257–265. doi:10.1111/j.1744-6570.1954.tb01599.x.

Kite, M. E., & Wagner, L. (2002). Attitudes toward older adults. In T. D. Nelson (Ed.), *Ageism: Stereotyping and prejudice against older persons* (pp. 129–161). Cambridge, MA: MIT Press.

Kite, M. E., Stockdale, G. D., Whitley Jr., B. E., & Johnson, B. T. (2005). Attitudes toward younger and older adults: An updated meta-analytic review. *Journal of Social Issues, 61*, 241–266. doi:10.1111/j.1540-4560.2005.00404.x.

Kogan, N., & Shelton, F. C. (1960). Differential cue value of age and occupation in impression formation. *Psychological Reports, 7*, 203–216. doi:10.2466/pr0.1960.7.2.203.

Kooij, D., De Lange, A., Jansen, P., & Dikkers, J. (2008). Older workers' motivation to continue to work: Five meanings of age. A conceptual review. *Journal of Managerial Psychology, 23*, 364–394. doi:10.1108/02683940810869015.

Krings, F., Sczesny, S., & Kluge, A. (2011). Age discrimination: The role of competence and warmth. *British Journal of Management, 22*, 187–201. doi:10.1111/j.1467-8551.2010.00721.x.

Kroon, A. C., Van Selm, M., ter Hoeven, C. L., & Vliegenthart, R. (2016). Reliable and unproductive? Stereotypes of older employees in corporate and news media. *Ageing & Society*, 1–26. doi:10.1017/So144686X160000982.

Kulik, C. T., Perera, S., & Cregan, C. (2016). Engage me: The mature-age worker and stereotype threat. *Academy of Management Journal, 59*, 2132–2156. doi:10.5465/amj.2015.0564.

Kunze, F., Boehm, S. A., & Bruch, H. (2011). Age diversity, age discrimination climate and performance consequences – a cross organizational study. *Journal of Organizational Behavior, 32*, 264–290. doi:10.1002/job.698.

Kunze, F., Boehm, S., & Bruch, H. (2013). Organizational performance consequences of age diversity: Inspecting the role of diversity-friendly HR policies and top managers' negative age stereotypes. *Journal of Management Studies, 50*, 413–442. doi:10.1111/joms.12016.

Kunze, F., Raes, A. M., & Bruch, H. (2015). It matters how old you feel: Antecedents and performance consequences of average relative subjective age in organizations. *Journal of Applied Psychology, 100*, 1511–1526. doi:10.1037/a0038909.

Lagacé, M., Charmarkeh, H., Tanguay, J., & Annick, L. (2015). How ageism contributes to the second-level digital divide: The case of Canadian seniors. *Journal of Technologies and Human Usability, 11*(4), 1–13. Retrieved from http://ijt.cgpublisher.com/product/pub.296/prod.25.

Lahey, J. N. (2006). How do age discrimination laws affect older workers? *Work Opportunities for Older Americans, 5*, 1–8. Retrieved from https://pdfs.semanticscholar.org/6b16/a269395f9fa8d6fd90426a185547c806fcd2.pdf.

Lamont, R. A., Swift, H. J., & Abrams, D. (2015). A review and meta-analysis of age-based stereotype threat: Negative stereotypes, not facts, do the damage. *Psychology and Aging, 30*, 180–193. doi:10.1037/a0038586.

Lawrence, B. S. (1988). New wrinkles in the theory of age: Demography, norms, and performance ratings. *Academy of Management Journal, 31*, 309–337. doi:10.2307/256550.

Lazazzara, A., Karpinska, K., & Henkens, K. (2013). What factors influence training opportunities for older workers? Three factorial surveys exploring the attitudes of HR professionals. *The International Journal of Human Resource Management, 24*, 2154–2172. doi:10.1080/09585192.2012.725077.

Lee, J. A., & Clemons, T. (1985). Factors affecting employment decisions about older workers. *Journal of Applied Psychology, 70*, 785–788. Retrieved from http://psycnet.apa.org/buy/1986-10591-001.

Lee, S. Y., Pitesa, M., Thau, S., & Pillutla, M. M. (2015). Discrimination in selection decisions: Integrating stereotype fit and interdependence theories. *Academy of Management Journal, 58*, 789–812. doi:10.5465/amj.2013.0571.

Levy, B. R., & Banaji, R. B. (2002). Implicit ageism. In T. D. Nelson (Ed.), *Ageism: Stereotyping and prejudice against older persons* (pp. 49–75). Cambridge, MA: MIT Press.

Levy, B., & Langer, E. (1994). Aging free from negative stereotypes: Successful memory in China among the American deaf. *Journal of Personality and Social Psychology, 66*, 989–997. doi:10.1037/0022-3514.66.6.989.

Leyens, J. P., Yzerbyt, V. Y., & Schadron, G. (1992). The social judgeability approach to stereotypes. In W. Stroebe & M. Hewstone (Eds.), *European review of social psychology* (pp. 92–120). Chichester, UK: Wiley.

Linville, P. W. (1982). The complexity-extremity effect and age-based stereotyping. *Journal of Personality and Social Psychology, 42*, 193–211. doi:10.1037/0022-3514.42.2.193.

Locke-Connor, C., & Walsh, R. P. (1980). Attitudes toward the older job applicant: Just as competent but more likely to fail. *Journal of Gerontology, 35*, 920–927. doi:10.1093/geronj/35.6.920.

Lyon, P., & Pollard, D. (1997). Perceptions of the older employee: Is anything really changing? *Personnel Review, 26*, 245–257. doi:10.1108/00483489710172051.

Marchiondo, L. A., Gonzales, E., & Ran, S. (2016). Development and validation of the workplace age discrimination scale. *Journal of Business and Psychology, 31*, 493–513. doi:10.1007/s10869-015-9425-6.

Marcus, J., & Fritzche, B. (2015). One size doesn't fit all: Toward a theory on the intersectional salience of ageism at work. *Organizational Psychology Review, 5*, 168–188.

Marcus, J., & Fritzche, B. (2016). The cultural anchors of age discrimination in the workplace: A multi-level framework. *Work, Aging and Retirement, 2*, 217–229.

Marcus, J., Fritzsche, B. A., Le, H., & Reeves, M. D. (2016). Validation of the work-related age-based stereotypes (WAS) scale. *Journal of Managerial Psychology, 31*, 989–1004 doi:2F10.1108%2FJMP-11-2014-0320.

Martens, A., Goldenberg, J. L., & Greenberg, J. (2005). A terror management perspective on ageism. *Journal of Social Issues, 61*, 223–239. doi:10.1111/j.1540-4560.2005.00403.x.

McCann, R., & Giles, H. (2002). Ageism in the workplace: A communication perspective. In T. D. Nelson (Ed.), *Ageism: Stereotyping and prejudice against older persons* (pp. 163–199). Cambridge, MA: MIT Press.

Morgeson, F. P., Reider, M. H., Campion, M. A., & Bull, R. A. (2008). Review of research on age discrimination in the employment interview. *Journal of Business and Psychology, 22*, 223–232. doi:10.1007/s10869-008-9066-0.

Min, J. Y., Park, S. G., Kim, S. S., & Min, K. B. (2014). Workplace injustice and self-reported disease and absenteeism in South Korea. *American Journal of Industrial Medicine, 57*, 87–96. doi:10.1002/ajim.22233.

North, M. S., & Fiske, S. T. (2013). Act your (old) age: Prescriptive ageist biases over succession, consumption, and identity. *Personality and Social Psychology Bulletin, 39*, 720–734. doi:10.1177/0146167213480043.

North, M. S., & Fiske, S. T. (2015). Modern attitudes toward older adults in the aging world: A cross-cultural meta-analysis. *Psychological Bulletin, 141*, 993–1021. doi:10.1037/a0039469.

Nussbaum, J. F., Pitts, M. J., Huber, F. N., Krieger, J. L., & Ohs, J. E. (2005). Ageism and ageist language across the life span: Intimate relationships and non-intimate interactions. *Journal of Social Issues, 61*, 287–306. doi:10.1111/j.1540-4560.2005.00406.x.

Perry, E. L. (1994). A prototype matching approach to understanding the role of applicant gender and age in the evaluation of job applicants. *Journal of Applied Social Psychology, 24*, 1433–1473. doi:10.1111/j.1559-1816.1994.tb01558.x.

Perry, E. L., & Bourhis, A. C. (1998). A closer look at the role of applicant age in selection decisions. *Journal of Applied Social Psychology, 28*, 1670–1697. doi:10.1111/j.1559-1816.1998.tb01340.x.

Perry, E. L., & Finkelstein, L. M. (1999). Toward a broader view of age discrimination in employment-related decisions: A joint consideration of organizational factors and cognitive processes. *Human Resource Management Review, 9*, 21–49. doi:10.1016/S1053-4822(99)00010-8.

Perry, E. L., & Parlamis, J. D. (2005). Age and ageism in organizations: A review and consideration of national culture. In A. M. Konrad, P. Prasad, & J. K. Pringle (Eds.), *Handbook of workplace diversity*. London, England: SAGE.

Perry, J. S., & Varney, T. L. (1978). College students' attitudes toward workers' competence and age. *Psychological Reports, 42*, 1319–1322. doi:10.2466/pr0.1978.42.3c.1319.

Perry, E. L., Kulik, C. T., & Bourhis, A. C. (1996). Moderating effects of personal and contextual factors in age discrimination. *Journal of Applied Psychology, 81*, 628–647. doi:10.1037/0021-9010.81.6.628.

Pitt-Catsouphes, M., Matz-Costa, C., & Brown, M. (2011). The prism of age: Managing age diversity in the twenty-first-century workplace. In E. Parry & S. Tyson (Eds.), *Managing an age-diverse workforce* (pp. 80–94). New York: Palgrave Macmillan.

Posthuma, R. A., & Campion, M. A. (2009). Age stereotypes in the workplace: Common stereotypes, moderators, and future research directions. *Journal of Management, 35*, 158–188. doi:10.1177/0149206308318617.

Poulston, J., & Jenkins, A. (2013). The persistent paradigm: Older worker stereotypes in the New Zealand hotel industry. *Journal of Human Resources in Hospitality & Tourism, 12*, 1–25. doi:10.1080/15332845.2013.723252.

Rauschenbach, C., Goritz, A. S., & Hertel, G. (2012). Age stereotypes about emotional resilience at work. *Educational Gerontology, 38*, 511–519. doi:10.1080/03601277.2011.567187.

Remery, C., Henkens, K., Schippers, J., & Ekamper, P. (2003). Managing an ageing workforce and a right labor market: Views held by Dutch employers. *Population Research and Policy Review, 22*, 21–40. doi:10.1023/A:1023543307473.

Riach, K., & Kelly, S. (2015). The need for fresh blood: Understanding organizational age inequality through a vampiric lens. *Organization, 22*, 287–305. doi:10.1177/1350508413508999.

Rosen, B., & Jerdee, T. H. (1976a). The nature of job-related age stereotypes. *Journal of Applied Psychology, 61*, 180–183. doi:10.1037/0021-9010.61.2.180.

Rosen, B., & Jerdee, T. H. (1976b). The influence of age stereotypes on managerial decisions. *Journal of Applied Psychology, 61*, 428–432. doi:10.1037/0021-9010.61.4.428.

Rosen, B., & Jerdee, T. H. (1977). Too old or not too old? *Harvard Business Review, 55*, 97–106.

Ruggs, E. N., Hebl, M. R., Walker, S. S., & Fa-Kaji, N. (2014). Selection biases that emerge when age meets gender. *Journal of Managerial Psychology, 29,* 1028–1043. doi:10.1108/JMP-07-2012-0204.

Rupp, D. E., Vodanovich, S. J., & Credé, M. (2005). The multidimensional nature of ageism: Construct validity and group differences. *Journal of Social Psychology, 145,* 335–364. doi:10.3200/SOCP.145.3.335-362.

Rupp, D. E., Vodanovich, S. J., & Credé, M. (2006). Age bias in the workplace: The impact of ageism and causal attributions. *Journal of Applied Social Psychology, 36,* 1337–1364. doi:10.1111/j.0021-9029.2006.00062.x.

Segers, J., Inceoglu, I., & Finkelstein, L. (2014). The age cube of work. In E. Parry (Ed.), *Generational diversity at work: New research perspectives* (pp. 11–36). New York: Routledge.

Shore, L. M., Cleveland, J. N., & Goldberg, C. B. (2003). Work attitudes and decisions as a function of manager age and employee age. *Journal of Applied Psychology, 88,* 529–537. doi:10.1037/0021-9010.88.3.529.

Shore, L. M., & Goldberg, C. B. (2004). Age discrimination in the workplace. In R. L. Dipboye & A. Colella (Eds.), *Discrimination at work* (pp. 203–226). Mahwah, NJ: Lawrence Erlbaum Associates.

Singer, M. S., & Sewell, C. (1989). Applicant age and selection interview decisions: Effect of information exposure on age discrimination in personnel selection. *Personnel Psychology, 42,* 135–154. doi:10.1111/j.1744-6570.1989.tb01554.x.

Snyder, M., & Miene, P. K. (1994). Stereotyping of the elderly: A functional approach. *British Journal of Social Psychology, 33,* 63–82. doi:10.1111/j.2044-8309.1994.tb01011.x.

Taylor, P., & Walker, A. (1998). Employers and older workers: Attitudes and employment practices. *Aging and Society, 18,* 641–658. doi:10.1017/s0144686x98007119.

Triandis, H. C. (1963). Factors affecting employee selection in two cultures. *Journal of Applied Psychology, 47,* 89–96. doi:10.1037/h0049334.

Truxillo, D. M., Finkelstein, L. M., Pytlovany, A. C., & Jenkins, J. S. (2017). Age discrimination at work: A review of the research and recommendations for the future. In A. Colella, & E. King, *The Oxford handbook of workplace discrimination* (pp. 1–37). New York: Oxford University Press.

Truxillo, D. M., Cadiz, D. M., & Hammer, L. B. (2015). Supporting the aging workforce: A review and recommendations for workplace intervention research. *Annual Review of Organizational Psychology and Organizational Behavior, 2,* 351–381. doi:10.1146/annurev-orgpsych-032414-111435.

Turner, J. C. (1985). Social categorization and the self-concept: A social cognitive theory of group behavior. In E. J. Lawler (Ed.), *Advances in group processes* (Vol. 2, pp. 77–122). Greenwich, CT: JAI Press.

Van Selm, M., & Van der Heijden, B. I. J. M. (2014). Media portrayals of older employees: A success story? *Journal of Organizational Change, 27,* 583–597. doi:10.1108/JOCM-05-2014-0102.

Vrugt, A., & Schabracq, M. (1996). Stereotypes with respect to elderly employees: The contribution of attribute information and representativeness. *Journal of Community and Applied Social Psychology, 6,* 287–292. doi:10.1002/(SICI)1099-1298(199610)6:4<287::AID-CASP376>3.0.CO;2-S.

Walker, A. (2005). The emergence of age management in Europe. *International Journal of Organizational Behavior, 10,* 685–697.

Weiss, E. M., & Maurer, T. J. (2004). Age discrimination in personnel decisions: A reexamination. *Journal of Applied Social Psychology, 34,* 1551–1562. doi:10.1111/j.1559-1816.2004.tb02786.x.

Wisdom, N. M., Connor, D. R., Hogan, L. R., & Callahan, J. L. (2014). The relationship of anxiety and beliefs toward aging in ageism. *Journal of Scientific Psychology*, 10–21.

Yuan, A. S. V. (2007). Perceived age discrimination and mental health. *Social Forces*, *86*, 291–311. doi:10.1353/sof.2007.0113.

Zaniboni, S. (2015). The interaction between older workers' personal resources and perceived discrimination affects the perceived retirement age and the expected adjustment. *Work, Aging and Retirement*, *1*, 266–273. doi:10.1093/workar/wav010.

Zenger, T. R., & Lawrence, B. S. (1989). Organizational demography: The differential effects of age and tenure distributions on technical communication. *Academy of Management Journal*, *32*, 353–378. doi:10.2307/256366.

APPENDIX 4.1 Categorization of age bias at work articles according to the tripartite view of bias

Source	Stereotyping	Prejudice	Discrimination
Ahmed, Andersson, & Hammarstedt (2012)			X
Averhart (2012)	X	X	X
Avolio & Barrett (1987)	X		X
Bakar & McCann (2014)		X	X
Bal, Reiss, Rudolph, & Baltes (2011)	X		X
Bertolino, Truxillo, & Fraccaroli (2013)	X		
Bilinska, Wegge, & Kliegel (2016)	X		
Billett, Dymock, Johnson, & Martin (2011)	X		
Bird & Fisher (1986)	X	X	
Busch, Dahl, & Dittrich (2009)			X
Calo, Patterson, & Decker (2013)	X		
Chen & Wang (2012)	X		X
Cheung, Kam, & Ngan (2010)	X		X
Chiu, Chan, Snape, & Redman (2001)	X	X	X
Cleveland & Landy (1983)	X		X
Cleveland & Landy (1987)	X		
Cleveland, Festa, & Montgomery (1988)	X		X
Connor, Walsh, Litzelman, & Alvarez (1978)	X	X	X
Cox & Barron (2012)	X	X	
Craft, Doctors, Shkop, & Benecki (1979)	X		X
Crew (1984)	X		
DeArmond, Tye, Chen, Krauss, Rogers, & Sintek (2006)	X		
Dedrick & Dobbins (1991)	X		X
Erber & Long (2006)	X	X	
Finkelstein & Burke (1998)	X		X
Finkelstein, Burke, & Raju (1995)	X		X
Finkelstein, Higgins, & Clancy (2000)	X		X
Finkelstein, Ryan, & King (2013)	X		
Fritzche & Marcus (2013)		X	X
Fusilier & Hitt (1983)	X		X

Source	Stereotyping	Prejudice	Discrimination
Gaillard & Desmette (2010)	X		
Gordon & Arvey (1986)	X		
Gordon & Arvey (2004)	X		X
Gordon, Rozelle, & Baxter (1988)	X	X	X
Gordon, Rozelle, & Baxter (1989)	X		X
Grima (2011)	X		X
Gringart, Helmes, & Speelman (2005)	X		X
Gringart, Jones, Helmes, Jansz, Monterosso, & Edwards (2012)	X		X
Haefner (1977)			X
Harteis, Billett, Goller, Rausch, & Seifried (2015)	X		X
Hassell & Perrewe (1995)	X		
Helmes (2012)	X	X	X
Henkens (2005)	X		
Henry, Zacher, & Desmette (2015)	X		
Heyma, van der Werff, Nauta, & van Sloten (2014)			X
Iweins, Desmette, & Yzerbyt (2012)	X		X
Iweins, Desmette, Yzerbyt, & Stinglhamber (2013)	X	X	X
James, McKenchie, Swanberg, & Besen (2012)			X
Jenkins (2008)			X
Kadefors & Hanse (2012)	X		
Kalavar (2001)	X	X	X
Karpinska, Henkens, & Schippers (2013)	X		
Kim & Mo (2014)	X		
Kogan & Shelton (1960)	X		
Krings, Sczesny, & Kluge (2011)	X		X
Kunze, Boehm, & Bruch (2011)			X
Kunze, Boehm, & Bruch (2013)	X		
Lawrence (1988)	X		X
Lazazzara, Karpinska, & Henkens (2013)			X
Lee & Clemons (1985)	X		X
Lee, Pitesa, Thau, & Pillutla (2015)			
Levin (1988)	X		
Liden, Stilwell, & Ferris (1996)	X		X
Lin, Dobbins, & Farh (1992)			X
Lindner, Graser, & Nosek (2014)			X
Locke-Connor & Walsh (1980)	X		X
Loretto, Duncan & White (2000)	X	X	X
Luoh, & Tsaur (2011)	X	X	
Luoh, & Tsaur (2014)	X		
Lyon & Pollard (1997)	X		
Marcus & Fritzche (2014)	X	X	X
McCann & Keaton (2013)	X		

continued

APPENDIX 4.1 Continued

Source	Stereotyping	Prejudice	Discrimination
Ng & Feldman (2012)	X		
North & Fiske (2015)	X	X	
Perry & Varney (1978)	X		
Perry (1994)	X		X
Perry & Bourhis (1998)	X		X
Perry, Kulik, & Bourhis (1996)	X		X
Poulston & Jenkins (2013)	X		X
Principi, Fabbietti, & Lamura (2015)	X		
Rabl & Triana (2013)			X
Rauschenbach, Goritz, & Hertel (2012)	X		
Remery, Henkens, Schippers, & Ekamper (2003)	X	X	X
Roscigno, Mong, Byron, & Tester (2007)			X
Rosen & Jerdee (1976)	X		X
Rosen & Jerdee (1977)	X		X
Ruggs, Hebl, Walker, & Fa-Kaji (2014)			X
Rupp, Vodanovich, & Credé (2006)	X	X	X
Schniter & Shields (2014)	X		X
Shore, Cleveland, & Goldberg (2003)			X
Singer & Sewell (1989)	X		X
Singer (1987)	X		
Sofica (2012)			X
Triandis (1963)			X
Truxillo, McCune, Bertolino, & Fraccaroli (2012)	X		
Vrugt & Schabracq (1996)	X		
Wanberg, Kanfer, Hamann, & Zhang (2015)			X
Weiss & Maurer (2004)	X		X

Note

We attempted a comprehensive search of published articles on age bias in the workplace at the time this chapter was written, yet cannot guarantee that every relevant study is represented in this table. Additionally, our categorization is based on our understanding of three components. We realize that other researchers may have different interpretations. We chose the term "prejudice" to capture the affective and evaluative category. Articles here may differ to the degree that they are capturing pure affect and not a more cognitively laden evaluation, as described further in the text.

References

Ahmed, A. M., Andersson, L., & Hammarstedt, M. (2012). Does age matter for employability? A field experiment on ageism in the Swedish labour market. *Applied Economics Letters, 199,* 403–406. doi:10.1080/13504851.2011.581199.

Averhart, V. (2012). Ageism in the workplace: Examining the influence of age conceptualization on the advancement opportunities of older workers *FIU Electronic Theses and Dissertations.* 585. Retrieved from http://digitalcommons.fiu.edu/.

Avolio, B. J., & Barrett, G. V. (1987). Effects of age stereotyping in a simulated interview. *Psychology and Aging, 2,* 56–63. doi:10.1037/0882-7974.2.1.56.

Bakar, H. A., & McCann, R. M. (2014). Matters of demographic similarity and dissimilarity in supervisor–subordinate relationships and workplace attitudes. *International Journal of Intercultural Relations, 41*, 1–16. doi:10.1016/j.ijintrel.2014.04.004.

Bal, A. C., Reiss, A. E., Rudolph, C. W., & Baltes, B. B. (2011). Examining positive and negative perceptions of older workers: A meta-analysis. *The Journals of Gerontology: Series B, 66*, 687–698. doi:10.1093/geronb/gbr056.

Bertolino, M., Truxillo, D. M., & Fraccaroli, F. (2012). Age effect on perceived personality and job performance. *Journal of Managerial Psychology, 28*, 867–885. doi:10.1108/JMP-07-2013-0222.

Biernat, M., Manis, M., & Nelson, T. E. (1991). Stereotypes and standards of judgment. *Journal of Personality and Social Psychology, 60*, 485–499. doi:10.1037/0022-3514.60.4.485.

Bilinska, P., Wegge, J., & Kliegel, M. (2016). Caring for the elderly but not for one's own old employees? *Journal of Personnel Psychology, 15*, 95–105. doi:10.1027/1866-5888/a000144.

Billett, S., Dymock, D., Johnson, G., & Martin, G. (2011). Last resort employees: Older workers' perceptions of workplace discrimination. *Human Resource Development International, 14(4)*, 375–389. doi:10.1080/13678868.2011.601571.

Bird, C. P., & Fisher, T. D. (1986). Thirty years later: Attitudes toward the employment of older workers. *Journal of Applied Psychology, 71*, 515–517. doi:10.1037/0021-9010.71.3.515.

Büsch, V., Dahl, S. A., & Dittrich, D. A. V. (2009). An empirical study of age discrimination in Norway and Germany. *Applied Economics, 41*, 633–651. doi:10.1080/00036840601007344.

Calo, T. J., Patterson, M. M., & Decker, W. H. (2013). Employee perceptions of older workers' motivation in business, academia, and government. *International Journal of Business and Social Science, 4(2)*, 1–10.

Chen, H. J., & Wang, Y. H. (2012). Age stereotypes of older primary teachers in Taiwan. *Educational Gerontology, 38(5)*, 362–371. doi:10.1080/10668926.2011.559839.

Cheung, C. K., Kam, P. K., & Man-hung Ngan, R. M. H. (2010). Age discrimination in the labour market from the perspectives of employers and older workers. *International Social Work, 54*, 118–136. doi:10.1177/0020872810372368.

Chiu, W. C. K., Chan, A. W., Snape, E., & Redman, T. (2001). Age stereotypes and discriminatory attitudes toward older workers: An East-West comparison. *Human Relations, 54*, 629–661. doi:10.1177/0018726701545004.

Cleveland, J. N., Festa, R. M., & Montgomery, L. (1988). Applicant pool composition and job perceptions: Impact on decisions regarding an older applicant. *Journal of Vocational Behavior, 32*, 112–125. doi:10.1016/0001-8791(88)90009-7.

Cleveland, J. N., & Landy, F. J. (1983). The effects of person and job stereotypes on two personnel decisions. *Journal of Applied Psychology, 68*, 609–619. doi:10.1037/0021-9010.68.4.609.

Cleveland, J. N., & Landy, F. J. (1987). Age perceptions of jobs: Convergence of two questionnaires. *Psychological Reports, 60*, 1075–1081. doi:10.2466/pr0.1987.60.3c.1075.

Connor, C. L., Walsh, P., Litzelman, D. K., & Alvarez, M. G. (1978). Evaluation of job applicants: The effects of age versus success. *Journal of Gerontology, 33*, 246–252. doi:10.1093/geronj/33.2.246.

Cox, C. B., & Barron. L. (2012). The effects of changing anti-discrimination legal standards on the evaluation of older workers. *Journal of Applied Social Psychology, 42*, 198–221. doi: 10.1111./j.1559-1816.2012.01040.x.

Craft, J. A., Doctors, S. I., Shkop, Y. M., & Benecki, T. J. (1979). Simulated management perceptions, hiring decisions and age. *Aging and Work, 2,* 95–102.

Crew, J. C. (1984). Age stereotypes as a function of race. *Academy of Management Journal, 27,* 431–435. doi:10.2307/255934.

DeArmond, S., Tye, M., Chen, P. Y., Krauss, A., Rogers, D. A., & Sintek, E. (2006). Age and gender stereotypes: New challenges in a changing workplace and workforce. *Journal of Applied Social Psychology, 36,* 2184–2214. doi:10.1111/j.0021-9029.2006.00100.x.

Dedrick, E. J., & Dobbins, G. H. (1991). The influence of subordinate age on managerial actions: An attributional analysis. *Journal of Organizational Behavior, 12(5),* 367–377. doi:10.1002/job.4030120502.

Erber, J. T., & Long, B. A. (2006). Perceptions of forgetful and slow employees: Does age matter? *The Journals of Gerontology Series B: Psychological Sciences and Social Sciences, 61(6),* 333–339. doi:10.1093/geronb/61.6.P333.

Finkelstein, L. M., & Burke, M. J. (1998). Age stereotyping at work: The role of rater and contextual factors on evaluations of job applicants. *The Journal of General Psychology, 125(4),* 317–345. doi:10.1080/00221309809595341.

Finkelstein, L. M., Burke, M. J., & Raju, M. S. (1995). Age discrimination in simulated employment contexts: An integrative analysis. *Journal of Applied Psychology, 80,* 652–663. doi:10.1037/0021-9010.80.6.652.

Finkelstein, L. M., Higgins, K. D., & Clancy, L. M. (2000). Justifications for ratings of older and young job applicants: An exploratory content analysis. *Experimental Aging Research, 26,* 263–283. doi:10.1080/036107300404895.

Finkelstein, L. M., Ryan, K. M., & King, E. B. (2013). What do the young (old) people think of me? Content and accuracy of age-based metastereotypes. *European Journal of Work and Organizational Psychology, 22,* 633–657. doi:10/1080/1359432X.2012.673279.

Fritzche, B., & Marcus, J. (2013). The senior discount: Biases against older career changers. *Journal of Applied Social Psychology, 43,* 350–362. doi:10.1111/j.1559-1816.2012.01004.x.

Fusilier, M. R., & Hitt, M. A. (1983). Effects of age, race, sex, and employment experience on students' perceptions of job applications. *Perceptual and Motor Skills, 57,* 1127–1134. doi:10.2466/pms.1983.57.3f.1127.

Gaillard, M., & Desmette, D. (2010). (In)validating stereotypes about older workers influences their intentions to retire early and to learn and develop. *Basic and Applied Social Psychology, 32,* 86–98. doi:10.1080/0197350903435763.

Gordon, R. A., & Arvey, R. D. (1986). Perceived and actual ages of workers. *Journal of Vocational Behavior, 28,* 21–28. doi:10.1016/0001-8791(86)90036-9.

Gordon, R. A., & Arvey, R. D. (2004). Age bias in laboratory and field settings: A meta-analytic investigation. *Journal of Applied Social Psychology, 34,* 468–492. doi:10.1111/j.1559-1816.2004.tb02557.x.

Gordon, R. A., Rozelle, R. M., & Baxter, J. C. (1988). The effect of applicant age, job level, and accountability on the evaluation of job applicants. *Organizational Behavior and Human Decision Processes, 41,* 20–33. doi:10.1016/0749-5978(88)90044-1.

Gordon, R. A., Rozelle, R. M., & Baxter, J. C. (1989). The effect of applicant age, job level, and accountability on perceptions of female job applicants. *The Journal of Psychology, 123,* 59–68. doi:10.1080/00223980.1989.10542962.

Grima, F. (2011). The influence of age management policies on older employee work relationships with their company. *The International Journal of Human Resource Management, 22,* 1312–1332. doi:10.1080/09585192.2011.559101.

Gringart, E., Helmes, E., & Speelman, C. P. (2005). Exploring attitudes toward older workers among Australian employers: An empirical study. *Journal of Aging & Social Policy, 17,* 85–103. doi:10.1300/J031v17n03_05.

Gringart, E., Jones, B., Helmes, E., Jansz, J., Monterosso, L., & Edwards, M. (2012). Negative stereotyping of older nurses despite contact and mere exposure: The case of nursing recruiters in Western Australia. *Journal of Aging and Social Policy*, 24, 400–416. doi:10.1080/08959420.2012.735170.

Haefner, J. E. (1977). Race, age, sex, and competence as factors in employer selection of the disadvantaged. *Journal of Applied Psychology*, 62, 199–202. doi:10.1037/0021-9010.62.2.199.

Harteis, C., Billett, S., Goller, M., Rausch, A., & Seifried, J. (2015). Effects of age, gender, and occupation on perceived workplace learning support. *International Journal of Training Research*, 13, 64–81. doi:10:1080/14480220.2015.1051349.

Hassell, B. L., & Perrewe, P. L. (1995). An examination of beliefs about older workers: Do stereotypes still exist? *Journal of Organizational Behavior*, 16, 457–468. doi:10.1002/job.4030160506.

Helmes, E. (2012). Attitudes toward older workers among undergraduates: Does status make a difference? *Educational Gerontology*, 38, 391–399. doi:10.1080/03601277.2011.559848.

Henkens, C. J. I. M. (2005). Stereotyping older workers and retirement: The managers' point of view. *Canadian Journal of Aging*, 24, 353–366. doi:10.1353/cja.2006.0011.

Henry, H., Zacher, H., & Desmette, D. (2015). Reducing age bias and turnover intentions by enhancing intergenerational contact quality in the workplace: The role of opportunities for generativity and development. *Work, Aging and Retirement*, 1, 243–253. doi:10.1093/workar/wav005.

Heyma, A., van der Werff, S., Nauta, A., & van Sloten, G. (2014). What makes older job-seekers attractive to employers? *De Economist*, 162, 397–414. doi:10.1007/s10645-014-9239-3.

Iweins, C., Desmette, D., & Yzerbyt, V. (2012). Ageism at work: What happens to older workers who benefit from preferential treatment? *Psychologica Belgica*, 52, 327–349. doi:10.5334.pb-52-4-327.

Iweins, C., Desmette, D., Yzerbyt, V., & Stinglhamber, F. (2013). Ageism at work: The impact of intergenerational contact and organizational multi-age perspective. *European Journal of Work and Organizational Psychology*, 23, 331–346. doi:10.1080/1359432X.2012.748656.

James, J. B., McKenchie, S., Swanberg, J., & Besen, E. (2012). Exploring the workplace impact of intentional/unintentional age discrimination. *Journal of Managerial Psychology*, 28, 907–927. doi:10.1108/JMP-06-2013-0179.

Jenkins, A. K. (2008, May). Age discrimination in hotel workplaces: HRM practices and their effects on the employment of "older" workers. Presented at the 17th annual CHME Conference, Glasgow, UK.

Kadefors, R., & Hanse, J. J. (2012). Employer's attitudes toward older workers and obstacles and opportunities for the older unemployed to reenter working life. *Nordic Journal of Working Life Studies*, 2, 29–47. doi:10.19154/njwls.v2i3.2362.

Kalavar, J. M. (2001). Examining ageism: Do male and female college students differ? *Educational Gerontology*, 27, 507–513. doi:10.1080/036012701316894199.

Karpinska, K., Henkens, K., & Schippers, J. (2013). Retention of older workers: Impact of managers' age norms and stereotypes. *European Sociological Review*, 29, 1323–1335. doi:10.1093/esr/jct017.

Kim, D. S., & Mo, S. H. (2014). Stereotypical beliefs on old Korean workers. *Ageing International*, 39, 385–402. doi:10.1007/s12126-014-9200-4.

Kogan, N., & Shelton, F. C. (1960). Differential cue value of age and occupation in impression formation. *Psychological Reports*, 7, 203–216. doi:10.2466/pr0.1960.7.2.203.

Krings, F., Sczesny, S., & Kluge, A. (2011). Age discrimination: The role of competence and warmth. *British Journal of Management*, *22*, 187–201. doi:10.1111/j.1467-8551.2010.00721.x.

Kunze, F., Boehm, S. A., & Bruch, H. (2011). Age diversity, age discrimination climate and performance consequences – a cross organizational study. *Journal of Organizational Behavior*, *32*, 264–290. doi:10.1002/job.698.

Kunze, F., Boehm, S., & Bruch, H. (2013). Organizational performance consequences of age diversity: Inspecting the role of diversity-friendly HR policies and top managers' negative age stereotypes. *Journal of Management Studies*, *50*, 413–442. doi:10.1111/joms.12016.

Lawrence, B. S. (1988). New wrinkles in the theory of age: Demography, norms, and performance ratings. *Academy of Management Journal*, *31*, 309–337. doi:10.2307/256550.

Lazazzara, A., Karpinska, K., & Henkens, K. (2013). What factors influence training opportunities for older workers? Three factorial surveys exploring the attitudes of HR professionals. *The International Journal of Human Resource Management*, *24*, 2154–2172. doi:10.1080/09585192.2012.725077.

Lee, J. A., & Clemons, T. (1985). Factors affecting employment decisions about older workers. *Journal of Applied Psychology*, *70*, 785–788. Retrieved from http://psycnet.apa.org/buy/1986-10591-001.

Lee, S. Y., Pitesa, M., Thau, S., & Pillutla, M. M. (2015). Discrimination in selection decisions: Integrating stereotype fit and interdependence theories. *Academy of Management Journal*, *58*, 789–812. doi:10.5465/amj.2013.0571.

Levin, W. C. (1988). Age stereotyping: College student evaluations. *Research on Aging*, *10*, 134–148. doi:10.1177/0164027588101007.

Liden, R. C., Stilwell, D., & Ferris, G. R. (1996). The effects of supervisor and subordinate age on objective performance and subjective performance ratings. *Human Relations*, *49*, 327–347. doi:10.1177/001872679604900304.

Lin, T. R., Dobbins, G. H., & Farh, J. L. (1992). A field study of race and age similarity effects on interview ratings in conventional and situational interviews. *Journal of Applied Psychology*, *77*, 363–371. doi:10.1037/0021-9010.77.3.363.

Lindner, N. M., Graser, A., & Nosek, B. A. (2014). Age-based hiring discrimination as a function of equity norms and self-perceived objectivity. *PloS ONE*, *9*, 1–6. doi:10.1371/journal.pone.0084752.

Locke-Connor, C., & Walsh, R. P. (1980). Attitudes toward the older job applicant: Just as competent but more likely to fail. *Journal of Gerontology*, *35*, 920–927. doi:10.1093/geronj/35.6.920.

Loretto, W., Duncan, C., & White, P. J. (2000). Ageism and employment: Controversies, ambiguities, and younger people's perceptions. *Ageing and Society*, *20*, 279–302. doi:10.1017/s0144686x00007741.

Luoh, H. F., & Tsaur, S. H. (2011). Customers' perceptions of service quality: Do servers' age stereotypes matter? *International Journal of Hospitality Management*, *30*, 283–289. doi:10.1016/j.ijhm.2010.09.002.

Luoh, H. F., & Tsaur, S. H. (2014). The effects of age stereotypes on tour leader roles. *Journal of Travel Research*, *53*, 111–123. doi:10.1177/0047287513482774.

Lyon, P., & Pollard, D. (1997). Perceptions of the older employee: Is anything really changing? *Personnel Review*, *26*, 245–257. doi:10.1108/00483489710172051.

Marcus, J., & Fritzsche, B. (2014). One too many categories: An experimental test on the effectiveness of a dual-identity recategorization intervention on age bias. *Current Psychology*, *33*, 578–599. doi:10.1007/s12144-014-9230-9.

McCann, R. M., & Keaton, S. A. (2013). A cross cultural investigation of age stereotypes and communication perceptions of older and younger workers in the USA and Thailand. *Educational Gerontology, 39*, 326–341. doi:10.1080/03601277.2012.700822.

Ng, T. W. H., & Feldman, D. C. (2012). Evaluating six common stereotypes about older workers with meta-analytical data. *Personnel Psychology, 65*, 821–858. doi:10.1111/peps.12003.

North, M. S., & Fiske, S. T. (2015). Modern attitudes toward older adults in the aging world: A cross-cultural meta-analysis. *Psychological Bulletin, 141*, 993–1021. doi:10.1037/a0039469.

Perry, E. L. (1994). A prototype matching approach to understanding the role of applicant gender and age in the evaluation of job applicants. *Journal of Applied Social Psychology, 24*, 1433–1473. doi:10.1111/j.1559-1816.1994.tb01558.x.

Perry, E. L., & Bourhis, A. C. (1998). A closer look at the role of applicant age in selection decisions. *Journal of Applied Social Psychology, 28*, 1670–1697. doi:10.1111/j.1559-1816.1998.tb01340.x.

Perry, E. L., Kulik, C. T., & Bourhis, A. C. (1996). Moderating effects of personal and contextual factors in age discrimination. *Journal of Applied Psychology, 81*, 628–647. doi:10.1037/0021-9010.81.6.628.

Perry, J. S., & Varney, T. L. (1978). College students' attitudes toward workers' competence and age. *Psychological Reports, 42*, 1319–1322. doi:10.2466/pr0.1978.42.3c.1319.

Poulston, J., & Jenkins, A. (2013). The persistent paradigm: Older worker stereotypes in the New Zealand hotel industry. *Journal of Human Resources in Hospitality & Tourism, 12*, 1–25. doi:10.1080/15332845.2013.723252.

Principi, A., Fabbietti, P., & Lamura, G. (2015). Perceived qualities of older workers and age management in companies: Does the age of HR managers matter? *Personnel Review, 44*, 801–820. doi:10.1108/PR-09-2013-0158.

Rabl, T., & Triana, M. (2013). How German employees of different ages conserve resources: Perceived age discriminatino and affective organizational commitment. *The International Journal of Human Resource Management, 24*, 3599–3612. doi:10.1080/09585192.2013.777936.

Rauschenbach, C., Goritz, A. S., & Hertel, G. (2012). Age stereotypes about emotional resilience at work. *Educational Gerontology, 38*, 511–519. doi:10.1080/03601277.2011.567187.

Remery, C., Henkens, K., Schippers, J., & Ekamper, P. (2003). Managing an ageing workforce and a right labor market: Views held by Dutch employers. *Population Research and Policy Review, 22*, 21–40. doi:10.1023/A:1023543307473.

Roscigno, V. J., Mong, S., Byron, R., & Tester, G. (2007). Age discrimination, social closure, and employment. *Social Forces, 86*, 313–334. doi:10.1353/sof.2007.0109.

Rosen, B., & Jerdee, T. H. (1976). The influence of age stereotypes on managerial decisions. *Journal of Applied Psychology, 61*, 428–432. doi:10.1037/0021-9010.61.4.428.

Rosen, B., & Jerdee, T. H. (1977). Too old or not too old? *Harvard Business Review, 55*, 97–106.

Ruggs, E. N., Hebl, M. R., Walker, S. S., & Fa-Kaji, N. (2014). Selection biases that emerge when age meets gender. *Journal of Managerial Psychology, 29*, 1028–1043. doi:10.1108/JMP-07-2012-0204.

Rupp, D. E., Vodanovich, S. J., & Credé, M. (2006). Age bias in the workplace: The impact of ageism and causal attributions. *Journal of Applied Social Psychology, 36*, 1337–1364. doi:10.1111/j.0021-9029.2006.00062.x.

Schniter, E., & Shields, T. W. (2014). Ageism, honesty, and trust. *Journal of Behavioral and Experimental Economics, 51*, 19–29. doi:10.1016/j.socec.2014.03.006.

Shore, L. M., Cleveland, J. N., & Goldberg, C. B. (2003). Work attitudes and decisions as a function of manager age and employee age. *Journal of Applied Psychology, 88*, 529–537. doi:10.1037/0021-9010.88.3.529.

Singer, M. S. (1987). Age stereotypes as a function of profession. *The Journal of Social Psychology, 126*, 697–692. doi:10.1080/00224545.1986.9713647.

Singer, M. S., & Sewell, C. (1989). Applicant age and selection interview decisions: Effect of information exposure on age discrimination in personnel selection. *Personnel Psychology, 42*, 135–154. doi:10.1111/j.1744-6570.1989.tb01554.x.

Sofica, A. (2012). The social network of actors influencing age discrimination in the human resources recruiting process. *Eastern Journal of European Studies, 3*, 169–188.

Triandis, H. C. (1963). Factors affecting employee selection in two cultures. *Journal of Applied Psychology, 47*, 89–96. doi:10.1037/h0049334.

Truxillo, D. M., McCune, E. A., Bertolino, M., & Fraccaroli, F. (2012). Perceptions of older versus younger workers in terms of big five facets, proactive personality, cognitive ability, and job performance. *Journal of Applied Social Psychology, 42*, 2607–2639. doi:10.1111/j.1559-1816.2012.00954.x.

Vrugt, A., & Schabracq, M. (1996). Stereotypes with respect to elderly employees: The contribution of attribute information and representativeness. *Journal of Community and Applied Social Psychology, 6*, 287–292. doi:10.1002/(SICI)1099-1298(199610)6:4<287::AID-CASP376>3.0.CO;2-S.

Wanberg, C., Kanfer, R., Hamann, D., & Zhang, Z. (2015). Age and reemployment success after job loss: An integrative model and meta analysis. *Psychological Bulletin, 142*, 400–426. doi:10.1037/bul0000019.

Weiss, E. M., & Maurer, T. J. (2004). Age discrimination in personnel decisions: A reexamination. *Journal of Applied Social Psychology? 34*, 1551–1562. doi:10.1111/j.1559-1816.2004.tb02786.x.

APPENDIX 4.2 A selected overview of bias research applicable to age bias at work

Theory	Example Citation	General Premise
Theories reflecting subtle bias (*core motives: understanding, enhancing self*)[a]		
Continuum Model of Stereotyping	Fiske & Neuberg (1990).	Stereotyping occurs unless individuating information is available, leading to more complex processing.
Stereotype Content Model	Cuddy, Norton, & Fiske (2005)	All social groups can be categorized on two dimensions: competence and warmth.
Social Role Theory	Kite & Wagner (2002)	We come to associate characteristics of a particular social role with groups who tend fill that role, resulting in stereotypes.
Illusory Correlation	Hamilton & Sherman (1994)	When a rare person and rare event co-occur, witnesses may perceive that they are related

Theory	Example Citation	General Premise
Communication Adaptation Theory; Communication Enhancement Theory	Nussbaum, Pitts, Huber, Raup Krieger, & Ohs (2005)	People adjust their speech depending on their communication partner to increase efficiency, gain approval, or remain distinctive
Prototype Matching Theory	Perry (1994)	Raters compare worker information to job information to make decisions
Complexity-Extremity Effect	Linville (1982)	People have less complex schemas regarding outgroups leading them to evaluate outgroups members more extremely
Shifting Standards Model	Biernat, Manis, & Nelson (1991)	The same absolute evaluation has a different meaning for members of different groups (e.g., smart when referring to a child versus an adult)
Implicit Ageism	Levy & Banaji (2002)	Some ageism is reflective of an implicit attitude, distinct from explicit, conscious ageism
Descriptive Norm Theory	Duguid & Thomas-Hunt (2015)	Messages designed to reduce stereotyping by pointing out prevalence ironically increase it by making a descriptive norm salient and sanctioning the stereotyping.
Social Development Theory	Wisdom, Connor, Hogan, & Callahan (2014)	Children learn at a very young age that age is an important source of categorization and that attractiveness declines with age.

Theories reflecting blatant bias (*core motives: control, belonging, enhancing self*)

Social Identity Theory; Self Categorization Theory	Turner (1985)	People categorize themselves into groups that allow them maintain a positive social identity
Career Timetables Perspective	Lawrence (1988)	Normative expectations of where a person should be in the organizational hierarchy at a given age
Social Judgability Theory	Leyens, Yzerbyt, & Schadron (1992)	People make judgments about others only when they feel entitled to do so
Terror Management Theory	Martens, Goldenberg, & Greenberg (2005)	When mortality is salient, the self is threatened leading people to respond negatively to outgroups

continued

APPENDIX 4.2 Continued

Theory	Example Citation	General Premise
Realistic Conflict Theory	Bobo (1983)	Prejudice develops over actual competition over scarce and valued resources
Cultural Anchors Theory, Marcus & Fritzche 2017		Core dimensions of culture impact salience of identity and importance of norms.

Note
a Categorization framework based on Fiske (2004).

References

Biernat, M., Manis, M., & Nelson, T. E. (1991). Stereotypes and standards of judgment. *Journal of Personality and Social Psychology, 60,* 485–499. doi:10.1037/0022-3514.60.4.485.

Bobo, L. (1983). Whites' opposition to busing: Symbolic racism or realistic group conflict? *Journal of Personality and Social Psychology, 45,* 1196–1210. doi:10.1037/0022-3514.45.6.1196.

Cuddy, A. J. C., Norton, M. I., & Fiske, S. T. (2005). This old stereotype: The pervasiveness and persistence of the elderly stereotype. *Journal of Social Issues, 61,* 267–286. doi:10.1111/j.1540-4560.2005.00405.x.

Duguid, M. M., & Thomas-Hunt, M. C. (2015). Condoning stereotyping? How awareness of stereotyping prevalence impacts expression of stereotypes. *Journal of Applied Psychology, 100,* 343–359. doi:10.1037/a0037908.

Fiske, S. T., & Neuberg, S. L. (1990). A continuum of impression formation, from category-based to individuating processes: Influences of information and motivation on attention and interpretation. *Advances in experimental social psychology, 23,* 1–74. doi:10.1016/S0065-2601(08)60317-2.

Hamilton, D. L., & Sherman, S. J. (1994). Illusory correlations: Implications for stereotype theory and research. In D. Bar-Tal, C. F. Graumann, A. W. Kruglanski, & W. Stroebe, *Stereotyping and prejudice: Changing conceptions* (pp. 59–82). New York: Springer Science & Business Media New York.

Kite, M. E., & Wagner, L. (2002). Attitudes toward older adults. In T. D. Nelson (Ed.), *Ageism: Stereotyping and prejudice against older persons* (pp. 129–161). Cambridge, MA: MIT Press.

Lawrence, B. S. (1988). New wrinkles in the theory of age: Demography, norms, and performance ratings. *Academy of Management Journal, 31,* 309–337. doi:10.2307/256550.

Levy, B. R., & Banaji, R. B. (2002). Implicit ageism. In T. D. Nelson (Ed.), *Ageism: Stereotyping and prejudice against older persons* (pp. 49–75). Cambridge, MA: MIT Press.

Leyens, J. P., Yzerbyt, V. Y., & Schadron, G. (1992). The social judgeability approach to stereotypes. In W. Stroebe & M. Hewstone (Eds.), *European review of social psychology* (pp. 92–120). Chichester, UK: Wiley.

Linville, P. W. (1982). The complexity-extremity effect and age-based stereotyping. *Journal of Personality and Social Psychology, 42,* 193–211. doi:10.1037/0022-3514.42.2.193.

Martens, A., Goldenberg, J. L., & Greenberg, J. (2005). A terror management perspective on ageism. *Journal of Social Issues, 61,* 223–239. doi:10.1111/j.1540-4560.2005.00403.x.

Nussbaum, J. F., Pitts, M. J., Huber, F. N., Krieger, J. L., & Ohs, J. E. (2005). Ageism and ageist language across the life span: Intimate relationships and non-intimate interactions. *Journal of Social Issues, 61,* 287–306. doi:10.1111/j.1540-4560.2005.00406.x.

Perry, E. L. (1994). A prototype matching approach to understanding the role of applicant gender and age in the evaluation of job applicants. *Journal of Applied Social Psychology, 24,* 1433–1473. doi:10.1111/j.1559-1816.1994.tb01558.x.

Turner, J. C. (1985). Social categorization and the self-concept: A social cognitive theory of group behavior. In E. J. Lawler (Ed.), *Advances in group processes* (Vol. 2, pp. 77–122). Greenwich, CT: JAI Press.

Wisdom, N. M., Connor, D. R., Hogan, L. R., & Callahan, J. L. (2014). The relationship of anxiety and beliefs toward aging in ageism. *Journal of Scientific Psychology,* 10–21.

5

LEGAL ISSUES AND THE AGING WORKFORCE

E. Patrick McDermott and Caren B. Goldberg

In this chapter, we provide an overview of employment law with regards to the aging workforce. As the average life span continues to increase and many employees find that they need to work into their later years, issues relating to age discrimination are apt to increase. We begin by providing some statistics on the prevalence of age discrimination and the types of personnel decisions that most commonly result in age discrimination claims. Next, we provide an in-depth examination of the scope of legal protection provided to an employee under the Age Discrimination in Employment Act (ADEA), as well as state and local statutes, with an emphasis on protections from adverse employment actions, such as discharge. In this section, we include the historical background of the ADEA and key differences between the ADEA and Title VII of the Civil Rights Act of 1964 (Title VII) and its amendment in 1991. Following this, we discuss other ADEA protections related to severance agreements, mandatory retirement, and pensions. We then discuss current trends such as how recent ADEA decisions, a judiciary dominated by conservative appointees, and our state and local governments, might influence future cases and the rights of older workers. With an eye toward the future, we finish with a discussion of how the gig economy's creation of work outside of the traditional employment relationship and increased reliance on technology portend less legal protection against age discrimination. Given that federal laws are inherently country-specific, we note that this chapter is limited US anti-discrimination legislation.

Background

Age discrimination charges accounted for 23.2 percent of all Equal Employment Opportunity Commission (EEOC) charges in 2016 (US Equal Employment

Opportunity Commission, 2017a); this figure has been relatively stable over the past ten years. With this number of charges comes great expense. Last year, employers paid out $88.2 million in monetary awards in EEOC cases, outside of litigation (Terrell, 2017). By far, the most commonly challenged employment practice is discharge, with approximately twice as many age discrimination charges coming from discharge (10,837) than from the next most common practices, terms/conditions[1] (5533 charges) and harassment (4185 charges). While charge statistics provide useful information, they only tell part of the story. As with other areas of discrimination, many people who believe they have encountered unfair treatment based on a protected characteristic do not file charges. For example, a recent EEOC report (US Equal Employment Opportunity Commission, 2017b) reported that an AARP survey revealed that nearly two-thirds of employers between 55 and 64 believed their age was an obstacle to obtaining employment. Although unreported access discrimination has always existed, recent technological changes have likely exacerbated the occurrence of it, an issue which we later discuss in the Future Directions section of this chapter.

To appreciate the rather large disparity between discharge challenges and other age-based challenges, it bears stating an obvious, but important fact: Pay and tenure are highly correlated (cf., Leslie, Manchester, & Dahm, 2017). With experience comes raises; with raises come higher personnel costs, both in terms of salary and benefits. Because older employees typically cost an employer more money, they are often targeted in downsizing efforts. Thus, cost savings is a common defense proffered by employers when older employees are disproportionately affected by downsizing. We elaborate on the courts' view on the cost-savings defense later in this section.

The relatively high proportion of age discrimination claims arising from discharge decisions is particularly problematic to older workers. As discussed in greater length in the Finkelstein, Hanrahan, and Thomas (2018) chapter of this book, discrimination takes a psychological toll on older workers, regardless of the type of employment decision. However, the burden is considerably larger for older workers who have been subject to discharge-related discrimination for at least two reasons. First, as we will discuss later in this chapter, at least some age discrimination likely stems from negative stereotypes regarding older workers' technological currency and trainability. While job-seekers of all ages may invest in updating their knowledge and skills, older workers have less time to realize a return on their investment, which may deter them from making such investments.

Second, senior employees who are terminated are likely to encounter additional discrimination in their subsequent job-seeking efforts. For example, Wanberg, Kanfer, Hamann, and Zhang's (2016) meta-analysis showed that the average duration of unemployment for individuals seeking re-employment increases with age: Job-seekers between 20 and 29 were unemployed for an average 14.7 weeks; job-seekers between 30 and 49 were unemployed for an average of 19.5 weeks;

and job-seekers over 50 remained unemployed for an average of 25.3 weeks. This portends double-jeopardy for those who are terminated because of their age – discharge-related discrimination is likely to be followed by subsequent re-employment-related discrimination.

The ADEA permits employers to base decisions on factors other than age, even if such factors disproportionately affect older workers. Thus, employers frequently cite cost savings (a factor other than age) as a means of defending layoff decisions that may adversely impact senior employees. Until 1993, federal courts were split on whether one could establish age discrimination where the employer's cost-based decision was highly correlated with age. The Supreme Court resolved this issue in the *Hazen Paper* decision, where it held that years of service and age were, "analytically distinct," so that termination decisions impacting older workers based on years of service, earnings, and other factors highly correlated with age were deemed permissible. *Hazen Paper Co. v. Biggins*, 507 U.S. 604 (1993). Spindler (2000) notes the legal scenario that exists today, where a "newly minted whipper-snapper MBA," can terminate older workers for profit and personal gain at the expense of the employees, "aging with grace."

While the foregoing discussion of Wanberg et al.'s (2016) meta-analysis and the Supreme Court's decision in *Hazen Paper* paint a somewhat bleak outlook for older workers, the future may not be so pessimistic. Forecasts indicate that a sizeable number of Baby Boomers are expected to retire over the next several years, creating what is expected to be one of the largest labor shortages in history (AARP, 2008). Given that labor economists (Becker, 1957) have long argued that discrimination is a, "taste or preference," that organizations engage in when the labor market is loose (i.e., when the supply of labor exceeds the demand for labor), the increased need for qualified employees is apt to be accompanied by a leveling of the playing field for older job-seekers. Just as Fields, Goodman, and Blum (2005) found that the difficulty an organization had in procuring and maintaining an adequate supply of human resources was positively related to the subsequent representation of Black employees, so too is it apt to be related to the representation of older employees. Shore and Goldberg (2005) argued that tight labor markets increase opportunities for older workers by increasing their value both inside (through retention efforts) and outside (through recruitment efforts) the organization.

The Age Discrimination in Employment Act of 1967

The ADEA is often viewed as the key piece of legislation aimed at protecting older workers; hence, it is the centerpiece of the current chapter. The legal context of age discrimination in the United States is complex. There is a patchwork of federal, state, and local laws that govern unlawful employment discrimination. Thus, a full discussion of the rights of a person alleging age discrimination is a function of federal, state, county, city, and other public law.[2]

Differences between the ADEA and Title VII of the Civil Rights Act

The ADEA was passed in 1967, three years after Title VII of the Civil Rights Act of 1964. In the ADEA, Congress elected to blend the concepts of Title VII with the remedial provisions of the Fair Labor Standards Act (FLSA) of 1938. The substantive provisions of the ADEA were borrowed *in haec verba* (i.e., incorporating verbatim text) from Title VII, with the word, "age," replacing the protected classifications of race, sex, color, religion, and national origin, found in Title VII. While both pieces of anti-discrimination legislation were passed in the same period, with similar intent, and with similar verbiage, there are key distinctions. One of the most notable of these reflects the definition of a "protected class." The Civil Rights Act of 1964 protects all categories, regardless of historical disadvantage. For example, men and Caucasians have the same protections provided to women and African-Americans. By contrast, the ADEA does not protect younger workers from age discrimination; rather, it only protects those persons age 40 or over from age discrimination. Under the ADEA, an employer is permitted to discriminate against younger workers in favor of older workers. *General Dynamics Land Systems* v. *Cline*, 540 U.S. 581 (2004).[3]

Differences in Damages for Unlawful Discrimination

From 1964 until its amendment in 1991, Title VII provided an employee who prevailed in litigation the limited remedies of reinstatement, back pay, and payment of attorneys' fees and costs of litigation;[4] in contrast, the ADEA provided the more generous Fair Labor Standards Act ("FLSA") remedies of reinstatement, back pay with possible liquidated (double) back pay, payment of attorneys' fees and costs of litigation, and a right to trial by jury.[5] Thus, until 1991, the ADEA had a more favorable remedial structure than Title VII, because of the liquidated damages and right to jury trial.

The different remedies for ADEA violations versus other unlawful discrimination under Title VII became more pronounced after the 1991 amendments to Title VII. Section 1981(a) of the Civil Rights Act amended Title VII by providing for the right to trial by jury and to compensatory damages for pain and suffering, as well as punitive damages in Title VII cases.[6] Specifically, the 1991 amendments allowed for a Title VII damages claim to include reinstatement, back pay, and the new remedies of noneconomic compensatory damages for, "pain and suffering," and punitive damages to be decided by a jury.[7] Compensatory damages are damages for existing and future pecuniary losses, emotional pain, suffering, inconvenience, mental anguish, loss of enjoyment of life, and other nonpecuniary losses; they are capped on a sliding scale based on company size, at up to $300,000.[8] As a result, as we will discuss later in detail, in most cases, a Title VII claim became more attractive to litigate than an age claim. This change, coupled with judicial hostility to age discrimination lawsuits, contributed to an increase in age cases that relied on fact patterns that included race or sex discrimination (in addition to age), allowing plaintiffs to frame their cases such that age was not the central basis of the discrimination claim.

Disparate Treatment Based on Stereotypes

There is often a disconnect between what social science research has established as knowledge and what is permissible evidence in litigating an age discrimination claim. As we discuss in this section, while there is a substantial body of research related to age stereotypes, legal protection against discrimination has gaps or procedural hurdles that allow employers to violate the law. In this section, we review the research on age stereotypes and discuss when this literature may be more or less helpful in an age discrimination case.

Researchers began investigating the effects of age stereotypes on work-related outcomes 40 years ago (Rosen & Jerdee, 1976). In the decades since then, others have largely confirmed the existence of the negative stereotypes articulated by Rosen and Jerdee; namely, that compared with their younger counterparts, older workers are perceived as less flexible (Chiu, Chan, Snape, & Redman, 2001; Henkens, 2005; Marcus, Fritzsche, Le, and Reeves, 2016), less trainable (Rosen & Jerdee, 1977; Taylor & Walker, 1998), less physically capable (Billet, Dymock, Johnson, & Martin, 2011), less interpersonally adept (Lyon & Pollard, 1997; Marcus et al., 2016), less technologically up-to-date (Busch, Dahl, & Dittrich, 2009), and less energetic (Levin, 1988).

Research further suggests that these stereotypes may, in fact, result in negative decisions concerning older workers. As the Finkelstein et al. (2018) chapter in the volume notes, most studies have not explicitly linked the extent of one's endorsement of these stereotypes to the likelihood of making a negative decision about older targets. However, applied research has shown the ages of actual applicants did have a small but significant influence on recruiters' perceptions of their interpersonal skills and flexibility/trainability (Goldberg & Shore, 2003). Given the limited number of studies directly linking stereotype endorsement to work outcomes and the relatively small effects in the few studies that have, from a legal perspective, building an age discrimination case based primarily on stereotypes can be a tall order. For example, while it may seem clear to a 60-year-old plaintiff that she was denied training because she was perceived as less trainable than her younger counterpart, without direct evidence that the manager who made the training decision thought this, the courts are not likely to be persuaded. While such admissions may seem unlikely, organizations often do (presumably unwittingly) make ageist statements in public. Consider how frequently organizations advertise that they are looking for stereotypically young candidates, with phrases such as, "energetic people," "fresh ideas," or a "fast-paced environment." For example, the authors did separate quick searches in Maryland, Virginia, and Washington, DC (the geographic areas of both authors) on Monster.com for the keyword, "energetic." In all three searches, they received over 1000 results.[9] Indeed, even the federal government, who is presumably under greater scrutiny with respect to equal employment opportunity, has numerous vacancies (71 as of February 28, 2018) posted with such age-laden language on USAJobs, the repository of all federal government positions. In contrast to more forthright ageist comments, where a judge or jury would have little trouble understanding that use of the term, "old fart" (*Ryther v. KARE 11*, 108 F.3D 132 (8th Cir. 1997), for example, suggests some age-related animus, in cases where organizations use more subtle age-stereotypic cues, an expert witness in psychology or human resources who is versed in the literature on age stereotypes might play an important role in helping a finder of fact understand how use of the term, "energetic people," might be a veiled indication of a preference for younger workers.

Regardless of whether such statements are subtle or overt, they are not likely to have enough standalone value to survive summary judgment. However, when combined with other facts, the articulation of statements regarding ageism and/or ageist stereotypes can tip the scales in a plaintiff's favor. One such common scenario is where an employer proffers a performance-related defense for a negative decision regarding an older employee. Generally speaking, such a defense is seen as a perfectly legitimate non-age-based reason for making negative decisions. However, when ageist comments are brought to bear, an otherwise reasonable defense can be viewed as a pretext by the courts. For example, in *Russell* v. *McKinney Hospital Venture*, 235 F.3d 219 (5th Cir. 2000), the Court of Appeals held that the plaintiff established that the employer's proffered reason for her termination, that the employer needed a, "change in management style," was pretextual. The record showed that the plaintiff had received very favorable evaluations and that she was terminated after the son of the CEO requested that she be fired. The son had frequently referred to the plaintiff as an, "old bitch." Likewise, in *Reeves* v. *Sanderson Plumbing Products, Inc.*, 530 U.S. 133, 120 S. Ct. 2097, 147 L.Ed.2d 105 (2000), the plaintiff, a 57-year-old supervisor, was terminated and replaced by a series of individuals in their 30s. Although the defendant indicated that Reeves had performance problems and placed him on a Performance Improvement Plan a few months before his termination, a decision-maker told the plaintiff that, "he was so old that he must have come over on the Mayflower," and that he, "was too damn old to do his job." The jury found that the employer had engaged in willful age discrimination based upon these comments and that the employer exaggerated the facts that allegedly led to the termination. It bears noting that these two cases were decided prior to the *Gross* decision and its "but-for," standard that we will discuss later. Thus, it is unclear whether the outcomes of these two cases would be the same today. The, "but-for," standard permits an employer to argue that age was not *the only* reason for the termination. If the jury believes this to be true, then the employee would not prevail under current interpretation of the law.

Disparate Impact

In addition to the disparate treatment theory cases, there can be liability under a disparate impact theory. This occurs where an employer's facially neutral policy disproportionality impacts older workers. The disparate impact theory of liability does not involve discriminatory intent; rather it occurs when an organization has a facially neutral policy, such as the ability to lift a certain amount of weight, which because of typical age-related declines in physical strength, has a disproportionately negative effect on older employees. In 2005, the Supreme Court found that this theory, used in Title VII cases, could apply in ADEA cases; *Smith* v. *City of Jackson*, 544 U.S. 228 (2005). This theory has been expanded to included age discrimination against certain subclasses of older workers. To prevail in such cases, the plaintiff needs to establish statistical disparity based on the neutral policy and also prove that this disparity was caused by the policy. This is shown by various forms of evidence, including 40-and-older comparisons, subgroup comparisons, or more sophisticated statistical modeling. Because age is not comparable to sex or race as it is a continuous and not discrete variable measure, the statistical analyses used in Title VII cases are not transferable to age cases. Also, while the focus in a Title VII case is on whether the neutral policy has a disparate impact on a protected class, under the ADEA there is another layer of complexity because an employer can offer the statutory defense of there being a reasonable factor other than age ("RFOA") that permits this disparate impact.

Disparate impact cases are often class action cases. These are more easily litigated by plaintiffs under Title VII than under the ADEA because the ADEA requires that a plaintiff opt in to the plaintiff class in the lawsuit, whereas Title VII automatically includes all members in a protected class, unless they actively choose to opt out to avoid being a plaintiff (Hoffman 2012). Furthermore, under the ADEA, the named plaintiff(s) must move the court for conditional class certification, so that notice can be provided to putative class members. The employer, on the other hand, will try to force the cases to be addressed individually. Plaintiff's counsel may sometimes maintain both a Title VII opt-out class action and an ADEA opt-in class action or use favorable state laws to be able to have a traditional class action with an opt-out class. Disparate impact cases often turn into a statistical battle of the experts, where the plaintiff identifies the policy, practice, or rule applicable to the plaintiff's theory of the similarly-situated class members and the defendant rebuts by narrowing the definition of the similarly-situated class at issue and/or performing statistical analyses on subsets of class members; *Karlo* v. *Pittsburgh Glass Works, LLC*, 849 F.3d 61 (3d Cir. 2017). Because statistical power is a function of sample size, this strategy of sub-categorizing members of the class may render a class-wide statistically significant difference nonsignificant.

Class action cases can expose the employer to significant damages and payment of the high costs of the plaintiffs' attorneys and experts, should the plaintiff prevail. This type of litigation is very costly and requires the ability to locate highly qualified counsel. Because expertise in class-action litigation is a highly specialized niche, the average worker terminated in these circumstances may have trouble finding an attorney who understands this complex area of litigation or is willing to engage in it.

Barriers to Pursuing Disparate Treatment Cases

Seeking Enforcement of the ADEA from a Cost–Benefit Perspective

As noted above, the Equal Employment Opportunity Commission (2017a) reports that most age discrimination cases address discharge. For these cases, the probability of a substantial payout is quite low. As discussed in the damages section, a worker who has been discriminated against due to age has a limited payout because that worker can, at most, only double his/her back pay in the case of a willful violation of the ADEA. In the case of a low-wage worker, this does not amount to very much money. In contrast, under a Title VII action, a low-wage worker could obtain up to $300,000 in pain and suffering and punitive damages with no cap, both of which are awarded on top of any back pay and other lost remuneration. All told, Terrell (2017) reports that the average settlement payout for ADEA cases that are not litigated is $26,600. In addition, given the more difficult, "but-for," standard of proof, the average management labor attorney can typically craft a defense by simply finding one negative issue with the worker's performance and exaggerating it, so that a federal court will grant summary judgment, effectively scoring a "win" for the employer. Thus, the ADEA moved from being a more favorable remedial statute to a less favorable remedial statute upon the 1991 amendments to Title VII. Indeed, fewer than 15 percent of ADEA charges result in a favorable outcome for plaintiffs (Terrell, 2017). For the majority of cases with damages claims within the Title VII cap limits set by size of employer, the ADEA pays outs lower damages than these Title VII or the American With Disabilities Act claims (Senn, 2012). However, in cases where the potential payout exceeds the Title VII cap (e.g., a highly-paid employee working for a small employer with a $50,000 damage cap), the ADEA has a better potential damages payout (Senn, 2012). This is more than a mere academic concept, because an attorney's strategy as to how to plead and try the case is affected by these remedies. If the case has lower damages, where there are mixed theories of discrimination, counsel is better off tailoring the case to the cause of action with the highest payout for the client.[10]

Age Discrimination Has a More Difficult Standard of Proof

The burden of proof required to sustain a discrimination case represents another good reason for plaintiffs' attorneys to avoid federal age discrimination cases when alternative causes of action can be pled. In *Gross* v. *FBL Financial Services*, the Supreme Court changed the interpretation of the ADEA, so that instead of having to prove that age was a "motivating factor," in an adverse employment action, a plaintiff had the much higher bar of proving that, "but for," the person's age, the adverse action would not have been taken; *Gross v. FBL Financial Services*, 557 U.S. 167 (2009). Foreman (2010) notes the irony that as the American workforce ages, the Supreme Court is removing protections against age discrimination. The Supreme Court nearly vitiated the ADEA with its decision in *Gross*. The Court has developed into a court that is not favorable to worker rights, as evidenced by its reinterpretation of existing age discrimination and retaliation statutes to favor employers.[11] Legal scholars see a broader trend of elevating employment-at-will, at the expense of employment nondiscrimination protections (Corbett, 1996; Widiss, 2012). Widiss describes the *Gross* decision as a, "fiction of statutory interpretation," pointing out the many flaws in this decision undermining older workers' rights (Widiss, 2012).

These cases were decided by Republican appointees Anthony Kennedy, John Roberts, Antonin Scalia, Clarence Thomas, and Samuel Alito. The appointment of Judge Neil Gorsuch, another justice whose legal decisions, to date, favor employers over workers' rights, to replace the late Scalia, presages that older workers will not find support in the federal legal system (*Denver Post*, 2017). The *Denver Post*, which covers the city where Gorsuch sat as a Court of Appeals judge, reported that Gorsuch sided with employers in 21 of 23 in cases involving workers' pension or benefit rights. His dissent in a retaliation case against a truck driver reveals a vantage point of finding fault with workers to avoid finding unlawful employer conduct; *TransAm Trucking, Inc. v. Department of Labor*, 2016 U.S. App. LEXIS 13071 (10th Cir. July 15, 2016). The trend of eroding older worker protection in the face of an aging workforce may continue under the current composition of the Supreme Court (Corbett, 2010). While this decision-making is a complex dynamic, it has been noted that the justices' use of interpretative theories and decision-making canons can, "reinforce judges' ideological positions rather than blunting the impact of those positions," and that there is "considerable evidence" of this at the Supreme Court (Brudney & Baum, 2017).

The EEOC's Role in Pursuing Age Discrimination Claims – Resources Limit Enforcement of the Law

In addition to the limited financial return for most ADEA claims, and the more rigorous legal standards of proof required to sustain them, the administrative agency that is supposed to champion employees discriminated against due to protected status, the Equal Employment Opportunity Commission ("EEOC") is underfunded and cannot represent most charge-filers in court. To pursue an age discrimination claim, an individual is required to file a charge with the EEOC or his/her local agency. However, the agency does not have the resources to provide enforcement (McDermott, Obar, Jose, & Bowers, 2000).

The first reality that most charge-filers learn is that the EEOC does not "investigate" cases, as that term is commonly used. A comparison of the complement of EEOC investigators to the number of charges filed annually easily demonstrates that there are not enough EEOC resources to fully investigate a case (EEOC, 2017b).

The experience of the first author, who has represented clients before the EEOC and who evaluated the EEOC mediation program, is that most cases are decided on paper alone, with the employer providing written position statements after the plaintiff files a charge explaining his/her story to the EEOC. At intake, the EEOC classifies cases as "A, B, or C" under its "Priority Charge Handling Procedures" (PCHP; McDermott et al. 2000). "A" charges are charges that, based on the opinion of the EEOC charge intake personnel, were likely to result in an EEOC finding of "probable cause" to believe that the law had been violated; "B" charges were those with possible merit with the final finding contingent on the results of the investigation; and "C" charges were those without merit on their face that should be dismissed outright. While each office may use modified procedures, the fact is that employees can be subject to the luck of the draw at intake, which is particularly precarious for non-represented plaintiffs. However, even where a skilled EEOC agent can gather the facts and clearly express the correct theories and facts for the relevant legal claims, the playing field may not always be level. Many companies have legal counsel or experienced human resource professionals preparing the position statements that are required to respond to a charge. Further, an enforcement agency can only be as effective as its budget permits. The EEOC budget has never provided for a full investigation of EEOC charges, so that early dispute resolution has been the best avenue for a non-represented charge-filer to obtain a modicum of justice. In recent years, the Congressional budget process has neglected the EEOC.

In 2014, the EEOC budget was reduced to $364 million and has remained at this level for the last few years (EEOC, 2017b), even though this period saw a 3 percent increase in number of charges filed (EEOC, 2017a). For decades, the EEOC has been prevented from being an effective enforcer of the various civil rights statutes at the EEOC investigation phase; GAO, 2009). The average charge-filer has little hope of prevailing on a claim, unless he or she can afford employment law counsel. This is best shown by the ubiquitous EEOC Right to Sue letter, in which the EEOC explains that it has "investigated," and the charge-filer either does not have a case, has a case, or the EEOC has not had time to determine whether the charge-filer has a case. Regardless of the verbiage of the Right to Sue letter, there has usually been little investigation and, after waiting, sometimes for years, the charge-filer has 90 days to find a lawyer and file suit in federal court or state court to vindicate his or her rights. Thus, after pinning their hopes on vindication at the EEOC, charging parties discover that the EEOC cannot help them, even where they have a case; rather, they have 90 days to find a lawyer who will usually require a retainer, which is often cost-prohibitive, particularly to those who have just lost their job.

The EEOC filer who does not have counsel is usually in a difficult position, where justice is difficult to obtain. This is a sad truth that many first experience when they seek to enforce their legal rights. Obtaining counsel for an ADEA claim is difficult, as many plaintiff's attorneys will not accept a case unless it has a strong guarantee of payout, which turns on "smoking gun" facts *and* whether the employee earns enough money for a high payout – particularly for age cases in jurisdictions that must rely on the federal, "but-for," standard and for states where the state law does not provide for pain and suffering damages. Even here, the attorney may request a retainer for expenses, which is typically beyond the means of a person living paycheck-to-paycheck who has lost his/her job. Moreover, as with other forms of discrimination, a victim of age discrimination has a duty to mitigate damage by seeking other employment. Any mitigation reduces the amount of the employee's damages for the unlawful termination. Obtaining subsequent employment, even if at lower pay, can often reduce the potential back pay amount to the point that pursuing a lawsuit, with its upfront retainer and subsequent costs of discovery, may be prohibitive. Persons often decide to move on and not hold the employer accountable.

When one puts together the challenging aspects of the age discrimination landscape for the most common age discrimination issues, we see two very different categories of plaintiffs with correspondingly different potential benefits from age discrimination legislation. On the one hand, those with lower damages cases, those who cannot afford private counsel, the overwhelming majority of employees on whose behalf the EEOC will decline to file suit, and those unable to gain the benefit of a class action lawsuit are unlikely to have the opportunity to vindicate their mistreatment. In contrast, for those who are pleading high-damages cases, those who can afford counsel (or who can find counsel who will represent them on a contingency basis), and/or those who have similarly-affected co-workers who can constitute a class, the law remains a powerful tool for exacting justice.

The ADEA's Other Protections

The Employee Retirement Income Security Act of 1974 (ERISA) and the ADEA combine to provide protection for older workers by preventing discrimination regarding employee benefits plans. The ADEA provides a wide range of protections against age discrimination in pensions; ADEA at 29 U.S.C. §623 (i). ERISA, which is related to favorable tax treatment for employers under the Internal Revenue Code, also provides that an employer cannot discriminate against an individual due to age; Internal Revenue Code ("I.R.C.") §411(b)(1)(H)(i); ERISA 29 U.S.C. at §204(b)(1)(H)(i), 29 U.S.C. §1054(b)(1)(H)(i).

A detailed discussion of these protections is beyond the scope of this chapter. However, it is important for aging workers to understand the importance of these pension protections. Traditional defined benefit plans pay a guaranteed monthly pension; the employer assumes the risk of the investments funding the employee pensions. These plans are receding in favor of the more recent trend of cash balance plans, where the investment risk is shifted to the employee; they are also considered defined benefit plans under the law.

Amendments to the ADEA

We have discussed the complex legal background of the law and age discrimination, the social science research evidencing systemic age discrimination in the workplace, and the practical difficulties in our legal and administrative forums that seek to protect workers from unlawful discrimination. We would be remiss if we did not identify a few other areas where the ADEA protects the worker where no harassment or discharge is at issue.

From its inception until 1986, the ADEA included mandatory retirement for certain professions. In 1986, the ADEA was amended to bar mandatory retirement provisions in most professions – Age Discrimination in Employment Amendments of 1986, Pub. L. No. 99–592, 100 Stat. 3342 (1986). The 1986 amendments did not include university professors, who were still required to retire at age 70; however, in 1993, an additional amendment was added, which eliminated mandatory retirement for university professors.

The Older Workers Benefit Protection Act (OWBPA) was added to the ADEA in 1990 to protect workers who are presented with a termination notice and offered severance in return for giving up any legal rights to sue for age discrimination. The timing provisions give a settling party time to reconsider and withdraw from a settlement before it becomes irrevocable. A person has up to 21 days to consider the settlement agreement and is provided seven days to revoke an executed agreement.[12] The waiver also must be, "knowing and voluntary," and cannot waive future causes of action that have not accrued and consideration (usually money) must be exchanged. The Act also provides additional notice requirements where there is a large-scale exit incentive program, so that the employee is aware of other employees who are being laid off and their ages.

State Courts or Local Government Statutes as a Legal Haven for Older Workers

While this chapter cannot fully address the extent to which state and local legislatures can supplement national labor policy and Supreme Court decisions, by enacting legislation, it is important to understand that our nation's federal structure and Constitution ensure the vibrancy of local law. While the ADEA may provide less-than-complete protection for older workers, it should be borne in mind that while the ADEA is the most comprehensive age-related anti-discrimination law, both in terms of types of employment decisions covered and national reach, it is by no means the only one. For cases involving any type of age-based decision, the federal statutory scheme is both complemented and complicated by state and local statutes that can effectively replace a federal employment discrimination cause of action. For example, some state and local statutes, often identified as governing "Human Rights," or "Human Relations," provide for pain and suffering for age discrimination. State courts and local statutes also have their own legal standards that may accept or reject federal case law on such issues as the *Gross*, "but-for," legal standard for age discrimination.[13] In such jurisdictions, one would be remiss to file a federal ADEA claim, when one can pursue stronger possible relief in state court or before local employment discrimination agencies (National Conference of State Legislators, 2015). Thus, one may have a better case outside of federal court and the ADEA.

Directions for Future Research

Because of the ever-changing nature of the legal landscape, it could be argued that the legal discussion above is more representative of the past than of the future. Indeed, when the previous edition of this book was published, the Supreme Court had not yet heard *Gross* v. *FBL Financial Services*, a decision that effectively erased decades of precedential decisions. While our courts and administrative agencies, whether by choice or by budget, make the protection of older workers a very challenging proposition, the changing nature of the employment relationship and technology are under-studied contextual factors that may affect the extent to which older workers encounter discrimination.

The Changing Employment Relationship

The standard employment relationship of an employer paying statutory wages to an employee working a set work schedule – usually 40 hours per week in the United States – is changing (Fenwick et al., 2017).[14] The Tax Cuts and Jobs Act of 2017 encourages some employees to move to independent contractor status and pay themselves through a limited liability corporation. While not practical for many, these changes continue the trend away from the traditional employment model. As employment shifts toward work performed through temporary employment, temporary employment agency work, part-time employment, and ambiguous work relationships (i.e., the gig economy), much of the law discussed above is not applicable; or where applicable, not tailored to protect workers in these relationships.[15] That is, the ADEA and similar legislation are designed to protect older *employees*.

As organizations move to work arrangements outside of the traditional employer–employee relationship, fewer legal protections are accorded to the individual, including protection against age discrimination. One exception where the law is addressing the new gig economy is in New York City, which recently enacted the first law protecting freelance workers entitled, the "Freelance Isn't Free Act" (New York City, Office of the Mayor, 2017). The law requires a written agreement setting forth the names and mailing addresses of the hiring business or individual and the freelance worker; an itemization of all services being provided by the freelance worker; the value of the services being provided by the freelance worker and the rate and method of payment of the freelance worker; and the date by which payment is due (or the process by which the payment date will be determined). The law also sets the time for payment, that the payment must be for the contract amount, and provides enforcement remedies.

New York City is the exception – all workers are now facing the accelerating trend toward non-standard employment relationships with little legal protection. This trend reduces the wide range of jobs where older workers had statutory protection.[16] We raise this issue of the lack of protection for the new forms of engagement of workers because this broader trend away from legal protection is arguably more threatening for older workers. Because they have spent much of their career in traditional employment, one can speculate that adjusting to the gig economy will represent a greater challenge for older workers than for their younger counterparts, who have not been socialized to expect a long-term employment relationship.

While the new frontier of freelance and other contingent work models reduces age discrimination protection, population realities are apt to also influence the extent to which protecting the employment rights of older workers becomes a priority. The World Economic Forum recently warned that we must adapt to a changing workplace because longevity is a major threat to the economic security of older persons (World Economic Forum, 2017). There is increasing evidence that many are not prepared for their retirement and may have to continue to work (Oakley and Keneally, 2017). A coherent national policy, with legislative action, is needed to protect the increasing number of older workers now exposed to weak legal protection juxtaposed with the changing context of employment relationships. The future social security of our elderly will be the reward. At the same time, the retirement of the Baby Boom generation will create a dearth of talent in many organizations, which Goldberg, Perry, Finkelstein, and Shull (2013) suggest, will likely make the pursuit and fair treatment of older workers an increasingly important aspect of organizations' diversity efforts. Thus, while legislative and/or judicial reform are needed as long-term solutions to the lack of protection from age discrimination, in the shorter-term, the labor market may constrain employers' ability to engage in age discrimination.

Technology

As society's reliance on technology increases, some of the implications of this trend for age discrimination should be mentioned. First, as noted previously, there is evidence that older workers are perceived as being less technologically adept than their younger counterparts (Busch et al., 2009; Rosen & Jerdee, 1976). The fact that job requirements are becoming increasingly likely to include technology-related knowledge, skills, abilities and other personal characteristics ("KSAO"s) does not bode well for older workers, who, by virtue of their age, may be deemed less suitable for hiring, training, or promotions.

Organizations are also becoming increasingly reliant on technology in recruitment and selection. Scanning applicants' online presence in social media such as Facebook or Linked-In (i.e., Social Media Assessments, or SMAs) has become a very common tool in the applicant screening process (Jeske & Shultz, 2016). Van Iddekinge, Lanivich, Roth, and Junco (2016) found that 63 percent of recruiters used SMAs occasionally, often, or always. Because of the plethora of information individuals include on their social media websites, the potential for adverse impact is not trivial. For example, people may include their date of birth in their profile, or provide a host of other less age-specific information or "likes" from which age may be reasonably inferred (High School reunions for a given graduating class year; posts about a child going off to college; "liking" AARP, etc.). Most organizations presumably do not conduct social media assessments with the intention of determining candidates' demographic characteristics. However, even if an organizational decision-maker is not setting out to determine the ages of applicants, there are a variety of cues about an individual's age that the recruiter might access, which could inadvertently indicate that the candidate is over 40 years of age.

While empirical research on social media assessments is still quite nascent, Van Iddekinge et al.'s (2016) study suggests that assessments of Facebook profiles are not predictive of performance, turnover intentions, or actual turnover. In addition, the authors found mean differences in SMA scores, across race and gender, suggesting a potential for adverse impact. While we are not aware of any studies that have examined the potential for SMAs to adversely impact older job-seekers, the potential certainly exists. And, given the non-significant predictive validity evidence, to the extent that older workers might be adversely affected, organizations that engage in such screening would find themselves in the undesirable position of attempting to defend a discriminatory practice that offers no predictive benefit.

In addition to age-related information that may be gleaned casually or inadvertently from a candidate's social media profile, technology creates another means through which age discrimination may occur. Specifically, data analytics allow advertisers to use targeted marketing with a level of precision that has not previously been available to them. This has resulted in great efficiency for marketers, who can dictate, for example, that they only want an online advertisement for cosmetics to be displayed to female users of a certain age group. However, Google and Facebook allow employers to use similar targeting strategies for employment advertisements (Angwin, Scheiber, & Tobin, 2017). A joint investigation conducted by ProPublica and the *New York Times* found 39 companies that used age-restricted employment ads, including some large, well-respected organizations, such as Microsoft, Facebook, Goldman Sachs, Ernst & Young, and Verizon (Larson, Varner, Tobin, & Angwin, 2017). Yet, more troubling than the fact that these companies prevented older workers from seeing the employment opportunities was Facebook's defense of the practice. Angwin et al. (2017) note that when asked about age-targeted recruitment advertisements, "Facebook defended the practice. 'Used responsibly, age-based targeting for employment purposes is an accepted industry practice and for good reason: it helps employers recruit and people of all ages find work,' said Rob Goldman, a Facebook vice president." A December 2017 class action lawsuit argues that age-restricted employment advertisements constitute intentional discrimination in violation of the ADEA and other local states. *Bradley* et al. v. *T-Mobile U.S. Inc.* et al., Case No: 5–17:07232 BLF (USDC California, Northern District). Given the potential reach and impact of this case, its outcome may set an important precedent in this uncharted territory of age discrimination.

Summary

In this chapter, we have provided the reader with both a retrospective and prospective view of the ADEA. Although it was initially created to largely mirror the Title VII of the Civil Rights Act of 1964, many earlier protections have been eroded based on case law. Despite these changes, the ADEA still has some teeth: Over the past several years, employers have paid between $75 million and $100 million per year, in federal age discrimination cases, excluding those that were litigated (Terrell, 2017). We also discussed important areas for future inquiry, noting that the shift from the traditional employment relationship to an arrangement in which individuals who perform work tasks are not employees, points to a gap in age discrimination legislation protection that needs to be filled. In addition, we discussed the role that technology may play in age discrimination. These include likely increased salience of age-related stereotypes relating to technological facility (Busch et al., 2009; Rosen & Jerdee, 1976), how the trend toward relying on social media assessments in evaluating applicants (Jeske & Shultz, 2016; Van Iddekinge et al., 2016) might result in older applicants being disqualified early in the selection process, and the recent evidence that organizations which rely on social media for recruitment may be explicitly excluding older individuals from their pools, through the use of age-targeted advertisements. These are burgeoning areas for scholars and practitioners in both the industrial psychology/human resources and legal spheres. It is our hope that readers in both areas will further the research in both fields.

Notes

1. Terms and conditions include remuneration, work assignment, scheduling of hours of work, transfer to another position, and a work environment free from unlawful harassment. Courts can sometimes limit protection under the law by finding a change in working terms or conditions to not be "materially adverse" to support a cause of action (Lidge, 1999; Bradshaw, 2006).
2. This chapter does not address the law of age discrimination at the state and local level. This can be a robust area of both protection and litigation and is discussed later.
3. Note that state, county, or municipal law may bar this conduct.
4. One can also obtain injunctive relief, but for most individuals receiving money and/or getting reinstated to the job is the predominant relief sought.
5. Compare Title VII at §§2000e5(e)(3)(A)(B) (authorizing back pay) and 2000e5(k) (authorizing award of attorneys' fees to prevailing party) with ADEA §626 (characterizing age discrimination damages as unpaid wages under the FLSA that can be liquidated (doubled) for willful violations of the law along with the award of attorney's fees.
6. The Civil Rights Act of 1991, Pub. L. No. 102–166, 105 Stat. 1071–1100 (codified as amended in scattered sections of 42 U.S.C. (Supp. III 1992)); ww.eeoc.gov/eeoc/history/35th/thelaw/cra_1991.html.
7. Punitive damages are awarded to discourage such unlawful conduct in society. The reader should not assume that allowing punitive damages creates a "lottery ticket" litigation mentality among those injured by unlawful discrimination. The Courts have used their powers to limit a jury's power to award these damages via the Due Process clause of the Constitution, and State legislatures and Congress have also placed limits on punishment for Title VII discrimination by use of damages caps that limit recovery, regardless of the actual injury a person suffers.
8. CRA of 1866 at 42 U.S.C. §1981a(b)(3). For a full discussion of the various changes to employment discrimination law flowing from the CRA of 1991 see Livingston (1993).
9. Monster.com does not enumerate values over 1000; rather it presents the search outcome as "1000+." Thus, the actual number of times the word "energetic" appears may be several times greater than 1000.
10. The first author represented management in employment litigation for almost two decades and subsequently represented plaintiffs for almost two decades and offers this observation based on personal experience.
11. After *Gross* heightened the legal burden to prevail in an age discrimination lawsuit, the Court did the same for cases addressing retaliation for protesting age discrimination and other unlawful employment discrimination. *Univ. of Tex. Southwestern Med. Ctr.* v. *Nassar*, 133 S. Ct. 2517, 186 L. Ed. 503 (2013).
12. 29 U.S.C. §626(f) (1999).
13. Many states that adopted the language of the federal anti-discrimination statutes in their state statutes have state case law holding that federal case law precedent should be used to interpret the state statute. Thus, as the Supreme Court narrows older worker protection there is a risk that the state courts will follow. See for example *Carsillo* v. *City of Lake Worth*, 995 So. 2d 1118, 1119 (Fla. 4th DCA 2008).
14. Fenwick et al. (2017) define the Standard Employment Relationship as

> work performed in the framework of full-time, formal and open-ended (non-time-bound) arrangements in a subordinate employment relationship. The central feature of the SER is its hierarchical organization: the employer has power to direct employees in their work; to control their work by monitoring their performance; and to discipline them for poor performance.

15. This "fissured workplace" is a worldwide challenge that has its unique impact based on the nation's industrial relations and legal model.
16. This trend includes many universities, where the rising use of non-tenure contingent professors and adjuncts creates a fissured workplace with protected tenured professors and tenure-track professors, working alongside colleagues who can be terminated for no reason at the end of their contract. As these contract professors age, they will have limited options if their contract is not renewed.

References

American Association of Retired Persons (2008). *Staying ahead of the curve 2007: The AARP Work and Career Study*. Washington DC: AARP Knowledge Management.

Angwin, J., Scheiber, N., & Tobin, A. (2017, December 20). Dozens of companies are using Facebook to exclude older workers from job ads. *ProPublica*.

Becker, G. S. (1957). *The economics of discrimination*. Chicago, IL: University of Chicago Press.

Billett, S., Dymock, D., Johnson, G., & Martin, G. (2011). Last resort employees: Older workers' perceptions of workplace discrimination. *Human Resource Development International, 14*, 375–389.

Bradshaw, C. (2006). A revised tangible employment action analysis: Just what is an undesirable reassignment? *Journal of Gender, Social Policy & the Law, 2*, 385–412.

Brudney, J., & L. Baum. (2017). Protean statutory interpretation in the courts of appeals. *William and Mary Law Review, 58*, 681–763.

Busch, V., Dahl, S. A., & Dittrich, D. A. V. (2009). An empirical study of age discrimination in Norway and Germany. *Applied Economics, 41*, 633–651.

Chiu, W. C. K., Chan, A. W., Snape, E., & Redman, T. (2001). Age stereotypes and discriminatory attitudes toward older workers: An East-West comparison. *Human Relations, 54*, 629–661.

Corbett, W. R. (1996). The "fall" of Summers, the rise of "pretext plus," and the escalating subordination of federal employment discrimination law to employment at will: lessons from Mckennon and Hicks. *Georgia Law Review, 30*, 305–384.

Corbett, W. R. (2010). Babbling about employment discrimination law: Does the master builder understand the blueprint for the great tower? *University of Pennsylvania Journal of Business Law, 12*, 683–729.

Denver Post (2017, February 17). Neil Gorsuch Often Sided with Employers in Workers' Rights Cases, Retrieved from www.denverpost.com/2017/02/27/neil-gorsuch-workers-rights-cases/.

Equal Employment Opportunity Commission (2017a). Statutes by Issue (Charges filed with EEOC) FY 2010 – FY – 2016. Retrieved from www.eeoc.gov/eeoc/statistics/enforcement/statutes_by_issue.cfm.

Equal Employment Opportunity Commission (2017b). EEOC Budget and Staffing History 1980 to present. Retrieved from www.eeoc.gov/eeoc/plan/budgetandstaffing.cfm.

Fenwick, C., Kucera, D., Curtis, K., Lapeyre, F., Tchami, G., Stavrakis, C., Hunter, D., & Marcadent, P. (2017). A challenging future for the employment relationship: Time for affirmation or alternatives? International Labor Organization, International Labour Office, Note in The Future of Work Centenary Series, 3 Issue Notes Series, Retrieved from www.ilo.org/wcmsp5/groups/public/-dgreports/-dcomm/documents/publication/wcms_534115.pdf.

Fields, D., Goodman, J., & Blum, T. (2005). Human Resource dependence and organizational demography: A study of minority employment in private sector companies. *Journal of Management, 31,* 167–185.

Foreman, M. (2010). Gross v. FBL Financial Service – Oh so gross! *University of Memphis Law Review, 40,* 681–703.

Finkelstein, L. M., Hanrahan, E. A., & Thomas, C. L. (2018). An expanded view of age bias in the workplace. In K. Shultz & G. Adams (Eds.), *Aging and Work in the 21st Century,* 2nd Ed. CA: Psychology Press.

Goldberg, C., & Shore, L. M. (2003). The impact of age of applicants and of referent others on recruiters' assessments: A study of young and middle-aged job seekers. *Representative Research in Social Psychology, 27,* 11–22.

Goldberg, C., Perry, E. L., Finkelstein, L. M., & Shull, A. (2013). Antecedents and outcomes of targeting older applicants in recruitment. *European Journal of Work and Organizational Psychology, 22,* 1–14.

Government Accounting Office (2009). *Pilot projects could help test solutions to long-standing concerns with the EEO complaint process.* Washington, DC: U.S. Government Printing Office. www.gao.gov/assets/300/293883.pdf (accessed February 24, 2018).

Henkens, C. J. I. M. (2005). Stereotyping older workers and retirement: The managers' point of view. *Canadian Journal of Aging, 24,* 353–366.

Hoffman, M. (2012). Fast's four factors: A solution to similarly situated discovery disputes in FLSA collective actions. *Houston Law Review, 49,* 491–530.

Jeske, D., & Shultz, K. (2016). Using social media content for screening in recruitment and selection: Pros and cons. *Work, Employment & Society, 30,* 535–546. doi: 10.1177/0950017015613746.

Larson, J., Varner, M., Tobin, A, & Angwin, J. (2017). These are the job ads you can't see on Facebook if you're older. http://projects.propublica.org/graphics/facebook-job-ads (accessed March 1, 2018).

Leslie, L., Manchester, C., & Dahm, P. (2017). Why and when does the gender gap reverse? Diversity goals and the pay premium for high potential women? *Academy of Management Journal, 60,* 402–419.

Levin, W. C. (1988). Age stereotyping: College student evaluations. *Research on Aging, 10,* 134–148.

Lidge, E. F. (1999). The meaning of discrimination: Why courts have erred in requiring employment discrimination plaintiffs to prove that the employer's action was materially adverse or ultimate. *Kansas Law Review, 37,* 333–411.

Livingston, D. R. (1993). The civil rights act of 1991 and EEOC enforcement. *Stetson Law Review, 13,* 53–100.

Lyon, P., & Pollard, D. (1997). Perceptions of the older employee: Is anything really changing? *Personnel Review, 26,* 245–257.

Marcus, J., Fritzsche, B. A., Le, H., & Reeves, M. D. (2016). Validation of the work-related age-based stereotypes (WAS) scale. *Journal of Managerial Psychology, 31,* 989–1004 doi:2F10.1108%2FJMP-11-2014-0320.

McDermott, P., Obar, R., Jose, A., and Bowers, M. (2000). An evaluation of the Equal Employment Opportunity Commission mediation program, at pp. 75–107 (discussion of various EEOC Commissioner strategies to reduce charge backlog with limited resources) Retrieved from www.eeoc.gov/eeoc/mediation/report/.

National Conference of State Legislators (2015, July). State employment related discrimination statutes. Retrieved from www.ncsl.org/documents/employ/Discrimination-Chart-2015.pdf (accessed November 12, 2017).

New York City, Office of the Mayor (2017, May 15). Freelancers aren't free: Mayor announces first in nation protections for freelance workers. Retrieved from www1.nyc.gov/office-of-the-mayor/news/307-17/freelancers-aren-t-free-mayor-first-nation-protections-freelance-workers.

Oakley, D. and Keneally, K. (2017). Retirement security 2017: A roadmap for policy makers Americans' views of the retirement crisis and solutions. *National Institute on Retirement Security*. www.nirsonline.org/wp-content/uploads/2017/06/2017_opinion_nirs_final_web.pdf.

Rosen, B., & Jerdee, T. H. (1976). The nature of job-related age stereotypes. *Journal of Applied Psychology, 61*, 180–183.

Rosen, B., & Jerdee, T. H. (1977). Too old or not too old? *Harvard Business Review, 55*, 97–106.

Savage, D. G. (June 19, 2009). Age bias much harder to prove: The Supreme Court shifts the burden of proof to the worker making the claim. Businesses cheer. *L.A. Times*, p. 1.

Senn, C. R. (2012). Ending discriminatory damages. *Alabama Law Review, 64*, 187–254.

Shore, L. M., & Goldberg, C. B. (2005). Age discrimination in the workplace. In R. L. Dipboye and A. Colella (Eds.), *Psychological and organizational bases of discrimination at work* (pp. 203–225). Mawhaw, NJ: Lawrence Erlbaum.

Spindler, K. (2000). Shareholder demands for higher corporate earnings have their price: How courts allow employers to fire older employees for their achievements. *Pepperdine University School of Law Review, 27*, 807–826.

Taylor, P., & Walker, A. (1998). Employers and older workers: Attitudes and employment practices. *Ageing Society, 18*, 641–658.

Terrell, K. (2017, December 17). Age discrimination goes online – 50 years after the landmark legislation to protect older workers bias is on the rise? *AARP Bulletin*, Retrieved from www.aarp.org/work/working-at-50-plus/info-2017/age-discrimination-online-fd.html.

US Equal Employment Opportunity Commission. (2017a). Charge statistics FY 1997 through FY 2016. www.eeoc.gov/eeoc/statistics/enforcement/charges.cfm.

US Equal Employment Opportunity Commission. (2017b, June, 14). Age discrimination and outdated views of older workers persist, experts tell commission. Press release. www.eeoc.gov/eeoc/newsroom/release/6-14-17a.cfm.

Van Iddekinge, C. H., Lanivich, S. E., Roth, P. L., & Junco, E. (2016). Social media for selection? Validity and adverse impact potential of a Facebook-based assessment. *Journal of Management, 47*, 1811–1835.

Wanberg, C., Kanfer, R., Hamann, D., & Zhang, Z. (2016). Age and reemployment success after job loss: An integrative model and meta-analysis. *Psychological Bulletin, 142*, 400–426.

Widiss, D. A. (2012). Undermining congressional overrides: The hydra problem in statutory interpretation. *Texas Law Review, 90*, 858–942.

World Economic Forum White Paper. (2017, May). We'll Live to 100 – How can we afford it? Retrieved from www3.weforum.org/docs/WEF_White_Paper_We_Will_Live_to_100.pdf, p. 11.

Case Law

Bradley et al. v. T-Mobile U.S. Inc. et al., Case No: 5–17:07232 BLF, (USDC California, Northern District).

Carsillo v. City of Lake Worth, 995 So. 2d 1118, 1119 (Fla. 4th DCA 2008).

Gen. Dynamics Land Sys. v. *Cline*, 540 U.S. 581 (2004).
Gross v. *FBL Financial Services*, 557 U.S. 167; 129 S. Ct. 2343; 174 L. Ed. 2d 119 (2009).
Hazen Paper Co. v. *Biggins*, 507 U.S. 604 (1993).
Reeves v. *Sanderson Plumbing Products, Inc.*, 530 U.S. 133, 120 S. Ct. 2097, 147 L.Ed.2d 105 (2000).
Russell v. *McKinney Hospital Venture*, 235 F.3d 219 (5th Cir. 2000).
Karlo v. *Pittsburgh Glass Works, LLC*, 849 F.3d 61 (3d Cir. 2017).
Ryther v. *KARE 11*, 108 F.3D 132 (8th Cir.1997).
Smith v. *City of Jackson*, 544 U.S. 228 (2005).
TransAm Trucking, Inc. v. *Admin. Review Board*, 2016 U.S. App. LEXIS 13071 (10th Cir. July 15, 2016).
Univ. of Tex. Southwestern Med. Ctr. v. *Nassar*, 133 S. Ct. 2517, 186 L. Ed. 503 (2013).

Statutes

Age Discrimination in Employment Act of 1967 (Pub. L. 90–202) (ADEA), as amended, 29 U.S.C. §621 et seq. www.eeoc.gov/laws/statutes/adea.cfm (last accessed October 8, 2017).
Employee Retirement Income Security Act of 1974, Pub. L. No. 93–403, as amended §204(b)(1)(H)(i), 29 U.S.C. §1054(b)(1)(H)(i).
Internal Revenue Code, 26 USCS prec §1 et seq. at §411 (b)(1)(H)(i).
Tax Cuts and Jobs Act of 2017, Public Law No: 115–9 (12/22/2017).
The Civil Rights Act of 1991, Pub. L. No. 102–166, 105 Stat. 1071–1100 (codified as amended in scattered sections of 42 U.S.C. (Supp. III 1992)); Retrieved from www.eeoc.gov/eeoc/history/35th/thelaw/cra_1991.html.
The Fair Labor Standards Act of 1938, as amended, 29 U.S.C. 201 et seq. Retrieved from www.dol.gov/whd/regs/statutes/FairLaborStandAct.pdf.
Title VII of the Civil Rights Act of 1964 Pub. L. 88–352,42 U.S.C. 2000e et seq. Retrieved from www.eeoc.gov/laws/statutes/titlevii.cfm.

6
EMPLOYEE AGE AND PERFORMANCE IN ORGANIZATIONS

Jerry W. Hedge and Walter C. Borman

Persons aged 55 and older are becoming a significant proportion of the population – and a growing part of the labor pool. The pace of change – technological, societal, economic, and in the workplace – has implications for employees who want to continue to grow and contribute to the organization in meaningful ways, and for employers who desire to retain the contributions of this valued segment of the workforce. In addition, older workers are becoming an increasingly important concern for organizations who may worry that as workers age their productivity may wane.

In this chapter, we review the available research literature on the relationship between age and work performance. In doing so we address a number of research issues, including:

- How is age conceptualized and operationalized?
- What do we know about the effects of aging on job performance?
- How are various components of performance influenced by the aging process and aspects of the work environment?
- What evolving frameworks might be useful for encouraging and evaluating sustained performance over time?
- How might human resource management programs be designed to support and sustain successful aging at work?

Conceptions of Age

The rapid expansion of research on work and aging in the last decade has increased scrutiny on how best to operationalize the age construct. There are no consistent *legal* benchmarks that can guide the researcher or practitioner to a definitive age at which an employee can be considered an older worker. In fact, there is much variability in how the term is operationally defined. For example, the Age Discrimination in Employment Act (ADEA) designates 40 years as the legal demarcation of an older worker; AARP identifies 50 years as eligibility for membership; and the Older Americans Act recognizes people aged 55 and older as older workers. Since 65 had been the traditional age for retirement and receipt of Social Security benefits in the US, that age is frequently cited as a transition point or cutoff (Hedge, Borman, & Lammlein, 2006).

Most research on work and aging has defined age from a chronological perspective, that is, the time that has passed since the birth of an individual (Schwall, 2012). Chronological age is a convenient measure, and one that is widely used and accepted, although, many studies seem to lack any strong rationale for choosing a particular age cutoff or age range to define a worker as "older." Simpson, Greller, and Stroh (2002) suggested that often the age range is expanded simply to compensate for lower numbers of people in the older category. Hertel and Zacher (2018) noted that more recent work and aging research tends to use chronological age as a continuous variable, typically ranging from 18 to 65 years and older.

More importantly, using chronological age exclusively is problematic because people age differently. Beier (2015) noted that different abilities change at different rates within an individual. Comparisons between people in different age groups may be less useful than considering physiological and psychological within-individual changes across a person's life span. Consequently, organizational researchers have begun to focus on other ways age can be conceptualized. For example, recent reviews (Hertel & Zacher, 2018; Schwall, 2012; Zabel & Baltes, 2016) have suggested age constructs such as functional, organizational, subjective, social, and relative age as useful alternatives. Although it is unlikely that chronological age will ever be completely abandoned (if for no other reason than it provides a useful point of reference for past research studies), it may not provide the rich source of information that other age constructs might offer. Empirical studies are only beginning to emerge that examine the content, construct, and predictive validity of these alternative age constructs.

One measure that has received increased research attention and stimulated considerable discourse is *successful aging at work* (see for example, Kooij, 2015; Zacher, 2015). While a common operational definition has yet to emerge, it is generally agreed that to be aging successfully at work, a person must maintain or experience positive change in some work outcome (e.g., work ability, productivity) over time, and must be an active participant in achieving that success (Olson & Shultz, in press). Conversely, a decline in these work outcomes would be considered unsuccessful aging at work (Hertel & Zacher, 2018).

In sum, age can be viewed through many lenses, but as noted by Bohlmann, Rudolph, and Zacher (2017), age itself is an "empty" variable, lacking information about changes in psychological variables such as workers' abilities, motives, experiences, or behavior over time. The concept also varies considerably across contexts and cultures, with a number of factors determining who is considered older. Furthermore, as Truxillo, Cadiz, and Hammer (2015) noted, the concept of an older worker seems to be evolving; that is, people appear to be aging more slowly, and working longer than has been true traditionally. Still, while it is important to keep these emerging definitions of age in mind as we explore the available literature on the relationship between age and work performance, until our research database begins to accumulate studies that use and/or compare alternate conceptions of aging, much of the research that is presently available and that will be discussed in the next section, relies on chronological age to examine differences in performance across the work life span.

Age and Job Performance

If older workers are to remain in the workforce later in life, as some wish and others need to do, jobs must be available and employers must be willing to hire and retain them. Workers should get and keep jobs based on their ability, not age, yet older workers face a variety of barriers in their efforts to remain employed or find new employment (Hedge & Borman, 2012). Age stereotypes and biases can be detrimental to individual and organizational productivity, and can lead to age discrimination when it negatively affects workplace decisions about employment, training, promotion, termination, benefits, or retirement. While age stereotyping is an important and relevant topic for a discussion on age and performance at work, these subjects have been covered thoroughly by Webster, Thoroughgood, and Sawyer (Chapter 3, this volume), and Finkelstein, Hanrahan, and Thomas (Chapter 4, this volume), and so will not be repeated here. Interested readers are referred to these chapters for more extensive discussions on the topic.

Although the popular consensus is that adults older than about age 55 show declines in several abilities, research correlating age with job performance generally finds almost no correlation between the two (Ng & Feldman, 2008). The following section focuses on four specific components of job performance and examines the literature on age-performance relationships for each component. It has long been recognized that job performance is best thought as a multidimensional construct (Campbell, McCloy, Oppler & Sager, 1993). There have been several attempts to identify possible taxonomies that might reflect this multidimensional job performance construct (see Borman, Grossman, Bryant, & Dorio, 2017 for a recent review). One that offers a summary depiction of the performance space is the task-contextual or citizenship performance distinction. *Task performance* refers to the technical proficiency component of job performance (cf., Williams & Anderson, 1991). Meanwhile, *citizenship performance* is defined by the helping, cooperating, and persisting activities that support task accomplishment (e.g., Borman & Motowidlo, 1993). Two additional performance dimensions have also been identified as important components, counterproductive work behavior (CWB: Robinson & Bennett, 1995) and adaptive performance (Pulakos, Arad, Donovan, & Plamondon, 2000). There is sufficient literature on links between age and each of these performance constructs to consider them individually.

Task–Overall Performance

In an early review, Rhodes (1983) concluded that there was evidence for a low correlation, and at least four different age–job performance relations: weak positive, weak negative, an inverted U, and nonsignificant. In their meta-analysis investigating this relationship, McEvoy and Cascio (1989) found a correlation of 0.06 between age and job performance, and Waldman and Avolio's (1986) meta-analysis found an overall mean correlation of near zero between these variables.

Sturman (2003) also conducted a meta-analysis that suggested the relationship between age and job performance approximated an inverted U shape. Specifically, for younger adults, age is positively correlated with job performance. The relationship gets progressively smaller until around age 50, where the correlation is estimated at zero. Beyond this age, the relationship becomes negative. The inverted U-shaped relationship is consistent with McDaniel, Pesta, and Banks' (2012) review, the theorizing of McEvoy and Cascio (1989), the empirical findings of Callahan (1998), Avolio, Waldman, and McDaniel (1990), Ng and Feldman's (2008) more recent meta-analysis, and the review of Salthouse (2012).

A more informative way of understanding this low age-performance correlation is to explore moderators of the relationship and thus the reasons for this result. Several explanations have been offered. Park (1994) suggested that older workers often have jobs they are very familiar with and thus considerable practice and experience with their job tasks, allowing for successful performance even if broader cognitive functioning declines. Older workers may have developed complex detailed knowledge structures (i.e., expertise) that compensate for any loss in general skills or abilities. Schooler, Caplan, and Oates (1998) suggested the following reasons for smaller or no age differences in job performance compared with the age differences in cognitive abilities found in laboratory settings: (1) expertise and experience may help make up for declines in cognitive functioning; (2) lab tasks tend to push people to their cognitive limits, whereas actual jobs usually do not; (3) older people with large declines in cognitive abilities have often left the workplace (i.e., selective attrition); and (4) older workers are more motivated and satisfied with their jobs and thus tend to try harder.

Older workers can compensate for overall cognitive deficits in other ways, as well. In fact, other explanations have been offered; as an example, Artistico, Cervone, and Pezzuti (2003) found that older employees were better than their younger counterparts when working on problems they have already encountered on the job. Moreover, older workers may have developed complex detailed knowledge structures (i.e., expertise) that compensate for any loss in general skills or abilities. Support for this contention comes from Thornton and Dumke (2005), who noted that professional expertise gained during a long career can often overcome deterioration in certain abilities. Specifically, a well-developed semantic memory system for job-relevant concepts can help the older adult buffer against declines in the process-dependent episodic memory system.

This effect is clearly displayed in the literature on expertise and aging (Charness & Tuffiash, 2008; Horton, Baker, & Shorer, 2008). Episodic memory decline is less relevant to the older worker who possesses a rich network of job facts acquired through decades of experience. Therefore, aging may have little effect (or even beneficial effects) in areas where expert knowledge systems are required for successful job performance. Lawyers, doctors, college professors, and other professional jobs where performance requires some level of expertise in domain-specific areas are examples. In other words, experts presumably possess a network of highly-organized, domain-specific knowledge, accumulated by experience, and stored efficiently in long-term memory. Retrieval from the network (a relatively automatic process) serves as a script, or template for processing and acting on familiar information as needed to perform well in a job (Charness & Bosman, 1990).

In a somewhat different vein, Kanfer and Ackerman (2004) observed that general declines in fluid intellectual abilities with age are often accompanied by increases in crystallized intellectual capabilities, and they suggest that a good strategy for older employees is to gravitate to jobs that emphasize the latter abilities, such as those with requirements for managerial skills. Finally, older workers may often have more access to co-worker support to help them with their tasks. Of course, in cases where jobs change frequently, and require significant retraining, age will probably correlate negatively with job performance.

Age and Organizational Citizenship Performance

Contextual or citizenship performance refers to such behavioral dimensions as: (1) Personal Support – helping others in the organization (e.g., peers or supervisors); cooperating with others and putting team objectives ahead of personal interests; (2) Organizational Support – favorably representing the organization by defending and promoting its objectives, as well as supporting the organization's mission and objectives; (3) Conscientious Initiative – persisting with extra effort despite difficult conditions; taking the initiative to do all that is necessary to accomplish objectives even if they are not normally a part of one's duties (Borman et al., 2001).

A useful way to view citizenship performance is by contrasting it with task performance. Citizenship activities differ from task activities in at least three important ways. First, task activities contribute either directly or indirectly to the technical core. Citizenship activities, on the other hand, do not support the technical core itself as much as they support the organizational, social, and psychological environment in which the technical core must function. Second, task activities usually vary between different jobs. Citizenship activities, however, are common to many or all jobs. Their peripheral details vary because they are performed in environments that change from job to job, but their central features are the same. Volunteering, persisting, helping, and cooperating are undoubtedly important for all jobs. And third, because the source of variation in task performance is proficiency with which task activities are carried out, the important human characteristics are knowledge, skills, and abilities that co-vary with task proficiency. The main source of variation in citizenship performance, however, is not proficiency, but volition and predisposition. Such behaviors are probably better predicted by variables related to individual differences in motivational characteristics and predispositional variables represented by personality characteristics.

In general, the correlation between age and citizenship performance is moderately positive. Older employees are somewhat more likely to engage in the helping or prosocial behaviors relevant to this category of performance (Borman, Penner, Allen, & Motowidlo, 2001). As we will note in a later section on age and personality, older people tend to stand higher on the traits of agreeableness and emotional stability, and this may in turn be associated with job behavior relative to citizenship performance.

More recently, further understanding of the relationship between age and citizenship performance was offered by Profili, Sammarra, and Innocenti (2016) who found that older workers (>35 years old) in a large sample displayed considerably higher levels of altruistic citizenship performance when they perceived their organization to offer high work-life balance. In contrast, younger employees (<35 years old) displayed higher altruistic citizenship when they perceived the climate as "fun."

Another study by the same authors (Profili Sammarra, and Innocenti, 2017) found a correlation of 0.16 between organizations' perceived age diversity and individual level altruistic organizational citizenship behavior. The correlation between age diversity and affective commitment was 0.55. Thus, there is limited evidence for the relationship between age and citizenship performance with most of it indirect, involving correlations between age and personality variables known to relate to age.

Age and Counterproductive Work Behavior

Counterproductive work behavior (CWB) can be defined broadly as volitional acts by employees that potentially violate the legitimate interests of, or do harm to, an organization or its stakeholders (Sackett & DeVore, 2001). It may include behaviors such as theft, improper substance use, misuse of time and resources, inappropriate verbal or physical actions toward co-workers or supervisors, or destruction of property at work. Recently, Marcus, Taylor, Hastings, Sturn, and Weigelt (2016) reviewed four models of CWB: 1-factor overall CWB; 2-factors (i.e., toward individuals and toward the organization); 5-factors (e.g., sabotage, withdrawal); and 11-factors (e.g., misuse of information, poor quality work). For our purposes, we will focus for the most part on the single factor version and its relationship with age.

Regarding direct age–CWB correlations, three meta-analyses provide estimates of this relationship. Ng and Feldman (2008) found mean corrected correlations of about −0.10. Berry, Ones, and Sackett (2007) reported slightly lower correlations of −0.05 for CWB directed at people within the organization and −0.09 for CWB directed at the organization. Similarly, Berry, Carpenter, and Barratt (2012) found a correlation of −0.05 against overall CWB. These findings indicate a small but consistent relationship between age and CWB; older employees are slightly less likely to engage in these negative, individually, and organizationally harmful behaviors.

More indirect evidence for this result comes from the literature on age–personality relationships and, in turn, personality links with CWB. Consistent findings show that older employees tend to stand higher on conscientiousness, agreeableness, and emotional stability (e.g., Hedge & Borman, 2012; Hedge, Borman, & Lammlein, 2006). At the same time, these personality traits also correlate (negatively) with CWB. Meta-analytic evidence shows corrected mean correlations actions of −0.15 to −0.29 for conscientiousness, −0.13 to −0.18 for agreeableness, and −0.04 for emotional stability (Berry, Carpenter, & Barratt, 2012; Salgado, 2002). This indirect evidence suggests that older employees are less likely to demonstrate CWB, perhaps at least in part because of their more conscientious and agreeable personalities.

Age and Adaptive Performance

There is evidence to support that the adaptive performance construct is an important component of job performance, distinct from the task, citizenship, and CWB performance constructs (Hesketh, Allworth, & Considine, 1996). One attempt to define adaptive performance is research by Pulakos and her colleagues (Pulakos, Arad, Donovan, & Plamondon, 2000). These researchers first reviewed the literature on adaptability relevant to the organizational context. The review yielded several candidate dimensions such as: Dealing with uncertain or unpredictable work situations (e.g., Hall & Mirvis, 1995); Learning new tasks, technologies, and procedures (e.g., Hesketh & Neal, 1999); and Demonstrating interpersonal adaptability (e.g., Bowen & Schneider, 1988). In a subsequent study with incumbents in 21 US Army jobs, critical incidents targeting adaptive job performance were generated and content analyzed, revealing two additional dimensions: Handling work stress and Handling emergencies or crisis situations. A confirmatory factor analysis of job analysis ratings on an inventory developed to reflect this content provided evidence for these eight dimensions. Thus, the eight-dimension depiction of the adaptability construct appears to be a reasonable way to summarize this performance construct.

There are very few studies that specifically target the correlation between age and adaptive performance. Rather, we can make inferences about this relationship by examining associations between certain cognitive and personality variables, and both age and adaptive performance. For example, emotional stability is a reasonably consistent predictor of adaptive performance (Huang, Ryan, Zabel, & Palmer, 2004), and this variable is also associated with older employees. As long as there is a theoretical or at least conceptual rationale for these age-adaptive performance relationships, we can use this pattern of correlations to hypothesize the relationship.

Regarding age and cognitive ability, the results of a large-scale longitudinal study by Schaie (1994) found that except for perceptual speed, which begins declining between age 25 and 32, all abilities show modest increases from age 25 until about age 45, when they level off or begin to decline slightly. Most relevant for the age-adaptability relationship, when abilities are categorized as *fluid* (i.e., abilities in reasoning and related higher mental processes) versus *crystallized* (i.e., abilities related to already acquired knowledge), fluid abilities decline in later middle age, especially in women (McArdle, Ferrer-Czaja, Hamagand, & Woodcock, 2002). In addition, cognitive abilities with a speed component, showed accelerating declines after age 65. This suggests that when jobs require more fluid abilities, especially with a significant speed component, older workers may be at a disadvantage.

Supporting this picture, Avolio and Waldman (1994) found correlations between age and the General Aptitude Test Battery subtests of motor coordination, finger dexterity, and manual dexterity of −0.28 to −0.35. Finally, Czaja and Sharit (1993) had 25- to 70-year-old participants performing computer-interactive tasks and found longer response times and more errors for the older people.

The findings are relevant for the age-adaptive performance relationship. In jobs that involve a lot of change and frequent rapid responses, often the reality for our current work landscape, older employees on average, may have challenges compared with their younger counterparts. We must emphasize the "on average" point here, as there are large individual differences in these cognitive declines. Schaie (1994), Warr and Birdi (1998), and others have pointed out that the standard deviation in abilities increases with older age. Also, there is strong evidence that older people who are involved in complex, intellectually stimulating activities show lower rates of decline in cognitive functioning (Masunaga & Horn, 2001). This extends to leisure activities where more engaged, mentally stimulating activities can contribute to lower rates of cognitive decline (Bosma et al., 2002; Gribbin, Schaie, & Parham, 1980).

On the personality side, research evidence is mixed for the age-adaptive performance relationship. A recent meta-analysis (Huang, Ryan, Zabel, & Palmer, 2014), found a positive relationship between both emotional stability and conscientiousness with adaptive performance, but there was considerable disagreement in findings across the primary studies. Helson, Jones, and Kwan (2002), conducted a large-scale longitudinal study and found that older persons scored higher on norm-adherence dimensions such as self-control. This finding suggests that older employees may be less likely to react favorably to change initiatives, preferring to stick with the usual procedures and practices. As mentioned, emotional stability has a significant positive correlation with adaptive performance, and longitudinal studies (Helson et al., 2002) demonstrate that emotional stability increases with age. Finally, a consistent result in this literature is that age correlates negatively with openness to experience (Pulakos et al., 2002), most notably the facet of behavioral flexibility, of obvious relevance to the age-adaptive performance relation. This finding ties in with the earlier-mentioned deficits for older people in speed-related and fluid intelligence. On balance, ability and personality lines of research suggest that older workers may be somewhat disadvantaged on this component of job performance. With the caveats mentioned, adaptive performance is probably not a strength for older employees.

Age, Personality, and Performance

A central question related to personality and age is, how coherent and consistent is personality across time? And, if there are reliable changes in traits across time, how are these changes likely related to job performance?

Although there is evidence for considerable consistency in personality across time (Costa & McCrae, 1988), more recent research has identified reliable differences across the lifespan for individual traits. For example, Roberts, Walton, and Viechtbauer's (2006) longitudinal study found that at the Five Factor Model (Goldberg, 1993) level, there are increases over time for the traits of conscientiousness and agreeableness. The cumulative effect sizes for these two traits show that there are changes of +0.60 to +0.85 standard deviations between ages 20 and about 70. With regard to emotional stability, Roberts et al. found a cumulative effect size of about +0.60 between the ages 20 and 70. Finally, with extraversion and openness to experience, there were decreases across the adult lifespan. For extraversion, the decline was almost all in the interpersonal aspects of the trait rather than the independence, confidence aspects. Regarding openness, the gradual decline was primarily after early adulthood.

These results were largely confirmed by a more recent study with a sample size of more than 1.2 million adults (Soto, John, Gosling, & Potter, 2011). Regarding older adults, for conscientiousness, the increases were primarily in self-discipline; for agreeableness, in both altruism and compliance; and for emotional stability, in both (negative) anxiety and depression, primarily after age 55.

Thus, research has found reliable shifts in some traits for older people. What this means for the age-performance relation is, with the possible exception of the openness findings, personality change results support the role of older workers in the workplace. They are likely to be less impulsive and more conscientious in carrying out their tasks. The higher level of agreeableness also means that they should get along more smoothly with supervisors, co-workers, and customers, compared with younger workers. From a management perspective, this is highly desirable, and provides support for the employment of older workers.

Technology-Based Performance and Aging

Emerging technological innovations have the potential to support or degrade the performance of older workers, who are increasingly operating in a high-tech environment. The widespread availability of personal computers, and associated technological advances (e.g., the internet) has transformed the way people interact with employers, fellow employees, and clients. As computers have grown increasingly powerful and have facilitated the automation of work tasks, there continues to be an increased movement away from hard physical work toward more knowledge-based work (Foster & Mayhorn, 2012). While a reduction in manual labor is a trend that is conducive to the health of many older workers who may be experiencing declines in physical work capabilities, it can place greater demands on cognitive abilities, such as speed of processing, working memory, and perceptual abilities, for which there are normative age-related declines (Sharit & Czaja, 2012).

It is essential that the older worker has the skills and the confidence to interact with technology. It has been shown that such issues can largely be alleviated through appropriate user–interface design and training strategies that accommodate the capabilities and limitations of older adults. For example, Beier, Teachout, and Cox (2012) point to the potential advantages of computer-based training (CBT) for older learners, including the fact that most CBT programs are self-paced, and that training can also easily be modified to take declining sensory abilities into account. They also note that this approach can foster a sense of anonymity, thus allowing trainees to try new things and explore the content being trained without worrying about impression management, which may be especially salient for older, more established, workers.

In addition, Wolfson, Cavanagh, and Kraiger (2014) proposed several recommendations to enhance older adult learning and transfer outcomes when employing technology-based instruction (TBI). They suggested that TBI for older workers should be highly structured, give feedback and adaptive guidance, and incorporate a user-friendly and consistent interface. Still, Beier et al. (2012), cautioned that while many age-related TBI usability issues may dissipate as those employees who grew up using technology age, it would be reasonable to assume that older cohorts will still lag behind their younger counterparts in the ease with which they adopt technology, and developers should keep this in mind when designing training.

Age and Performance in the Broader Organizational Context

Stimulating and nurturing older workers' careers is advantageous for both employees and organizations. Employability, work ability, and sustainability are emerging, interrelated concepts that, when integrated in the organization's work structure and procedures, can support both the organization's need to maintain a competitive edge in a changing business environment, and an individual's desire for career growth and success across the lifespan. Rapid technological innovations, increased competition, and reduced job security mean work environments are increasingly dynamic and unpredictable, and require employees of all ages to update their skill sets, modify existing work behaviors, and adapt to new organizational roles. In order for individuals and organizations to continually maintain and strengthen their capabilities, it is important that they focus (individually and in concert) on practices that facilitate career sustainability.

Employability

Employability has been defined in the literature in a variety of ways (see Forrier & Sels, 2003, for a more detailed examination of the employability construct). Forrier, Verbruggen, and De Cuyper (2015) succinctly describe employability as an individual's chance of obtaining a job in the internal or external labor market, and differentiate three of the more frequently used approaches as focusing on: (a) an individual's appraisal of chance (perceived employability); (b) personal strengths that influence the chance (occupational and generic competencies); and (c) the realization of chance (job transitions). Thus, employability is closely linked to a person's skill set and formal and informal job qualifications. Employees with high employability are seen as having skills and experience that are transferable across different jobs, and that are in demand within or across organizations (De Cuyper, Mäkikangas, Kinnunen, Mauno, & De Witte, 2012).

The employability concept is important in the current context because of the benefits to organizations of both retaining the valued contributions of their aging workforce and in maintaining optimal levels of engagement and performance from these workers. It is also important because of its significance to aging workers as they strive to secure and maintain employment against the background of changes in the nature of employment contracts and in the rapidly-changing demands of the labor market.

Kirves, Kinnunen, De Cuyper, and Mäkikangas (2014) argued that when employees feel in control of their careers and have faith in their prospects in the labor market (internal or external), then well-being at work increases. Veld, Semeijn, and van Vuuren (2015) found that HR management practices and employees' willingness (to adapt) are positively related to employability, and suggested that both organizations and employees are responsible for enhancing employability. Nauta et al. (2009) suggested that organizations that need to adapt to changing environments should implement a strong employability culture (where employers and employees continuously invest in keeping knowledge and skills up-to-date), because it stimulates an employability mindset among employees and decreases turnover intention.

Work Ability

The work ability concept is based on the assumption that work ability is determined by an individual's perception of the demands of work and the ability to cope with those demands. Because the operational environment of organizations is dynamic, work ability is about continuously finding a balance between a person's abilities and work demands (Ilmarinen, 2009). High levels of work ability occur when there is a good fit between the features of work and the individual's resources (Ilmarinen & Ilmarinen, 2015).

Much of the early work ability studies were conducted in Europe, and Ilmarinen and Ilmarinen (2015) reported that work ability tends to decline with age, although it remains in the good to excellent range for 20- to 65-year-old workers. A study by Costa and Sartori (2007) showed a general decreasing trend in work ability over time as well. They also found that work ability levels tended to vary due to working conditions and personal health status. Work ability remained high and stable over time in jobs with higher mental involvement and autonomy, but lower physical constraints, but showed marked decreases as the physical work load increased and job control decreased.

A recent study by McGonagle, Fisher, Barnes-Farrell, and Grosch (2015) failed to support a negative relationship between age and perceived work ability, but did find that personal resources (i.e., sense of control and health status) were particularly important for participants' current work ability perceptions across diverse occupations. Interestingly, these researchers also found that perceived work ability had consistent lagged effects on absenteeism, retirement, and disability leave in the studies; that is, when the researchers examined lagged (1.6 years later) work ability perceptions, they found evidence of relationships between job demands and perceived work ability. They suggested that job demands might contribute to work ability levels through a strain process over time, and, as strains accumulate, this could have further detrimental effects on health and well-being, and it may be particularly true for workers in physically demanding jobs.

The concept of work ability differs from conventional work performance concepts and measures as it examines the interplay of personal resources in relation to physical and mental job demands (Maertens, Putter, Chen, Diehl, & Huang, 2012). Maintaining and promoting work ability throughout the life course depend on both employees' efforts and employers' commitment to actively producing opportunities and making the employment environment suitable for older employees.

Sustainability

The reality of an aging workforce emphasizes the importance of focusing on sustainable employment; that is, the extent to which workers are able and willing to remain working now and in the future (van Dam, van Vuuren, & Kemps, 2017). Viewing successful aging at work from a sustainability perspective underscores the notion of continual striving to maintain person–job fit. Kooij (2015) suggested that the Person–Job fit framework characterizes the notion of sustainability in ways that will hopefully balance health, motivation, and work ability components and lead to successful aging at work. Optimal sustainability depends on both short and long-term commitments from employees and employers to strengthen employability, work ability, and productivity of employees (De Lange, Kooij, & Van der Heijden, 2015).

While constructs such as employability, work ability, and sustainability are not the primary focus of this chapter, the research base continues to expand for all three, and suggest potential links to individual and organizational performance in important ways. We encourage continued refinement of how employability, work ability, and sustainability are operationally defined, and how they impact work performance, as well as a closer look at their interrelationships within the context of performance over the course of one's work life.

Human Resource Management of an Aging Workforce

As older workers become a significantly larger portion of the workforce, a strategic human resource management challenge will be to create new and attractive opportunities that are not only designed in ways that will encourage and promote continued investment in older employees, but that strengthen and support the organizational contributions of older workers. In order to meet these challenges, organizations need to create structures, policies, and procedures that foster an environment supportive of older workers' performance, work attitudes and motivation, and physical and psychological well-being.

Despite the empirical evidence that human resource management (HRM) practices contribute in important ways toward attracting, employing, and retaining workers, and despite the reality of an ever-expanding diversity of the workforce, relatively little is known about the influence of HRM practices on job performance across the work lifespan (Kooij, De Lange, Jansen, & Dikkers, 2008). In addition, age differences have been examined primarily in terms of *employee perceptions* of HR, and the effects of different actual HR practices on older and younger people have not been examined. As noted by Truxillo et al. (2015), this is an important point given that actual HR practices and the way that employees perceive them may be quite different.

Still, in terms of worker perceptions, available research has shown that organizations' HR practices can influence older workers' motivations to continue working, retire, or re-enter the workforce. For example, Armstrong-Stassen (2008) found that people in post-retirement jobs are drawn to organizations that provide HR practices tailored to the needs and desires of older workers, and suggested that if employers are interested in encouraging retirees to return to the workforce, they are going to have to implement those HR practices that are important to this group. Armstrong-Stassen and Ursel (2009) found that implementing training and development HR practices targeting older workers and tailored to their needs, and providing interesting and challenging job assignments, are important to perceptions of organizational support and career satisfaction, and ultimately to the retention of older workers. The main conclusion of this research is that organizations that are perceived to be providing their employees with developmental HR practices are communicating that they want to invest in their employees, and this relates to positive attitudes and motivation.

Over the last several years, Bal and colleagues (Bal, De Jong, Jansen, & Bakker, 2012; Bal & Jansen, 2016) have studied HRM practices for a diverse workforce and emphasized the notion of workplace flexibility in relation to older workers. They suggested that within the context of human resource management, the awareness among employees that flexibility practices are available to them when they need it, will enhance their motivation and performance. Employees will feel valued by their organization and know that in the future if they face difficulties in maintaining balance between work and nonwork obligations, they will be able to use these practices (Bal et al., 2012).

A series of conceptual (Kooij, De Lange, Jansen, & Dikkers, 2008), meta-analytic (Kooij, Jansen, Dikkers, & De Lange, 2010; Kooij, De Lange, Jansen, Kanfer, & Dikkers, 2011), and empirical (Kooij, Jansen, Dikkers, & De Lange, 2014) studies on the differential effects of perceived HR practices on older and younger workers led to the classification of HR practices into four clusters, which the authors suggest influence worker outcomes differentially over the lifespan. These clusters are: development practices (e.g., OJT training and development), maintenance practices (e.g., job security and flexible work hours), utilization practices (e.g., horizontal job movement, task enrichment), and accommodative practices (e.g., part-time work). Additional research is needed to test the effectiveness of these HR bundles in the context of an aging worker.

Truxillo et al. (2015) in their review of the work and aging literature, were able to identify only a few published studies that extended the HRM-age research beyond perceptions to a closer examination of which interventions are more and less effective and why. They noted that there are just a small number of empirically tested studies of workplace interventions and best practices to support older workers (e.g., job crafting, workplace flexibility, age-inclusive HR practices), and suggest that far more age-related interventions need to be examined to support effective practice.

Kulik, Ryan, Harper, and George (2014) suggest that companies should ensure that they offer employees, regardless of their age, equal opportunities for continuous (i.e., life-long) learning, training, and development, as well as opportunities for promotions, transferals, and career progression. To achieve this Person–Environment fit across time, they suggest that a life-span-aware and diversity-friendly HRM perspective is crucial in order to diagnose reliably what workers need, in terms of specific HR practices, and at what stages in their career in order to experience successful aging at work.

Directions for Future Research

The body of knowledge pertaining specifically to the age–job performance relationship has not grown particularly rapidly since the previous edition of this volume (see Cleveland & Lim, 2007), or since more recent reviews by Hedge and Borman (2012) or McDaniel, Pesta, and Banks (2012). Still, our knowledge continues to accumulate around the broader concept of performance at work and how older workers and organizations can strive to optimize that performance. In many ways our understanding is still in its infancy, and much research remains to be done.

The data on job performance of older workers are relatively sparse, because although some large meta-analyses have been completed (e.g., Callahan, 1998; McEvoy & Cascio, 1989; Ng & Feldman, 2008; Sturman, 2003), few large samples include workers over 60. What the available data suggest is that, on average, age is a weak predictor of job performance. In addition, age likely has an inverted U relationship with job performance, such that after around age 50 performance in most jobs starts to decline. However, the inverted U shape relationship is found primarily in less cognitively demanding jobs, and workers in high complexity jobs, where performance relies on an already-acquired knowledge structure, can be expected to maintain performance.

Future researchers should study age–performance relationships across industries, job complexity, and subgroups of older workers (e.g., by gender and education level), to establish whether these patterns of age–performance relationships vary and whether different age trajectories emerge. Additional research is also necessary to further understand the age–performance relationships of the various performance components (i.e., citizenship, adaptive performance, and counterproductive work behaviors). Also, as suggested by Tishman, Van Looy, and Bruyère (2012) researchers and practitioners should explore the match between the skills required by growth industries and the job skills of older workers, which has implications for the transfer of skills that will enable older workers to extend their careers to industries where job growth is projected.

Researchers should continue to study age-related variables that are more psychologically meaningful than chronological age. There continues to be a growing discussion about the use of alternative measures, and, in fact, over the last decade, increased use of such measures by researchers, as well as suggestions for including other alternatives to chronological age as well (Beier, 2016; Hanscom & Cleveland, 2017; Hertel & Zacher, 2018). For example, Zabel and Baltes (2016) suggested that organizational age measures such as job tenure or career stage may be more relevant when studying the effectiveness of workplace interventions. Finally, the concept of successful aging at work has received particular attention in the last few years (see, for example, Kooij, 2015; Zacher, 2015), and we encourage further activity to reach a common operational definition, and to explore its incorporation in empirical studies of aging and work performance.

Expanding the discussion of aging and job performance to include the broader organizational context, we discussed several emerging concepts important for sustaining the performance of older workers. Including concepts such as employability, work ability, and sustainability emphasize maintaining or improving productivity and successful aging at work over time. As these types of topics move to the mainstream of discussion and research in the work and aging literature, we expect that innovative perspectives will continue to emerge and enrich the broader conversation around work and aging. For example, concepts such as work ability and successful aging at work emphasize the notion of positive worker adjustment (e.g., health, competencies, attitudes, and motivation) over time, and it might be wise to include performance and engagement indicators of positive adaptation (an idea suggested by Rudolph, De Lange, & Van der Heijden, 2015).

Implications for Practice

While some solid empirical research has begun to provide insight into useful HR strategies available to organizations for sustaining the job performance of older workers, it seems clear that different approaches and work policies will be necessary to take full advantage of the talents of these workers moving into later career stages. In addition, as noted by Truxillo et al. (2015), more empirical work is needed to identity not only what HR programs are most successful for different situations and age groups, but why they are more or less effective.

Sustainable career management involves career policies that facilitate the ability of the workforce in working longer, more effectively, and efficiently in ways that contribute to individual and organizational success. It also involves a shared responsibility between employers and employees. As suggested by

De Vos, Dujardin, Gielens, and Meyers (2016), such management necessitates using processes and practices that support the development of individuals along a path of experiences and jobs.

One promising strategy for building and sustaining the competencies of employees and organizations is to implement formalized career pathways systems; that is, a structured HR management system that facilitates the growth and advancement of employees across work positions or roles over the span of their work history in an organization (Hedge & Rineer, 2017). While individual employees can and should take an active role in their career development, they can really only continue to age successfully at work if their organizations' systems are structured in a way that support them in reaching their goals. Employees' access to training strongly decreases with age, with lower-performing older workers receiving even less training opportunities than their higher-performing counterparts (Lazazzara, Karpinska, & Henkens, 2013). A training and development program that is informed by a structured career pathways system is more likely to identify key knowledge and skills gaps and promote growth opportunities for later-career individuals.

As older workers become a significantly larger portion of the workforce, organizations must retain the special talents, extensive knowledge, and relevant experience of older workers in order to stay competitive. Kulik, Ryan, Harper, and George (2014) argue that an aging population could open the door to creating workplaces that are more inclusive and provide employees greater flexibility to achieve work–life balance.

References

Armstrong-Stassen, M. (2008). Organizational practices and the post-retirement employment experience of older workers. *Human Resource Management Journal, 18*, 36–53.

Armstrong-Stassen, M., & Ursel, N. D. (2009). Perceived organizational support, career satisfaction, and the retention of older workers. *Journal of Occupational and Organizational Psychology, 82*, 201–220.

Artistico, D., Cervone, D., & Pezzuti, L. (2003). Perceived self-efficacy and everyday problem solving among young and older adults. *Psychology and Aging, 18*, 68–79.

Avolio, B. J., Waldman, D. A., & McDaniel, M. A. (1990). Age and work performance in nonmanagerial jobs: The effects of experience and occupation type. *Academy of Management Journal, 32*, 407–422.

Avolio, B. J., & Waldman, D. A. (1994). Variations in cognitive, perceptual, and psychomotor abilities across the working life span: Examining the effects of race, sex, experience, education, and occupational type. *Psychology and Aging, 9*, 430–442.

Bal, M., & Jansen, P. G. W. (2016). Workplace flexibility across the lifespan. In R. Buckley, J. Halbesleben, & A. Wheeler (Eds.), *Research in Personnel and Human Resources Management* (Vol. 34, pp. 43–99). Bingley, UK: Emerald Group Publishing.

Bal, P. M., De Jong, S. B., Jansen, P. G. W., & Bakker, A. B. (2012). Motivating employees to work beyond retirement: A multi-level study of the role of I-deals and unit climate. *Journal of Management Studies, 49*, 306–331.

Beier, M. (2015). The aging workforce and the demands of work in the 21st century. In L. M. Finkelstein, D. M. Truxillo, F. Fraccaroli, & R. Kanfer (Eds.), *Facing the challenges of a multi-age workforce: A use-inspired approach* (pp. 108–133). New York: Routledge.

Beier, M. E. (2016). The aging workforce and the demands of work in the 21st century. In L. M Finkelstein, D. M Truxillo, F. Fraccaroli, & R. Kanfer (Eds.), *Facing the Challenges of a multi-age workforce: A use-inspired approach,* pp. 108–133. New York: Routledge.

Beier, M. E., Teachout, M. S., & Cox, C. B. (2012). The training and development of an aging workforce. In J. W. Hedge & W. C. Borman (Eds.), *The Oxford handbook of work and aging* (pp. 436–453). New York: Oxford University Press.

Berry, C. M., Carpenter, N. C., & Barratt, C. L. (2012). Do other-reports of counterproductive work behavior provide an incremental contribution over self-reports? A meta-analytic comparison. *Journal of Applied Psychology, 97,* 613–636.

Berry, C. M, Ones, D. S., & Sackett, P. R. (2007). Interpersonal deviance, organizational deviance, and their common correlates: A review and meta-analysis. *Journal of Applied Psychology, 92,* 410–424.

Bohlmann, C., Rudolph, C. W., and Zacher, H. (2017). Methodological recommendations to move research on work and aging forward. *Work, Aging & Retirement.* Advance online publication. doi.org/10.1093/workar/wax023.

Borman, W. C., Buck, D. E., Hanson, M. A., Motowidlo, S. J., Stark, S., & Drasgow, F. (2001). An examination of the comparative reliability, validity, and accuracy of performance ratings made using computerized adaptive rating scales. *Journal of Applied Psychology, 86,* 965–973.

Borman, W. C., Grossman, M., Bryant, R. H., & Dorio, J. (2017). The measurement of task performance as criteria in selection research second edition. In J. L. Farr & N. Tippins (Eds.), *Handbook of employee selection second edition* (pp. 429–447). New York: Psychology Press.

Borman, W. C., & Motowidlo, S. M. (1993). Expanding the criterion domain to include elements of contextual performance. In N. Schmitt & W. C. Borman (Eds.), *Personnel selection* (pp. 71–98). San Francisco: Jossey Bass.

Borman, W. C. Penner, L. A., Allen, T. D., & Motowidlo, S. J. (2001). Personality predictors of citizenship performance. *International Journal of Selection and Assessment, 9,* 52–69.

Bosma, H., Van Boxtel, M. P. J., Ponds, R. W. H. M., Jelicic, M., Houx, P. S. H., Metsemakers, J., & Jolles, J. (2002). Engaged lifestyle and cognitive function in middle and old-aged, non-demented persons: A reciprocal association? *Journal for the German Society of Gerontology and Geriatrics, 35,* 575–581.

Bowen, D. E., & Schneider, B. (1988). Services marketing and management: Implications for Organizational Behavior. In B. M. Staw & L. L. Cummings (Eds.), *Research in organizational behavior* (Vol. 10, pp. 43–80). Greenwich, CT: JAI.

Callahan, C. M. (1998). *An examination of four occupational moderators of age-job performance relationship* (unpublished dissertation). University of Akron. Akron, Ohio.

Campbell, J. P., McCloy, R. A., Oppler, S. H., & Sager, C. E. (1993). A theory of performance. In H. Schmitt & W. C. Borman (Eds.). *Personnel selection in organizations* (pp. 35–70). San Francisco, CA: Jossey-Bass.

Charness, N., & Bosman, E. (1990). Expertise and aging: Life in the lab. In T. H. Hess (Ed.), *Aging and cognition: Knowledge organization and utilization* (pp. 343–385). Amsterdam, the Netherlands: North-Holland.

Charness, N., & Tuffiash, M. (2008). The role of expertise research and human factors in capturing, explaining, and producing superior performance. *Human Factors, 50*, 427–432.

Cleveland, J. N., & Hanscom, M. (2017). What is old at work? Moving past chronological age. In E. Parry & J. McCarthy (Eds.), *The Palgrave handbook of age diversity and work* (pp. 17–46). London: Palgrave Macmillan.

Cleveland, J. N., & Lim, A. S. (2007). Employee age and performance in organizations. In K. S. Shultz & G. A. Adams (Eds.), *Aging and work in the 21st century* (pp. 109–137). Mahwah, NJ: Lawrence Erlbaum.

Costa, P. T., & McCrae, R. R. (1988). Personality in adulthood: A six-year longitudinal study of self-reports and spouse ratings on the NEO Personality Inventory. *Journal of Personality and Social Psychology, 54*, 853–863.

Costa, G., & Sartori, S. (2007). Ageing, working hours and work ability. *Ergonomics, 50*, 1914–1930.

Czaja, S. J., & Sharit, J. (1993). Age differences in the performance of computer-based work. *Psychology and Aging, 8*, 59–67.

De Cuyper, N., Mäkikangas, A., Kinnunen, U., Mauno, S., & De Witte, H. (2012). Cross-lagged associations between perceived external employability, job insecurity, and exhaustion: Testing gain and loss spirals according to the Conservation of Resources Theory. *Journal of Organizational Behavior, 33*, 770–788.

De Lange, A. H., Kooij, D. T. A. M., & Van der Heijden, B. I. J. M. (2015). Human resource management and sustainability at work across the lifespan: An integrative perspective. In L. M. Finkelstein, D. M. Truxillo, F. Fraccaroli, & R. Kanfer (Eds.), *Facing the challenges of a multi-age workforce: A use-inspired approach* (pp. 50–79). New York: Routledge.

De Vos, A., Dujardin, J.-M., Gielens, T., & Meyers, C. (2016). *Developing sustainable careers across the lifecourse*. Cham, Switzerland: Springer.

Forrier, A., & Sels, L. (2003). The concept employability: A complex mosaic. *International Journal of Human Resources Development and Management, 3*, 102–124.

Forrier, A., Verbruggen, M., & De Cuyper, N. (2015). Integrating different notions of employability in a dynamic chain: The relationship between job transitions, movement capital and perceived employability. *Journal of Vocational Behavior, 89*, 56–64.

Foster, L. F., & Mayhorn, C. B. (2012). Aging workers and technology. In J. W. Hedge & W. C. Borman (Eds.), *The Oxford handbook of work and aging* (pp. 341–361). New York: Oxford University Press.

Goldberg, L. R. (1993). The structure of phenotypic personality traits. *American Psychologist, 48*, 26–34.

Gribbin, K., Schaie, K. W., & Parham, I. A. (1980). Complexity of life style and maintenance of intellectual abilities. *Journal of Social Issues, 36*, 47–61.

Hall, D. T., & Mirvis, P. H. (1995). The new career contract: Developing the whole person at midlife and beyond. *Journal of Vocational Psychology, 47*, 269–289.

Hanscom, M. E., & Cleveland, J. N. (2017). The influence of successful aging at work upon simulated performance decisions. *Work, Aging and Retirement*. Advance online publication. doi:10.1093/workar/wax021.

Hedge, J. W., & Borman, W. C. (2012). Work and aging. In S. W. J. Koslowski (Ed.), *The Oxford handbook of organizational psychology* (Vol. 2, pp. 1245–1283). New York: Oxford University Press.

Hedge, J. W., & Rineer, J. R. (2017). *Improving career development opportunities through rigorous career pathways research* (RTI Press Publication No. OP-0037). Research Triangle Park: NC: RTI Press.

Hedge, J. W., Borman, W., & Lammlein, S. L. (2006). *The aging workforce: Realities, myths, and implications for organizations.* Washington, DC: APA Books.

Helson, R., Jones, C., & Kwan, V. S. Y. (2002). Personality change in adulthood: Hierarchical liner modeling analyses of two longitudinal samples. *Journal of Personality and Social Psychology, 83*, 752–766.

Hertel, G., & Zacher, H. (2018). Managing the aging workforce. In D. S. Ones, N. Anderson, C. Viswesvaran, & H. K. Sinangil (Eds.), *The SAGE handbook of industrial, work and organizational psychology* (2nd ed., Vol. 3, pp. 396–428). Thousand Oaks, CA: Sage.

Hesketh, B., & Neal, A. (1999). Technology and performance. In D. R. Ilgen & D. P. Pulakos (Eds.), *The changing nature of performance: Implications for staffing, motivation and development* (pp. 21–55). San Francisco: Jossey-Bass.

Hesketh, B., Allworth, E., & Considine, G. (1996). *Preliminary report on phase one of the selection project for the Hilton Hotel.* Unpublished paper, Department of Psychology, Macquarie University, Sydney, Australia.

Horton, S., Baker, J., & Shorer, J. (2008). Expertise and aging: Maintaining skills throughout the lifespan. *European Review of Aging and Physical Activity, 5*, 89–96.

Huang, J. L., Ryan, A. M., Zabel, K. L., & Palmer, A. (2004). Personality and adaptive performance at work. *Journal of Applied Psychology, 99*, 162–179.

Ilmarinen, J. (2009). Work ability: A comprehensive concept for occupational health research and prevention. *Scandinavian Journal of Work, Environment & Health, 35*, 1–5.

Ilmarinen, J., & Ilmarinen, V. (2015). Aging and work ability. In L. Finkelstein, D. M. Truxillo, F. Fraccaroli, & R. Kanfer (Eds.), *Facing the challenges of a multi-age workforce: A use-inspired approach* (pp. 177–207). New York: Routledge.

Kanfer, R., & Ackerman, P. L. (2004). Aging, adult development and work motivation. *Academy of Management Review, 29*, 440–458.

Kirves, K., Kinnunen, U., De Cuyper, N., & Mäkikangas A. (2014). Trajectories of perceived employability and their associations with well-being at work: A three-wave study. *Journal of Personnel Psychology, 13*, 46–57.

Kooij, D. T. (2015). Successful aging at work: The active role of employees. *Work, Aging and Retirement, 1*, 309–319.

Kooij, D. T. A. M., De Lange, A. H., Jansen, P. G. W., & Dikkers, J. S. E. (2008). Older workers' motivation to continue to work: Five meanings of age. *Journal of Managerial Psychology, 23*, 364–394.

Kooij, D. T. A. M., De Lange, A. H., Jansen, P. G. W., Kanfer, R., & Dikkers, J. S. E. (2011). Age and work-related motives: Results of a meta-analysis. *Journal of Organizational Behavior, 32*, 197–225.

Kooij, D. T. A. M., Jansen, P. G. W., Dikkers, J. S. E., & De Lange, A. H. (2010). The influence of age on the associations between HR practices and both affective commitment and job satisfaction: A meta-analysis. *Journal of Organizational Behavior, 31*, 1111–1136.

Kooij, D. T., Jansen, P. G., Dikkers, J. S., & De Lange, A. H. (2014). Managing aging workers: A mixed methods study on bundles of HR practices for aging workers. *The International Journal of Human Resource Management, 25*, 2192–2212.

Kulik, C. T., Ryan, S., Harper, S., & George, G. (2014). From the editors: Aging populations and management. *Academy of Management Journal, 57*, 929–935.

Lazazzara, A., Karpinska, K., & Henkens, K. (2013). What factors influence training opportunities for older workers? Three factorial surveys exploring the attitudes of HR professionals. *The International Journal of Human Resource Management, 24*, 2154–2172.

Maertens, J. A., Putter, S. E., Chen, P. Y., Diehl, M., & Huang, Y.-H. (2012). Physical capabilities and occupational health of older workers. In J. W. Hedge & W. C. Borman (Eds.), *The Oxford handbook of work and aging*. New York: Oxford University Press.

Marcus, B., Taylor, O. A., Hastings, S. B., Sturn, A., and Weigelt, O. (2016). She structure of counterproductive behavior: A review, structural meta-analysis, and a primary study. *Journal of Management, 42*, 203–233.

Masunaga, H., & Horn, J. L. (2001). Expertise and age-related changes in components of intelligence. *Psychology and Aging, 16*, 293–311.

McArdle, J. J., Ferrer-Czaja, E., Hamagand, F., & Woodcock, R. W. (2002). Comparative longitudinal structural analyses of the growth and decline of multiple intellectual abilities over the life span. *Developmental Psychology, 38*, 115–142.

McDaniel, M. A., Pesta, B. J., & Banks, G. C. (2012). Job performance and the aging worker. In J. W. Hedge & W. C. Borman (Eds.), *The Oxford Handbook of work and aging* (pp. 280–297). New York: Oxford University Press.

McEvoy, G. M., & Cascio, W. F. (1989). Cumulative evidence of the relationship between employee age and job performance. *Journal of Applied Psychology, 74*, 11–17.

McGonagle, A., Fisher, G. G., Barnes-Farrell, J. L., & Grosch, J. (2015). Individual and work factors related to perceived work ability and labor force outcomes. *Journal of Applied Psychology, 100*, 376–398.

Nauta, A., Van Vianen, A., Van der Heijden, B., Van Dam, K., & Willemsen, M. (2009). Understanding the factors that promote employability orientation: The impact of employability culture, career satisfaction, and role breadth self-efficacy. *Journal of Occupational and Organizational Psychology, 82*, 233–251.

Ng, T. W. H., & Feldman, D. C. (2008). The relationship of age to ten dimensions of job performance. *Journal of Applied Psychology, 93*, 392–423.

Olson, D. A., & Shultz, K. S. (in press). Lifespan perspective on successful aging at work. In B. Baltes, C. Rudolph, & H. Zacher (Eds.), *Work across the lifespan*. New York: Elsevier.

Park, D. C. (1994). Aging, cognition, and work. *Human Performance, 7*, 181–205.

Profili, S., Sammarra, A., & Innocenti, L. (2016). Can age make a difference? A moderated model of altruistic organizational counterproductive behavior antecedent. *International Journal of Business Science and Applied Management, 11*, 18–31.

Profili, S., Sammarra, A., & Innocenti, L. (2017). Exploring organizational citizenship behavior through the lens of age. *International Journal of Business Administration, 8*, 22–33.

Pulakos, E. D., Arad, S., Donovan, M. A., & Plamondon, K. E. (2000). Adaptability in the workplace: Development of a taxonomy of adaptive performance. *Journal of Applied Psychology, 55*, 612–624.

Pulakos, E. D., Schmitt, N., Dorsey, D. W., Arad, S., Hedge, J. W., & Borman, W. C. (2002). Predicting adaptive performance: Further tests of a model of adaptability. *Human Performance, 15*, 299–323.

Rhodes. S. R. (1983). Age-related differences in work attitudes and behaviors: A review and conceptual analysis. *Psychological Bulletin, 93*, 328–367.

Roberts, B. W., Walton, K. E., & Viechtbauer, W. (2006). Patterns of mean-level change in personality traits across the life course: A meta-analysis of longitudinal studies. *Psychological Bulletin, 132*, 1–25.

Robinson, S. L., Bennett, R. J. (1995). A typology of deviant workplace behaviors: A multidimensional scaling study. *Academy of Management Journal, 38*, 555–572.

Rudolph, C., De Lange, A. H., & Van der Heijden, B. I. J. M. (2015). Adjustment processes in bridge employment: Where we are and need to go. In P. Bal, T. Kooij & D. Rousseau (Eds.), *Aging workers and the employment relationship* (pp. 221–242). New York: Springer.

Sackett, P. R., & DeVore, C. J. (2001). Counterproductive behaviors at work. In: N. Anderson, D. Ones, H. Sinangil, & C. Viswesvaran (Eds.), *Handbook of industrial, work, and organizational psychology* (pp. 145–164). London: Sage Publications.

Salgado, J. F. (2002). The Big Five personality dimensions and counterproductive behaviors. *International Journal of Selection and Assessment, 10,* 117–125.

Salthouse, T. (2012). Consequences of age-related cognitive declines. *Annual Review of Psychology, 63,* 201–226. http://doi.org/10.1146/annurev-psych-120710-100328.

Schaie, K. W. (1994). The course of adult intellectual development. *American Psychologist, 49,* 304–313.

Schooler, C., Caplan, L., & Oates, G. 1998. "Aging and work: An overview." In K. W. Schaie & C. Schooler (Eds.), *Impact of work on older adults* (pp. 1–19). New York: Springer.

Schwall, A. R. (2012). Defining age and using age-relevant constructs. In J. W. Hedge & W. C. Borman (Eds.), *The Oxford handbook of work and aging* (pp. 169–186). New York: Oxford University Press.

Sharit, J., & Czaja, S. J. (2012). Job design and redesign for older workers. In J. W. Hedge & W. C. Borman (Eds.), *The Oxford handbook of work and aging* (pp. 454–482). New York: Oxford University Press.

Simpson, P. A., Greller, M. M., & Stroh, L. K. (2002). Variations in human capital investment activity by age. *Journal of Vocational behavior, 61,* 109–138.

Soto, C. J., John, O. P., Gosling, S. D., & Potter, J. (2011). Age differences in personality traits from 10 to 65: Big Five domains and facets in a large cross-sectional sample. *Journal of Personality and Social Psychology, 100,* 330–348.

Springer. A. B. (1998). Career trajectories and the older worker. In K. W. Schaie & C. Schooler (Eds.), *Impact of work on older adults* (pp. 207–234). New York: Springer.

Sturman, M. C. (2003). Searching for the inverted U-shaped relationship between time and performance: Meta-analyses of the experience/performance, tenure/performance, and age/performance relationships. *Journal of Management, 29,* 609–640.

Thornton, W. J. 1., & Dumke, H. A. (2005). Age differences in everyday problem-solving and decision-making effectiveness: A meta-analytic review. *Psychology and Aging, 20,* 85–99.

Tishman, F., Van Looy, S., & Bruyère, S. (2012). *Employer strategies for responding to an aging workforce.* Prepared for the NTAR Leadership Center for submission to the Office of Disability Employment Policy, US Department of Labor.

Truxillo, D. M., Cadiz, D. M., & Hammer, L. B. (2015). Supporting the aging workforce: A research review and recommendations for workplace intervention research. *Annual Review of Organizational Psychology and Organizational Behavior, 2,* 351–381.

van Dam, K., van Vuuren, T., & Kemps, S. (2017). Sustainable employment: The importance of intrinsically valuable work and an age-supportive climate. *The International Journal of Human Resource Management, 28,* 2449–2472.

Veld, M., Semeijn, J. H., & van Vuuren, T. (2015). Enhancing perceived employability. *Personnel Review, 44,* 866–882.

Waldman, D. A., & Avolio, B. J. (1986). A meta-analysis of age differences in job performance. *Journal of Applied Psychology, 71,* 33–38.

Warr, P., & Birdi, K. (1998). Employee age and voluntary development activity. *International Journal of Training and Development, 2,* 190–204.

Williams, L. J., & Anderson, S. E. (1991). Job satisfaction and organizational commitment as predictors of organizational citizenship and in-role behaviors. *Journal of Management, 17,* 601–617.

Wolfson, N., Cavanagh, T., & Kraiger, K. (2014). Older adults and technology-based instruction: Optimizing learning outcomes and transfer. *Academy of Management: Learning and Education, 13,* 26–44.

Zabel, K. L., & Baltes, B. B. (2016). Workplace intervention effectiveness across the lifespan. In L. Finkelstein, D. Truxillo, F. Fraccaroli, & R. Kanfer (Eds.). *Facing the challenges of a multi-age workforce: A use-inspired approach* (pp. 284–311). New York: Routledge.

Zacher, H. (2015). Successful aging at work. *Work, Aging and Retirement, 1,* 4–25.

7

AGE(ING) AND WORK ATTITUDES

Janet L. Barnes-Farrell, Gretchen A. Petery, Jeanette N. Cleveland, and Russell A. Matthews

How people feel about the work they do, the jobs they hold, the people they work with, and the organizations that employ them represent important phenomena in any consideration of how employees respond to their work situations. Work attitudes have been the topic of literally thousands of studies in the fields of industrial and organizational psychology, organizational behavior, and related behavioral science disciplines. It is also well understood that individual characteristics of workers as well as features of their jobs, working conditions, and the larger sphere in which their work lives operate all contribute to such feelings.

A worker's age represents a key individual characteristic that has the potential to shape the work experiences and conditions to which an individual will be exposed (e.g., the nature of work assignments, opportunities for advancement, and rewards available to a worker). Affective reactions to work and features of the work environment may likewise be linked to age. The consistent growth of the older segments of our workforce and the development of new organizational structures and career/retirement patterns place increased emphasis on the importance of understanding when and how age and age-related processes are related to work attitudes. In particular, a clearer understanding of the attitudes and motives of older workers can help to guide management practices and organizational policy aimed at meeting the needs of an aging workforce and encouraging older workers to remain engaged and active members of the workforce.

In the first edition of this book, Barnes-Farrell and Matthews (2007) concluded their chapter with some suggestions for future research into age and attitudes to fill gaps in our understanding of how worker age contributes to work attitudes and motivation processes. A decade later, we are pleased to see that some of those questions and gaps have begun to receive attention. We have tried to reflect this progress in the current chapter, in which we summarize key features of published evidence regarding the relationship of worker age with the work attitudes employees espouse and their motivation to invest themselves in their jobs, careers, and organizations. This is accompanied by a consideration of several functional and theoretical explanations for age differences in worker affective reactions toward their work situations. We also provide an overview of research questions and methodological considerations that should be addressed for a fuller understanding of how our aging workforce responds to their work situations.

Work Attitudes

Our first goal is to examine how worker age is related to beliefs and attitudes that workers develop regarding their jobs, their work organizations, and their careers. These include attitudes such as job satisfaction, job involvement, and organizational commitment, as well as attitudes toward work processes such as skill development and technological change, and attitudes toward other age-relevant issues such as retirement.

Age and Job Satisfaction

Overall Job Satisfaction

One of the most consistently reported findings regarding age and work attitudes is a positive relationship between worker age and overall job satisfaction. The first major review of work attitudes as they relate to worker age, published by Rhodes in 1983, summarized the results of 60 studies conducted between 1957 and 1982 that included bivariate or multivariate analyses of this relationship. Rhodes concluded that, in general, older workers report more positive attitudes toward their jobs than younger workers do, citing that "...there is overwhelming evidence that overall job satisfaction is positively associated with age" (Rhodes, 1983, p. 331).

Since the publication of that review, a number of studies have provided additional evidence consistent with this broad-brush statement about the relationship between worker age and overall job satisfaction. Much of this work is summarized in a meta-analytic review of evidence regarding the relationship between age and work attitudes, which likewise reported a positive relationship between worker age and overall job satisfaction, based on an accumulated set of 169 studies (Ng & Feldman, 2010). Furthermore, although most of the research addressing this issue has been conducted in the United States and western European countries, the positive age–job satisfaction relationship has been observed in a variety of cultural settings. Specifically, similar findings have been reported in studies conducted in China (Siu, Spector, Cooper, & Donald, 2001), Japan (Kalleberg & Loscocco, 1983), and Turkey (Nichols, Sugur, & Tasiran, 2003). However, it should be pointed out that this finding, while typical, is by no means uniform. For example, Rhodes indicated that several individual studies in her review reported no significant relationship between age and overall job satisfaction, or they reported age–job satisfaction relationships that were limited to particular sub-samples in the study. Further, a number of studies published after the Rhodes review have reported that they did not observe a reliable relationship between worker age and job satisfaction. These have included studies based on samples of full-time white-collar workers (Cleveland & Shore, 1992; Glisson & Durick, 1988; Spreitzer, Kizilos, & Nason, 1997), blue-collar workers (Pond & Geyer, 1991), and part-time workers (Feldman, Doerpinghaus, & Turnley, 1995; Kaye, Alexander, & Kauffman, 1999). Other studies only find the positive relationship with age for those in relatively attractive work situations (cf. Riordan, Griffith, & Weatherly, 2003).

Taken together, findings pertinent to aging and job satisfaction suggest that although the *general* relationship between worker age and overall job satisfaction may be positive, there is much more to the story. In the following sections we examine some of what is known and speculated about the nature of that story. Then we will turn to a consideration of what is known about other relevant work attitudes.

Facet Satisfaction

A number of studies that directly or indirectly studied the relationship between age and job satisfaction have moved beyond assessments of global satisfaction to examine satisfaction with various aspects of work. From the perspective of age relationships, the most frequent distinction has been between those aspects of job satisfaction that are concerned with intrinsic satisfactions (e.g., the meaningfulness of work) and those that are primarily concerned with extrinsic satisfactions (e.g., pay and promotions). A reliable positive relationship between age and intrinsic work satisfaction (the meaningfulness of work) has been demonstrated across a variety of samples and occupational groups (Rhodes, 1983; Ng & Feldman, 2010). Satisfaction with this aspect of work seems to increase with age up until the period immediately preceding retirement (Bourne, 1982). However, satisfaction with extrinsic facets of work, such as pay and promotions, does not show the same consistent pattern of results (Rhodes, 1983; Kacmar & Ferris, 1989; Ng & Feldman, 2010). As such, it has been argued that the frequently reported positive associations between age and job satisfaction are largely driven by reactions to intrinsically satisfying aspects of work and by satisfaction with "people" aspects of work such as supervisor satisfaction (Ng & Feldman, 2010).

What is the Form of the Relationship between Age and Job Satisfaction?

Although it has typically been assessed and reported as a positive linear relationship, some researchers have argued that the age–satisfaction relationship may be nonlinear in form. Herzberg and colleagues proposed many years ago that the relationship between age and job satisfaction was U-shaped (Herzberg, Mausner, Peterson, & Capwell, 1957). Examples of research that supports this position include a study conducted by Kacmar and Ferris (1989), which argued that the relationship between age and satisfaction with intrinsic and extrinsic aspects of one's job takes different forms. Consistent with their theorizing, they found a U-shaped relationship between age and extrinsic job satisfaction, and the usual positive linear relationship between age and intrinsic satisfaction. In addition, a large-scale study of British workers carefully examined the U-shaped hypothesis. Clark, Oswald, and Warr (1996) analyzed data from a sample of over 5000 employed individuals who participated in the 1991 wave of the British Household Panel Study. They found robust evidence consistent with a U-shaped relationship between worker age and job satisfaction. When they examined the pattern of job satisfaction across the age span, they found a clear pattern of satisfaction that initially declined, bottoming out at about age 31, then increased in a fairly linear fashion until one's early 60s. After controlling for a total of 80 potential covariates and controlling for general wellbeing, the U-shaped relationship remained, although the age at which job satisfaction was at a minimum shifted to age 36.

Rather than a direct relationship between age and work attitudes, other research has reported that age influences the strength of relationships between features of the work environment and job satisfaction. For example, Pond and Geyer (1987, 1991) proposed that the perceived availability of work alternatives is less important to older workers, so there should be only a weak relationship between perceived work alternatives and job satisfaction for this group. On the other hand, younger workers should report lower job satisfaction when they are aware that there are work alternatives available to them. In a pair of studies conducted with a white collar sample and a blue collar sample, respectively, they found that age was unrelated to job satisfaction, but it did moderate the negative relationship between perceived work alternatives and job satisfaction as they hypothesized.

In a similar vein, Kooij and colleagues reported the results of a meta-analysis in which they tested the hypothesis that age would strengthen the relationship of high maintenance HR practices (which should be of particular interest to older workers) with job satisfaction and affective commitment and weaken the relationship of high development HR practices with these work attitudes (Kooij, Jansen, Dikkers, & De Lange, 2010). Likewise, Innocenti, Profili and Sammarra (2012) reported that worker age moderates relationships between HR development practices and positive work attitudes such as job satisfaction and affective commitment; consistent with Kooij et al.'s findings, weaker (and even negative) relationships were observed for older employees.

Retirement as a Psychological Option for Older Workers: Implications for Job Satisfaction

The shift to thinking about retirement as an alternative role also represents a unique feature of the work-lives of older workers that has implications for how they evaluate their jobs. As workers approach the timeframe when retirement becomes a socially acceptable and economically viable alternative, their evaluation of the work role is carried out in the context of concomitant evaluations of the desirability of the retirement role (Barnes-Farrell, 2003). Satisfaction with the work role may be partly a function of whether it serves to hinder movement to a more desired role (the *pull* of an attractive retirement role) or allows one to avoid a less desirable role (the *push* force associated with negative attitudes toward retirement).

Retirement researchers report that a sense of personal control over the decision to work or retire is of primary importance to the wellbeing of older adults; this seems to be more important than whether they are working or retired (Heckhausen & Schulz, 1995; Isaksson & Johansson, 2000; Shultz, Morton, & Weckerle, 1998). As such, job satisfaction for employed older workers may be partly a function of the voluntariness of their employment status. Moreover, attitudes toward early retirement appear to be related to age-related social categories with which employees identify, such as the category of "older worker." Distinct from chronological age, individuals who self-categorize themselves as older workers report less commitment to career development and a stronger desire to retire early (Desmette & Gaillard, 2008). The recent development and use of alternative age assessment and measures in age/work research is a critical contribution for our understanding of aging and work attitudes. In a section later in this chapter, we will briefly discuss the importance of this emerging research.

In another interesting study, Ekerdt and DeViney (1993) suggest that the increasing salience of retirement as a contextual feature may influence the relationship between age and job satisfaction. They propose that attitudes toward work may become more positive with age, in part, due to gravitation to more satisfying positions and, in part, due to developmental processes that allow older workers to re-evaluate what they expect from their work situations. Further, they argue that a second ongoing and perhaps opposite process for older workers is the gradual increase in salience of "time remaining" at work. Specifically, as workers approach planned retirement dates, they begin the process of disengaging from the workplace, and this includes increasingly harsh assessments of their work conditions. Based on data from a large sample of male workers ages 50–69 (drawn from the US Veteran's Administration Normative Aging Study) who were not retired yet approaching a fixed retirement, their analyses demonstrated that as participants grew older (ignoring planned retirement age), job attitudes became more positive. Yet as they came closer to retirement age (ignoring age), job attitudes became more negative. Because retirement age has become a more fluid concept, these findings suggest that the interplay between age and job attitudes is likely to be further complicated by the attention that workers give to their plans to shift from the work role to the retirement role.

Another more recent study that likewise focuses on the concept of "time remaining" used data from the Sax Institute 45 and Up Study in Australia to look at the impact of chronological age (as a proxy for time remaining until retirement) on the relationship between career adaptability and job satisfaction (Zacher & Griffin, 2015). In this older worker sample, they found that the positive relationship between career adaptability and job satisfaction was weaker for those who were approaching retirement age than it was for those who were relatively distant from retirement age. Studies of "time remaining" highlight an important issue that will be taken up more fully in later sections of this chapter – i.e., that alternate measures of age can sometimes lead to important new insights. That is, rather than looking solely at a worker's age, we might look at time until expected retirement as a type of age measure, particularly since the literature reviewed here suggests that it is being close to retirement and not age per se that might trigger particular reactions to the job. Literature we review in later sections shows, similarly, that measures of how old you feel, or how old you see yourself in comparison with others can predict a number of criteria that are not fully accounted for by chronological age alone.

Cognitive and Affective Attitudes towards Work: Job Involvement, Organizational Commitment, and Attitudes towards Change and Development

Job Involvement and Organizational Commitment

Job satisfaction is but one of an array of important attitudes that workers develop regarding aspects of work. Two work-related attitudes that have received significant attention in recent years as important contributors to valued work behaviors are job involvement and organizational commitment. In her review 35 years ago, Rhodes (1983) concluded that there was evidence supporting a positive relationship between age and job involvement and a somewhat less consistent, positive relationship between age and organizational commitment. More recently, the meta-analysis conducted by Ng and Feldman (2010) reported a moderate relationship between age and job involvement; positive relationships of age with affective and normative commitment; and no significant relationship with continuance commitment.

As is true with much of the research that provides the basis for the well-known relationship between age and job satisfaction, many studies concerned with attitudes such as job involvement and organizational commitment measure chronological age and include it as a statistical control in analyses. Studies that examine age as a focal variable are much less common, but they offer some insight into the ways that investment in one's job or one's organization might be associated with worker age. For example, Finegold, Mohrman, and Spreitzer (2002) investigated the sources of organizational commitment for workers of different ages. In a large multi-organization sample of technical workers, they found that older workers exhibited higher levels of organizational commitment than younger workers. When they investigated the sources of commitment, results showed that commitment was driven more by job security issues than anything else for older workers; for younger workers, satisfaction with work–life balance was the primary predictor of levels of organizational commitment. In a related vein, Kacmar and her colleagues reasoned that age should be positively correlated with organizational commitment because older workers have fewer alternatives available to them and generally longer investments in their employing organizations. However, among hospitality managers, age was not a significant predictor of any aspect of organizational commitment (Kacmar, Carlson, & Brymer, 1999).

Finally, Lorence (1987) examined data from panels of workers who participated in the Quality of Employment surveys conducted in the US during 1972–1973 and 1977. He made the distinction between labor force involvement in general and psychological involvement with a particular job. He concluded that labor force involvement is positively associated with age and is best accounted for by developmental explanations (e.g., changes in motivational pressures over time) while psychological involvement with a particular job seems to be driven more strongly by cohort differences and differences in job characteristics for workers of different ages (i.e., differences in expectations and job characteristics for different generations).

Attitudes toward Change and Development

Organizations today are characterized by constant change including unexpected work requirement changes, the routine update of knowledge and skills, and significant employment changes. Positive attitudes toward change, whether it be organizational change, adapting to new technology, or acquiring new skills may be important to workers and organizations that want to succeed in this kind of environment. Although most of us are familiar with stereotypes about older workers' general unwillingness to engage in change (Ng & Feldman, 2010), a few empirical studies have reported data relevant to workers' attitudes toward personal and organizational change.

Self-Efficacy Beliefs and Developmental Changes

Maurer (2001) proposed a model of career-relevant development that explicitly considers the role that age plays in attitudes toward development and motivation to engage in development activities. Briefly, he theorizes that age will be negatively associated with important antecedents to the development of self-efficacy beliefs for development – mastery experiences, vicarious experiences, persuasion, and physiological influences – resulting in reduced levels of self-efficacy for development. This, in turn, affects attitudes toward development and intention to engage in development activities. An empirical study testing this model supported the basic premises of the model (Maurer, Weiss, & Barbeite, 2003). The authors noted that age effects were small, yet the findings point to the value of developing interventions aimed at older workers' access to the kinds of experiences that are likely to enhance their sense of self-efficacy for development.

Organizational Changes: Technology, Teams, and Significant Employment Changes

As the structure of jobs changes, it is important to understand the extent to which age affects reactions to features of jobs that are modified. For example, a common modification of many jobs is the increasing integration of technology to perform specific job tasks. Some evidence relevant to this issue is provided by Morris and Venkatesh (2000), who investigated user reactions and technology usage behavior for workers who were being introduced to new software. They found that although age was negatively associated with attitudes toward technology adoption, younger workers' technology usage behaviors were actually more strongly influenced by their attitudes than were older workers' behaviors. In contrast, more recent work (Elias, Smith, & Barney, 2012) examined the role of worker age as a moderator of relationships between attitude towards technology and outcomes such as job satisfaction and work motivation. They found that a positive attitude toward technology was more strongly linked to both intrinsic and extrinsic motivation for older workers than it was for younger workers. Finally, the introduction of self-managing team structures for accomplishing work tasks is another common change to work design that has the potential for differential reactions among younger and older workers. A study of employee age and perceptions of work in self-managing and traditional work groups found that older workers reacted positively to self-managing work groups (Hayslip et al., 1996).

In a study of Canadian workers' reactions to plant closures, Mazerolle and Gangaram (1999) examined evidence for the relative preponderance of three possible reactions to plant closings: the "discouraged worker effect" (i.e., feeling discouraged from seeking re-employment), the "poisoning effect" (development of negative attitudes toward all employers), and the "career growth effect" (feeling that the plant closing had a net positive effect for the worker). Older workers (those older than 55 years of age) who had been laid off were less likely to report negative attitudes and more likely to report positive career outcomes than younger workers who were laid off. Another study that focused specifically on the reactions of older workers to downsizing examined a sample of employees at a Swedish insurance company that offered early retirement options to some of its workers during a downsizing effort. A comparison of workers who stayed or took early retirement during the downsizing showed that attitude toward the downsizing was primarily dependent on whether the worker's status (employed or retired) was voluntary (Isaksson & Johansson, 2000).

Age-Related Reactions to Other Forms of Organizational Treatment

It is reasonable to expect that worker age and the manner in which workers of different ages are treated may also be associated with the extent to which the work environment is experienced as a supportive and welcoming place by younger and older workers. For example, age discrimination, which is encountered by many older workers in a variety of intended and unintended ways, should have consequences for perceptions of fair treatment at work. Consistent with this expectation, Van Yperen and colleagues reported evidence that worker age is negatively associated with perceptions of procedural and interactional justice (Van Yperen, Hagedoorn, Zweers, & Postma, 2000). However, meta-analytic evidence does not show any significant relationship of worker age with variables such as job insecurity and psychological contract breach (Ng & Feldman, 2010).

A study that specifically focused on the work engagement of "mature-age" (45 and older) workers in Australia examined stereotype threat (in the form of work conditions such as working with a primarily young work group) and reported that these conditions were predictive of lower work engagement a year later (Kulik, Perera & Cregan, 2016). Finally, James, McKechnie and Swanberg (2011) made the argument that older workers are "differently" engaged than younger workers, based on their observation that the job quality factors (e.g., supervisor support, schedule satisfaction, career development) that contributed to employee engagement in a large US retail organization differed among the five age/career groups that they studied.

Are Older Workers Easier to Please or Just Better Off?

Some of the more interesting issues raised by the observation that age is generally associated with increasingly positive job satisfaction, organizational commitment, and similar attitudes include *why* and *when* age should be associated with positive work attitudes. As pointed out by Warr (1994), much of the work published prior to the 1990s on age–job satisfaction relationships had not taken into account or explored the causes of the relationships between age and job satisfaction. However, a number of reasons for age-related increases in job satisfaction have been posited since then. These include (1) functional reasons that rely on the covariation of age with job circumstances that produce satisfaction and (2) developmental explanations that emphasize systematic changes in the central life interests and emotional functioning of adults that unfold as workers age.

Functional Bases

To begin with, any consideration of the relationship between age and worker feelings or behaviors must recognize several possible sources of covariation between the two. For example, a number of variables that are also associated with job satisfaction, such as work experience, organizational tenure, job level, and income, tend to be correlated with age. Older workers typically have longer tenure and more work experience, and have advanced to higher occupational levels, providing them with jobs that offer many features that contribute to job satisfaction. Thus, the bivariate relationship that is observed between age and job satisfaction may be an artifact of other events that come along with spending time in the workforce – older workers may simply have had more time to reap the rewards embedded in occupational structures. Some investigations that report positive relationships between age and job satisfaction have statistically controlled for these relationships; others have not. In some studies, especially those based on data from a single organization, these variables are so closely intertwined as to make it almost impossible to tease apart their independent effects. Multivariate studies that control for such opportunity biases generally do account for some of the relationship between age and job satisfaction. However, large-scale population studies that have statistically controlled for relevant covariates typically report that opportunity variables do not completely account for the age–satisfaction relationship (cf. Clark, Oswald, & Warr, 1996; Rhodes, 1983).

In addition, changes in organizational structures and career patterns that disrupt the normative association between worker age and work status variables likewise have the potential to affect the relationship between age and job satisfaction. For example, the classic career development model can be loosely characterized as an age-graded sequence of entry and development, maintenance, withdrawal and exit phases, followed by retirement from the workforce. Within the last 25 years, models of careers (cf. Hall & Mirvis, 1995; Sterns & Miklos, 1995) propose that workers may engage in multiple cycles of entry, development, and withdrawal that involve entry and exit from multiple organizations and several distinct *careers* over the course of a working life. Increasingly, workers in their 50s and 60s will choose (voluntarily or involuntarily) to enter new fields in which they have no more status or experience than workers in their 20s and 30s. To the extent that job tenure, occupational level, and similar variables are responsible for positive job attitudes, the assumption that older workers can be expected to report higher levels of job satisfaction than their younger co-workers may not be tenable in the future.

A second functional explanation for age differences in job satisfaction and other work attitudes is cohort based. Cohort and generational explanations emphasize common socio-cultural experiences that affect the perspectives and values of adults born during a particular period of time. For example, adults who grew up during the Depression developed ideas about job security and the meaning of work in a very different economic and political climate than members of the Baby Boom generation. Age differences in job satisfaction reported in any particular study are likely to confound worker age with worker cohort. Thus, for example, age differences in work attitudes observed in a cross-sectional study that includes workers from multiple generations are likely to mask the fact that adults born during the Baby Boom generation may react differently to work conditions than Generation X adults and Millennial adults will react when they reach the same age. However, critical and meta-analytic reviews of works that have examined generational explanations for age differences in work attitudes and work values (Costanza, Badger, Fraser, Severt, & Gade, 2012; Parry and Urwin, 2011; Twenge, 2010) have concluded that the evidence on this issue is decidedly mixed, providing sparse support of meaningful or practical differences in either work attitudes or work values that can be confidently attributed to generational effects, despite popular press claims to the contrary. In addition to small effect sizes and inconsistent findings across studies, the bulk of empirical studies of generational differences in work values and work attitudes have relied on cross-sectional data, which do not allow researchers to disentangle generational effects from age and period effects.

Another *external* explanation for age differences in job satisfaction is the so-called *job change* hypothesis, which argues that, over time, workers gravitate to jobs that are a closer fit with their needs and expectations. Because job satisfaction is often conceptualized as a response to the congruence between worker desires/needs/values and job characteristics, this logic leads to the expectation that older workers, on average, will report more positive reactions to their job situations. Support for this explanation was provided in a study that examined the job satisfaction of government managers (White & Spector, 1987). These researchers found that locus of control and job congruence explained the bulk of the relationship between age and job satisfaction in their sample.

Developmental Explanations

Developmental processes (i.e., aging) refer to patterns of feelings and behaviors that unfold in largely the same way for all people as time passes. Thus, older workers may report more satisfaction with their jobs, for example, because they have mellowed with time. For example, one alternative theoretical explanation suggests that aging is associated with a gradual lowering of expectations and aspirations. According to this line of thought, as workers age, they adjust their standards from overly idealistic standards to more realistic (and lower) ones. This allows older workers to be well satisfied with situations that would not have been satisfying at an earlier point in their lives. Thus, we would expect gradually increasing levels of job satisfaction, even for individuals whose work circumstances have not improved in any objective way.

Other possible explanations for the age–satisfaction relationship draw on the idea that workers experience developmental shifts in role concerns from those of "getting by and getting ahead" that characterize the early years of adulthood, to concerns with attaching meaning to one's life that have been posited by lifespan theorists as characterizing later stages of adulthood. This corresponds with a tendency to reflect on positive experiences and the ability to savor them. Research on emotional regulation throughout the life course provides evidence consistent with this position. A longitudinal study that examined age-related differences and changes in positive and negative affect found that levels of positive affect remain fairly stable until late in life, but negative affect decreases with age (Charles, Reynolds, & Gatz, 2001). Similarly, a study of daily emotional experiences reported that the frequency with which adults experience positive affect remains constant, but the frequency with which negative affect is experienced declines until about age 60. Furthermore, among older adults, highly positive emotional experiences tend to endure and highly negative emotional experiences tend to dissipate (Carstensen, Pasupathi, Mayr, & Nesselroade, 2000). In other words, older workers are better able to recognize the good and let go of the bad.

Work Motivation and Work Motives

In its most general sense, work motivation refers to workers' willingness to direct their energies toward organizationally valued behaviors and outcomes. A whole host of issues arise when we begin considering the issue of motivating older workers. First, and perhaps most obvious, is whether or not older workers exhibit generally different overall levels of work motivation and work engagement than younger workers. Initially, empirical findings indicated that age is negatively associated with aspiration levels and overall levels of motivation (Sturman, 2003). However, other work provides evidence of positive relationships between age and motivation. For example, Bégat, Ellefsen, and Severinsson (2005) observed a positive correlation between age and measures of motivation and work engagement for a sample of Norwegian nurses. Nonetheless, most recent research on the relationship between age and work motivation is somewhat more nuanced. For example, a study of full-time US workers (Kordbacheh, Shultz, & Olson, 2014) reported that worker age was indirectly related to both intrinsic motivation and work engagement via its positive relationship with work meaningfulness.

In light of the importance of continuous learning among workers of all ages, motivation to engage in training and career development activities has received particular attention. As noted earlier, Maurer and his colleagues (Maurer et al., 2003) have presented evidence that worker age is negatively associated with motivation to engage in development activities, mediated by opportunities to develop self-efficacy for development. Work by others (Bertolino, Truxillo, & Fraccaroli, 2011) supports the position that age also influences the relationship of development-oriented personal characteristics with training motivations and beliefs. In a survey study of Italian municipal workers, they observed that relationships of proactive personality with training motivation, career development beliefs, and training behavioral intentions were systematically stronger for younger workers than they were for their older counterparts.

Based on human capital theory, Renaud, Lakhdari, and Morin (2004) argued that older workers should have lower motivation to voluntarily engage in training because of the shorter time that they have available to recoup their investments, making it an unwise investment of their time and energies. Data from a large Canadian financial organization was consistent with this hypothesis. In contrast, Simpson, Greller, and Stroh (2002) questioned the usefulness of human capital theory as an explanation for older workers' career and work development motivation. Instead, they argued that a life-span career development model, which proposes older workers can and do invest in their own careers, provides a better description of workers on-the-job and off-the-job career development activities. By recognizing workers' off-the-job career development activities as additional reflections of career and work motivation, they presented data indicating that late-career workers (ages 50–65) were actually *more* active in pursuing focused career development activities outside the workplace than were earlier-career workers.

In a study that examined the effectiveness of change management attempts in a number of organizations, Caldwell, Herold, and Fedor (2004) found that older workers were less motivated to participate in change and adapted less well to implemented management changes. They suggested that the kinds of change management practices required to encourage change in older workers may be different from the kinds of traditional suggestions for motivating change that have been developed in the context of studies of younger workers – that is, extrinsic rewards and training. In particular, they identified perceived organizational support as a construct that may appeal more directly to the kinds of motives that become salient as workers age – that is, feeling secure and valued.

Work Motives and Values

Most of what is known about work motivation and aging is that workers of different ages will have varying motives and values that may affect the kinds of outcomes and experiences that they will find attractive. Empirical data and theory drawn from the fields of lifespan psychology and career development provide some insight into this question. Lifespan theories of human development provide information about the kinds of motives that adults of different ages will seek to satisfy at work. For example, finding meaning in existing relationships is a central life task that emerges in late life (Carstensen et al., 2000). This should increase the importance of opportunities to maintain social connections at work as a source of satisfaction and as a motive for investing efforts in one's work. In this vein, Greller and Stroh (1995) suggest a particularly important role for outcomes that meet intrinsic needs and relationship needs for older workers. With respect to relationship needs, Greller and Simpson (1999) suggest further that the types of relationships people prefer may change as we age. As they move into our 50s and 60s, individuals tend to seek or build emotional value from their relationships rather than instrumental value. For example, older workers may be more concerned with developing and maintaining work (and life) situations that provide them with warm, nurturing social relationships in preference to seeking to develop networks of people who can provide career assistance. This argues for the importance of providing opportunities for high-quality social interactions and social/emotional support for older workers.

Building on Alderfer's ERG theory of work motivation, Mor-Barak (1995) proposed a four factor theoretical framework for understanding the meaning of work for older adults seeking employment. The first three – Financial, Social, and Personal – generally correspond to Alderfer's Existence, Relatedness, and Growth needs. The fourth factor is Generativity, which refers to opportunities to transfer knowledge and experience to younger generations, which she posited may be of particular value to older adults. A recent study of public sector workers in Italy (Vignoli, Guglielmi, Depolo, Chiesa, & Wang, 2017), which focused on individual and group triggers of work engagement for older employees (i.e. workers over the age of 50), illustrated how the generativity motive is relevant to concepts such as work engagement. For this "older worker" subgroup, they found that team-level collaboration processes and individual level generativity striving were both associated with work engagement. In addition, work from the Netherlands suggests that generativity operates at the task level (Stamov-Roßnagel & Biemann, 2012). In a study of production and office workers in the building industry, they observed that worker age was positively related to motivation, but this was specific to generativity-related tasks.

Although her review of the literature supported the expectation of increasing interest in meeting affiliation needs with increasing age, Rhodes (1983) generally did not offer consistent evidence of reliable relationships between age and the desire to satisfy growth or self-actualization needs. Later, however, in a study of kibbutz workers, Leviatan (1992) found support for the argument that older workers' motives are dominated by a desire to meet higher order needs. Job characteristics that allowed workers to meet higher-order needs explained more variance in work satisfaction and motivation to contribute to the job than did features such as physical conditions that allowed them to meet lower-order needs. More recent meta-analytic work by Kooij and her colleagues (Kooij, De Lange, Jansen, Kanfer, & Dikkers, 2011) likewise supports the argument that the nature of work motives shifts with age, from more extrinsically focused motives (e.g., pay, advancement) to more intrinsically focused motives such as interesting work.

Turning to motives that are particularly pertinent to task performance, Kanfer and Ackerman (2000) presented evidence regarding age differences in motivational traits indicating that age is negatively correlated with the strength of competitive excellence motives, such as mastery and competitiveness. Likewise, work in the Netherlands (De Lange, Van Yperen, Van der Heijden & Bal, 2010) suggests that dominant achievement goals differ by age, with older workers tending to emphasize mastery-avoidance goals (avoidance of performance loss) and younger workers tending to emphasize mastery-approach goals. Kanfer and Ackerman (2004) have made the argument that current theories of work motivation do not accommodate the realities of changing motive structures. Salient motives may operate as positive incentives for work motivation when organizational conditions provide opportunities for motive satisfaction. As such, they point to age-related changes in the salience of motives as examples of why organizations and work motivation theorists should integrate age into their thinking about motivation processes and motivational interventions.

Work Motives in Understudied Populations

With the exception of unwanted exits from the workforce, the typical work pattern for men is one of continued work until late life, at which point exit from the workforce is generally contemplated in terms of partial or complete retirement from the workforce. For women, working lives may exhibit a more complicated pattern, with one or more entries and exits, prompted by childbearing and changes in marital status, before retirement is contemplated. Doorewaard, Hendrick, and Verschuren (2004) studied a large sample of European *returners* to examine the relationship between age and work motives among women who have chosen to return to work after an absence from the workforce. They found that older female workers who return to work have stronger job and people orientations to work than younger female workers who return; in contrast, younger women who return to work had significantly stronger money orientations.

Dendinger, Adams, and Jacobson (2005) conducted a study that focused specifically on an understudied, but growing, segment of the older workforce: bridge employees. As described in other chapters in this book, bridge employment is a form of employment that represents a stage in a worker's transition from the role of full-time career worker to the role of full retirement. They drew on Mor-Barak's (1995) theoretical argument that there are four primary reasons for work among older workers: social, personal, financial, and generative. In particular, they speculated that the reasons non-retired older workers continue to work and the reasons that bridge employee older workers engage in work may be different, with implications for their work attitudes. Because generativity has been suggested as a motive that becomes central during late mid-life, it may be a particularly relevant motive for those engaging in bridge employment. They found that the strength of the generativity motive in bridge employment was systematically related to job satisfaction of bridge employees. Presumably, the jobs of the bridge employees they studied provided the opportunity to satisfy that motive. Another recent study that examined motives for continuing to work among career workers, bridge workers, and self-employed workers noted that work centrality, career satisfaction and perceived contribution were all predictors of the work fulfillment motive for bridge employees, but they were unrelated to the generativity motive (Templer, Armstrong-Stassen, & Cattaneo, 2010). Findings of this kind point out that for older adults, employment serves a variety of functions beyond providing income, including social contact and social status, structure, and opportunities for developing self-esteem.

Looking Ahead: Key Issues and Concepts to Keep an Eye On

Intersectionality and Multiple Discrimination

We want to emphasize the importance of the discussion presented in Webster, Thoroughgood and Sawyer's Chapter 3 on diversity issues and aging. Chapter 3 provides a more nuanced discussion of these issues although we would like to identify a few points where an intersectional or multiple discrimination approach would advance our understanding of aging and work as it relates to work attitudes and motivation (Crenshaw, 1989). This paradigm recognizes that any individual is simultaneously a member of several different categories (e.g., old, male, White), that these categories may combine in a number of ways, and that the salience of particular categories or combinations of categories can change across different contexts (Crenshaw, 1989; Hankivsky, Cormier, & de Merich, 2009). Second, power and social inequalities are central to intersectional analyses (Collins, 2015). Specifically, valued rewards and outcomes are not distributed equally across groups (e.g., greater poverty among older women than similarly aged men), and those groups with more power and resources work to retain their advantages. Intersectional research and multiple discrimination research recognize the barriers faced by different individuals and recognize that the strategies for overcoming those barriers are likely to vary as a function of different combinations of demographic and identity constructs. Thus, the major themes of intersectional research are critical to understanding the diversity of aging at work.

To be sure, women and other diverse groups have been largely ignored in social gerontological and aging research and absent from theories on aging except as control or nuisance variables (Krekula, 2007). Little attention is given to middle age or mature women who have either worked most of their lives in professional careers or clerical jobs or who have worked largely within the home with little or no external pay, benefits or retirement. Few psychological or work theories incorporate the salience and fluidity of multiple social categories and multiple identities into understanding the diversity of aging employees at work. Webster et al. (Chapter 3, this volume) identifies a number of diversity identities that require more attention within an intersectional, multiple discrimination research paradigm in research on age and work, including gender, sexual orientation/gender identity, and race/ethnicity. We would expand these diversity identities to include socio-economic status, education, and native/non-native born employees and believe that part-time/full-time employment, occupational sex segregation, early retirement and retirement planning as well as the role and meaning of work in ones' lives are related topics to investigate.

Beyond Chronological Age: Emerging Aging Measures

A number of scholars have argued that it is misguided to limit our thinking about the relationship between age and work attitudes and motives to operationalizations of age based solely on chronological age ("distance from birth" indices of age), which is by far the most common way of representing worker age in empirical studies. Earlier, we pointed out that alternative conceptualizations of age (e.g. psychosocial indices such as relative age, age similarity, and psychological age) are often more useful predictors of work attitudes than chronological age has been.

For example, Cleveland and Shore (1992) reported a complex relationship between age variables and several job attitudes, including job involvement and organizational commitment, in a sample of over 400 workers in a US-based multinational firm. They found that alternative age measures were related to job involvement and organizational commitment (for example, older workers who were old relative to others in their work groups and also "felt" older). Importantly, chronological age was not related to any of the work attitudes they measured.

Other research that has focused on work engagement as a focal variable has highlighted the role of organizational context features such as age composition of the workforce relative to the employee. A study drawing on Gallup data from employed adults in the UK reported that perceived age similarity played a greater role in work engagement for older workers (those over the age of 55) than it did for younger workers (Avery, McKay, & Wilson, 2007). Similarly, Green and colleagues theorized that age dissimilarity, rather than age per se, should have a negative impact on the quality of leader-member relationships, with consequences for a variety of work attitudes, including organizational commitment. In their study of public library employees, they did not find any support for this position (Green, Anderson, & Shivers, 1996). A recent study concerned with demographic dissimilarity as an antecedent of attitudes that mediate deviant behaviors likewise reported that age dissimilarity was unrelated to levels of organizational commitment (Liao, Joshi, & Chuang, 2004).

Likewise, alternative conceptualizations of age, including those grounded in lifespan theories and social identity theories may be helpful in understanding how and why age relates to work motives and motivation-related attitudes and behaviors. This approach is exemplified by a recent study in the Netherlands by Akkermans and colleagues (Akkermans et al., 2016), which demonstrated that indices of subjective age that focus on "time and opportunities remaining" rather than "time passed" had stronger relationships with motives such as intrinsic motivation and extrinsic motivation. In their study of taxi drivers, those with a longer future time horizon reported higher levels of intrinsic and extrinsic motives as well as higher overall work motivation. Other recent studies conducted by Kooij and her colleagues have also focused on the age-related notion of future time perspective (FTP). In one study, the researchers provided evidence from a four-wave study of Dutch university employees consistent with the argument that changing FTP mediated relationships between chronological age and relevant downstream motivation variables such as promotion focus, growth motives, and motivation to continue working (Kooij, Bal, & Kanfer, 2014). In a second study they reported that open-ended FTP mediated relationships between chronological age and several work motives, including growth motivation, and esteem motivation, with consequent implications for work engagement (Kooij, De Lange, Jansen & Dikkers, 2013). In a third study that focused on job crafting and its relationship with work engagement, Kooij, Tims, & Akkermans (2017), reported that increases in open-ended FTP were associated with increased levels of work engagement, mediated by job crafting (individualized proactive job redesign) that emphasized increased job resources and challenging job demands. Kooij, De Lange, Jansen, and Dikkers (2007) reviewed studies that examined relationships between five alternative conceptualizations of age and the motivation to continue working. They concluded that all five conceptualizations have implications for motivation to continue in the work role, but they operate via somewhat different mechanisms. This work has definite implications for organizations that are interested in strategies for retention of their older workers.

Other researchers have examined evidence for generational differences in work values (an *environmental* explanation for differences in work values) as an alternative or a complement to arguments that work values change as we age (a *personological* explanation). However, as noted earlier, most work that has examined generational explanations for work attitudes and work values has concluded that the evidence on this count was not very compelling (Lyons &

Kuron, 2013; Parry & Urwin, 2011; Twenge, 2010). One notable exception is a study by Smola and Sutton (2002), who compared the results of a survey they conducted with previous work value survey research conducted by Cherrington in the 1970s. When they attempted to tease apart the influence of aging and generational differences in Cherrington's report of age differences in work values they found evidence that Gen X (younger) workers put more emphasis on quick promotions than Boomers (older workers) did and put more value on the Moral Importance of work. Boomers, in contrast, placed more importance on Work as Primary in One's Life. They also found evidence that workers' values change as they mature – unexpectedly, rather than becoming more responsible, workers develop a less idealized view of work as they age. Probably the most interesting finding in their analysis is that the stronger of the two effects found in their data (generational versus aging) was generational. That is, differences in work values between groups of workers of different ages were primarily a function of whether they were members of the Boomer Generation or the Gen-X generation, rather than their ages per se.

Recommendations for Future Research and Theorizing

Probably the most consistent take-away point from previous research is that older workers are likely to value work and express generally positive attitudes toward work that satisfies motives and needs that are important to them. However, evaluation of the existing body of work in this field makes it clear that there is substantial room for rigorous research that contributes to our understanding of the role that worker age plays in the development and consequences of important work attitudes and the manner in which work motivation processes are affected by aging processes.

The review of existing theoretical and empirical work in this domain reveals several kinds of contributions that could make a real difference to our ability to make sense of the complex relationships between age and worker attitudes and motivations.

- First, and most basic, is a continued need for additional theoretically grounded empirical research that includes worker age as a *focal* issue. By virtue of its status as a demographic marker, worker chronological age is one of the most commonly included variables in most studies of work attitudes and work behavior. However, it is typically treated as a *noise* variable that is statistically controlled rather than treated as an important and interesting worker characteristic that forms the centerpiece of a study. As a result, we are often left trying to stitch together patterns of relationships involving age, often based on the observation of simple correlational associations extracted from studies and analyses that do not take into consideration the variety of contextual features that contribute to those relationships. Placing age front and center from the

standpoint of theorizing and research design could do much to reduce the piecemeal nature of our knowledge.
- A related need is for additional research that takes on the challenge of assessing age in meaningful ways. Undoubtedly, some of the conflicting findings that abound in the published research can be traced to differing, and often arbitrary, classifications of workers as older or younger. Thoughtful operationalizations of age variables that flow from extant information about the nature and meaning of age are needed. There have been repeated calls for recognition that "calendar age" is only one aspect of the multifaceted concept of age; several studies described in this chapter have highlighted the value that concepts such as subjective age, relative age, and future time perspective can have for our understanding of how workers of all ages think about and respond to this very personal but context-bound characteristic that is an ever-changing part of our lives and our identities. Conceptualizations and empirical research that incorporates these alternate ways of thinking about and assessing age can help to advance our understanding of how age fits into the landscape of work attitudes and motivations.
- From the standpoint of methodology, research designs that speak more directly to the kinds of questions being addressed in studies concerned with aging and work attitudes are needed. Longitudinal designs and multiple cohort designs that include measures of the kinds of constructs relevant to questions in this field are challenging to carry out, but they provide substantial value in reducing ambiguity about the interpretation of findings. We are heartened to see much more work in the past decade that has incorporated these designs and we hope to see continued movement in this direction in the next decade.
- Finally, we are beginning to see important movement in the direction of context-sensitive research on age and work attitudes. We see this in studies that address person-centric, job-centric, organization-centric, and "worldview"-centric (e.g., family situation, cultural, and socioeconomic context) moderators of age relationships with work attitudes; we likewise see this in studies that address the theoretical reasons and conditions under which age itself serves as a modifier of other important relationships. More research in this vein is needed.
- Importantly, greater research attention to the diversity of aging that builds on conceptions of intersectionality and multiple discrimination is critically needed. In order to advance our understanding of aging it is imperative to recognize the other identities and roles that workers occupy simultaneously with their age identities. A more intersectional approach would help to clarify the complex realities of how workers of different ages/generations, genders, ethnicities, and cultural backgrounds experience work as they age. These approaches are likely to be some of the more fruitful ways of coming to terms with when and why and how age "matters."

References

Akkermans, J., De Lange, A. H., van der Heijden, B. I. J. M., Kooij, D. T. A. M., Jansen, P. G. W., & Dikkers, J. S. E. (2016). What about time? Examining chronological and subjective age and their relation to work motivation. *Career Development International, 21,* 419–439. doi: 10.1108/CDI-04-2016-0063.

Avery, D. R., McKay, P. F., & Wilson, D. C. (2007). Engaging the aging workforce: The relationship between perceived age similarity, satisfaction with coworkers, and employee engagement. *Journal of Applied Psychology, 92,* 1542–1556. doi: 10.1037/0021-9010.92.6.1542.

Barnes-Farrell, J. L. (2003). Beyond health and wealth: Attitudinal and other influences on retirement decision-making. In G. Adams & T. Beehr (Eds.), *Retirement: Reasons, processes, and results* (pp. 159–187). New York: Springer.

Barnes-Farrell, J., & Matthews, R. (2007). Age and work attitudes. In K. Shultz & G. Adams (Eds.), *Aging and work in the 21st century* (pp. 139–162). Mahwah, NJ: LEA Laurence Erlbaum Associates.

Bégat, I., Ellefsen, B., & Severinsson, E. (2005). Nurses' satisfaction with their work environment and the outcomes of clinical nursing supervision on nurses' experiences of wellbeing – a Norwegian study. *Journal of Nursing Management, 13,* 221–230.

Bertolino, M., Truxillo, D. M., & Fraccaroli, F. (2011). Age as moderator of the relationship of proactive personality with training motivation, perceived career development from training, and training behavioral intentions. *Journal of Organizational Behavior, 32,* 248–263. doi: 10.1002/job.670.

Bourne, B. (1982). Effects of aging on work satisfaction, performance, and motivation. *Research on Aging, 5,* 37–47.

Caldwell, S. D., Herold, D. M., & Fedor, D. B. (2004). Toward an understanding of the relationships among organizational change, individual differences, and changes in person–environment fit: A cross-level study. *Journal of Applied Psychology, 89,* 868–882.

Carstensen, L. L., Pasupathi, M., Mayr, U., & Nesselroade, J. R. (2000). Emotional experience in everyday life across the adult life span. *Journal of Personality and Social Psychology, 79,* 644–655.

Charles, S. T., Reynolds, C. A., & Gatz, M. (2001). Age-related differences and change in positive and negative affect over 23 years. *Journal of Personality and Social Psychology, 80,* 136–151.

Clark, A., Oswald, A., & Warr, P. (1996). Is job satisfaction U-shaped in age? *Journal of Occupational and Organizational Psychology, 68,* 57–81.

Cleveland, J. N., & Shore, L. M. (1992). Self- and supervisor perspective on age and work attitude and performance. *Journal of Applied Psychology, 77,* 469–484.

Collins, P. H. (2015). Intersectionality's definitional dilemmas. *Annual Review of Sociology, 41,* 1–20.

Costanza, D. P., Badger, J. M., Fraser, R. L., Severt, J. B., & Gade, P. A. (2012). Generational differences in work-related attitudes: A meta-analysis. *Journal of Business Psychology, 27,* 375–394. doi: 10.1007/s10869-012-9259-4.

Crenshaw, K. (1989). Demarginalizing the intersection of race and sex: A black feminist critique of antidiscrimination doctrine, feminist theory and antiracist politics. *University of Chicago Legal Forum,* 139–167.

De Lange, A. H., Van Yperen, N. W., Van der Heijden, B. I. J. M., & Bal, P. M. (2010). Dominant achievement goals of older workers and their relationship with motivation-related outcomes. *Journal of Vocational Behavior, 77,* 118–125. doi: 10.1016/j.vb.2010.02.013.

Dendinger, V. M., Adams, G. A., & Jacobson, J. D. (2005). Reasons for working and their relationship to retirement attitudes, job satisfaction, and occupational self-efficacy of bridge employees. *International Journal of Aging and Human Development, 61*, 21–35.

Desmette, D., & Gaillard, M. (2008). When a "worker" becomes an "older worker": The effects of age-related social identity on attitudes towards retirement and work. *Career Development International, 13*, 168–185. doi: 10.1108/13620430810860567.

Doorewaard, H., Hendrick, J., & Verschuren, P. (2004). Work orientation of female returners. *Work, Employment, and Society, 18*, 7–27.

Ekerdt, D., & DeViney, S. (1993). Evidence for a preretirement process among older male workers. *Journal of Gerontology: Social Sciences, 48*, S35–S43.

Elias, S. M., Smith, W. L., & Barney, C. E. (2012). Age as a moderator of attitude toward technology in the workplace: Work motivation and overall job satisfaction. *Behaviour & Information Technology, 31*, 453–467. doi: 10.1080/014492X.2010.513419.

Feldman, D. C., Doerpinghaus, H. I., & Turnley, W. H. (1995). Employee reactions to temporary jobs. *Journal of Managerial Issues, 7*, 127–141.

Finegold, D., Mohrman, S., & Spreitzer, G. M. (2002). Age effects on the predictors of technical workers' commitment and willingness to turnover. *Journal of Organizational Behavior, 23*, 655–674.

Glisson, C., & Durick, M. (1988). Predictors of job satisfaction and organizational commitment in human service organizations. *Administrative Science Quarterly, 33*, 61–81.

Green, S. G., Anderson, S. E., & Shivers, S. L. (1996). Demographic and organizational influences on leader-member exchange and related work attitudes. *Organizational Behavior and Human Decision Processes, 66*, 203–214.

Greller, M. M., & Simpson, P. (1999). In search of late career: A review of contemporary social science research applicable to the understanding of late career. *Human Resource Management Review, 9*, 309–347.

Greller, M. M., & Stroh, L. K. (1995). Careers in midlife and beyond: A fallow field in need of sustenance. *Journal of Vocational Behavior, 47*, 232–247.

Hall, D. T., & Mirvis, P. H. (1995). The new career contract: Developing the whole person at midlife and beyond. *Journal of Vocational Behavior, 47*, 269–289.

Hankivsky, O., Cormier, R., & de Merich, D. (2009). *Intersectionality: Moving women's health research and policy forward* (p. 68). Vancouver: Women's Health Research Network.

Hayslip, B. Jr., Metheny, W., Miller, C., Yeatts, D., Beyerlein, M., & Johnson, D. (1996). Employee age and perceptions of work in self-managing and traditional work groups. *International Journal of Aging and Human Development, 42*, 291–312.

Heckhausen, J., & Schulz, R. (1995). A life-span theory of control. *Psychological Review, 102*, 284–304.

Herzberg, F. I., Mausner, B., Peterson, R. O., & Capwell, D. R. (1957). *Job attitudes: Review of research and opinion*. Pittsburgh: Psychological Service of Pittsburgh.

Innocenti, L., Profili, S., & Sammarra, A. (2012). Age as moderator in the relationship between HR development practices and employees' positive attitudes. *Personnel Review, 42*, 724–744. doi: 10.1108/PR-Jan-2012-2009.

Isaksson, K., & Johansson, G. (2000). Adaptation to continued work and early retirement following downsizing: Long-term effects and gender differences. *Journal of Occupational and Organizational Psychology, 73*, 241–256.

James, J. B., McKechnie, S., & Swanberg, J. (2011). Predicting employee engagement in an age-diverse retail workforce. *Journal of Organizational Behavior, 32*, 173–196. doi: 10.1002/job.681.

Kacmar, K. M., Carlson, D. S., & Brymer, R. A. (1999). Antecedents and consequences of organizational commitment: A comparison of two scales. *Educational and Psychological Measurement, 59*, 976–994.

Kacmar, K. M., & Ferris, G. R. (1989). Theoretical and methodological considerations in the age-job satisfaction relationship. *Journal of Applied Psychology, 74*, 201–207.

Kalleberg, A. L., & Loscocco, K. A. (1983). Aging, values, and rewards: Explaining age differences in job satisfaction. *American Sociological Review, 48*, 78–90.

Kanfer, R., & Ackerman, R. L. (2000). Individual differences in work motivation: Further explorations of a trait framework. *Applied Psychology: An International Review, 49*, 470–482.

Kanfer, R., & Ackerman, R. L. (2004). Aging, adult development, and work motivation. *Academy of Management Review, 29*, 440–458.

Kaye, L. W., Alexander, L. B., & Kauffman, S. (1999). Factors contributing to job quality and satisfaction among ethnically diverse, lower income, elderly part-timers. *Journal of Gerontological Social Work, 31*, 143–166.

Kooij, D. T. A. M., Bal, P. M., & Kanfer, R. (2014). Future time perspective and promotion focus as determinants of intraindividual change in work motivation. *Psychology and Aging, 29*, 319–328. doi: 10.1037/a0036768.

Kooij, D., De Lange, A., Jansen, P., & Dikkers, J. (2007). Older workers' motivation to continue to work: Five meanings of age: A conceptual review. *Journal of Managerial Psychology, 4*, 364–394. doi: 10.1108/02683940810869015.

Kooij, D. T. A. M., De Lange, A. H., Jansen, P. G. W., Kanfer, R., & Dikkers, J. S. E. (2011). Age and work-related motives: Results of a meta analysis. *Journal of Organizational Behavior, 32*, 197–225. doi: 10.1002/job.665.

Kooij, D. T. A. M., De Lange, A. H., Jansen, P. G. W., & Dikkers, J. S. E. (2013). Beyond chronological age: Examining perceived future time and subjective health as age-related mediators in relation to work-related motivations and well-being. *Work & Stress, 27*, 88–105. doi: 10.108/02678373.2013.769328.

Kooij, D. T. A. M., Jansen, P. G. W., Dikkers, J. S. E., & De Lange, A. H. (2010). The influence of age on the associations between HR practices and both affective commitment and job satisfaction: A meta analysis. *Journal of Organizational Behavior, 31*, 1111–1136. doi: 10.1002/job.666.

Kooij, D. T. A. M., Tims, M., & Akkermans, J. (2017). The influence of future time perspective on work engagement and job performance in the role of job crafting. *European Journal of Work and Organizational Psychology, 26*, 4–15. doi: 10.1080/1359432X.2016.1209489.

Kordbacheh, N., Shultz, K., & Olson, D. A. (2014). Engaging mid and late career employees: The relationship between age and employee engagement, intrinsic motivation, and meaningfulness. *Journal of Organizational Psychology, 14*, 11–25.

Krekula, C. (2007). The intersection of age and gender: Reworking gender theory and social gerontology. *Current Sociology, 55*(2), 155–171.

Kulik, C. T., Perera, S., & Cregan, C. (2016). Engage me: The mature-age worker and stereotype threat. *Academy of Management Journal, 59*, 2132–2156. doi: 10.5465/amj.2015.0564.

Leviatan, U. (1992). Determinates of work motivation and work satisfaction among kibbutz workers. *Canadian Journal of Community Mental Health, 11*, 49–64.

Liao, H., Joshi, A., & Chuang, A. (2004). Sticking out like a sore thumb: Employee dissimilarity and deviance at work. *Personnel Psychology, 57*, 969–1000.

Lorence, J. (1987). Age differences in work involvement: Analyses of three explanations. *Work and Occupations, 14*, 533–557.

Lyons, S., & Kuron, L. (2013). Generational differences in the workplace: A review of the evidence and direction of future research. *Journal of Organizational Behavior, 35*, S139-S157. doi: 10.1002/job.1913.

Maurer, T. J. (2001). Career-relevant learning and development, worker age, and beliefs about self-efficacy for development. *Journal of Management, 27*, 123–140.

Maurer, T. J., Weiss, E. M., & Barbeite, F. G. (2003). A model of involvement in work-related learning and development activity: The effects of individual, situational, motivational, and age variables. *Journal of Applied Psychology, 88*, 707–724.

Mazerolle, M. J., & Gangaram, S. (1999). Older workers' adjustments to plant closures. *Relations Industrielles, 54*, 313–336.

Mor-Barak, M. (1995). The meaning of work for older adults seeking employment: The generativity factor. *International Journal of Aging and Human Development, 41*, 325–344.

Morris, M. G., & Venkatesh, V. (2000). Age differences in technology adoption decisions: Implications for a changing work force. *Personnel Psychology, 53*, 375–403.

Ng, T. W. H., & Feldman, D. C. (2010). The relationship of age with job attitudes: A meta analysis. *Personnel Psychology, 63*, 677–718.

Nichols, T., Sugur, N., & Tasiran, A. C. (2003). Signs of change in Turkey's working class: Workers' age-related perceptions in the modern manufacturing sector. *British Journal of Sociology, 54*, 527–545.

Parry, E., & Urwin, P. (2011). Generational differences in work values: A review of theory and evidence. *International Journal of Management Review, 13*, 79–96. doi: 10.1111/j.1468-2370.2010.00285.x.

Pond, S. B., & Geyer, P. D. (1987). Employee age as a moderator of the relation between perceived work alternatives and job satisfaction. *Journal of Applied Psychology, 72*, 552–557.

Pond, S. B., & Geyer, P. D. (1991). Difference in the relation between job satisfaction and perceived work alternatives among older and younger blue-collar workers. *Journal of Vocational Behavior, 39*, 251–262.

Renaud, S., Lakhdari, M., & Morin, L. (2004). The determinants of participation in non-mandatory training. *Relations Industrielles, 59*, 724–743.

Rhodes, S. R. (1983). Age-related differences in work attitudes and behavior: A review and conceptual analysis. *Psychological Bulletin, 93*, 328–367.

Riordan, C. M., Griffith, R. W., & Weatherly, E. W. (2003). Age and work-related outcomes: The moderating effects of status characteristics. *Journal of Applied Social Psychology, 33*, 37–57.

Shultz, K. S., Morton, K. R., & Weckerle, J. R. (1998). The influence of push and pull factors on voluntary and involuntary early retirees' retirement decision and adjustment. *Journal of Vocational Behavior, 53*, 45–57.

Simpson, P. A., Greller, M. M., & Stroh, L. K. (2002). Variations in human capital investment activity by age. *Journal of Vocational Behavior, 61*, 109–138.

Siu, O., Spector, P. E., Cooper, C. L., & Donald, I. (2001). Age differences in coping and locus of control: A study of managerial stress in Hong Kong. *Journal of Applied Psychology, 16*, 707–710.

Smola, K. W., & Sutton, C. D. (2002). Generational differences: Revisiting generational work values for the new millennium. *Journal of Organizational Behavior, 23*, 363–382.

Spreitzer, G. M., Kizilos, M. A., & Nason, S. W. (1997). A dimensional analysis of the relationship between psychological empowerment and effectiveness, satisfaction, and strain. *Journal of Management, 23*, 679–704.

Stamov-Roßnagel, C., & Biemann, T. (2012). Ageing and work motivation: A task-level perspective. *Journal of Managerial Psychology, 27,* 459–487. doi: 10.1108/0268394121 1235382.

Sterns, H. L., & Miklos, S. (1995). The aging worker in a changing environment: Organizational and individual issues. *Journal of Vocational Behavior, 47,* 248–268.

Sturman, M. C. (2003). Searching for the inverted U-shaped relationship between time and performance: Meta-analyses of the experience/performance, tenure/performance, and age/performance relationships. *Journal of Management, 29,* 609–640.

Templer, A., Armstrong-Stassen, M., & Cattaneo, J. (2010). Antecedents of older workers' motives for continuing to work. *Career Development International, 15,* 479–500. doi: 10.1108/13620431011075349.

Twenge, J. M. (2010). A review of the empirical evidence on generational differences in work attitudes. *Journal of Business Psychology, 25,* 201–210. doi: 10.1007/s10869-010-9165-6.

Van Yperen, N. W., Hagedoorn, M., Zweers, M., & Postma, S. (2000). Injustice and employees' destructive responses: The mediating role of state negative affect. *Social Justice Research, 13,* 291–312.

Vignoli, M., Guglielmi, D., Depolo, M., Chiesa, R., & Wang, M. (2017, November). *Individual and group triggers of work engagement and team performance in older workers.* Poster presented at the *Age in the Workplace* Meeting, Lüneburg, Germany.

Warr, P. (1994). Age and employment. In H. C. Triandis, M. D. Dunnette, & L. M. Hough (Eds.), *Handbook of industrial and organizational psychology* (2nd ed., Vol. 4, pp. 485–550). Palo Alto, CA: Consulting Psychologists Press.

White, A. T., & Spector, P. E. (1987). An investigation of age-related factors in the age-job-satisfaction relationship. *Psychology and Aging, 2,* 261–265.

Zacher, H., & Griffin, B. (2015). Older workers' age as a moderator of the relationship between career adaptability and job satisfaction. *Work, Aging and Retirement, 1,* 227–236. doi: 10.1093/worker/wau009.

8
EMPLOYEE DEVELOPMENT AND TRAINING ISSUES RELATED TO THE AGING WORKFORCE

Deborah A. Olson and Debora Jeske

The effectiveness and viability of organizations across industries and geographic locations are increasingly dependent upon both organizational knowledge management practices and policies, along with employee expertise, their learning strategies and attitudes towards continuous training and development. This underscores the importance of organizations attracting and retaining younger and older employees who possess these attributes (Kogovsek, Znidarsic, & Kogovsek, 2016; Loretto & White, 2006). This is the outcome of two specific trends. First, many organizations recognize that organizational growth and innovation are dependent on the skills and knowledge of their workers. In order to meet those challenges, however, it is important to motivate workers to engage in continuous learning and development activities (Tims, Bakker, & Derks, 2012; Wang, Olson, & Shultz, 2013). And second, given the aging global workforce, many organizations striving for growth and innovation are cognizant of the need to invest in the growth and development of both younger as well as older workers as their skills, talent, and knowledge are essential elements in the process of facilitating organizational effectiveness (Kooij, 2015). In this chapter, we focus specifically on the aspects related to training, development and learning processes for older workers in the workplace. We reflect on a number of theories, processes and practices relevant to their training and development.

Theoretical Frameworks

A number of theories in the area of human resource management, psychology and cognition provide frameworks to understand the circumstances that facilitate professional development and training, particularly among older workers.

These frameworks include human capital theory (Becker, 1964), attribution theory (Kelley & Michela, 1980), and implicit person theories (Dweck, 1986). We introduce each briefly and relate them to existing research.

Human capital theory was initially conceptualized by Becker (1964) as a way to describe the importance of the acquisition of skills, experiences, and knowledge that individuals gain over the course of their careers. The concept of human capital describes individuals' accumulated knowledge, experience, know-how, and education combined with the personal and professional experiences and networks that impact their career advancement, performance, and success within their careers. Human capital theory is relevant in this context since older workers possess a unique accumulation of resources that have been gathered and refined over the course of their careers. For older workers, it is the accumulation of this capital which brings value to the organization and increases their "worth" to organizations. However, older workers are often subjected to stereotypes and biases which have the potential to negatively impact their motivation and willingness to engage in learning and development activities (Finkelstein, Burke, & Raju, 1995).

According to the human capital theory, providing learning, training, and development opportunities for older workers is a rational investment that will increase the value of the organization's human capital. However, in 1976, Rosen and Jerdee published research results which reported that older workers were perceived by younger workers to have limited interest in training and development and therefore were less motivated than their younger counterparts to learn new skills. Ageism also affects the severity with which performance errors are judged by managers of older workers (Rupp, Vodanovich, & Crede, 2006). Many organizations continue to base their decisions on such research results, using them as justification to limit access to training for older workers and thus inadvertently fostering negative stereotypes about the learning ability and motivation of older workers. However, many stereotypes have been disconfirmed (Ng & Feldman, 2012). The only stereotype that has been supported is that older workers tend to be less willing to participate in training and developmental opportunities (Ng & Feldman, 2012). However, the question arises to what extent this lack of willingness is related to the presence of barriers to learning, the absence of a supportive learning climate (Froehlich, Segers, & van den Bossche, 2014; Stamov Roßnagel & Jeske, 2017) or design of training and development opportunities that disregard including approaches that optimize learning for older workers (Jeske & Stamov Roßnagel, 2012).

Attribution theory is another theoretical framework relevant to our discussion. Attribution theory asserts that when individuals evaluate the successes or failures of others, they do so with the intention to identify patterns of causes for the behaviors observed (Kelley & Michela, 1980). Attribution theory plays a role in explaining how biases based on causal assumptions influence the allocation of training and development resources, oftentimes in favor of the development of younger versus older employees (Finkelstein et al. 1995; see also Costanza & Finkelstein, 2015). A recent study that illustrates the impact of attribution theory and biases related to age was conducted by Cox and Beier (2014). These authors investigated the impact of attributions of older workers by both older and younger managers. Their results showed that when older managers evaluated older workers' performance (compared with younger counterparts), lower levels of performance were attributed to external and controllable causes. However, their lower performance was attributed to stable causes when younger managers were rating the same performance (Cox & Beier, 2014). These attributions have direct implications for decisions regarding the perceived potential payoff resulting from making investments in training and development for older workers. If managers take the first perspective (performance is perceived as linked to aging), older workers may be viewed as less able to learn new skills. As a result, investments in the training and development for older workers would not be seen as yielding a return on investment given the associated costs (Dedrick & Dobbins, 1991).

Implicit person theories may also explain training participation and engagement of older workers. These theories are related to attribution theory. Rather than stable or unstable causes, these theories consider how different beliefs about the malleability of certain personal attributes (e.g., ability, motivation, and personality) may impact work-related behavior and learning (Dweck, 1986; Dweck & Leggett, 1988; Heslin, Latham, & VandeWalle, 2005). Two types of implicit theories are relevant to our discussion. First, there is entity theory. This theory posits that the attributes of the person are fixed therefore investment in development activities would have a limited impact on growth since the attribute is resistant to developmental interventions. The second perspective here is incremental theory. This asserts that personal attributes are changeable and learning occurs through persistent investment of time and effort. In this context, taking the initiative to invest time and resources to learn directly impacts development and growth of new skills. Incremental theory is linked to adaptive learning strategies that sustain individual motivation and effort over time (Dweck, 1986; Heckhausen, Shane, & Kanfer, 2017).

Implicit person theories may also contribute to older workers' self-perceptions and their perceived ability to learn new skills. In a longitudinal study conducted by Rothermund and Brandtstadter (2003), they found that negative stereotypes about older individuals were subsequently reflected in their self-appraisals. Wrenn and Maurer (2004) studied the specific beliefs held about older workers related to entity and incremental theories. They found that those workers who believed that abilities decline with age tended to avoid learning opportunities so as to minimize the chance of making mistakes. In addition, they were more likely to believe that mistakes reflected a lack of ability, thereby making any investment of effort futile. These findings may explain why older workers are less willing to engage in training and development activities (Ng & Feldman, 2012). The impact of entity theory and negative stereotypes held about older workers persists over time and negatively impacts older workers' self-efficacy, their retention likelihood (Karpinska, Henkens, & Schippers, 2013), their hiring chances (Abrams, Swift, & Drury, 2016), and perceived job suitability when they are seeking a career change (Fritzsche & Marcus, 2013). All these factors can therefore negatively affect the growth of human capital in terms of skills and knowledge within organizations.

The mindset of supervisors has an important role in understanding training willingness of older workers as well (see also Kanfer & Ackerman, 2005). When managers hold entity theory beliefs about the performance of workers, they tend to rely on initial impressions when judging individuals' work and were reluctant to change their ratings of performance, even when new data demonstrated improvements in the performance of older workers over time (see Heslin et al., 2005). Managers who held incremental beliefs about workers were more likely to change their ratings of individuals' performance over time when new performance data emerged that demonstrated their improvement and growth (Heslin et al., 2005). Given the connection between performance appraisal reviews and the investment decisions about who will receive training and development, older workers whose managers subscribe to entity theories would not deem older workers as yielding the expected payoff for the continued investment by the organization nor receive the same opportunities to participate in learning and development initiatives sponsored by the organization.

Contextual and Individual Predictors of Learning Motivation and Performance

As demonstrated in the previous section, learning motivation and performance of older workers may be influenced by the beliefs and theories held by both older workers and managers. Implicit biases and attributions can either facilitate or pose obstacles to the continued learning and development-related activities of older workers. A number of research studies provide further clues to other influencers on learning motivation and performance (Heckhausen et al., 2017). This evidence suggests that there is a difference between how learning motivation and performance may be evaluated by managers, compared with by older workers themselves. For example, the meta-analysis conducted by Finkelstein et al. (1995) revealed that younger workers were rated as having more potential for development than older workers. Further research showed that older workers were perceived as less able and less motivated to perform well in training and development activities when compared to their younger counterparts (Maurer, 2001).

However, these findings are not necessarily in line with how older workers view training and development opportunities. Older workers are interested in actively learning and developing. Kerman and Keenan (2017) found that 71 percent of adults are interested in continued opportunities to engage in training and development, with 61 percent of employees age 55 and older expressing that they are "extremely or very interested" in taking action to keep their skills and knowledge up-to-date. More than 50 percent of employees 55 and older expressed that they were interested in developing skills to facilitate both continued career development, as well as training to position themselves for new opportunities in jobs that are completely different from the ones they currently hold (Kerman & Keenan, 2017). These trends are in line with the growing number of people aged 55 and older in the USA who were working or actively seeking work in 2014 (40 percent according to Toossi & Torpey, 2017). The rate of participation in the labor force for those aged 65 to 74 years old and working is also expected to increase faster than the rate for other age groups (Toossi & Torpey, 2017).

This suggests that preconceived notions about learning motivation are misguided and that efforts to create inclusive learning practices are needed to sustain this willingness to learn and participate in training, despite older research suggesting the contrary (Ng & Feldman, 2012). Participation in and engagement with learning appear to be changing among older workers. These emerging trends however are not necessarily captured in current training and development practices in organizations (Kerman & Keenan, 2017). The need for inclusive training and development processes will only continue to increase over time, especially in light of the increasingly multi-generational workplace (Costanza, Badger, Fraser, Severt, & Gade, 2012; Lyons & Kuron, 2014), since many older workers are actively choosing to remain in the workforce longer than in previous generations (Toossi & Torpey, 2017).

Some positive advances can be noted already. More recent lifespan approaches to motivation and learning are changing generalized and age-stereotypic preconceptions about the learning ability of older workers (Heckhausen et al., 2017). For example, the age-related motivation perspective (Gegenfurtner & Vauras, 2012) asserts that the motivation to actively engage in development and learning activities remains constant over the life course. From this perspective, the motivation to learn and implement new ideas and approaches is sustained over the life course (Wanberg, Kanfer, Hamann, & Zhang, 2016). Recent research outcomes support the proposition that age-related motivational maintenance exists and demonstrates that as workers age their learning motivation remains constant (Bal & Dorenbosch, 2015; Kogovsek et al., 2016; Setti, Dordoni, Piccoli, Bellotto, & Argentero, 2015). In support of age-related motivational maintenance, Krapp (2005) proposed that over the life course, individuals proactively take action to learn and expand their skills in areas they find interesting. These learning activities translate into the development of deeper knowledge and new skills related to those areas of interest (Hidi, 2006). The willingness to learn new skills and the belief that learning enables an individual to reach more complex long-term goals are important additional predictors of engagement with learning activities (Walker, Greene, & Mansell, 2006).

Worker's motivated learning in areas of interest and their search for ways to apply what is learned may also contribute to the maintenance of older worker's performance over time. In 2012, Gegenfurtner and Vauras published a meta-analysis of 38 studies on motivational changes over time. These authors found support for age-related motivational maintenance (rather than age-related decline) indicating that learning motivation and the desire to transfer learning remains constant as one ages (Gegenfurtner & Vauras, 2012). However, other factors may also influence motivation to learn and subsequent performance on the newly learned tasks. For example, relevance of the training content, support from supervisors and coworkers to implement new processes and practices, may all directly impact motivation to learn and actively engage in strategies to transfer the training to improve performance (Dweck, 1986; Volet, Vauras, & Salonen, 2009). If motivation to engage in ongoing learning is not present, then transfer of training will not occur, and attributions about older workers' disinterest in learning may result.

The willingness to continue to engage in development activities and increasing one's performance is facilitated by a supportive learning climate within the organization (Armstrong-Stassen & Schlosser, 2008; see also Froehlich, Segers, & van den Bossche, 2014). Organizational actions that demonstrate support for ongoing development of worker's skills and expansion of their knowledge are perceived as symbols of the organization's commitment to them and their continued effectiveness in their roles (Allen, Shore, & Griffeth, 2003). Moreover, Bal, van Kleef, and Jansen (2015) found that older workers who received active support from their supervisors for continued career development activities were more engaged in their work and learning opportunities when compared with older workers who did not receive active support from their managers. Understanding the impact of perceived support for older workers' motivation to engage in ongoing learning and development activities is an important factor within any organizational context (Hedge, 2008).

These findings therefore point to the need to consider the context in which learning occurs (Jeske & Stamov Roßnagel, 2015) and specifically the presence or absence of resources that may hinder or facilitate learning (Jeske, Stamov Roßnagel, & Strack, 2017; Skule, 2004). The willingness to participate in training and development may also depend on the extent to which such development constitutes an additional burden for the worker, particularly when job demands may be high and resources low (Bal, Hofmans, & Polat, 2017). This suggests that development and training may generate short-term negative effects on workers' willingness to participate in training under specific learning conditions. The recognition of these factors and findings provides new ways to support learning generally, rather than adhering to established training curricula set by organizations. By encouraging and supporting workers who seek to gain new insights, skills and knowledge on topics of interest, a climate of learning is generated that is likely to benefit the organization. For example, if learning is encouraged, it may increase development of ideas related to strategic objectives of the organization as well as reduce the negative influence of attributional biases and perceptions held by both the workers and managers about the learning ability and motivation of different generations (Finkelstein, Ryan, & King, 2013; Lester, Standifer, Shultz, & Windsor, 2012).

In addition to the insights gained from theoretical frameworks, the research on motivation and individual predictors of learning motivation and performance, the work and practice around employee development and training have also benefited from new approaches. We introduce job crafting as one of these in the next section.

Informal Learning and Job Crafting

Learning and development occurs when people expand their knowledge and skills and in turn refine new approaches that impact task performance (Marsick & Watkins, 2001). According to aging theory (Nelson & Dannefer, 1992), the needs and motivations of individuals change over time and will become more diverse. Such individual differences have been found to predict engagement in voluntary training and development activities (Crant, 2000; Major, Turner, & Fletcher, 2006). Similarly, the centrality of work may also change over the course of one's working life (Bal & Kooij, 2011). The main challenge is to identify the strategies that older workers use to optimize their continued development and learning (Zacher & Frese, 2011). The focus is specifically on how they engage in learning and how their behavior may be motivated by the aforementioned personal as well as organizational circumstances. In the following section, we focus on two training and development-oriented approaches that may complement more traditional training schemes: informal learning and job crafting.

Informal learning is initiated by the individual with the intention to engage in continuous learning and growth in an unstructured, experiential manner that focuses on developmental areas that are important to the individual (Cross, 2007; Jeske & Stamov Roßnagel, 2015; Marsick & Volpe, 1999). In this context, informal learning is integrated into daily tasks and activities (Hodkinson, Colley, & Malcolm, 2003). It can be reactive and unplanned as well as intentional and moderately structured. Regardless of the approach, the results of engaging in informal learning are perceptible and impact performance and effectiveness (Berg & Chyung, 2008). This is consistent with the finding that adult learners are more self-directed and engaged in development activities on an ongoing basis (Knowles, Holton, & Swanson, 2005). Berg and Chyung (2008) found that, when compared with younger workers, older workers engaged in more informal learning activities (e.g., web searches, reading professional journals) as meaningful strategies to learn new information and develop new skills. Additional evidence indicates that age predicts a more positive informal learning attitude at work (Jeske & Stamov Roßnagel, 2016), while Tornau and Frese (2013) observed a positive association between age and personal initiative.

These trends may be reconciled if we consider the following. First, informal learning may be a matter of choice and opportunity that arises in the work context, independently from what the organization provides. Such learning activities may also exclude performance evaluations (e.g., such as comparing training performance and transfer between younger and older workers). This is relevant because work-related informal learning includes trial and error learning (e.g., Schürmann & Beausaert, 2016). The less structured and self-initiated nature of such learning may also reduce the fear of negative performance reviews. This is an important consideration since work and learning experiences are a source of perceived competence for both younger and older workers (Paloniemi, 2006). In addition, the participation of older workers in informal learning opportunities may be impacted by the characteristics of the social context in which learning takes place, such as access to available supports for learning and the sense of inclusiveness when others are involved in a learning activity. A number of social contexts factors positively impact informal learning and continuous development of new skills, acquisition of up-to-date knowledge and opportunities to hone interests through working on projects and assignments individuals find meaningful and engaging (Grossman & Salas, 2011). Older workers also tend to participate in training programs for recreational reasons, to feel connected to colleagues and maintain their social networks (Krapp, 2005; Maurer, Weiss, & Barbeite, 2003). Informal learning may also be more likely when colleagues and supervisors are available as trainers (Jeon & Kim, 2012).

Opportunities for feedback, coaching and reflection have all been shown to contribute to informal learning at work (Janssens, Smet, Onghena, & Kyndt, 2016). However, the results of a large study on informal and formal learning among employees indicated that employees of different age groups also reported different degrees of learning at work (Kyndt, Dochy, & Nijs, 2009). For example, employees in their 60s and those with greater seniority were less likely to experience coaching while employees in their 30s and those with low seniority also scored highest on feedback and knowledge acquisition (Kyndt et al., 2009). Unfortunately, the research did not provide insight into the quantity or quality of the experience reported by different age groups.

Nevertheless, these findings suggest that certain learning opportunities are more likely to be given to younger rather than to older workers (Kyndt et al., 2009). Moreover, only 20 percent of organizations designed processes to support individuals in informal learning to enhance their performance and continued development (Cross, 2007). This makes informal learning dynamics one of the areas that requires further investigation given its impact on learning and development.

Job crafting is another concept relevant to training and development. This concept captures 'the physical and cognitive changes individuals make in the task or relational boundaries of their work' (Wrzesniewski & Dutton, 2001, p. 179). This definition recognizes the proactive role that workers take in determining job-related boundaries in order to improve their work experience and perceived meaningfulness of their work. When crafting, workers attempt to change the nature of the tasks they are completing, the degree to which they interact with others, and how they view and cognitively evaluate their job (reflecting task, relational, and cognitive crafting) (Wrzesniewski & Dutton, 2001). Through self-initiated changes, the worker attempts to balance demands and resources in line with their abilities and needs (see Tims et al., 2012). Rudolph, Katz, Lavigne, and Zacher (2017, p. 6) explain that: "physical changes refer to actual alterations of job characteristics, cognitive changes involve psychological redefinitions and reinterpretations of job characteristics without actual changes, and relational boundary changes entail altering the quantity or quality of workplace relationship."

Some evidence is already available regarding the relationship between job crafting and age. A meta-analysis conducted by Rudolph et al. (2017) showed that age and job crafting were negatively related, but the coefficient was very small. This result is in direct opposition to the human capital theory (Becker, 1964) which would suggest older workers may be in a better position to craft their jobs given their longer tenure and greater expertise. This underscores the importance of understanding the preconditions that set the stage for job crafting to take place. Several interpretations may be offered. First, older workers may have established more routine work processes that may not support job crafting initiatives (see also Zacher, Hacker, & Frese, 2016). And second, interdependence, such as found in terms of task interdependence in teams, may further limit opportunities for individual job crafting (Cullinane, Bosak, Flood, & Demerouti, 2017; Le Blanc, Demerouti & Bakker, 2017). And third, workers may lack skills, seniority (Cullinane et al., 2017) and sufficient awareness of how to adjust their job to meet their own needs in ways that increases their engagement with and meaningfulness of their work (an issue addressed in the intervention outlined by van den Heuvel, Demerouti, & Peeters, 2015). Since older workers are traditionally less likely to be supported in their personal development or receive the same training opportunities as their younger counterparts, they may find it more challenging to engage in job crafting due to lack of experience with self-initiated learning and development.

Job crafting has several potential benefits. Job crafting may allow individuals to make changes to their job, rebalancing job demands and personal resources, all elements that enhance work motivation, productivity, and health (Kanfer, Beier, & Ackerman, 2013). As job crafting also encourages individuals to reach out to others to identify new opportunities for development, participants in interventions have reported more resources and higher levels of self-efficacy (van den Heuvel et al., 2015). This may contribute to workers becoming more responsive and adaptive to change (Le Blanc et al., 2017). And lastly, personally negotiated training may, like job crafting, be particularly essential for older workers in order to maintain their person–job fit (see Kooij, Tims, & Kanfer, 2015).

While self-initiated, job crafting is unlikely to emerge in a vacuum. On an individual level, the meta-analysis by Rudolph et al. (2017) suggests that general self-efficacy, proactivity, and a promotion focus contribute to job crafting. At a job level, opportunities for skill utilization (Cullinane et al., 2017), job autonomy and workload are linked to job crafting (Rudolph et al., 2017; Wrzesniewski & Dutton, 2001), while expectations of future job changes and uncertainty may also motivate job crafting to expand tasks and one's relational environments and network (e.g., Wang, Demerouti, & Bakker, 2016). Indeed, while most job crafting is initiated by individuals and may thus not be the result of employers' decision making (Hornung, Rousseau, Glaser, Angerer, & Weigl, 2010), collaborative crafting in cooperation with managers and one's organization has also been proposed and examined (e.g., Cheng, Chen, Teng, & Yen, 2016). The role of supervisory support is important to both job crafting and training, particularly in terms of the resources provided to workers that allow them to balance job demands and their own (e.g., training) needs. For example, supervisors can demonstrate their support by accepting individual job crafting and designating job holders to be responsible for the outcomes (see work by Hornung et al., 2010). Without supervisory support, particularly when managers do not recognize (older) workers' interest in expanding their skills, workers are unlikely to be presented with the option to select or even participate in training. Therefore, the degree to which training, like job crafting, is utilized effectively by older workers may depend on the support given to such workers that encourages this behavior.

While job crafting is one approach that may support employee development and learning, we would now like to turn to an additional area that is rarely discussed in the literature on aging. Creativity and innovation are topics more frequently discussed in relation to entrepreneurship. We believe that this area may be worthwhile exploring in more detail in the future as the potential innovative and creative contribution of workers of all ages may be facilitated by equal access to development and training opportunities.

Creativity and Innovation

According to Alfonso-Benlliure, Meléndez, and García-Ballesteros (2013, p. 113), "creativity is a process in which divergent as well as convergent thinking abilities are used, each more or less prominently depending on the moment in the creative process." Creativity has been assessed in multiple ways, for example, using ink-blots (to assess creative fluency, flexibility and originality; Andersson,

Berg, Lawenius, & Ruth, 1989) as well as self-reported and peer-rated creative ability in the workplace (Choi, Anderson, & Veillette, 2009; Zhou, 2003).

The link between creativity and age has already been explored in a number of papers. Research on older participants, of 70 years, has not found evidence of age-related changes in creativity when measured over a 13 year period (Andersson et al., 1989). More recent work has shown that older adults think divergently using similar strategies when compared with younger counterparts (Palmiero, Di Giacomo, & Passafiume, 2014). Many eminent artists, inventors, and scientists produce very high quality work in late adult life, often past regular retirement age (Simonton, 1994; Kim & Pierce, 2013). However, researchers also acknowledge that barriers to creativity exist in terms of motivation, confidence and context factors (such as pressures to conform; Kim & Pierce, 2013). This may further limit the extent to which individuals exhibit creativity in different stages of their lives. This is also considered in relation to creativity over the lifespan (e.g., Nakamura & Csikszentmihalyi, 2006).

Creativity may also depend on learning opportunities and the characteristics of the job in question. Research focused on creativity exhibited by older workers underscores the importance of job resources (Bakker, 2011; Langfred & Moye, 2004; Schaufeli, Bakker & Van Rhenen; 2009). Two important job resources are job control and support for creativity in one's work role. Job control is defined as the degree of influence individuals have over the sequence of work that needs to be completed within a specific time frame and the context in which the work needs to be completed. Employees who have high levels of job control have more freedom to act, which creates an optimal context in which to generate new ideas and approaches (Perry-Smith & Mannucci, 2017). Having job control also creates opportunities to take responsibility to solve problems using new and potentially untested approaches to improve work outcomes and processes (Ohly, Sonnentag, & Pluntke, 2006; Rosing & Zacher, 2016).

The experience of job control contributes to positive feelings that energize employees and motivates them to persist in their creative pursuits despite obstacles and setbacks. However, age stereotypes held by supervisors and co-workers about older workers can have a negative impact on perceived social support, which could reduce the level of encouragement that older workers receive. Stereotypes can negatively impact older worker's self-efficacy. Specifically, stereotypes about older workers' ability to generate creative options and implement innovative solutions have a direct impact on their innovation self-efficacy. Indeed, Binneweis, Ohly, and Niessen (2008) found that older workers who reported high job control and support for creativity generated more creative ideas, while older workers who experienced low job control did not. Job control creates a context which fosters creativity by encouraging learning and experimentation through providing opportunities to apply knowledge and skills in new ways. Job control and supervisor support for engaging in creative approaches encourage older workers to resist succumbing to negative stereotypes.

Ng and Feldman (2013) conducted a meta-analysis to examine the relationship between age and innovation. Their results showed no support for the hypothesis that as age and tenure increase, innovation-related behavior decreases. However, they found that older and longer-tenure workers performed as well as their younger counterparts in terms of contributing to innovation within their organizations (Ng & Feldman, 2013). These findings suggest several insights for organizations. For older workers, innovation-related behaviors are optimized as a result of their accumulated knowledge and experience. This contributes to the ability of older workers to generate ideas and distinguish high-value ideas from those that are less likely to impact results. Likewise, older workers have developed and nurtured a broader network of colleagues whom they can turn to in order to obtain feedback on the viability of innovative ideas. Older workers therefore possess the ability to both generate ideas and develop realistic implementation strategies. Having the ability to develop and implement innovations helps to explain why no curvilinear relationship was found by Ng and Feldman (2013) in the relationship between innovation-related behavior and age.

Overall, the research to date indicates that age does not result in a decline in innovation-related behaviors. Understanding the evidence and using that information to make data-based decisions to invest in older workers is essential for continued organizational growth and change. As the global workforce continues to age, it is imperative to understand and delineate the conditions that motivate older workers to continue to learn as well as develop creative approaches and ideas at work (Kinsella & Phillips, 2005). Organizational leaders who invest in their human capital by expanding the knowledge, experience and skills of individuals will reap the benefits of the investments they make in older workers. With this evolution, research questions and practical implications emerge that need to be addressed to build on and expand our understanding of the dynamics of facilitating learning and development for older workers.

Directions for Future Research

As part of our review, we identified a number of future research areas. Urick, Hollensbe, Masterson, and Lyons (2016) also noted the role of values and role identity between generations at work. The evidence on generational differences in work values tends to be mixed (see also Lyons & Kuron, 2014). Indeed, some trends may be more influenced by the change in labor market dynamics (e.g., changes in jobs security and stability in employment) and changing perceptions about the importance of work–life balance (compared with work centrality). Many perceptions of differences may not be substantiated in reality (Costanza, Darrow, Yost, & Severt, 2017). Future research may wish to consider the role of work centrality, job–person (mis)fit, social identity, and conflict between younger and older employees to identify which combination of factors represents facilitators and barriers to engagement with training initiatives and job crafting. This research may be able to expand on existing job crafting interventions and research (e.g., Cullinane et al., 2017; van den Heuvel et al., 2015). Identifying circumstances when current job demands, resources and supervisory support may not sufficiently facilitate (informal) learning and job crafting is significant since participation in such activities may be a matter of context (e.g., job, team) rather than subject to the proactivity and initiative of individual employees. Relatedly, the meta-analysis of Rudolph et al. (2017) showed a small but negative relationship between job crafting and age. This relationship needs to be explored further. For example, the research on learning conditions has identified a number of circumstances that support informal learning (see Eraut, 2007; Hoekstra, Korthagen, Brekelmans, Beijaard, & Imants, 2009; Janssens et al., 2016; Kyndt et al., 2009). This research may also help to explain when job crafting takes place and how reframing this as an activity promoting employability may impact motivation and willingness to engage in continuous learning and development over the course of one's career (see also Jeon & Kim, 2012).

Implications for Practice

Research by Joshi, Dencker, and Franz (2011) emphasized the importance of inter-generational interaction to transmit values, skills and resources. Urick et al. (2016) also noted that more interactions with employees of different ages also facilitated more positive perceptions of the other group. As a result, we propose that interventions are needed to identify and respond to (mis)perceptions of older and younger workers. Preconceptions exist not only about older workers but also influence beliefs held about younger workers, despite the fact that generational differences at work are not substantiated (e.g., Costanza et al., 2012). Initiatives such as training, reverse mentoring, and coaching (see also Urick et al., 2016) may help generate greater willingness to work with employees of different ages by overcoming biases and concerns about competition (for jobs and promotions). Managers may also benefit from training to identify behaviors such as withdrawal from and avoidance of learning opportunities. These behaviors may be traced to a general unfamiliarity, out-group bias or anticipated conflict with other age groups at work. This may also mean tackling these issues, facing uncomfortable truths about how managerial and training practices may inadvertently foster age-related and generational stereotypes. A number of questionnaires and resources already exist to assess intergenerational work climate and age-based job stereotypes at work (e.g., Furunes & Mykletun, 2010; Marcus, Fritzsche, Le, & Reeves, 2016; King & Bryant, 2017), and build interventions based on findings. Another human resource implication applies to the need to revisit how learning is appraised at work. Most appraisals take account of traditional training forms, but do not provide a means to address and record activities related to informal learning, job crafting, and innovative or creative contributions. As a result, employees' learning activities may be largely invisible to managers or the organizations (see also de Laat & Schreurs, 2013). This is compounded by a lack of awareness of how individuals may learn (Eraut, 2007), or in the case of job crafting, how employees develop skills and expertise through the process of making changes to their job. While job crafting has been linked to the identification of more developmental opportunities via increased interaction with supervisors and resource seeking (e.g., van den Heuvel et al., 2015), managers can help to maintain and support such behaviors through frequent interactions, appraisals and regular feedback (the last point is also a key component in the literature on learning conditions, see also Kyndt et al., 2009). Such managerial behaviors will also help to sustain the motivation of employees to continue their development. Finally, consistent and continuous managerial support may also prompt individuals who are hesitant about learning to try to engage in learning – in line with the suggestion that organizations need to develop a culture of support and learning (e.g., Eraut, 2007). This may be an important step forward, particularly for older workers, who may be hesitant to venture into new knowledge or skills domains unless their managers support their journey, including when failures occur that are an inherent part of the learning and development process (Dweck, 1986).

References

Abrams, D., Swift, H. J., & Drury, L. (2016). Old and unemployable? How age-based stereotypes affect willingness to hire job candidates. *Journal of Social Issues, 72*, 105–121.

Alfonso-Benlliure, V., Meléndez, J. C., & García-Ballesteros, M. (2013). Evaluation of a creativity intervention program for preschoolers. *Thinking Skills and Creativity, 10*, 112–120.

Allen, D. G., Shore, L. M., & Griffeth, R. W. (2003). The role of perceived organizational support and supportive human resource practices in the turnover process. *Journal of Management, 29*, 99–118.

Andersson, E., Berg, S., Lawenius, M., & Ruth, J.-E. (1989). Creativity in old age: A longitudinal study. *Aging, 1*, 159–164.

Armstrong-Stassen, M., & Schlosser, F. (2008). Benefits of a supportive development climate for older workers. *Journal of Managerial Psychology, 23*, 419–437.

Bakker, A. B. (2011). An evidence-based model of work engagement. *Current Directions in Psychological Science, 20*, 265–269.

Bal, P. M., & Dorenbosch, L. (2015). Age-related differences in the relations between individualised HRM and organisational performance: A large-scale employer survey. *Human Resources Management Journal, 25*, 41–61.

Bal, P. M., Hofmans, J., & Polat, T. (2017). Breaking psychological contracts with the burden of workload: A weekly study of job resources as moderators. *Applied Psychology: An International Review, 66*, 143–167.

Bal, P. M., & Kooij, D. (2011). The relations between work centrality, psychological contracts, and job attitudes: The influence of age. *European Journal of Work and Organizational Psychology, 20*, 497–523.

Bal, P. M., van Kleef, M., & Jansen, P. G. (2015). The impact of career customization on work outcomes: Boundary conditions of manager support and employee age. *Journal of Organizational Behavior, 36*, 421–440.

Becker, G. (1964). *Human capital: A theoretical and empirical analysis with special reference to education.* New York: Columbia University Press.

Berg, S. A., & Chyung, S. Y. (2008). Factors that influence informal learning in the workplace. *Journal of Workplace Learning, 20*(4), 229–244.

Binneweis, C., Ohly, S., & Niessen, C. (2008). Age and creativity at work: The interplay between job resources, age and idea creativity. *Journal of Managerial Psychology, 23*, 438–457.

Cheng, J.-C., Chen, C.-Y., Teng, H.-Y., & Yen, C.-H. (2016). Tour leaders' job crafting and job outcomes: The moderating role of perceived organizational support. *Tourism Management Perspectives, 20*, 19–26.

Choi, J. N., Anderson, T. A., & Veillette, A. (2009). Contextual inhibitors of employee creativity in organizations. The insulating role of creative ability. *Group & Organization Management, 34*, 330–357. doi: 10.1177/1059601108329811.

Costanza, D. P., Badger, J. M., Fraser, R. L., Severt, J. B., & Gade, P. A. (2012). Generational differences in work-related attitudes: A meta analysis. *Journal of Business Psychology, 27*, 375–394. doi:10.1007/s10869-012-9259-4.

Costanza, D. P., Darrow, J. B., Yost, A., & Severt, J. B. (2017). A review of analytical methods used to study generational differences: Strengths and limitations. *Work, Aging, & Retirement, 3*, 149–165.

Costanza, D. P., & Finkelstein, L. M. (2015). Generationally based differences in the workplace: Is there a there there? *Industrial and Organizational Psychology: Perspectives on Science and Practice, 8*, 308–323.

Cox, C. B., & Beier, M. E. (2014). Too old to train or reprimand: The role of intergroup attribution bias in evaluating older workers. *Journal of Business and Psychology, 29*, 61–70.

Crant, J. M. (2000). Proactive behavior in organizations. *Journal of Management, 26*, 435–462.

Cross, J. (2007). *Informal learning: Rediscovering the natural pathways that inspire innovation and performance.* San Francisco, CA: Pfeiffer.

Cullinane, S. J., Bosak, J., Flood, P. C., & Demerouti, E. (2017). Job crafting for lean engagement: The interplay of day and job-level characteristics. *European Journal of Work and Organizational Psychology, 26*, 541–554.

de Laat, M., & Schreurs, B. (2013). Visualizing informal professional development networks: Building a case for learning analytics in the workplace. *American Behavioral Scientist, 57*, 1421–1438.

Dedrick, E. J., & Dobbins, G. H. (1991). The influence of subordinate age on managerial actions: An attributional analysis. *Journal of Organizational Behavior, 12*, 367–377.

Dweck, C. S. (1986). Motivational processes affecting learning. *American Psychologist, 41*, 1040–1048.

Dweck, C. S., & Leggett, E. L. A. (1988). A social-cognitive approach to motivation and personality. *Psychological Review, 95*, 256–273.

Eraut, M. (2007). Learning from other people in the workplace. *Oxford Review of Education, 33*, 403–422.

Finkelstein, L. M., Burke, M. J., & Raju, N. S. (1995). Age discrimination in simulated employment contexts: An integrative analysis. *Journal of Applied Psychology, 80*, 652–663.

Finkelstein, L. M., Ryan, K. M., & King, E. B. (2013). What do the young (old) people think of me? Content and accuracy of age-based meta-stereotypes. *European Journal of Work and Organizational Psychology, 22*, 633–657.

Fritzsche, B., & Marcus, J. (2013). The senior discount: Biases against older career changers. *Journal of Applied Social Psychology, 43*, 350–362.

Froehlich, D. E., Segers, M. S. R., & van den Bossche, P. (2014). Informal workplace learning in Austrian banks: The influence of learning approach, leadership style, and organizational learning culture on managers' learning outcomes. *Human Resource Development Quarterly, 25*, 29–57.

Furunes, T., & Mykletun, R. J. (2010). Age discrimination in the workplace: Validation of the Nordic Age Discrimination Scale (NADS). *Scandinavian Journal of Psychology, 51*, 23–30.

Gegenfurtner, A., & Vauras, M. (2012). Age-related differences in the relation between motivation to learn and transfer of training in adult continuing education. *Contemporary Educational Psychology, 37*, 33–46.

Grossman, R., & Salas, E. (2011). The transfer of training: What really matters? *International Journal of Training and Development, 15*(2), 103–120.

Heckhausen, J., Shane, J., & Kanfer, R. (2017). Competence and motivation at work throughout adulthood: Making the most of changing capacities and opportunities. In A. J. Elliot, C. S. Dweck, & D. S. Yeager (Eds.), *Handbook of competence and motivation* (2nd ed., pp. 449–470). New York: The Guilford Press.

Hedge, J. W. (2008). Strategic human resource management and the older worker. *Journal of Workplace Behavioral Health, 23*, 109–123.

Heslin, P. A., Latham, G. P., & VandeWalle, D. (2005). The effect of implicit person theory on performance appraisals. *Journal of Applied Psychology, 90*, 842–856.

Hidi, S. (2006). Interest: A unique motivational variable. *Educational Research Review, 1*(2), 69–82.

Hodkinson, R., Colley, H., & Malcolm, J. (2003). The interrelationships between informal and formal learning. *Journal of Workplace Learning, 15*(7/8), 313–318.

Hoekstra, A., Korthagen, F., Brekelmans, M, Beijaard, D., & Imants, J. (2009). Experienced teachers' informal workplace learning and perceptions of workplace conditions. *Journal of Workplace Learning, 21*(4), 276–298.

Hornung, S., Rousseau, D. M., Glaser, J., Angerer, P., & Weigl, M. (2010). Beyond top-down and bottom-up work redesign: Customizing job content through idiosyncratic deals. *Journal of Organizational Behavior, 31*, 187–215.

Janssens, L., Smet, K., Onghena, P., & Kyndt, E. (2016). The relationship between learning conditions in the workplace and informal learning outcomes: A study among police inspectors. *International Journal of Training and Development, 21*(2), 91–112.

Jeon, K. S., & Kim, K.-K. (2012). How do organizational and task factors influence informal learning in the workplace? *Human Resource Development International, 15*, 209–226.

Jeske, D., & Stamov Roßnagel, C. (2012). Success by inclusion: 'Age fair' e-learning practices. *Organizational Dynamics, 41*, 302–307.

Jeske, D., & Stamov Roßnagel, C. (2015). Learning capability and performance in later working life: Towards a contextual view. *Education + Training, 57*(4), 1–15.

Jeske, D., & Stamov Roßnagel, C. (2016). Understanding what drives informal learning at work: A resource-based view. *International Journal of Management, Knowledge, and Learning, 5*, 25–44.

Jeske, D., Stamov Roßnagel, C., & Strack, J. (2017). Training older workers: Resource-oriented strategies. *International Journal of Training & Development, 21*(2), 167–176.

Joshi, A., Dencker, J. C., & Franz, G. (2011). Generations in organizations. *Research in Organizational Behavior, 31*, 177–205.

Kanfer, R., & Ackerman, P. L. (2005). Aging, adult development and work motivation. *Academy of Management Review, 29*, 1–19.

Kanfer, R., Beier, M. E., & Ackerman, P. L. (2013). Goals and motivation related to work in later adulthood: An organizing framework. *European Journal of Work and Organizational Psychology, 22*, 253–264.

Karpinska, K., Henkens, K., & Schippers, J. (2013). Retention of older workers: Impact of managers' age norms and stereotypes. *European Sociological Review, 29*, 1323–1335.

Kelley, H. H., & Michela, J. L. (1980). Attribution theory and research. *Annual Review of Psychology, 31*, 457–501.

Kerman, S. C., & Keenan, T. A. (2017). *The multi-generational labor force: Perceptions of jobs among Millennials, Gen-Xers, and Boomers*. Washington, DC: AARP Research.

Kim, K. H., & Pierce, R. A. (2013). Creativity and age. In D. K. Simonton (Ed.), *Encyclopedia of creativity, invention, innovation and entrepreneurship* (pp. 364–368). New York: Springer.

King, S. P., & Bryant, F. B. (2017). The Workplace Intergenerational Climate Scale (WICS): A self-report instrument measuring ageism in the workplace. *Journal of Organizational Behavior, 38*, 124–151.

Kinsella, K. G., & Phillips, D. R. (2005). Global aging: The challenge of success. *Population Bulletin, 60*, 5–42.

Knowles, M. S., Holton, E. F, III, & Swanson, R. A. (2005). *The adult learner: The definitive classic in adult education and human resource development* (6th ed.). San Diego: Elsevier.

Kogovsek, M., Znidarsic, J., & Kogovsek, M. (2016). Strategies to enhance the learning results of older versus younger workers. *Anthropologist, 24*, 292–299.

Kooij, D. T. A. M. (2015). Successful aging at work: The active role of employees. *Work, Aging and Retirement, 1*, 309–319.

Kooij, D. T. A. M., Tims, M., & Kanfer, R. (2015). Successful aging at work: The role of job crafting. In P. M. Bal, D. T. A. M. Kooij & D. M. Rousseau (Eds.), *Aging workers and the employee-employer relationship* (pp. 145–161). New York: Springer.

Krapp, A. (2005). Structural and dynamic aspects of interest development: Theoretical considerations from an ontogenetic perspective. *Learning and Instruction, 12*(4), 383–409.

Kyndt, E., Dochy, F., & Nijs, H. (2009). Learning conditions for non-formal and informal workplace learning. *Journal of Workplace Learning, 21*(5), 369–383.

Langfred, C. W., & Moye, N. A. (2004). Effects of task autonomy on performance: An extended model considering motivational, informational, and structural mechanisms. *Journal of Applied Psychology, 89*, 934–945.

Le Blanc, P. M., Demerouti, E., & Bakker, A. B. (2017). How can I shape my job to suit me better? Job crafting for sustainable employees and organizations. In N. Chmiel (Ed.), *An introduction to work and organizational psychology: An international perspective* (pp. 48–63). Oxford, UK: Wiley.

Lester, S. W., Standifer, R. L., Shultz, N. J., & Windsor, J. M. (2012). Actual versus perceived generational differences at work an empirical examination. *Journal of Leadership & Organizational Studies, 19*, 341–354.

Loretto, W., & White, P. (2006). Population ageing and older workers: Employers' perceptions, attitudes, and policies. *Population, Space and Place, 12*, 341–352.

Lyons, S., & Kuron, L. (2014). Generational differences in the workplace: A review of the evidence and directions for future research. *Journal of Organizational Behavior, 35*(S1), S139–S157. doi: 10.1002/job.1913.

Major, D. A., Turner, J. E., & Fletcher, T. D. (2006). Linking proactive personality and the big five to motivation to learning and development activity. *Journal of Applied Psychology, 91,* 927–935.

Marsick, V. J., & Volpe, M. (1999). The nature and need for informal learning, *Advances in Developing Human Resources, 1,* 1–9.

Marsick, V. J., & Watkins, K. E. (2001). Informal and incidental learning. *New Directions for Adult and Continuing Education,* (89), 25–34.

Maurer, T. J. (2001). Career-relevant learning and development, worker age, and beliefs about self-efficacy for development. *Journal of Management, 27,* 123–140.

Maurer, T. J., Weiss, E. M., & Barbeite, F. G. (2003). A model of involvement in work-related learning and development activity: The effects of individual, situational, motivational, and age variables. *Journal of Applied Psychology, 88,* 707–724.

Marcus, J., Fritzsche, B. A., Le, H., & Reeves, M. D. (2016). Validation of the work-related age-based stereotypes (WAS) scale. *Journal of Managerial Psychology, 31,* 989–1004.

Nakamura, J., & Csikszentmihalyi, M. (2006). Creativity through the life span from an evolutionary systems. In C. Hoare (Ed.) *Handbook of adult development and learning* (pp. 243–254). New York: Oxford University Press.

Nelson, E. A., & Dannefer, D. (1992). Aged heterogeneity: Fact of fiction? The fate of diversity in gerontological research. *The Gerontologist, 32,* 17–23.

Ng, T. W. H., & Feldman, D. C. (2012). Evaluating six common stereotypes about older workers with meta-analytical data. *Personnel Psychology, 65,* 1744–6570.

Ng, T. W. H., & Feldman, D. C. (2013). A meta-analysis of the relationships of age and tenure with innovation-related behaviour. *Journal of Occupational and Organizational Psychology, 86,* 585–616.

Ohly, S., Sonnentag, S., & Pluntke, F. (2006). Routinization and its relationship with creative and proactive outcomes. *Journal of Organizational Behavior, 27,* 257–279.

Palmiero, M., Di Giacomo, D., & Passafiume, D. (2014). Divergent thinking and age-related changes. *Creativity Research Journal, 26,* 456–460.

Paloniemi, S. (2006). Experience, competence and workplace learning. *Journal of Workplace Learning, 18*(7/8), 439–450.

Perry-Smith, J. E., & Mannucci, P. V. (2017). From creativity to innovation: The social network drivers of the four phases of the idea journey. *Academy of Management Review, 42,* 53–79.

Rosen, B., & Jerdee, T. H. (1976). The nature of job-related age stereotypes. *Journal of Applied Psychology, 61,* 180–183.

Rosing, K., & Zacher, H. (2016). Individual ambidexterity: The duality of exploration and exploitation and its relationship with innovative performance. *European Journal of Work and Organizational Psychology, 25,* 1–16.

Rothermund, K., & Brandtstadter, J. (2003). Age stereotypes and self-views in later life: Evaluating rival assumptions. *International Journal of Behavioral Development, 27,* 549–554.

Rudolph, C. W., Katz, I. M., Lavigne, K. N., & Zacher, H. (2017). Job crafting: A meta-analysis of relationships with individual differences, job characteristics, and work outcomes. *Journal of Vocational Behavior, 102,* 112–138.

Rupp, D. E., Vodanovich, S. J., & Crede, M. (2006). Age bias in the workplace: The impact of ageism and causal attributions. *Journal of Applied Social Psychology, 36,* 1337–1364.

Setti, I., Dordoni, P., Piccoli, B. Bellotto, M., & Argentero, P. (2015). Proactive personality and training motivation among older workers: A mediational model of goal orientation. *European Journal of Training and Development, 39*(8), 681–699.

Schaufeli, W. B., Bakker, A. B., & Van Rhenen, W. (2009). How changes in job demands and resources predict burnout, work engagement, and sickness absenteeism. *Journal of Organizational Behavior, 30*, 893–917.

Schürmann, E., & Beausaert, S. A. J. (2016). What are drivers for informal learning? *European Journal of Training and Development, 40*(3), 130–154.

Simonton, D. K. (1994). *Greatness: Who makes history and why.* New York: Guilford Press.

Skule, S. (2004). Learning conditions at work: A framework to understand and assess informal learning in the workplace. *International Journal of Training and Development, 8*(1), 8–20.

Stamov Roßnagel, C., & Jeske, D. (2017). Successful ageing in the workplace. A resources-oriented intervention perspective. In L. Riby (Ed.), *Handbook of gerontology research methods* (pp. 95–117). London & New York: Routledge.

Tims, M., Bakker, A. B., & Derks, D. (2012). Development and validity of the job crafting scale. *Journal of Vocational Behavior, 80*, 173–186.

Toossi, M., & Torpey, E. (2017, May). *Older workers: Labor force trends and career options.* May, US Bureau of Labor Statistics report. Retrieved from: www.bls.gov/career outlook/2017/article/older-workers.htm (accessed July 24, 2017).

Tornau, K., & Frese, M. (2013). Construct clean-up in proactivity research: A meta-analysis on the nomological net of work-related proactivity concepts and their incremental validities. *Applied Psychology: An International Review, 62*, 44–96. doi:10.1111/j.1464-0597.2012.00514.x.

Urick, M. J., Hollensbe, E. C., Masterson, S. S., & Lyons, S. T. (2016). Understanding and managing intergenerational conflict: An examination of influences and strategies. *Work, Aging and Retirement, 3*, 166–185.

van den Heuvel, M., Demerouti, E., & Peeters, M. (2015). The job crafting intervention: Effects on job resources, self-efficacy, and affective well-being. *Journal of Occupational and Organizational Psychology, 88*, 511–532.

Volet, S., Vauras, M., & Salonen, P. (2009). Self- and social regulation in learning contexts: An integrative perspective. *Educational Psychologist, 44*, 215–226.

Walker, C. O., Greene, B. A., & Mansell, R. A. (2006). Identification with academics, intrinsic/extrinsic motivation, and self-efficacy as predictors of cognitive engagement. *Learning and Individual Differences, 16*, 1–12.

Wanberg, C. R., Kanfer, R., Hamann, D. J., & Zhang, Z. (2016). Age and reemployment success after job loss: An integrative model and meta-analysis. *Psychological Bulletin, 142*, 400–426.

Wang, M., Olson, D. A., & Shultz, K. S. (2013). *Mid and late career issues: An integrative perspective.* New York: Routledge.

Wang, H., Demerouti, E., & Bakker, A. B. (2016). A review of job crafting research: The role of leader behaviors in cultivating successful job crafters. In S. K. Parker, & U. K. Bindl (Eds.), *Proactivity at work*: Making things happen in organizations (pp. 77–104). London: Routledge.

Wrenn, K. A., & Maurer, T. J. (2004). Beliefs about older workers' learning and development behavior in relation to beliefs about malleability of skills, age-related decline, and control. *Journal of Applied Social Psychology, 34*, 223–242.

Wrzesniewski, A., & Dutton, J. E. (2001). Crafting a job: Revisioning employees as active crafters of their work. *Academy of Management Review, 26*, 179–201.

Zacher, H., & Frese, M. (2011). Maintaining a focus on opportunities at work: The interplay between age, job complexity, and the use of selection, optimization, and compensation strategies. *Journal of Organizational Behavior, 32*, 291–318.

Zacher, H., Hacker, W., & Frese, M. (2016). Action regulation across the adult lifespan (ARAL): A meta-theory of work and aging. *Work, Aging and Retirement, 2*, 286–306.

Zhou, J. (2003). When the presence of creative coworkers is related to creativity: Role of supervisor close monitoring, developmental feedback, and creative personality. *Journal of Applied Psychology, 88*, 413–422. doi: 10.1037/0021-9010.88.3.413.

9

CAREER EMBEDDEDNESS AND CAREER CRAFTING AMONG OLDER WORKERS

Daniel C. Feldman and Kenneth S. Shultz

Over the past two decades, there has been considerable attention paid to the idea of a *boundaryless career* (Arthur & Rousseau, 1996; Feldman, 2002a) and the fact that few individuals are staying with any one organization or career for their entire work lives. While these contemporary career theories are often viewed from a positive perspective (i.e., employees now have more agency in their career paths), some contemporary authors have suggested the need to look at the "dark side" of contemporary careers as well (e.g., Baruch & Vardi, 2016; Carse, Griffin, & Lyons, 2017). Regardless of the perspective, while the career mobility of young adults has been widely researched (e.g., Morrison, 2002; Scandura, 2002; Stumpf, 2014), the career mobility of older adults has been largely ignored (Wang, Olson, & Shultz, 2013). By and large, researchers have not studied the career mobility of workers over age 50. Thereafter, older workers' career mobility has only been examined in a few contexts, most notably, CEO succession (Ward, Sonnenfeld, & Kimberly, 1995), retirement (Feldman, 1994), and bridge employment (Kim & Feldman, 1998, 2000).

In this chapter we seek to redress those shortcomings by exploring career embeddedness and career crafting in late career. In trying to make sense of the lower career mobility of older workers, people have often made the fundamental attribution error (Kelly, 1973) and assumed that older workers don't change careers because they have no motivation to do so and that this lack of motivation to change is a relatively stable individual difference over time. Here, we argue that older workers' mobility is not only a function of their *motivation* to change careers, but also their *ability* to do so. Moreover, the forces for and against career change are both *internal* (within the person) and *external* (inherent in the situation) in nature.

Building on the research on job embeddedness (Mitchell, Holtom, Lee, Sablynski, & Erez, 2001), we first discuss the construct of career embeddedness and suggest that older workers' career mobility and stability are a function of: (a) older workers' networks and *links* to the current career path; (b) their *fit* with current career paths; (c) *sacrifices* that would be associated with leaving a career; and (d) *barriers* to entering new careers. We use this construct to understand the individual-level, job-level, and occupational-level factors that influence whether older workers are stable in their current career paths until retirement or change careers after age 50.

The Construct of Career Change

We define *careers* as the series of jobs that a person holds over the course of a work life and *career change* as "entry into a new occupation which requires fundamentally different skills, daily routines, and work environments from the present one" (Feldman, 2002b, p. 76). Although career change may be conceptually similar to other types of job transitions, it can also be clearly distinguished from them.

For example, the term *job change* refers to taking a different position within an organization (e.g., moving from being an auditor in one department to be an auditor in another department). A job change is not, in and of itself, a career change; in the example above, there are no major changes in important skills or daily routines. However, moving from being an internal auditor to be an accounting professor would be considered a career change because of the magnitude of difference in requisite skills, daily routines, and work environments. Using the same logic, then, the term *organization change* refers to taking a position with a different employer. If the organization change does not entail any fundamental changes in skills or work environments, such a transition would not be considered a career change (e.g., moving from being a customer service representative at Target to being one at Walmart). On the other hand, moving from being a customer service supervisor at Target to being head of sales at a car dealership would be considered a career change because of the degree of novelty in the new tasks and work routines (Feldman, 2002b).

In the context of older workers' careers, an additional clarification is warranted. Many older workers *retire* from a long-held job or career, but then continue to be employed for several years thereafter (Feldman, 1994). If that subsequent employment is part-time or temporary in nature and is a low-involvement activity, we consider such work *bridge employment* (Feldman, 2002b, p. 77). For example, an archaeology professor who retires and then occasionally leads tours to historic sites would be considered to be engaging in such bridge employment. On the other hand, a physician who leaves medicine, earns an MBA, and starts a full-time consulting business would be considered to have changed careers. In this latter case, the older worker is sustaining the same level of psychological involvement in the new position as in the old position, and at the same time is experiencing fundamental changes in required skills, daily routines, and work contexts. As we will see next, there are both internal and external forces which influence older workers' motivation to change careers and their ability to do so in practice.

The Motivation to Change Careers Among Older Workers

As Feldman (2002b) notes, there is always some uncertainty and risk associated with a major career change. Moreover, the motivation to change careers varies across career stages. For example, the number of children to support may be an important motivator for young adults to change careers so that they can increase their earnings and provide their families with greater financial stability; that motivation, though, is largely absent for older workers. At the same time, the physical demands of an occupation may be a greater motivator of career change for older adults than for younger adults (Loi & Shultz, 2007). While we will not attempt to provide a comprehensive list of all the factors that may motivate older workers to change careers, we will highlight the individual-level, job-level, and occupational-level factors that are most likely to impel late-career employees to make this transition.

Individual-Level Factors

While research suggests that individuals' personalities are not fully formed by age 21 but continue to evolve in early adulthood, there appears to be much less fluidity of personality later in life (Eysenk, 1994). Consequently, enduring personality attributes may play a significant role in individuals' motivation to change careers after age 50. One particularly relevant disposition is having a proactive personality regarding one's career (Sonnentag, 2017). Individuals high on proactive personality with regard to their career tend to engage in a wide variety of proactive behaviors to enhance their careers (e.g., social networking, career planning and goal setting, seeking out a mentor, engaging in career enhancing training). Thus, individuals high in proactive personality with regard to their career are more likely to both change careers after age 50 and, if they don't change careers, be more satisfied in their long-held career due to a higher sense of agency in the choice to stay.

Of the *Big 5* personality traits most frequently studied in organizational research (Digman, 1989), the two that seem most likely to influence career change are *openness to experience* and *neuroticism*. Because career change always entails some risk, older workers who are open to experience are more likely to perceive alternative careers positively and to not exaggerate the potential hazards of major transitions. In addition, older workers who are in good mental health and who have realistic and positive self-regard are also more likely to estimate their chances of success in a new career to be higher as well. Some other personality variables which might be important here are *extraversion* and *self-efficacy*.

Two other individual-level factors are also likely to predispose older workers to change careers, namely, *health* and *wealth* (Kim & Feldman, 1998; Wang et al., 2013). As workers experience greater cognitive deficits and more physical problems, they are often pressured to find new careers as they get older. Thus, poor health appears to be a strong motivator to change careers while, unfortunately, also making it harder for older workers to enter alternative careers.

In addition, in the case of many older workers, a change of career can mean a temporary loss in income and potentially a significantly lower stream of income well into the future. Changing careers can also entail investments in new training, new offices, and geographical relocation, all of which can require considerable resources. Thus, older workers with more financial resources may be more motivated (and better able) to undertake career changes despite the financial uncertainty associated with doing so (Feldman, 1994). For example, a recent empirical study by Vogelsang, Shultz, and Olson (in press) found that for those individuals who are successful in their career change at older ages, those with higher financial resources experienced significantly higher emotional well-being than those who lacked financial resources.

Job-Level Factors

The motivation to change careers later in life can be a function of both the attributes of the present occupation and the perceived attributes of alternative careers. In other words, the decision to change careers later in life is a function of both the *pushes* out of the present job and the *pulls* exerted by other occupations (Wang, Adams, Beehr, & Shultz, 2009).

It appears that many of the *push* factors related to late-career change revolve around *job stress* (Kahn & Byosiere, 1992). Much of the research on late adult development, for example, suggests that people in their 50s and 60s prefer to increase the time they spend with families and friends; many older workers start shifting their priorities from accumulating professional accomplishments to developing and sustaining more intimate relationships (Baltes & Graf, 1996). Consequently, older workers, particularly those with financial means, may be more willing to leave highly stressful occupations and seek out those which they find more socially meaningful or personally fulfilling (Feldman, Leana, & Bolino, 2002; Johnson, Kawachi, & Lewis, 2009; Shultz & Olson, 2014).

Another set of factors that motivate older workers to change careers revolve around *boredom* and *lack of appreciation*. After 25–30 years in an occupation, some older workers feel like they are merely going through the motions on tasks they have performed hundreds (or thousands) of times previously (Shultz, Morton, & Weckerle, 1998). In addition, sometimes older workers feel like they are taken for granted. Enormous amounts of resources may go into attracting and rewarding younger workers while the salaries of older workers performing the same jobs remain flat (in real dollar terms) or grow much more slowly. In some cases, there is even serious salary inversion, where neophytes with little or no experience are being hired at more than competent veterans earn (Godshalk & Fender, 2015). These factors, too, energize older workers to consider changing occupations in late career.

Occupation-Level Factors

Probably the occupation-level factor that most motivates older workers to enter new careers is the *degree of change in skills and work context* over the course of a 20–30 year period (Hermans & Oles, 1999). This change can come from a variety of sources. In some cases, the skills that used to be critical in a career are no longer valued highly or the skills themselves are obsolescent. Thus, people who entered medicine in the 1980s with a motivation to provide patient care may now be spending much more time digitizing their medical records, justifying medical procedures requested to hospital utilization committees, and tracking down insurance reimbursements.

In other cases, the motivation to change may stem from declines in the quality of work relationships or work climates in an occupation. For instance, young adults who became high school teachers in the 1980s with an enthusiasm for sharing their knowledge may now find themselves working in buildings with metal detectors, alarmed by the level of violence and drug use in their schools, and hamstrung by state and federal regulations on how and what they can teach. In short, the careers they originally entered no longer bear much resemblance to the careers they now hold (Kruger, 1994; Wang, Adams, Beehr, & Shultz, 2009). As a result, some older workers are motivated to change careers despite their investments in their current occupations.

Another factor that may play a role in whether older workers are motivated to change careers is the *decline in the demand for labor* in their occupation (Albrecht, Edin, Sundstrom, & Vroman, 1999). Over time, the demand for labor in different occupations varies depending upon a series of environmental factors. For example, in the 1960s there was a shortage of aeronautical engineers as the space race heated up; today, there is an excess of aeronautical engineers in the wake of shuttle disasters and government funding cuts for space travel. Some older workers see the handwriting on the wall and are motivated to change careers because their future professional prospects look bleak.

Using the same logic, older workers are motivated to change careers when there is *perceived age discrimination* in the occupation (Wang et al., 2013; see also Chapter 4 by Finkelstein et al. in this volume). This age discrimination can affect how older workers experience their careers on a day-to-day basis at work. Thus, older advertising executives often see themselves being shuttled to more peripheral activities and assignments, not because they are less competent than their younger peers but because they are perceived as being less *edgy*. Over time, the corrosive effects of this perceived discrimination can motivate older workers to seek out new careers – a goal, as we shall see later, that is often easier set than achieved (Beehr & Bowling, 2002).

Career Stability and Career Embeddedness

Without question, we have seen dramatic changes in the context of career development over the past few decades. There are new forms of employment that have emerged as important alternatives to "normal" 9-to-5 permanent jobs, including telecommuting, outsourcing, contract labor, and off-shoring (Shultz & Olson, 2013). In addition, there are forms of employment that once appealed to small segments of the labor market but are now held by much higher percentages of workers, including self-employment, part-time work, temporary work, subcontracting, leased workers, and loaned executives (Feldman, 2002a). Not surprisingly, the academic community and the popular press alike have paid considerable attention to these changes in the career landscape (Arthur & Rousseau, 1996).

Nonetheless, underneath the surface of these dramatic environmental changes, there is an impressive amount of stability within individuals' careers over time (Feldman, 2002a, p. 4). Individuals' first few jobs are pivotal in shaping their work skills and personal values for years to come (Habermas & Bluck, 2000). Moreover, as the research on career anchors suggests, work skills and personal values developed in one's 20s play a major role in anchoring lifelong career decisions (Feldman & Bolino, 1997; Schein, 1990). And, even in the literature that examines "lack of fit" as a predictor of occupational change, the findings have been at best mixed (Spokane, Meir, & Catalano, 2000; Tinsely, 2000). As Ostroff, Shin, and Feinberg (2002) suggest, it is often hard to untangle the disparate effects of poor person–job fit, person–group fit, and person–organization fit from those of poor person–occupation fit.

The lack of widespread career changes among older workers, though, has often been attributed primarily to the aging process itself rather than to systematic forces within the labor market that anchor the vast majority of people to their current career paths. Nonetheless, there is some research that suggests that older workers are somewhat more reluctant to change occupations voluntarily (Warr, 1994). Below, we consider why older workers may be more "embedded" in their occupations than their younger colleagues.

Job and Career Embeddedness

In a seminal article, Mitchell and his colleagues (2001) introduced the construct of *job embeddedness*. Rather than focusing on the traditional turnover approach that looks at why people leave their jobs, Mitchell and his colleagues examine the reasons why people stay. They describe job embeddedness as "a net or a web in which an individual can get stuck" (p. 1104). More specifically, they identify the three key elements of job embeddedness as: (1) the extent to which people have *links* to other people and activities; (2) the extent to which their jobs and communities *fit* other aspects of their lives, and (3) the *sacrifices* that would have to be made to break these links. While Mitchell et al. (2001) acknowledge that job attitudes (e.g., job satisfaction and organizational commitment) certainly contribute to decisions to stay or leave, they make an important observation about the role of embeddedness in explaining mobility patterns. That is, low embeddedness makes employees more susceptible to job dissatisfaction and increases their likelihood of looking for new jobs when they do become dissatisfied. This hypothesis was affirmed by a recent empirical study by Allen, Peltokorpi, and Rubenstein (2016) that included samples from both the US and Japan.

We suggest that there is an analogous phenomenon here that we will call *career embeddedness*. People don't only get embedded in jobs; they get embedded in careers as well (Adams, Webster, & Buyarski, 2010). Thus, we suggest that individuals will become embedded in their career paths (i.e., show greater occupational stability) when: (1) they have extensive *links* to other people in the profession and occupational activities; (2) their current career paths *fit* with other aspects of their lives; (3) they would have to make great *sacrifices* to break their occupational ties; and (4) there are significant *constraints* on their ease of entry into alternative careers. And, because individuals typically remain in careers longer than they remain in any given job or organization, we have good reason to expect that career embeddedness would be even higher for older workers than job embeddedness is.

Links

One link to the current career path is the *amount of time spent within a career*. The longer people have been in an occupation, the more contacts they have, the more tacit knowledge they have about work responsibilities and professional politics, and the more enmeshed they become in professional associations and activities. For older workers with high occupational tenure, then, their roots in the current career path run deep. Moreover, since older workers, as a group, have greater occupational tenure than their younger colleagues, their career embeddedness is likely to be greater as well.

Along similar lines, the *amount of task interdependence* is also likely to increase career embeddedness (O'Reilly, Caldwell, & Barnett, 1989). For example, working closely with a wide variety of colleagues, customers, suppliers, and contractors can help enmesh employees in both job activities and social networks. In situations where there is high task interdependence, people can come to feel that others depend upon them and this, too, creates greater attachment to the present occupation. Because older workers are more likely to have supervisory jobs, to have "boundary crossing" responsibilities, and to have leadership positions in professional activities, this greater task interdependence embeds them more deeply in their careers.

It is also important to note that Mitchell et al. (2001) suggest that links to the community as well as links to the job can embed an individual in his/her current position. Thus, in general, we would expect *length of time in a community* to enmesh older workers in their current career paths as well. However, in terms of career embeddedness, we also have to consider *the extent to which career alternatives are location-specific*. For instance, if someone in the field of agribusiness decided he wanted to be an options trader, such a career change would almost certainly require a move out a rural community. In this case, the probability of being able to simultaneously change careers and stay in the same community (or even the same type of community) would be very low – and career embeddedness would be correspondingly high. In contrast, it is fairly easy to become a nurse or a public-school teacher in any location, so older workers who want to transition into these occupations should feel much less embedded in their current careers.

Fit

There are a variety of ways fit can be conceptualized (Kristof, 1996). At its broadest level, fit refers to some sort of congruence between an individual's attributes and a specific position's requirements and work context. For instance, there can be fit in terms of matching individual skills with job demands (person–job (P-J) fit), matching an individual's personal style with the personal styles of workgroup members (person–group (P-G) fit), or matching an individual's needs and values with the culture of the organization as a whole (person–organization (P-O) fit).

The research evidence suggests that different types of poor fit motivate different kinds of career transitions (Ostroff et al., 2002, pp. 70–72). In particular, it appears that changes in occupation are most likely to occur *when both P-J fit and P-G fit are low*. In such cases, workers will not be enmeshed by either the work itself or by fulfilling social relationships with colleagues. Consequently, it will not take a powerful external force to pry them loose from their current career trajectory.

In contrast, when only person–organization fit is low, there is much less likelihood that individuals will look for new occupations. That is because context factors (organizational values and norms) play a much less significant role in driving occupational change than P-J fit and P-G fit do (Austin & Hanish, 1990). When the source of dissatisfaction is the organization itself, the most likely reaction is to look for a new place to work rather than to reject the career itself. In colloquial terms, people are less likely to "throw the baby out with the bath water" just because they are unhappy with a particular employer.

Like the *links* construct, the *fit* construct can also be conceptualized in terms of both work and community (Mitchell et al., 2001). In terms of fit with the community, the biggest predictors of career stability are likely to be *value-fit* and *lifestyle-fit*. The values component refers to personal congruence with prevailing religious and social norms in the present community; for example, a person likes the liberal/conservative values that underlie the education and cultural opportunities in the community. Meanwhile, the lifestyle-fit component refers to personal congruence with the kinds of leisure activities and daily routines available in a community, be they athletic pursuits such as skiing or lifestyle issues such as low cost of living and low crime rates. To the extent that career changes require leaving a particular community, career embeddedness would be much higher. Moreover, because older workers have typically lived in their communities a longer time than their younger colleagues and have adjusted to a particular way of life, we would expect community fit to embed older workers even more strongly (Feldman & Vogel, 2009).

Sacrifices

Changing careers is not a cost-free activity. As noted earlier, there can be expensive transaction costs associated with winding down a career, moving geographically, obtaining additional training, and even potentially earning less money in a new career. Emotionally, people can experience considerable stress as they are stripped of old routines and have to develop new ones (Kim & Feldman, 2000; Richardson & Kilty, 1991). Furthermore, the costs associated with a career change are not borne solely by the individual. Spouses, partners, extended family members, and children may bear some of those costs, too, since their careers and daily routines may be disrupted as well (Stroh, Brett, & Reilly, 1996; Vogelsang et al., in press).

Chief among the sacrifices that might embed people in their careers are *employee benefits*, particularly those that are *longevity-based* (Kim & Feldman, 1998, 2000). For example, older workers may have to stay with their present employers for a given number of years (and thus, most likely, in their present careers) in order to be eligible for lifetime insurance coverage or to earn maximum pension benefits. Some organizations also grant sick leave, annual leave, and vacation leave on the basis of longevity, and these, too, might be put at risk with a career change. Since older workers are those who have accrued the greatest rewards associated with longevity-based benefits, such benefits play a much larger role in embedding older workers in their careers (Shaw, Delery, Jenkins, & Gupta, 1998), particularly when those benefits are not portable.

Another sacrifice to be considered here is the level of initial financial investment in obtaining occupational training, either in terms of past outlays of funds or current indebtedness for past education. A neurosurgeon who has invested hundreds of thousands of dollars in an education and has accumulated substantial debt doing so would have to make an enormous sacrifice to change careers – a much greater sacrifice of income, for example, than a pre-school teacher would be making to enter the business world.

Other work factors that might embed older workers in their careers are *opportunities for promotion and advancement* (Mitchell et al., 2001; Shaw et al., 1998). In career paths where years of service are very highly correlated with promotions and rank (e.g., the military and civil service), older individuals may be especially reluctant to change careers before they accrue the full measure of rewards they expected at the start of their careers. In addition, when employees change careers later in life, their opportunities for reaching equally senior positions in the next career are also lower.

Family responsibilities also serve to embed older workers in their current careers (Eby, Allen, & Douthitt, 1999). These responsibilities can impact the career embeddedness of older workers in numerous ways. For example, people with *working spouses* might be more "career embedded" because any career changes on their part might cause disruptions for their partners. Moreover, because working spouses also have concerns about pensions and other employee benefits, the financial sacrifices associated with such transitions would have greater ripple effects. In addition, the research on retirement suggests that spouses try to time their retirements together (Szinovacz, 2013; Talaga & Beehr, 1995). Thus, some older workers may simply "hang on" to their current careers until their spouses are ready to retire, too. *Responsibilities for elderly parents* may also embed older workers in their communities, a factor of much less concern to younger workers.

Constraints on Entry into Alternative Careers

While the embeddedness literature focuses on the factors that enmesh older workers in their current career paths, another issue that needs to be considered here is barriers to entry into other occupations. Older workers may be highly motivated to change careers, but don't make the transition because they perceive there aren't suitable alternatives in the labor market.

Chief among these concerns is *age discrimination in employment.* Even assuming older workers exhibit minor decrements in cognitive skill or physical ability over time, there remains considerable age bias against older workers trying to obtain new jobs (Hassell & Perrewe, 1995; see also Chapter 4 by Finkelstein et al. and Chapter 5 by McDermott and Goldberg in this volume), particularly when they involve between versus within career job transitions (Fritzsche & Marcus, 2013). While there are fewer hard data available on this next issue (Cascio, 1995), there also seems to be some *age discrimination in access to training* (Beehr & Bowling, 2002; see also Chapter 8 by Olson and Jeske in this volume). It is often hard for older workers who want to go back to school to earn academic degrees to start new careers. Even in academia, which is reputably liberal in its attitudes, one rarely sees PhD students in their 50s or new faculty in their 60s (Kim & Feldman, 1998). Moreover, older workers are somewhat less likely to want to engage in new training and they tend to take longer to train than younger workers (Kubeck, Delp, Haslett, & McDaniel, 1996). Thus, to the extent that career changes require new training, older workers are somewhat more reluctant and somewhat less successful in obtaining it.

Another impediment to seeking new careers is the extent to which those occupations require *extensive exposure to new technology*. In a particularly relevant study, Czaja and Sharit (1993) found that age is associated with slower response times and more errors on computer-based tasks. Moreover, age has a negative impact on performance on computer-based tasks even when previous computer experience was held constant. Beehr and Bowling (2002, p. 218) interpret these findings as suggesting that it is the aging process itself, and not just the lack of computer experience, that is associated with poorer performance with technology. Not surprisingly, then, as more careers are becoming technologically complex, older workers may perceive there are fewer alternative careers for them to enter. Whether this phenomenon will change in the next generation, where children grow up with extensive exposure to computer technology before even entering school, remains to be seen (see also Chapter 11 by Charness and Czaja in this volume).

Job and Career Crafting

Just as career embeddedness is a logical extension of job embeddedness, the concept of career crafting (Valcour, 2015) is a logical extension of job crafting (Rudolph, Katz, Lavigne, & Zacher, 2017; Wrzesniewski & Dutton, 2001). Therefore, below we briefly describe and distinguish job and career crafting. In addition, we discuss how career crafting relates to career embeddedness and career change after age 50.

Job crafting is typically defined as the ways in which employees use various opportunities to customize their jobs by actively shifting their tasks and interactions with others at work. Wrzesniewski and Dutton (2001) identified three primary dimensions of job crafting behaviors: task, cognitive, and relational. With *task crafting*, individuals focus on changing the boundaries of their work and the approaches they use to complete tasks. This form of crafting allows individuals to adapt to changes in performance requirements in response to outside pressures (i.e., to increase performance related to new competitors in the market, implementation of technology that changes the approaches and processes used to complete tasks). Task crafting also allows individuals to develop new ways to improve task performance and increase efficiency by applying knowledge and experience in new ways. Changes associated with task crafting benefit the organization and team by increasing performance and efficiency related to achieving key goals set by the organization. Task crafting also benefits individuals by maintaining interesting and challenging work that provides opportunities for continuous learning and developing new approaches to complete tasks.

Cognitive crafting is the process of reframing how one views one's role. Individuals may reframe the tasks they need to complete by focusing on the overall purpose of their work and view their work as an integrated whole. For example, teachers may focus on the purpose of facilitating the development of students to expand their critical thinking skills in ways that allow them to navigate the overabundance of information they receive on a daily basis more successfully rather than focusing on the details associated with writing lesson plans, grading assignments, and managing disruptive classroom behaviors. As a result, cognitive crafting changes the boundaries of how individuals see their jobs (e.g., I am influencing students' lives by fostering and nurturing the development of their critical thinking and leadership skills).

Relational crafting emphasizes the importance of who individuals work with as they complete tasks. Individuals seek out others whom they prefer to work with as they complete tasks and assignments. This includes individuals whom they enjoy working with who may: (1) possess complementary skills that assist them in completing work in a high-quality way; (2) provide unique perspectives to help them develop creative approaches and innovations; as well as, (3) fulfill social needs through working with and developing collaborative relationships and meaningful attachments at work.

Similar to job crafting, career crafting is typically defined as the ways in which employees use various opportunities to customize their careers by actively shifting their tasks and interactions with others at work. As with job crafting (Berg, Wrzesniewski, & Dutton, 2010), career crafting takes a distinctly agentic approach to one's career (Grimland, Vigoda-Gadot, & Baruch, 2012; Hall, 2004). That is, it is assumed that the individual takes a proactive role in guiding and directing their career (Sonnentag, 2017). Also, like job crafting, career crafting included three components. *Cognitive Career Crafting* conceptualizes an ideal career goal and includes self-awareness, prioritizing, redefining tasks and/or relationships, as well as reframing perceptions of one's personal and professional life. Meanwhile, *Task Career Crafting* is about managing activities toward the fulfilment of the career goals, as well as taking on additional tasks to achieve desired career related outcomes. Finally, *Relational Career Crafting* focuses on the role of important others, altering the nature and extent of relationships, adding relationships, as well as selecting and nurturing relationships with key people in order to enact career goals. Thus, career crafting allows people to individualize and prioritize the key facets needed to realize the idealized career goals.

As with career embeddedness, career crafting also acknowledges that there are both internal and external factors that contribute to career change and stability after age 50. A recent qualitative study by Sukhapure and Cohen (2015) identified several consistent, identifiable characteristics of people who take control over their careers (i.e., internal factors of career crafters). They can be summarized as an ability to, (1) conceptualize their ideal career; (2) engage in cognitive, task, and/or relational career crafting; (3) make the change happen in their lives including navigational changes if necessary; (4) express passion with regard to both their work and personal life; (5) equip themselves with the necessary skills to maintain and/or change careers; and (6) have clarity about their career goals. In addition, external organizational factors such as developmental human resource practices (e.g., employees are empowered to make decisions, performance appraisals include developmental feedback) and perceived organizational support have also been shown to enhance career crafting or what Jung and Takeuchi (2017) refer to as *career self-management*.

Relatedly, a recent meta-analysis of the career adaptability concept by Rudolph, Lavigne, and Zacher (2017) has shown that career adaptability (i.e., a psychosocial resource for managing career-related tasks and transitions) is positively related to career-related adapting responses such as career planning, career exploration, and career decision-making self-efficacy. Age was positively (though weakly) associated with career adaptability. Thus, not surprisingly, older workers with more "human capital" (i.e., tenure) demonstrated higher levels of career adaptability.

Directions for Future Research

The career embeddedness and career crafting perspectives, then, can be usefully employed to understand the forces that keep older workers in their current positions or to energize them to seek alternative career paths. In this section, we consider some other directions for future research on this increasingly important topic.

Career Embeddedness of CEOs

The work of Sonnenfeld and his colleagues (Sonnenfeld, 1988; Ward, Sonnenfeld, & Kimberly, 1995) highlights the particular career challenges faced by senior executives forced out of their jobs. In many ways, the stripping away of these positions is as painful psychologically as it is financially. Because their work lives are so entwined with their personal lives and friendship networks, executives who lose top management positions feel like the fabric of virtually every aspect of life has been ripped away.

How does this particular group of older workers face the thought of changing careers? To date, the evidence doesn't appear that they embrace such forced change well. As Sonnenfeld and his colleagues note, there is often a profound sense of loss associated with exits from senior management positions and more energy seems to go into trying to hang on to former power and glory than into moving on.

One avenue for future research that might prove fruitful here is considering the career embeddedness of CEOs more fully in the context of broader network theory. In network theory, Zukin and Dimaggio (1990) have identified four forms of embeddedness: structural, cognitive, political, and culture. What all these forms of embeddedness have in common is the concept of a relationship tie (Granovetter, 1985) that keeps individuals tethered to their existing career paths. In the case of senior executives, the possession of a top management seat gives them entrée into the political and cultural elite, too. By virtue of their positions as senior executives, they are also often given seats on the boards of directors of interlocking businesses, major not-for-profit organizations, and even local and national policy-making positions (Useem, 1984). For this population in particular, embeddedness in broader corporate elites has to be considered alongside career embeddedness.

Career Embeddedness, Retirement, and Bridge Employment

The construct of career embeddedness might also dovetail nicely with the research on retirement and bridge employment (Bamberger & Bacharach, 2014; Wang et al., 2009). In early and mid-career, those who switch occupations typically continue to work full-time at their new vocations. In late career, however, the career options are somewhat different (Wang et al., 2013). Many individuals have the financial luxury of not working at all (retirement), continuing to work but with less intensity (bridge employment), or shift to an alternate career altogether. Thus, the career embeddedness construct might also help researchers get a better handle on retirement and bridge employment decisions (Furunes et al., 2015).

For instance, the retirement research paradigm has typically examined individual-level factors and organizational-level factors that predict whether older workers will retire (Wang & Shultz, 2010). At the individual level, for example, researchers have looked at employees' financial holdings, their physical and mental abilities, and their current job performance (what Kim and Feldman, 1998, refer to as "healthy, wealthy, or wise"). Similarly, at the organizational level, researchers have examined the structure of early retirement packages, the amount of pre-retirement counseling, and age discrimination in the workplace (Beehr & Bowling, 2002).

What the career embeddedness construct suggests is that the retirement and bridge employment literature could be enriched by considering the social context in which exit decisions and career change decisions are made. To date, network ties within the present organization and the present occupation are rarely explored in retirement research, yet social and professional ties to co-workers may indeed keep older workers from retiring or retiring fully from their jobs. (Academe is just one of many professions where this employment pattern can be discerned.)

Alternatively, it can also happen that older workers' network ties to people in *other* occupations or in *other* organizations could be major enabling factors for career mobility. For example, employees might network extensively with major clients and, in so doing, form stronger bonds with clients than with those in the current firm or occupational group. Thus, the knowledge of alternative careers and the potential attractiveness of those careers may be driven by "receiving" networks, as well as current occupational networks. (This has certainly been a common phenomenon in the military, where "retired" military officers become "Beltway bandits" working for companies bidding for defense contracts.) And, while "years in community" has often been used to study attachment in the retirement literature, "extent of involvement in community" has been largely ignored.

Career Embeddedness, Career Crafting, and Career Anchors

A third potential avenue for future research is examining the relationships between Schein's (1990) construct of career anchors and the present constructs of career embeddedness and career crafting. By the term *career anchor*, Schein means the set of self-defined interests, skills, and values that constrain individuals in making career choices. They typically develop between ages 30–35 and result in individuals making subsequent career choices within a narrowly circumscribed set of mobility options. For example, an individual with a *technical/functional* career anchor would try to find positions that capitalize on the use of specific technical skills and minimize managerial activity, while individuals with an *autonomy* career anchor would try to find positions that give maximum freedom around scheduling and work procedures and minimize close supervision.

While the career embeddedness and career crafting constructs give us some insight into whether individuals are willing to change careers, the career anchors literature gives us some insight into how far away from their current careers individuals are willing to move and where they are likely to land (Chapman & Brown, 2014; Feldman & Bolino, 1997). For example, Feldman and Bolino's octagonal model suggests that career anchors can be arrayed in terms of *degrees of difference* – and that these degrees of difference may be helpful in understanding to where older career changers are likely to migrate. Thus, individuals with an autonomy career anchor might be willing to move into careers with an entrepreneurial orientation, but individuals with a *challenge* career anchor are much less likely to move into careers which have *lifestyle* or *service* orientations.

Over the course of a career, individuals are much more likely to change organizations than they are occupations (Ng, Eby, Sorensen, & Feldman, 2005). Individuals make investments in developing certain sets of skills and, over time, the set of career paths that utilize those skills becomes somewhat circumscribed. In addition, what is often called "poor fit" with a job is often the result of dissatisfaction with co-workers, supervisors, and organizational values rather than with the work per se (Ostroff et al., 2002). Consequently, there is much more mobility across organizations than across occupations, particularly for older workers. Integrating career anchors research with future research on career embeddedness and career crafting would be helpful in understanding how far, and in what direction, older workers are willing to stretch themselves in order to find careers that are more satisfying and fulfilling.

Implications for Practice

Changes in the environment over the past several decades have resulted in the re-questioning of many long-held assumptions about what a "successful" career means (Akkermans & Tims, 2017; Arthur & Rousseau, 1996; Wang & Wanberg, 2017). Where once staying with one occupation (and, indeed, with one organization) an entire career was the norm, widespread layoffs, corporate restructurings, globalization, and technological advances have made the likelihood of such career trajectories highly unlikely. And, even if such career stability were possible, is it necessarily desirable (Wang & Wanberg, 2017)? Is career stability a sign of personal stability, as was widely believed in the 1950s and 1960s, or simply a lack of ambition? Can any one occupation or organization provide enough growth opportunities to keep individuals fully engaged over a 40-year period? Ultimately, then, is career embeddedness "good" or "bad" for individuals and organizations?

For individuals, it can be argued that career embeddedness is beneficial if it is a *conscious choice* rather than a default option. If individuals, as young adults, have chosen careers wisely and after careful consideration, career embeddedness can actually create a self-reinforcing, positive cycle. That is, the better an individual performs in a career path, the more likely s/he is to stay in it, the more likely s/he is to make contributions, and the more likely s/he is to get positive feedback. However, there is a paucity of research in this area, and thus there is limited empirical evidence that supports this hypothesis (e.g., Howes & Goodman-Delahunty, 2015).

On the other hand, if career embeddedness results from a series of bad choices and lack of initiative, then this embeddedness can result in a long period of plateaued performance and frustration instead. For instance, if middle-aged individuals who have fallen out of step with their careers for whatever reason – changes in job duties, work environments, or occupational values – fail to change occupations, they might find themselves stranded in a painful "hanging on" process. The "long-timer" who is simply trying to get in six, eight, or ten more years so s/he can collect full retirement is a sad, and all too frequent, career end for many older workers. And, given the current uncertainty about Social Security benefits and increased concerns about pension fund security, there may well be even more older workers in this situation.

For individuals themselves, then, probably the best advice would be: "hope for the best, but prepare for the worst." That is, make the kinds of decisions that maximize the likelihood one could experience career longevity – doing research on the occupation before entering it, continuously upgrading skills, and building constructive relationships with others in the occupation. At the same time, there are no guarantees that careers will not change dramatically over time, and indeed the probabilities are high that such change will occur (Feldman, 2002a, 2002b; Wang & Wanberg, 2017). Older workers would be unwise to write off a decade (or more) of their lives to careers they don't like, particularly if alternatives – indeed, alternatives that might draw on the same skill set and value set – are readily available. For example, recent research on late career entrepreneurship by Kautonen, Kibler, and Minniti (2017) found that late career entrepreneurs had higher ratings of quality of life after starting their own business; however, they also had reduced incomes, at least in the short term.

For organizations, the research on career embeddedness points to the need to move away from longevity-based incentives as the primary strategy for retaining employees. Particularly in organizations with defined benefit plans, many older workers are forced to remain in their current jobs (and occupations) way too long so they won't get "penalized" for retiring before age 65 or 30 years of service. Such compensation schemes force employees to stay well beyond their welcome – and age discrimination laws often make it difficult for companies to terminate older workers who are competent, if not stellar, in their jobs.

At the same time, the research on career embeddedness highlights another reason why bridge employment opportunities are a valuable tool for moving older workers gracefully out of the workforce and refreshing the talent pool. If there are, in fact, inertial forces that act against older workers' willingness to leave, then bridge employment represents a less painful and less dramatic way of weaning people away from long-held careers (Wang et al., 2009). Even in the worst-case scenario, where people have hated their jobs for a long period of time, older workers still fear losing their positions and experiencing what life without work will be like – the career equivalent of the Stockholm syndrome. Thus, gradual disintegration of career ties might be more effective in lessening dysfunctional career embeddedness than the wrenching apart of those ties.

Robert Frost famously wrote that "before I built a wall, I'd ask what I was walling in and what I was walling out." Much the same can be said about career embeddedness. It can provide a long-term, nourishing environment or it can entrap people in a perpetually frustrating, no-exit, career dead end. The seeds of dysfunctional late-career embeddedness, then, are often sown much earlier in life through poor initial job choices, lack of skill updating, and insufficient scanning of the environment. Being mindful and purposeful about managing one's own career, then, is as important late-career as it is as early career (Wang et al., 2013).

References

Adams, G. A., Webster, J. R., & Buyarski, D. M. (2010). Development of an occupational embeddedness measure. *Career Development International, 15*, 420–436. doi: 10.1108/13620431011075312.

Akkermans, J., & Tims, M. (2017). Crafting your career: How career competencies relate to career success via job crafting. *Applied Psychology, 66*, 168–195. doi: 10.1111/apps.12082.

Albrecht, J. W., Edin, P. A., Sundstrom, M., & Vroman, S. B. (1999). Career interruptions and subsequent earnings: A reexamination using Swedish data. *Journal of Human Resources, 24*, 294–311.

Allen, D. G., Peltokorpi, V., & Rubenstein, A. L. (2016). When "embeddedness" means "stuck": Moderating effects of job embeddedness in adverse work environments. *Journal of Applied Psychology, 101*, 1620–1686. http://dx.doi.org/10.1037/apl0000134.

Arthur, M. B., & Rousseau, D. M. (1996). *The boundaryless career: A new employment principle for a new organizational era.* New York: Oxford University Press.

Austin, J. T., & Hanish, K. A. (1990). Occupational attainment as a function of abilities and interests: A longitudinal analysis using Project TALENT data. *Journal of Applied Psychology, 75*, 77–86.

Baltes, P. B., & Graf, P. (1996). Psychological aspects of aging: Facts and frontiers. In D. Magnusson (Ed.), *The lifespan development of individuals: Behavioral, neurobiological, and psychosocial perspectives* (pp. 427–460). Cambridge, UK: Cambridge University Press.

Bamberger, P. A., & Bacharach, S. B. (2014). Predicting retirement upon eligibility: An embeddedness perspective. *Human Resource Management, 53*, 1–22. doi:10.1002/hrm.21548.

Baruch, Y., & Vardi, Y. (2016). A fresh look at the dark side of contemporary careers: Toward a realistic discourse. *British Journal of Management, 27*, 355–372. doi:10.1111/1467-8551.12107.

Beehr, T. A., & Bowling, N. A. (2002). Career issues facing older workers. In D. C. Feldman (Ed.), *Work careers: A developmental perspective* (pp. 214–241). San Francisco: Jossey-Bass.

Berg, J. M., Wrzesniewski, A., & Dutton, J. E. (2010). Perceiving and responding to challenges in job crafting at different ranks: When proactivity requires adaptivity. *Journal of Organizational Behavior, 32*, 158–186.

Cascio, W. F. (1995). Whither industrial and organizational psychology in a changing world of work? *American Psychologist, 50*, 928–939.

Carse, T., Griffin, B., & Lyons, M. (2017). The dark side of engagement for older workers. *Journal of Personnel Psychology, 16*(4), 161–171. http://dx.doi.org/10.1027/1866-5888/a000173.

Chapman, J. R., & Brown, B. L. (2014). An empirical study of the career anchors that govern career decisions. *Personnel Review, 43*, 717–740. doi:10.1108/PR-01-2013-0017.

Czaja, S. J., & Sharit, J. (1993). Age differences in the performance of computer-based work. *Psychology and Aging, 8*, 59–67.

Digman, J. M. (1989). Five robust trait dimensions: Development, stability, and utility. *Journal of Personality, 57*, 195–214.

Eby, L. T., Allen, T. D., & Douthitt, S. S. (1999). The role of nonperformance factors on job-related relocation opportunities: A field study and laboratory experiment. *Organizational Behavior and Human Decision Processes, 79*, 29–55.

Eysenk, M. W. (1994). *Individual differences*. Hillsdale, NJ: Erlbaum.

Feldman, D. C. (2002a). Stability in the midst of change: A developmental perspective on the study of careers. In D. C. Feldman (Ed.), *Work careers: A developmental perspective* (pp. 3–26). San Francisco: Jossey-Bass.

Feldman, D. C. (2002b). Second careers and multiple careers. In R. J. Burke & C. L. Cooper (Eds.), *The new world of work* (pp. 75–94). Oxford, UK: Blackwell.

Feldman, D. C. (1994). The decision to retire: A review and reconceptualization. *Academy of Management Review, 19*, 285–311.

Feldman, D. C., & Bolino, M. C. (1997). Careers within careers: Reconceptualizing the nature of career anchors and their consequences. *Human Resource Management Review, 6*, 145–163.

Feldman, D. C., Leana, C. R., & Bolino, M. C. (2002). Underemployment among downsized executives: Test of a mediated effects model. *Journal of Occupational and Organizational Psychology, 75*, 453–471.

Feldman, D. C., & Vogel, R. M. (2009). The aging process and person-environment fit. In S. G. Baugh and S. E. Sullivan (Eds.), *Maintaining focus, energy, and options over the life span* (Chapter 1, pp. 1–26). Charlotte, NC: Information Age Publishing.

Fritzsche, B., & Marcus, J. (2013). The senior discount: Biases against older career changers. *Journal of Applied Social Psychology, 43*, 350–362. doi: 10.1111/j.1559-1816.2012.01004.x.

Furunes, T., Mykletun, R. J., Solem, P. E., De Lange, A. H., Syse, A., Schaufeli, W. B., & Ilmarinen, J. (2015). Late career decision-making: A qualitative panel study. *Work, Aging and Retirement, 1*, 284–295. doi:10.1093/workar/wav011.

Godshalk, V. M., & Fender, C. M. (2015). External and internal reasons for career plateauing: Relationships with work outcomes. *Group & Organization Management, 40*, 529–559.

Granovetter, M. (1985). Economic action and social structure: The problem of embeddedness. *American Journal of Sociology, 19*, 481–510.

Grimland, S., Vigoda-Gadot, E., & Baruch, Y. (2012). Career attitudes and success of managers: The impact of chance event, protean, and traditional careers. *The International Journal of Human Resource Management, 23*, 1074–1094.

Habermas, T., & Bluck, S. (2000). Getting a life: The emergence of the life story in adolescence. *Psychological Bulletin, 126*, 748–769.

Hall, D. T. (2004). The protean career: A quarter-century journey. *Journal of Vocational Behavior, 65*, 1–13.

Hassell, B., & Perrewe, P. L. (1995). An examination of beliefs about older workers: Do stereotypes still exist? *Journal of Organizational Behavior, 16*, 457–468.

Hermans, H. J. M., & Oles, P. K. (1999). Midlife crisis in men: Affective organization of personal meanings. *Human Relations, 52*, 1403–1426.

Howes, L. M., & Goodman-Delahunty, J. (2015). Predicting career stability and mobility: Embeddedness and boundarylessness. *Journal of Career Development, 42*, 244–259. doi: 10.1177/0894845314548722.

Johnson, R. W., Kawachi, J., & Lewis, E. K. (2009). *Older workers on the move: Recareering in later life*. The Urban Institute, prepare for AARP Public Policy Institute. Accessed at www.urban.org/research/publication/older-workers-move-recareering-later-life.

Jung, Y., & Takeuchi, N. (2017). A lifespan perspective for understanding career self-management and satisfaction: The role of developmental human resource practices and organizational support. *Human Relations*. On-line first publication.

Kahn, R. L., & Byosiere, P. (1992). Stress in organizations. In M. D. Dunnette & L. M. Hough (Eds.), *Handbook of industrial and organizational psychology* (2nd ed., Vol. 3, pp. 571–650). Palo Alto, CA: Consulting Psychologists Press.

Kautonen, T., Kibler, E., & Minniti, M. (2017). Late-career entrepreneurship, income and quality of life. *Journal of Business Venturing, 32*, 318–333. http://dx.doi.org/10.1016/j.jbusvent.2017.02.005.

Kelly, H. H. (1973). The processes of causal attribution. *American Psychologist, 28*, 107–128.

Kim, S., & Feldman, D. C. (1998). Healthy, wealthy, or wise: Predicting actual acceptances of early retirement incentives at three points in time. *Personnel Psychology, 51*, 623–642.

Kim, S., & Feldman, D. C. (2000). Working in retirement: The antecedents and consequences of bridge employment and its consequences for quality of life in retirement. *Academy of Management Journal, 39*, 367–380.

Kristof, A. L. (1996). Person-organization fit: An integrative review of its conceptualizations, measurement, and implications. *Personnel Psychology, 49*, 1–49.

Kruger, A. (1994). The midlife transition: Crisis or chimera? *Psychological Reports, 75*, 1299–1305.

Kubeck, J. E., Delp, N. D., Haslett, T. K., & McDaniel, M. A. (1996). Does job-related training performance decline with age? *Psychology and Aging, 11*, 92–107.

Loi, J. L. P., & Shultz, K. S. (2007). Why older adults seek employment: Differing motivations among subgroups. *Journal of Applied Gerontology, 26*, 274–289. doi: 10.1177/0733464807301087.

Mitchell, T. R., Holtom, B. C., Lee, T. W., Sablynski, C. J., & Erez, M. (2001). Why people stay: Using job embeddedness to predict voluntary turnover. *Academy of Management Journal, 44*, 1102–1121.

Morrison, E. W. (2002). The school-to-work transition. In D. C. Feldman (Ed.), *Work careers: A developmental perspective* (pp. 126–158). San Francisco: Jossey-Bass.

Ng, T. W. H., Eby, L. T., Sorensen, K. L., & Feldman, D. C. (2005). Predictors of objective and subjective career success: A meta-analysis. *Personnel Psychology, 58*, 367–408.

O'Reilly, C. W., Caldwell, D. F., & Barnett, W. P. (1989). Work group demography, social integration, and turnover. *Administrative Science Quarterly, 34*, 21–37.

Ostroff, C., Shin, Y., & Feinberg, B. (2002). Skill acquisition and person-environment fit. In D. C. Feldman (Ed.), *Work careers: A developmental perspective* (pp. 63–90). San Francisco: Jossey-Bass.

Richardson, V., & Kilty, K. M. (1991). Adjustment to retirement: Continuity vs. discontinuity. *International Journal of Aging and Human Development, 33*, 151–169.

Rudolph. C. W., Katz, I. M., Lavigne, K. N., & Zacher, H. (2017). Job crafting: A meta-analysis of relationships with individual differences, job characteristics, and work outcomes. *Journal of Vocational Behavior, 102*, 112–138.

Rudolph, C. W., Lavigne, K. N., & Zacher, H. (2017). Career adaptability: A meta-analysis of relationships with measures of adaptivity, adapting responses, and adaptation results. *Journal of Vocational Behavior, 98*, 17–34. http://dx.doi.org/10.1016/j.jvb.2016.09.002.

Scandura, T. A. (2002). The establishment years: A dependence perspective. In D. C. Feldman (Ed.), *Work careers: A developmental perspective* (pp. 159–185). San Francisco: Jossey-Bass.

Schein, E. A. (1990). *Career anchors: Discovering your real values.* San Diego, CA: Pfeiffer.

Shaw, J. D., Delery, J. E., Jenkins, G. D., & Gupta, N. (1998). An organization-level analysis of voluntary and involuntary turnover. *Academy of Management Journal, 41*, 511–525.

Shultz, K. S., Morton, K. R., & Weckerle, J. R. (1998). The influence of push and pull factors on voluntary and involuntary early retirees' retirement decision and adjustment. *Journal of Vocational Behavior, 53*, 45–57.

Shultz, K. S., & Olson, D. A. (2013). The changing nature of work and retirement. In M. Wang (Ed.), *The Oxford handbook of retirement* (Chapter 33, pp. 543–558). New York: Oxford University Press.

Shultz, K. S., & Olson, D. A. (2014). Heavy work investment, bridge employment, and the transition to retirement. In I. Harpaz, & R. Snir (Eds.), *Heavy work investment: Its nature, sources, outcomes, and future directions* (Ch. 13, pp. 267–284). New York: Psychology Press.

Sonnenfeld, J. A. (1988). *The hero's farewell: What happens when CEOs retire*. New York: Oxford University Press.

Sonnentag, S. (2017). Career proactivity. In S. K. Parker & U. K. Bindl (Eds.), *Proactivity at work: Making things happen in organizations* (Ch. 30, pp. 49–76). New York: Routledge.

Spokane, A. R., Meir, E., & Catalano, M. (2000). Person-environment congruence and Holland's theory: A review and reconsideration. *Journal of Vocational Behavior, 57*, 137–187.

Stroh, L. K., Brett, J. M., & Reilly, A. H. (1996). Family structure, glass ceiling, and traditional explanations for the differential rate of turnover of female and male managers. *Journal of Vocational Behavior, 49*, 99–118.

Stumpf, S. A. (2014). A longitudinal study of career success, embeddedness, and mobility of early career professionals. *Journal of Vocational Behavior, 85*, 180–190. http://dx.doi.org/10.1016/j.jvb.2014.06.002.

Sukhapure, M., & Cohen, D. A. (2015). Hazy "career clarity" can career crafting bring it into focus? *Labour, Employment, and Work in New Zealand*. Downloaded on 12/19/2017 from: https://ojs.victoria.ac.nz/LEW/article/viewFile/2208/2047.

Szinovacz, M. (2013). A multilevel perspective for retirement research. In M. Wang (Ed.), *The Oxford handbook of retirement* (Ch. 11, pp. 152–173). New York: Oxford University Press.

Talaga, J. A., & Beehr, T. A. (1995). Are there gender differences in predicting retirement? *Journal of Applied Psychology, 80*, 16–28.

Tinsley, H. E. A. (2000). The congruence myth: An analysis of the efficacy of the person-environment fit model. *Journal of Vocational Behavior, 56*, 147–179.

Useem, M. (1984). *The inner circle: Large corporations and the rise of business political activity in the U.S. and U.K.* New York: Oxford University Press.

Valcour, M. (2015). Facilitating the crafting of sustainable careers in organizations. In A. De Vos and B. I. J. M. Van der Heijden (Eds.), *Handbook of research on sustainable careers* (Ch. 2, pp. 20–34). London, UK: Edward Elgar Publishing.

Vogelsang, E. M., Shultz, K. S., & Olson, D. A. (in press). Emotional well-being following a late life career change: The role of agency and resources. *International Journal of Aging and Human Development*.

Wang, M., & Shultz, K. S. (2010). Employee retirement: A review and recommendations for future investigation. *Journal of Management, 36*, 172–206. doi:10.1177/0149206309347957.

Wang, M., & Wanberg, C. R. (2017). 100 years of applied psychology research on individual careers: From career management to retirement. *Journal of Applied Psychology, 102*, 546–563. doi: 10.1037/apl0000143.

Wang, M., Adams, G. A., Beehr, T. A., & Shultz, K. S. (2009). Career issues at the end of one's career: Bridge employment and retirement. In S. G. Baugh and S. E. Sullivan

(Eds.), *Maintaining focus, energy, and options over the life span* (Ch. 6, pp. 135–162). Charlotte, NC: Information Age Publishing (IAP).

Wang, M., Olson, D. A., & Shultz, K. S. (2013). *Mid and late career issues: An integrative perspective*. New York: Routledge Academic Press/Taylor & Francis Group.

Ward, A. J., Sonnenfeld, J. A., & Kimberly, J. R. (1995). In search of a kingdom: Determinants of subsequent career outcomes for chief executives who are fired. *Human Resource Management, 34*, 117–139.

Warr, P. (1994). Age and employment. In H. C. Triandis, M. D. Dunnette, & L. M. Hough (Eds.), *Handbook of industrial and organizational psychology* (2nd ed., Vol. 4, pp. 485–550). Palo Alto, CA: Consulting Psychologists Press.

Wrzesniewski, A., & Dutton, J. E. (2001). Crafting a job: Revisioning employees as active crafters of their work. *Academy of Management Review, 26*, 179–201.

Zukin, S., & DiMaggio, P. (1990). *Structures of capital: The social organization of the economy*. New York: Cambridge University Press.

10
AGING AND OCCUPATIONAL HEALTH

Yisheng Peng, Steve M. Jex, and Mo Wang

Using psychological theories and interventions to understand and enhance employee health and well-being is an important goal of the interdisciplinary field of Occupational Health Psychology (Barling & Griffiths, 2011; Tetrick & Quick, 2011). Recently, both researchers and practitioners have suggested that more attention should be paid to older employees' health and well-being (e.g., Conen, Henkens, & Schippers, 2012; Ng & Feldman, 2013) considering the increasing number of older workers in the workforce (Anxo, Ericson, & Jolivet, 2012; Toossi, 2009). As such, it is important to understand how age (and the aging process) relates to employee health.

What is Employee Health?

From a traditional medical perspective, health is equated with the *absence of physical pathology* (Boorse, 1975). Based on this perspective, a person is deemed healthy if a medical examination shows the result is "normal." The primary strength of this perspective is its simplicity, as a person is either healthy or unhealthy. Unfortunately, the simplicity is also a primary weakness of this traditional medical perspective. This model fails to recognize that there are degrees of health, and that health is more than just a physical concept. Additionally, as this model emphasizes the existence of pathology, there is little recognition of the potential for future health problems (e.g., risk). For instance, to say that a person is "healthy" is misleading at best if this individual has a very poor diet, engages in little or no physical activity, and participates in a number of risky behaviors, although according to the traditional medical perspective this person would likely be identified as healthy.

Another way to view health is from a *wellness* model, which is based on the World Health Organization's (WHO) constitution, which states that health is "a state of complete physical, mental, and social well-being" (Larson, 1999). According to this view, health is much more than just the absence of physical pathology. Specifically, being healthy not only means the absence of physical pathology, but also means being mentally healthy and being able to establish and maintain meaningful social relationships.

Another aspect of note in the wellness model is that it focuses on individuals' strength and ability to overcome illnesses. It also emphasizes an individual's continued striving to achieve better physical and psychological functioning. Given these emphases, this model is preventative by nature. That is, health is not just an issue to think about when one becomes ill. Rather, this model proposes that people should continually examine their lifestyles and determine whether they are as healthy as they could be. Organizational intervention programs that offer options such as fitness programs, nutritional counseling, and stress management training are all based on this model.

A third way to view health is from an *environmental perspective* (Parsons, 1991), which looks at health in terms of the relationship between the employee and the environment. The primary difference between this and the wellness model is that the latter focuses primarily on the individual. The environmental perspective, in contrast, focuses on the interaction between the employee and his or her environment. As an example of how this perspective works, an employee would be deemed "healthy" if the demands of his or her job were compatible with his or her skills, abilities, and emotional temperament. Conversely, being unhealthy would involve being in a work environment that was not compatible. In the occupational stress literature this is best reflected in the Person-Environment (P-E) Fit perspective (Edwards, 1996). It should be noted that the environmental perspective is not only psychological, but also physical in nature. That is, an employee with a history of upper respiratory problems would not be healthy if he or she works in an environment with a high level of smoke or other air pollutants.

One recent perspective on employee health, *Total Worker Health* (TWH; Schill & Chosewood, 2013), represents both the reduction and elimination of workplace hazards, while at the same time promoting employee health and well-being. In fact, this has become a major theme at NIOSH (www.cdc.gov/niosh/twh/totalhealth.html) and the broader Occupational Health Psychology literature (Anger et al., 2015). It focuses not only on preventing worker injury and illness but also emphasizes the promotion of employee health and well-being. This perspective looks at health in a very comprehensive way, by integrating both organizational and individual approaches to reducing stress and injury in the workplace (Anger et al., 2015).

Effects of Physical, Cognitive, and Social-Emotional Aging Processes

Chronological age in and of itself is of little interest to researchers. Rather, it is the changes that occur as one ages that researchers have attempted to study. Thus, it is important to discuss the impact of aging processes on occupational health. In this section, we particularly focus on three broad categories of aging changes, namely, physical aging, cognitive aging, and social-emotional aging. While other changes occur with aging, these three were chosen because they have obvious relevance and connections to employee health.

Effects of Physical Aging at Work

With aging, people generally experience gradual declines in many physical aspects that include (but are not limited to) hearing (e.g., Hull, 2011), vision (e.g., Owsley, 2011), mobility (e.g., Satariano et al., 2012), and vital functions (e.g., Hawkley, Thisted, Masi, & Cacioppo, 2010). Research has shown a general trend toward decreasing energy, and, as a result, reduced capacity for physically demanding tasks with increasing age. The implication of this, obviously, is that age-related physical changes may make it more difficult for older employees to perform physically demanding tasks and this has in fact been shown (e.g., Seitsamo & Martikainen, 1999). As an example, due to decreased aerobic and musculoskeletal capacity, people between the ages of 40 and 60 years generally report an average decline of 20 percent in physical work capacity, leading to decreased job-related work capacity and increased work-related injuries and illnesses (Kenny, Yardley, Martineau, & Jay, 2008).

Another general job condition that would appear to cause difficulty for many older employees would be having to perform tasks very quickly. Many service-oriented jobs require employees to perform tasks very quickly in order to satisfy customers. For example, cashiers are usually required to complete sales transactions (e.g., scan items and print receipts) both quickly and accurately. As people get older they can certainly perform such tasks accurately, but compared with younger employees they may experience more difficulty performing those tasks very rapidly. Not only is this due to physical changes associated with aging, but also due to the cognitive changes.

Finally, it should be noted that while there is an overall negative relationship between age and health, older workers who are active in the workforce are generally able to maintain their health well enough until they approach normal retirement age (Ng & Feldman, 2013). It would be worthwhile to identify potential risky and protective factors at work that may harm and benefit older workers' health and well-being.

Effects of Cognitive Aging at Work

Although many researchers have recognized that cognitive functioning is an important aspect of health that is related to daily functioning and physical health (e.g., Clouston et al., 2013), researchers have only recently started attending to the effects of cognitive functioning at work (see the review by Fisher, Chaffee, Tetrick, Davalos, & Potter, 2017).

As people grow older, they tend to experience declines in some cognitive functions (Cavanaugh & Blanchard-Fields, 2010), including processing speed, working memory, inhibition function, and fluid intelligence (Lindenberger & Ghisletta, 2009; Salthouse, 2013). Such cognitive constraints may impair older workers' work volition (Cheung, Yeung, & Wu, 2017). Furthermore, these age-related cognitive changes may be disruptive to older workers' sense of well-being and to their job performance. For instance, cognitive aging could be a barrier that hinders older workers from solving novel problems (e.g., McArdle, Vasilaki, & Jackson, 2002), probably because it requires the retention of large amounts of information.

Due to these age-related cognitive changes, older workers' health could be negatively impacted under situations that have high time pressure and cognitive demands. Supporting this, it has been found that having sufficient time to complete tasks, as well as autonomy and schedule flexibility, can buffer the impact of time deadlines and problem solving on older workers' self-reported stress (Shultz, Wang, Crimmins, & Fisher, 2010). It is believed that other aspects of cognitive functioning, such as working memory and inhibition, may also affect older workers' health in different working conditions.

Effects of Social-Emotional Aging at Work

As people grow older, they also experience emotional changes. Specifically, they generally experience less frequent negative affect (e.g., Carstensen et al., 2011; Charles, Luong, Almeida, Ryff, Sturm, & Love, 2010) and greater overall positive affective well-being (Carstensen et al., 2011; Chen, Peng, & Fang, 2016). The socioemotional selectivity theory (SST; Carstensen, Isaacowitz, & Charles, 1999) suggests that with age, people generally change from an open-ended to a limited future time perspective. Unlike younger adults who focus on learning new knowledge, developing skills, and planning for careers, older adults place more emphasis on social-emotionally meaningful goals (Carstensen et al., 1999).

Furthermore, with increasing age, people may also experience motivational changes (e.g., Inceoglu, Segers, & Bartram, 2012). Meta-analytic results have shown a positive relationship between age and intrinsic motives, and a negative relationship between age and strength of growth and extrinsic motives (Kooij, De Lange, Jansen, Kanfer, & Dikkers, 2011). Motivational orientations that can help older workers to maintain meaningful social relationships and to acquire pleasant rewards from these relationships become particularly important as people get older (Kanfer & Ackerman, 2004; Kooij, De Lange, Jansen, & Dikkers, 2013).

Due to these social-emotional changes, older workers could have stronger motivation to regulate their emotions and may be better able to do so (Blanchard-Fields Mienaltowski, & Seay, 2007; Carstensen, 2006). For example, research has found that older workers' emotional suppression is associated with lower intensity of negative emotions and higher levels of sales productivity (Yeung & Fung, 2012), as well as lower levels of physical strain and higher levels of affective well-being (Peng, Tian, Jex, & Chen, 2016). It is believed that age-related advantages in emotion regulation may positively contribute to older workers' health and well-being (Ng & Feldman, 2013; Scheibe & Zacher, 2013).

Furthermore, age-related changes in work motivations may also have important effects on older workers (Kanfer & Ackerman, 2004; Kooij et al., 2011). Older workers' work motivations have been well demonstrated to be closely related to subjective health (Kooij & Van De Voorde, 2011; Kooij et al., 2013). Research has also found that as people get older, they tend to perceive less remaining time and thus have lower levels of promotion orientation. This change in promotion focus could in turn weaken older workers' goal strivings related to aspirations and accomplishments and result in lower work-related growth motive, making older workers less motivated to continue working (Kooij, Bal, & Kanfer, 2014).

Effect of Workplace Environment on Older Workers

In considering the impact of age on occupational health, we suggest that age operates not only as a main effect, but may also function as a *moderator* variable. The main effects of age on occupational health are due to age-related changes that occur over time, which are independent of the workplace. A moderator variable is a variable that changes the strength or form of the relationship between two or more other variables (Baron & Kenny, 1986). As such, this means that employees may react differently to certain organizational or job conditions depending upon their age.

Effects of Job Characteristics and Stressors

Since the first edition of this chapter appeared, researchers have started to pay more attention to job characteristics and aging (e.g., Ng & Feldman, 2015; Shultz et al., 2010; Zaniboni, Truxillo, & Fraccaroli, 2013). Theoretical arguments and empirical findings suggest that younger and older workers react differently to certain job characteristics (e.g., Truxillo, Cadiz, Rineer, Zaniboni, & Fraccaroli, 2012; Zacher & Schmitt, 2016). Specifically, compared with younger workers, interactions outside the organization (Goštautaitė & Bučiūnienė, 2015), skill variety (Zaniboni et al., 2013), job autonomy and feedback (Bos, Donders, Schouteten, & Van der Gulden, 2013; Ng & Feldman, 2015) were all found to result in more positive outcomes (e.g., higher engagement, lower turnover intentions) for older workers.

Unfortunately, very little occupational stress research has examined whether age impacts reactions to other job stressors. In one of the few studies of this type conducted, Mayes et al. (1991) found in a sample consisting of police officers, fire fighters, electricians, and managers that in terms of mental and physical health, older employees responded more negatively to role conflict and underutilization of skills compared with younger employees. The fact that role conflict was more bothersome was possibly because balancing these conflicts may have required higher levels of cognitive or physical resources than older employees possessed.

Another stressor that employees may react to differently depending on age is job insecurity (Sverke, Hellgren, & Näswall, 2002). Since older workers stand to lose much more financially if laid off, and may have limited prospects for reemployment as compared with younger employees, they may exhibit more negative psychological reactions to job insecurity. Supporting this argument, research has found that older workers' job satisfaction is more negatively affected than that of younger workers when they experience high levels of job insecurity (Mauno, Ruokolainen, & Kinnunen, 2013).

Another stressor that may have a stronger effect on older workers is workload. Given the previously described age-related physical changes, it is certainly possible that older employees would have more physical health problems when performing jobs requiring a heavy workload or long hours. Indeed, research has found that workload was positively related to burnout among a group of Dutch older workers (50+) (Henkens & Leenders, 2010), and physical demands were negatively related to older workers' perceived work ability (McGonagle, Fisher, Barnes-Farrell, & Grosch, 2015).

Effects of Organizational Climate

Organizational climate has received a great deal of recent attention in organizational research, although the trend has been to examine climate with respect to specific organizational domains. One aspect of climate that may impact older employees, and which also has not received a great deal of attention, is simply the organizational climate with regard to older employees. Recently there have been some preliminary studies on general age-related climate. Specifically, Kunze, Boehm, and Bruch (2011) conducted a cross-organizational study on age diversity, age discrimination climate, and performance consequences. Age discrimination climate reflects organizational members' shared perceptions (Kozlowski & Klein, 2000) of the extent to which organizational actions, procedures, and behavior toward different age groups are fair or unfair. Kunze et al. (2011) found that age diversity was positively related to the emergence of an age discrimination climate in companies, which was negatively related to overall firm performance through the mediation of affective commitment. Boehm, Kunze, and Bruch (2014) further found the positive effect of age-inclusive HR practices on the development of an organization-wide age diversity climate, which in turn was positively related to employees' collective perceptions of social exchange and indirectly related to firm performance and employees' collective turnover intentions. These two organizational-level studies on age diversity provide important messages that organizations should pay attention to such organizational climates with regard to older employees.

In addition, Zacher and Yang (2016, p. 1) proposed the term *organizational climate for successful aging*, which is defined as "employees' shared perceptions of the extent to which their organization facilitates successful aging at work." They found that organizational climate for successful aging was an important contextual resource that can buffer the negative relationship between employee age and focus on opportunities (i.e., beliefs about future goals and possibilities at work), even after controlling for organizational tenure, psychological climate for successful aging (i.e., individuals' perceptions), and the psychological and organizational age discrimination climate. In conclusion, studies on general age-related climate are relatively limited, and future research needs to further examine the impact of the age-related climate on older workers' health and well-being, as well as their job performance.

Interventions for Improving Older Employees' Health

While understanding the impact of age on employee health is an important goal in and of itself, the primary reason for studying this issue is ultimately to take steps to improve the health of older employees. Furthermore, since this group represents the fastest growing segment of the population, it is an important overall occupational health priority for organizations and society as a whole. Thus, we describe a number of interventions that can be used to increase older employees' health. Readers will note that most of the interventions described in this section could in fact be used to improve the health of all employees regardless of age. Our emphasis, however, will be on using the intervention(s) for enhancing the health of older employees.

Job Redesign

Generally speaking, jobs can be designed from four primary perspectives: *mechanistic, motivational, perceptual/motor,* and *biological* (Campion & Thayer, 1987; Morgeson & Campion, 2003). The mechanistic approach to job design is primarily concerned with increasing efficiency and decreasing training time. The discipline most closely identified with this approach is industrial engineering. The motivational approach aims to design jobs to maximize outcomes such as employee motivation, job satisfaction, and job involvement. The discipline most closely associated with the motivational approach is organizational psychology. The perceptual-motor approach is concerned with designing jobs to minimize employees' information processing and sensory demands. The discipline most closely identified with the perceptual-motor approach is human factors or engineering psychology. Finally, the biological approach to job design is concerned with designing jobs to maximize employees' physical comfort. The disciplines most closely associated with this approach are ergonomics and biomechanics.

Organizations wishing to enhance older workers' health would not be well-served emphasizing the mechanistic approach to redesign jobs. This is because the focus on production efficiency may lead an organization to speed up work processes to a point that may be problematic for older employees. Also, this approach emphasizes simplification of work, something that may be detrimental to older employees, as they may react more negatively than younger employees to underutilization of skills (Mayes et al., 1991).

In contrast, job redesign which emphasizes the other three approaches in Campion's model could potentially be used to enhance the health and well-being of older workers. In the case of the motivational approach, increased control or discretion has been shown to provide health-related benefits to employees regardless of age (e.g., Spector, 1986). As such, redesigning jobs in this manner has the potential to benefit all employees. In the case of the perceptual motor approach, redesigning jobs by analyzing the information processing demands (e.g., memory load to operate the machine) would appear to especially benefit older employees given the previously described age-related cognitive changes. For example, redesigning jobs so that the information processing demands are reduced, or in such a way that employees are not required to process information as quickly, would appear to be particularly beneficial to older workers. The work environment could also be redesigned to make information easier to read, and perhaps steps could be taken to cut down on excessive noise if the job requires a high level of concentration. It should also be noted that complex jobs and cognitively demanding jobs may allow older workers to fully use their age-related gains in experiential knowledge, which may in turn, lead to increased satisfaction and engagement for older workers (e.g., Truxillo et al., 2012; Zacher & Frese, 2011).

Job redesign based on the biological approach would also appear to be well-suited to the physical changes associated with aging. This might include an assessment of the physical demands of a job, ergonomic assessment of employees' work stations, or perhaps a consideration of work hours or schedules. Any job redesign intervention that enhances physical comfort would probably prove beneficial to older employees, due to the fact that age-related physical changes tend to increase the difficulty of performing physically demanding jobs or working in difficult shifts (Kenny et al., 2008).

In addition to the above four approaches to job design, the more recent relational job design approach places more emphasis on the social and relational context of jobs (Grant, 2007, 2008). In his theoretical model, Grant (2007) illustrated how the job relational architecture (e.g., frequency and duration of contact with people influenced by one's work) shapes the motivation to exert a positive impact on other people's lives. Supporting this, having opportunities to do something valuable for others at work was found to promote a sense of work meaningfulness among employees (Grant, Dutton, & Rosso, 2008). Relational mechanisms, such as perceived social impact and social worth, have been found to mediate the positive impact of task significance on job dedication and helping behavior (Grant, 2008). Given the previously described age-related social-emotional changes, relational job design is particularly beneficial to older workers.

The recent lifespan perspective on job design further suggests that more attention should be paid to the role of age in job design (Truxillo et al., 2012). Owing to age-related social-emotional changes, certain job characteristics, such as generativity opportunities, might be particularly influential for older workers. Specifically, generativity opportunities represent an important kind of job resource that might be particularly important to meet older workers' generativity needs (Henry, Zacher, & Desmette, 2015). Generativity refers to "the concern in establishing and guiding the next generation" (Erikson, 1950, p. 267). Older adults, who typically perceive their remaining time to be limited, tend to treat generativity as more salient (Carstensen, 2006; Lang & Carstensen, 2002). Middle-aged and older adults typically express generativity through teaching, helping, and guiding the younger generation (McAdams & de St. Aubin, 1998). In the workplace, generativity opportunities allow older workers to share their knowledge and experience, as well as skills, with younger colleagues in the workplace (Templer, Armstrong-Stassen, & Cattaneo, 2010). Such opportunities have been found to be positively related to older workers' higher quality intergenerational contact (Henry et al., 2015) and intentions to continue working after retirement (Fasbender, Wang, Voltmer, & Deller, 2015; Mor-Barak, 1995). As such, organizations could encourage older workers to mentor younger workers and pass on their knowledge and experience in the workplace. Such activities not only allow older workers to fulfill generativity needs but they also meet the development needs of younger workers (Henry et al., 2015).

Job Crafting

As a bottom-up process where employees can play an active role in creating their job boundaries (Berg, Dutton, & Wrzesniewski, 2013), job crafting involves "the self-initiated changes individuals make in the task or relational boundaries of their work aimed at improving person-job fit" (Kooij, Tims, & Kanfer, 2015, p. 147; see also Tims, Bakker, & Derks, 2012). Job crafting can be divided into three different types: task, relational, and cognitive crafting. Task crafting occurs when employees change the type, number, content or scope of tasks that they do as part of their job. Employees may choose to perform certain types of job tasks more or less frequently. Relational crafting can be achieved when employees alter the range, nature, or number of their social interactions at work. Employees may choose to communicate with certain people at work more or less frequently based on personal preferences. And finally, cognitive crafting occurs when employees change the way they perceive the tasks and relationships that make up their jobs. Employees could view their work as a trivial piece or as having broader impact on others, the organization, or society.

All three types of job crafting mentioned above could be beneficial to older employees. Task crafting would appear to be well-suited to the physical and cognitive changes associated with aging. Task crafting that reduces physical demands at work allows older employees to perform tasks under their control, lowering risks of injury and accidents. Task crafting that reduces cognitive demands also allows older workers to perform tasks that they can apply their experiences and skills to. Relational job crafting seems to be particularly suited to older workers, as social-emotional goals increase in salience with age (Carstensen et al., 1999). As relational job crafting mainly involves changes in social relationships at work by altering with whom and how they develop connections and relationships (Berg et al., 2013), it could be particularly meaningful for older workers because it can help meet their increased communion needs. Older workers are likely to craft their jobs by altering relational boundaries through which they can establish meaningful relationships, impact, and help others at work (Kooij et al., 2015).

Finally, cognitive crafting also appears to be well suited to older workers. It has been found that as people grow older, work-related growth and extrinsic motives (e.g., advancement and compensation) decrease, and work-related intrinsic motives (e.g., generativity, contributing to society, and autonomy) increase (Kooij et al., 2011; see also Kooij et al., 2013; McAdams & de St. Aubin, 1998). Cognitive crafting allows older employees to perceive the tasks and relationships at work in a different way, which can be consistent with their age-related changes in work motivations. For instance, cognitive crafting may help older workers to perceive the totality of assignments to increase task identity and significance (Kooij et al., 2015).

Organizational Climate Development

Changing any aspect of an organization is not easy; changing the climate or culture of an organization is especially difficult. Nevertheless, this represents another potential way to enhance the health and well-being of older employees. What type(s) of changes in organizational climate would be most beneficial to older employees? Based on the earlier discussion of organizational climate, people should be concerned about a perceived age discrimination climate not only because of ethical considerations but also because of its business consequences. Organizations need to regularly attend to the age composition of their employees in order to be aware of the potential occurrence of a perceived age discrimination climate (Kunze et al., 2011). If serious levels of perceived age discrimination climate were identified, actions should be taken to lower the perception of age discriminatory behavior in the organization. Organizations may consider age awareness training (Armstrong-Stassen & Templer, 2005), diversity training (Kunze et al., 2011), and improving management's commitment to anti-age-discriminatory behavior and making their age-related human resource practices more transparent (Avery, McKay, & Wilson, 2008).

Furthermore, one would assume that positive changes in an organization's general organizational climate with regard to older workers (e.g., organizational climate for successful aging) would prove beneficial. This may involve developing greater awareness of the concerns of older employees, offering more training opportunities to older employees, and providing more flexible career paths for older employees whose career trajectory has plateaued. Organizations may also implement human resource strategies (e.g., recruitment, training, work design, and promotion) conveying the message that organizations care about older workers' successful aging and development at work (Boehm & Dwertmann, 2015; Boehm et al., 2014; Zacher & Yang, 2016). Development of a more positive climate with regard to older employees has the potential to enhance older employees' Organization-Based Self-Esteem (OBSE), which in turn may have positive effects on both mental and physical health (Jex & Elacqua, 1999). It is also possible that such a change in climate may help with the retention of younger employees, as they see that they will be treated well as they grow older.

Productivity and Safety Training

Another intervention that may enhance the health and well-being of older employees is training. Training is defined as "the systematic acquisition of skills, rules, concepts, or attitudes that result in improved performance in another environment" (Goldstein & Ford, 2002, p. 1). As applied to older employees, this may include training interventions to help compensate for physical and/or cognitive changes associated with age. Training may also be used to increase younger employees' understanding of changes associated with increased age, and therefore may potentially increase empathy toward their older colleagues. Another use of training may be to enhance older employees' adaptation to changes in work methods and technology. These issues certainly apply to employees of all ages, but may be particularly salient for older employees. This is because older employees may have been performing their jobs in a certain way for long periods of time, and thus adjusting to new methods or technology may be more challenging.

Older workers are often less likely and willing to participate in training and development activities, probably due to decreased self-efficacy for development

(Maurer, 2001) and the high-entity self-theory and the low perceived developmental support, as well as supervisors' beliefs about older workers' learning avoidance orientation (Van Vianen, Dalhoeven, & De Pater, 2011). They may also experience less opportunity for training, feel less prepared to learn (Maurer, Weiss, & Barbeite, 2003), and their needs are less likely to be considered when designing training methods (Armstrong-Stassen & Templer, 2005). All challenges must be overcome if training is to be helpful to older workers.

Health Promotion

Health promotion represents a set of activities that are designed to promote health and health behaviors among employees (Griffiths & Munir, 2003). The most common health promotion intervention in organizations is probably providing employees with opportunities for physical activity, but others such as nutritional counseling, smoking cessation, and weight loss programs are also quite common. While organizations may develop health promotion interventions for a variety of reasons, the most common is the goal of reducing organizational health care costs. The idea is that when employees become healthier they will have less need to utilize health services, and because of decreased use, health insurance premiums will go down.

While there is no empirical evidence that health promotion should necessarily be specially targeted toward older employees, there are valid reasons why health promotion might be especially beneficial to this group. This is because the speed with which many physical changes associated with increased age occur depend on an individual's lifestyle and health habits. It has been well documented, for example, that individuals who are physically active throughout their lives will not age as quickly as those who are more sedentary (Griffiths, 1996). Other health habits such as eating a balanced diet and avoidance of smoking will also slow the progression of the physical aging process.

From an organization's point of view, there are reasons why health promotion activities aimed at older employees may ultimately have more impact than the same activities aimed at younger employees. Specifically, since older people in general utilize health care services at a higher rate than younger employees, improving older workers' health may have a much higher financial impact than improving the health of younger employees. This impact may be even greater considering that many organizations also pay at least a portion of the health insurance premiums of their retirees.

Scheduling Flexibility

Flexibility in scheduling allows employees to have a say in scheduling their work (Paullin & Whetzel, 2012). Given that older workers may have caregiver responsibilities (National Alliance for Caregiving & AARP, 2015), scheduling flexibility may allow them to better meet their caregiving needs at home. Furthermore, as older workers generally experience age-related declines in cognitive and physical capacities (Cavanaugh & Blanchard-Fields, 2010), scheduling flexibility also makes it easier for them to adjust to their job demands. Survey results have shown that both employers and employees recognize the importance of scheduling flexibility in job design and redesign for older workers (e.g., UK Department for Work & Pensions, 2013).

Legal Interventions and Wage/Benefit Protection

There are several pieces of employment legislation that may benefit older workers, although they cover all employees. One such piece of employment legislation is the Americans with Disabilities Act (ADA), which requires employers to make a "reasonable accommodation" for employees with disabilities who are able to perform major job functions. According to the ADA, a disability is defined as: (a) a physical or mental impairment that substantially limits one or more major life activities of an individual, as, for example, walking, talking seeing, hearing, or caring for oneself; (b) a record of such impairment; or (c) being regarded as having such an impairment. The ADA may help older workers who have performed work that has left them physically impaired in some manner. This is particularly the case due to the fact that many occupational injuries are cumulative over time (Schibye, Hansen, Sogaard, & Christensen, 2001). An older employee, for example, may experience damage to his or her back due to repetitive motion injuries at work yet may not be ready or able to retire. He or she may be covered under the ADA if these cumulative trauma injuries have been sufficiently documented and/or have been shown to interfere with major life activities.

Another law that may benefit older employees is the Occupational Safety and Health (OSH) Act of 1970. By developing and enforcing health and safety standards and by providing training, outreach, education and assistance, the Occupational Safety and Health Administration (OSHA) aims to create safe and healthy working environment for all employees. In addition to public sector employers and workers, most private sector employers and their employees are covered by the OSH Act. As a result of the OSHA act, organizations need to ensure programs are in place in order to prevent complaints, injuries, and even death of employees. Given that the population of older workers has increased (Toossi, 2009), management of OSH for an increasingly aging workforce becomes important. For instance, employers may need to pay attention to older workers' normal age-related changes in their physical and sensory functions. Such changes should be considered in risk assessment, and job tasks and work environment need to be modified in order to address these age-related changes.

Finally, a collection of interventions under the general umbrella of "income replacement" may also enhance the health and well-being of older workers.

While these programs (with the exception of Social Security and Medicare) were not specifically created for older workers, there may be certain instances when they are especially beneficial for older employees. For example, if older employees are performing work which they find to be too physically demanding, they may be able to leave such work and collect unemployment benefits until they are able to secure less physically demanding work. In addition, workers who are 65 or older or have a severe disability are eligible for Medicare, and those who have a very low income might be eligible for Medicaid. Older workers could be eligible for both Medicare and Medicaid such that these two social insurance programs could work together to provide them with good health coverage. Overall, legal intervention and wage/benefit programs have protected older workers from unfair treatment and unsafe working environments and have supplied those suffering severe disability and low income with legal protection and financial support.

Employee Assistance Programs

Employee Assistance Programs (EAPs) represent a variety of organizational programs that help employees who have a variety of problems, most typically mental health problems, substance abuse, and financial problems. The scope of EAPs varies considerably; some provide only referrals, while others may include on-site services such as mental health and financial counseling. The primary difference between EAPs and wellness programs is that the former focuses on employees who already have problems, while the latter focuses on prevention.

Like the other interventions described in this section, EAPs are not meant specifically for older employees. Nevertheless, it is possible for organizations to provide services within the context of EAPs that are more beneficial to older employees. For example, through EAPs, organizations may offer counseling to older employees who have difficulties in retirement planning. Organizations may also offer services to older employees who are going through difficult transitions such as children moving out.

Conclusions

Employee health is more than simply the "absence of physical disease," and it is wise for organizations to consider employees' age in their efforts to enhance employee health. As was shown in this chapter, employees experience a number of age-related changes that are independent of the workplace. Although the rate of these changes will vary from employee to employee, they will nevertheless occur for employees at all ages.

Given the age-related changes, what job and organizational conditions are most troublesome to older employees? A consistent theme in the literature is that, on average, older employees have the most difficulty with physically-demanding jobs.

It has also been shown that older employees may have more difficulty than younger employees with jobs that require great amounts of cognitive resources, or require very rapid processing of information. Finally, because older employees may have limited employment prospects, they may find job insecurity much more stressful than their younger colleagues.

Directions for Future Research

Based on the current literature, we would like to add that the current research regarding age and occupational health is quite sparse. More research is needed to document the job and organizational conditions (as well as job stressors) that are most troublesome for older workers. Such research should not only examine the vulnerability of older employees, but should also examine ways in which they may be more resilient than their younger colleagues. While older employees may have difficulty with physically demanding jobs, they may also have experiences and possess coping resources that enhance their capacity to handle many complex social situations in the workplace.

For future research, we strongly recommend that more attention be paid to the research samples employed. This is particularly true when age is examined as a continuous variable. Given that most research on aging in the workplace is focused on age-related changes that occur as employees approach retirement, samples should include substantial numbers of research participants who are approaching retirement age (even older workers who are engaging in bridge employment; Zhan, Wang, Liu, & Shultz, 2009). If samples include mainly young and middle-aged employees, results may be misleading and not apply to older employees.

A final suggestion for future research would be to investigate job and organizational conditions that might moderate the relationship between age and health. Most occupational health research has examined age itself as a moderator variable (e.g., Mayes et al., 1991), but it is equally plausible that the effects of age could be moderated by other variables. The recent lifespan perspective on job design (Truxillo et al., 2012) suggests that certain job characteristics might be particularly beneficial for older workers. For example, an organizational climate that is supportive of older employees might moderate the age–occupational health relationship such that age and occupational health might be positively related when employees work in organizations that value and support employees as they get older. Future research could empirically test such propositions.

Implications for Practice

What can organizations do to enhance the health and well-being of older workers? To a large extent, the answer to this question would be to do the same things that organizations would do to enhance the health and well-being of all employees. However, employees' age should be taken into account when designing and redesigning jobs. Specifically, physical and/or cognitive processing demands might be stressful for older workers, while generativity opportunities and interactions outside the organization might be beneficial for them. Organizations can also promote job crafting as a bottom-up process for older workers to craft their own jobs. Other interventions such as climate change, training, health promotion, and employee assistance (all of which are commonly used in organizations) can also be tailored to the needs of older employees.

In conclusion, older workers represent a large percentage of the workforce worldwide, and this will not change in the near future. It is also the case that more and more organizations have a vested interest in improving employees' health and well-being. Given these two trends, it is important for organizations to consider age in their efforts to enhance employee health. Such a consideration will result in improved health of the overall workforce. Furthermore, given the time and loyalty older employees have often put into an organization, it is certainly the right and moral thing for organizations to do.

References

Anger, W. K., Elliot, D. L., Bodner, T., Olson, R., Rohlman, D. S., Truxillo, D. M., … & Montgomery, D. (2015). Effectiveness of total worker health interventions. *Journal of Occupational Health Psychology, 20*, 226–247.

Anxo, D., Ericson, T., & Jolivet, A. (2012). Working longer in European countries: Underestimated and unexpected effects. *International Journal of Manpower, 33*, 612–628.

Armstrong-Stassen, M., & Templer, A. (2005). Adapting training for older employees: The Canadian response to an aging workforce. *Journal of Management Development, 24*, 57–67.

Avery, D. R., McKay, P. F., & Wilson, D. C. (2008). What are the odds? How demographic similarity affects the prevalence of perceived employment discrimination. *Journal of Applied Psychology, 93*(2), 235–249.

Barling, J., & Griffiths, A. (2011). A history of occupational health psychology. In J. C. Campbell & L. E. Tetrick (Eds.), *Handbook of occupational health psychology* (2nd ed., pp. 21–34). Washington, DC: APA.

Baron, R. M., & Kenny, D. A. (1986). The moderator – mediator variable distinction in social psychological research: Conceptual, strategic and statistical considerations. *Journal of Personality and Social Psychology, 51*, 1173–1182.

Berg, J. M., Dutton, J. E., & Wrzesniewski, A. (2013). Job crafting and meaningful work. In B. J. Dik, Z. S. Byrne, & M. F. Steger (Eds.), *Purpose and meaning in the workplace* (pp. 81–104). Washington, DC: American Psychological Association.

Blanchard-Fields, F., Mienaltowski, A., & Seay, R. B. (2007). Age differences in everyday problem-solving effectiveness: Older adults select more effective strategies for interpersonal problems. *The Journals of Gerontology Series B: Psychological Sciences and Social Sciences, 62*, 61–64.

Boehm, S. A., & Dwertmann, D. J. (2015). Forging a single-edged sword: Facilitating positive age and disability diversity effects in the workplace through leadership, positive climates, and HR practices. *Work, Aging and Retirement, 1*, 41–63.

Boehm, S. A., Kunze, F., & Bruch, H. (2014). Spotlight on age – diversity climate: The impact of age – inclusive HR practices on firm – level outcomes. *Personnel Psychology*, *67*, 667–704.

Boorse, C. (1975). On the distinction between disease and illness. *Philosophy and Public Affairs*, *5*, 49–68.

Bos, J. T., Donders, N. C. G. M., Schouteten, R. L. J., & Van der Gulden, J. W. J. (2013). Age as a moderator in the relationship between work-related characteristics, job dissatisfaction and need for recovery. *Ergonomics*, *56*, 992–1005.

Cavanaugh, J. C., & Blanchard-Fields, F. (2010). *Adult development and aging* (6th Ed). Belmont, CA: Wadsworth Publishing.

Campion, M. A., & Thayer, P. W. (1987). Job design: Approaches, outcomes, and tradeoffs. *Organizational Dynamics*, *15*, 66–79.

Carstensen, L. L. (2006). The influence of a sense of time on human development. *Science*, *312*, 1913–1915.

Carstensen, L. L., Isaacowitz, D. M., & Charles, S. T. (1999). Taking time seriously: A theory of socioemotional selectivity. *American Psychologist*, *54*, 165–181.

Carstensen, L. L., Turan, B., Scheibe, S., Ram, N., Ersner-Hershfield, H., Samanez-Larkin, G. R., ... Nesselroade, J. R. (2011). Emotional experience improves with age: Evidence based on over 10 years of experience sampling. *Psychology and Aging*, *26*, 21–33.

Charles, S. T., Luong, G., Almeida, D. M., Ryff, C., Sturm, M., & Love, G. (2010). Fewer ups and downs: Daily stressors mediate age differences in negative affect. *The Journals of Gerontology Series B: Psychological Sciences and Social Sciences*, *65B*, 279–286.

Chen, Y., Peng, Y., & Fang, P. (2016). Emotional intelligence mediates the relationship between age and subjective well-being. *The International Journal of Aging and Human Development*, *83*, 91–107.

Cheung, F., Yeung, D. Y., & Wu, A. M. (2017). Occupational future time perspective and successful aging at work. *Journal of Career Development*. Online first publication.

Clouston, S. A., Brewster, P., Kuh, D., Richards, M., Cooper, R., Hardy, R., ... & Hofer, S. M. (2013). The dynamic relationship between physical function and cognition in longitudinal aging cohorts. *Epidemiologic Reviews*, *35*, 33–50.

Conen, W. S., Henkens, K., & Schippers, J. (2012). Employers' attitudes and actions towards the extension of working lives in Europe. *International Journal of Manpower*, *33*, 648–665.

Erikson, E. H. (1950). *Childhood and society*. New York: W. W. Norton.

Edwards, J. R. (1996). An examination of competing versions of the person-environment fit approach to stress. *Academy of Management Journal*, *39*, 292–339.

Fasbender, U., Wang, M., Voltmer, J. B., & Deller, J. (2015). The meaning of work for post-retirement employment decisions. *Work, Aging and Retirement*, *2*, 12–23.

Fisher, G. G., Chaffee, D. S., Tetrick, L. E., Davalos, D. B., & Potter, G. G. (2017). Cognitive functioning, aging, and work: A review and recommendations for research and practice. *Journal of Occupational Health Psychology*, *22*, 314–336.

Goldstein, I. L., & Ford, J. K. (2002). *Training in organizations* (4th ed.). Belmont, CA: Wadsworth.

Goštautaitė, B., & Bučiūnienė, I. (2015). Work engagement during life-span: The role of interaction outside the organization and task significance. *Journal of Vocational Behavior*, *89*, 109–119.

Grant, A. M. (2007). Relational job design and the motivation to make a prosocial difference. *Academy of Management Review*, *32*, 393–417.

Grant, A. M. (2008). The significance of task significance: Job performance effects, relational mechanisms, and boundary conditions. *Journal of Applied Psychology, 93*, 108–124.

Grant, A. M., Dutton, J. E., & Rosso, B. D. (2008). Giving commitment: Employee support programs and the prosocial sensemaking process. *Academy of Management Journal, 51*, 898–918.

Griffiths, A. (1996). Employee exercise programs: Organizational and individual perspectives. In J. Kerr, A. Griffiths, & T. Cox (Eds.). *Workplace health: Employee fitness and exercise* (pp. 1–28). London: Taylor & Francis.

Griffiths, A., & Munir, F. (2003). Workplace health promotion. In D. A. Hofmann & L. E. Tetrick (Eds.), *Health and safety in organizations: A multilevel perspective* (pp. 316–340). San Francisco: Jossey-Bass.

Hawkley, L. C., Thisted, R. A., Masi, C. M., & Cacioppo, J. T. (2010). Loneliness predicts increased blood pressure: 5-year cross-lagged analyses in middle-aged and older adults. *Psychology and Aging, 25*, 132–141.

Henkens, K., & Leenders, M. (2010). Burnout and older workers' intentions to retire. *International Journal of Manpower, 31*, 306–321.

Henry, H., Zacher, H., & Desmette, D. (2015). Reducing age bias and turnover intention by enhancing intergenerational contact quality in the workplace: The role of opportunities for generativity and development. *Work, Aging & Retirement, 1*, 243–253.

Hull, R. H. (2011). *Hearing and aging*. San Diego, CA: Plural Publishing.

Inceoglu, I., Segers, J., & Bartram, D. (2012). Age-related differences in work motivation. *Journal of Occupational and Organizational Psychology, 85*, 300–329.

Jex, S. M., & Elacqua, T. C. (1999). Self-esteem as a moderator: A comparison of global and organization-based measures. *Journal of Occupational and Organizational Psychology, 72*, 71–81.

Kanfer, R., & Ackerman, P. L. (2004). Aging, adult development, and work motivation. *Academy of Management Review, 29*, 440–458.

Kenny, G. P., Yardley, J. E., Martineau, L., & Jay, O. (2008). Physical work capacity in older adults: implications for the aging worker. *American Journal of Industrial Medicine, 51*, 610–625.

Kooij, D. T., Bal, P. M., & Kanfer, R. (2014). Future time perspective and promotion focus as determinants of intraindividual change in work motivation. *Psychology and Aging, 29*, 319–328.

Kooij, D. T., De Lange, A. H., Jansen, P. G., & Dikkers, J. S. (2013). Beyond chronological age. Examining perceived future time and subjective health as age-related mediators in relation to work-related motivations and well-being. *Work & Stress, 27*, 88–105.

Kooij, D. T., De Lange, A. H., Jansen, P. G., Kanfer, R., & Dikkers, J. S. (2011). Age and work-related motives: Results of a meta-analysis. *Journal of Organizational Behavior, 32*, 197–225.

Kooij, D. T., Tims, M., & Kanfer, R. (2015). Successful aging at work: The role of job crafting. In P. M. Bal, D. T. A. M. Kooij, & D. M. Rousseau (Eds.), *Aging workers and the employee-employer relationship* (pp. 145–161). New York: Springer.

Kozlowski, S. W. J., & Klein, K. J. (2000). A multilevel approach to theory and research in organizations: Contextual, temporal, and emergent processes. In K. J. Klein & S. W. J. Kozlowski (Eds.), *Multilevel theory, research, and methods in organizations: Foundations, extensions, and new directions* (pp. 3–90). San Francisco, CA: Jossey-Bass.

Kunze, F., Boehm, S. A., & Bruch, H. (2011). Age diversity, age discrimination climate and performance consequences – a cross organizational study. *Journal of organizational behavior, 32*, 264–290.

Lang, F. R., & Carstensen, L. L. (2002). Time counts: Future time perspective, goals, and social relationships. *Psychology and Aging, 17*, 125–139.

Larson, J. S. (1999). The conceptualization of health. *Medical Care Research and Review, 56*, 123–136.

Lindenberger, U., & Ghisletta, P. (2009). Cognitive and sensory declines in old age: Gauging the evidence for a common cause. *Psychology and Aging, 24*, 1–16.

Mauno, S., Ruokolainen, M., & Kinnunen, U. (2013). Does aging make employees more resilient to job stress? Age as a moderator in the job stressor–well-being relationship in three Finnish occupational samples. *Aging & Mental Health, 17*, 411–422.

Maurer, T. J. (2001). Career-relevant learning and development, worker age, and beliefs about self-efficacy for development. *Journal of Management, 27*, 123–140.

Maurer, T. J., Weiss, E. M., & Barbeite, F. G. (2003). A model of involvement in work-related learning and development activity: The effects of individual, situational, motivational, and age variables. *Journal of Applied Psychology, 88*(4), 707–724.

Mayes, B. T., Barton, M. E., & Ganster, D. C. (1991). An exploration of the moderating effect of age on job stressor–employee strain relationships. *Journal of Social Behavior and Personality, 6*, 289–308.

McAdams, D. P., & de St. Aubin, E. (1998). *Generativity and adult development: How and why we care for the next generation* (1st ed.). Washington, DC: American Psychological Association.

McArdle, A., Vasilaki, A., & Jackson, M. (2002). Exercise and skeletal muscle aging: Cellular and molecular mechanisms. *Aging Research Reviews, 1*, 79–93.

McGonagle, A. K., Fisher, G. G., Barnes-Farrell, J. L., & Grosch, J. W. (2015). Individual and work factors related to perceived work ability and labor force outcomes. *Journal of Applied Psychology, 100*, 376–398.

Mor-Barak, M. (1995). The meaning of work for older adults seeking employment: The generativity factor. *International Journal of Aging & Human Development, 41*, 325–344.

Morgeson, F. P., & Campion, M. A. (2003). Work design. In W. C. Borman & D. R. Ilgen (Eds.), *Handbook of psychology: Industrial and organizational* (Vol. 12, pp. 423–452), Hoboken, NJ: John Wiley & Sons.

National Alliance for Caregiving and AARP. (2015). *Caregiving in the U.S. 2015.* Bethesda, MD: National Alliance for Caregiving.

Ng, T. W., & Feldman, D. C. (2013). Employee age and health. *Journal of Vocational Behavior, 83*, 336–345.

Ng, T. W., & Feldman, D. C. (2015). The moderating effects of age in the relationships of job autonomy to work outcomes. *Work, Aging and Retirement, 1*, 64–78.

Owsley, C. (2011). Aging and vision. *Vision Research, 51*, 1610–1622.

Park, D. C. (2000). The basic mechanisms accounting for age-related decline in cognitive function. In D. C. Park & N. Schwarz (Eds.), *Cognitive aging: A primer* (pp. 3–22). Philadelphia: Psychology Press.

Parsons, R. (1991). The potential influences of environmental perception on human health. *Journal of Environmental Psychology, 11*, 1–23.

Paullin, C., & Whetzel, D. L. (2012). Retention strategies and older workers. In J. W. Hedge, & W. C. Borman (Eds.), *The Oxford handbook of work and aging* (pp. 392–418). New York: Oxford University Press.

Peng, Y., Tian, B., Jex, S. M., & Chen, Y. (2016). Employees' age moderates relationships of emotional suppression with health and well-being. *Work, Aging and Retirement, 3*, 89–101.

Salthouse, T. A. (2013). Within-cohort age-related differences in cognitive functioning. *Psychological Science, 24*, 123–130.

Satariano, W. A., Guralnik, J. M., Jackson, R. J., Marottoli, R. A., Phelan, E. A., & Prohaska, T. R. (2012). Mobility and aging: New directions for public health action. *American Journal of Public Health, 102*, 1508–1515.

Scheibe, S., & Zacher, H. (2013). A lifespan perspective on emotion regulation, stress, and well-being in the workplace. In P. L. Perrewe, J. Halbesleben, & C. C. Rosen (Eds.), *Research in occupational stress and well-being* (Vol. 11, pp. 167–197). Bingley, UK: Emerald.

Schibye, B., Hansen, A. F., Sogaard, K., & Christensen, H. (2001). Aerobic power and muscle strength among young and elderly workers with and without physically demanding work tasks. *Applied Ergonomics, 32*, 425–431.

Schill, A. L., & Chosewood, L. C. (2013). The NIOSH Total Worker Health program: An overview. *Journal of Occupational and Environmental Medicine, 55*(Suppl.), S8–S11.

Seitsamo, J., & Martikainen, R. (1999). Changes in capability in a sample of Finnish aging workers. *Experimental Aging Research, 25*, 345–352.

Shultz, K. S., Wang, M., Crimmins, E. M., & Fisher, G. G. (2010). Age differences in the demand – control model of work stress: An examination of data from 15 European countries. *Journal of Applied Gerontology, 29*, 21–47.

Spector, P. E. (1986). Perceived control by employees: A meta-analysis of studies concerning autonomy and participation at work. *Human Relations, 11*, 1005–116.

Sverke, M., Hellgren, J., & Näswall, K. (2002). No security: A meta-analysis and review of job insecurity and it consequences. *Journal of Occupational Health Psychology, 7*, 242–264.

Templer, A., Armstrong-Stassen, M., & Cattaneo, J. (2010). Antecedents of older workers' motives for continuing to work. *Career Development International, 15*, 479–500.

Tetrick, L. E., & Quick, J. C. (2011). Overview of occupational health psychology: Public health in occupational settings. In J. C. Campbell & L. E. Tetrick (Eds.), *Handbook of occupational health psychology* (2nd ed., pp. 3–20). Washington, DC: APA.

Tims, M., Bakker, A. B., & Derks, D. (2012). Development and validation of the job crafting scale. *Journal of Vocational Behavior, 80*, 173–186.

Toossi, M. (2009). Labor force projections to 2018: Older workers staying more active. *Monthly Labor Review, 132*, 30–51.

Truxillo, D. M., Cadiz, D. M., Rineer, J. R., Zaniboni, S., & Fraccaroli, F. (2012). A lifespan perspective on job design: Fitting the job and the worker to promote job satisfaction, engagement, and performance. *Organizational Psychology Review, 2*, 340–360.

UK Department for Work & Pensions. (2013). *Employing older workers: An employer's guide to today's multi-generational workforce*. Retrieved from www.dwp.gov.uk.

Van Vianen, A. E., Dalhoeven, B. A., & De Pater, I. E. (2011). Aging and training and development willingness: Employee and supervisor mindsets. *Journal of Organizational Behavior, 32*, 226–247.

Yeung, D. Y., & Fung, H. H. (2012). Impacts of suppression on emotional responses and performance outcomes: An experience sampling study in younger and older workers. *The Journals of Gerontology, Series B: Psychological Sciences and Social Sciences, 67*, 666–676.

Zacher, H., & Frese, M. (2011). Maintaining a focus on opportunities at work: The interplay between age, job complexity, and the use of selection, optimization, and compensation strategies. *Journal of Organizational Behavior, 32*, 291–318.

Zacher, H., & Schmitt, A. (2016). Work characteristics and occupational well-being: The role of age. *Frontiers in Psychology*, 7. 1411.

Zacher, H., & Yang, J. (2016). Organizational climate for successful aging. *Frontiers in Psychology*, 7, 1007.

Zaniboni, S., Truxillo, D. M., & Fraccaroli, F. (2013). Differential effects of task variety and skill variety on burnout and turnover intentions for older and younger workers. *European Journal of Work and Organizational Psychology*, 22, 306–317.

Zhan, Y., Wang, M., Liu, S., & Shultz, K. S. (2009). Bridge employment and retirees' health: A longitudinal investigation. *Journal of Occupational Health Psychology*, 14, 374–389.

11

AGE AND TECHNOLOGY FOR WORK

Neil Charness and Sara J. Czaja

The nature of work has changed significantly in developed countries over the past century. We have moved from a labor force that was employed primarily in physically-demanding industries such as agriculture, manufacturing, and mining to one that is increasingly mentally-challenging: service-sector work. The typical life course has also shifted. In the 19th century if you were a man in the paid labor force (women didn't join in large numbers until the 1950s onward) you worked until you were physically unable to do so or died, usually in your sixth decade. In the 21st century, the more typical pattern is for both men and women to engage at least part-time in the paid labor force until pensionable age, usually occurring in one's 60s, with some post-retirement part-time work, with death following closer to two decades after retirement (Henkens et al., 2017). Accompanying the shift to a service-based economy and the change in workplace demographics, has been the rapid rise of technology, mainly in the form of microchip technology.

Why worry about technology for work, particularly for older workers? As economists have known for years, productivity in the workplace depends highly on capital investment. A fast-writing clerk with a quill, inkwell, and paper files cannot compete even with a slow-typing clerk who is trained and equipped with a database, email, word processor, and internet access. However, the training costs to use earlier office technology were probably considerably smaller than those necessary to use today's technology, especially as technology continues to change in a relatively rapid fashion. Worker education and training thus become potential bottlenecks for workers of all ages, for assuring productivity increases as technology advances. Further, we are now experiencing, as prior chapters have indicated, a rapidly aging labor force thanks to the large baby boom cohort that is beginning to retire and smaller cohorts following that one. Normative changes in perceptual, cognitive, and psychomotor abilities accompany increased age, and these can have an impact on work performance. For instance, learning rate slows with increased age, particularly for unfamiliar material. Older adults (age 65+ years) can be expected to take between 50 and 100 percent more time than younger workers to self-train on a new word processor (Charness, Kelley, Bosman & Mottram, 2001; mean age of the old groups was 63 years versus 25 and 27 years for the youngest groups in the two studies).

Despite expected functional declines with increased age, there is little relationship between age and work productivity measures (e.g., Ng & Feldman, 2008) suggesting that adaptation and acquired knowledge may protect older workers from losses in productivity. See Krampe and Charness (2018) for discussion of potential compensation mechanisms that revolve around the trade-offs between making use of domain-specific knowledge and domain general abilities. Other reasons have been offered for the mismatch between lab-based and work-based performance. Salthouse (2012) suggests that most work environments do not routinely demand peak performance in the same way that lab-based tasks do. Further, there are contextual cues in work environments that are not typically available in laboratory testing situations. However, it is important to note that the well-recognized learning rate slowdown with age may become increasingly important in an economy where the pace of technology adoption is accelerating and worldwide competition for jobs is increasing.

This chapter will first provide some definitions of aging and technology, and will then briefly examine some of the demographics relating to age and technology use. Next, we outline a framework for understanding how older adults interact with technology. We then look more specifically at how we can derive principles for selecting and designing technological artifacts to be useful for older workers. We outline some practical implications for workplace and training design that are based on our existing knowledge of aging and work. We close with some speculations about the future of work and then a summary of recommendations for future research in this area.

Definitions of "Older Worker"

When is someone considered "old"? The definition varies by culture and era. For instance, an EU report noted:

> When a person is considered old varies, in terms of the geographical location and context. According to a 2011 Eurobarometer survey, a person is considered 'old' at about 57 years in Slovakia but only at more than 70 years in the Netherlands. Though in some contexts, such as employment, people may be considered 'older' as of age 55 or even 50, on average in

the EU a person is thought of as old just before he or she reaches 64 years of age. We expect that this definition will continue to evolve as the face of aging continues to change.

In an important sense, all those in the labor force are *aging workers*, so it is difficult to select a specific cut-off age for defining an "older worker." However, the laws of the land can provide some guidelines. In the US, the Age Discrimination in Employment Act provides protection for adults 40 years of age and older: www.eeoc.gov/eeoc/publications/age.cfm, accessed September 23, 2017). The median age of the employed labor force in the US was 42.2 years in 2016 (www.bls.gov/cps/cpsaat11b.pdf, accessed September 23, 2017). If we look at high performance environments, even earlier ages might define "older worker." In many professional sports domains, for example, athletes are probably nearing (forced) retirement in their mid-30s. The rise of a seniors' tour in golf and of age bands in Masters' athlete competitions is a creative way to compensate for inevitable age-related negative changes in skill in sports domains.

A National Research Council panel in the US examined the health and safety needs of older workers, and adopted age 45 as their arbitrary cut-off point (National Research Council, 2004). Also, although work is usually equated with paid work, those age 45+ years who are caring for children or older parents, serve as unpaid volunteers, and are currently unemployed and intending to re-enter the labor force, could be considered as older workers too. Finally, things blur even further when you consider part-time workers in the so-called "gig economy." Part-time work is an increasingly popular option for those who are at or beyond pensionable retirement age.

There is a clear trend in US data for more people to be working past normal retirement age. Toossi (2016) indicates that the fastest growing group, those age 75+, is expected to reach 25 million people by 2024. Similarly, there have been strong efforts by governments in the EU to encourage people to remain in the labor force to ease fiscal pressures for governments providing pensions and medical care for their aging populations (Sinclair, Watson & Beach, 2013), leading to similar longevity trends for workers in the EU. Thus, although roughly 80 percent of the US workforce retires from full-time work by age 65, that is unlikely to hold for the future and the growing trend to return to part-time work is unlikely to dissipate either. Hence, much of the research we cite that includes an "older" group (typically with a mean age of 70–75) will be increasingly useful in understanding our future labor force. Nonetheless, for convenience, we can take the age bound 50–64 years as a useful way to encompass "older" workers. Finally, the prototypic older worker is a white male. Growing participation rates of women in the paid labor force as well as minorities (Toossi, 2016) make it clear that the workforce of the future will be diverse: increasingly female gendered and non-Caucasian (see Webster, Thoroughgood, & Sawyer, Chapter 3 this volume). Given that most research findings are based on samples of white males (and more recently females), it seems necessary to broaden sampling in our research to improve generalization.

Technology

Trying to define technology is rather like shooting at a moving target. Although the construct of technology is broad (one *Oxford English Dictionary* definition: a particular practical or industrial art), our focus is on high-technology which the OED defines as:

> **high-technology** applied attrib. to a firm, industry, etc., that produces or utilizes highly advanced and specialized technology, or to the products of such a firm.

As this definition implies, we are looking at highly advanced and specialized products or processes. The manual typewriter was an incredible advance on paper and pen at its introduction, but would be a quaint-looking piece of technology (low-technology) today compared with a computer equipped with word processing software.

Given the ubiquity of embedded and non-embedded microprocessors in many devices today, a good first approximation definition of technology would be anything with a microprocessor, either in it or controlling its function. A more function-oriented definition would be any device that serves as an information processing system by accepting variable inputs and generating variable outputs. Such a definition would cover many devices found in the typical office environment today: computers, mobile phones, monitors, copying machines, scanners, telephone systems, networking equipment, printers, etc. Office work is not the only place where technology has advanced. A look at the instrument panel in a modern tractor shows how far farming has advanced from the days of animal-driven plows. Similar comments can be made for the types of technologies now used in manufacturing and other types of industries. Think of computer-aided manufacturing (CAM), material handling robots, and 3D printing devices that are routinely used in the production of manufactured goods.

The word, "gerontechnology," was coined (e.g., Bouma, 1992; Kwon, 2016) to encompass issues related to both age and technology. Gerontechnology was originally defined as: "The study of technology and aging for the improvement of the daily functioning of the elderly" (Bouma, 1992). Thus, our chapter can also be seen as addressing gerontechnology for work.

Age-Related Use of Technology

One potential concern for older workers is whether they are up-to-date with technology. In general, older adults in the United States report lower use of technology than younger adults, and particularly as users of computer technology, the internet, and mobile devices (Anderson & Perrin, 2017). Surveys in European countries have identified similar trends with only half of people age 65–74 being internet users in OECD countries in 2014 (http://dx.doi.org/10.1787/888933274795, accessed September 24, 2017).

Although, as some have noted, the older adult population is the fastest growing segment in terms of computer and internet adoption, it is probably because younger cohorts are approaching asymptote and over successive cross-sectional panels younger cohorts have aged into older cohort categories carrying their technology habits with them. A representative example is shown in Figure 11.1 for percentage use of the internet by age group and year.

However, our interest is mainly in the comparison of older workers to younger workers in Figure 11.1, which corresponds roughly to the 50–64 group versus the two younger ones, that is, the top three curves. There is still a significant 10 percent gap in internet use even when comparing the 50–64 age group with 18–29 and 30–49 age groups. Although many people have left the paid workforce by age 65, there is a striking 20 percent gap between the bottom curve (those 65+) and the one for the age 50–64 group. In the next sections, we provide an overview of changes with age that may affect work performance and the ability to use technology, and outline some

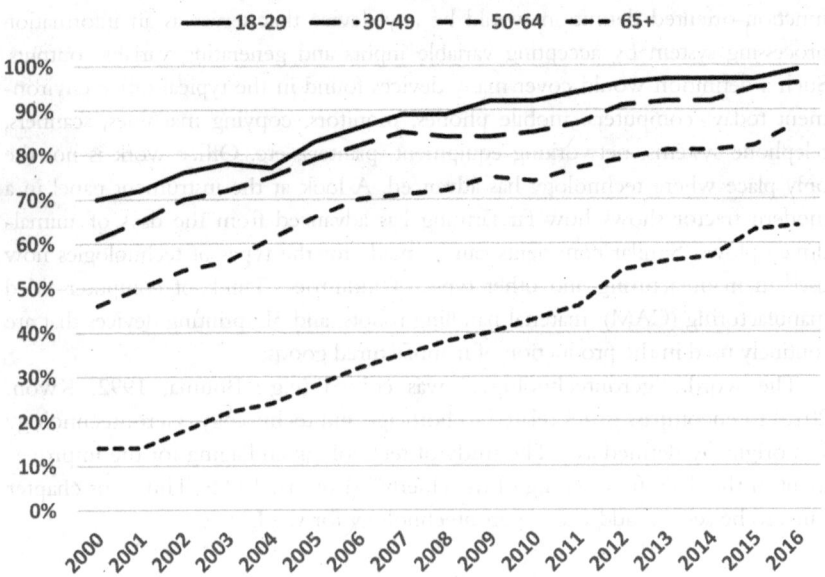

FIGURE 11.1 Internet use by age group and year in the US.

Source: Data from Pew Internet & American Life Project, www.pewinternet.org/fact-sheet/internet-broadband/ (accessed September 20, 2017).

principles for how to design technology products to avoid handicapping older workers. More detailed discussion of principles of design for older users can be found in Fisk et al. (2009).

A Framework for Understanding Technology Interaction

Why are older adults, and by implication, older workers less frequent users of technology such as computers and the internet? It is helpful to consider the benefit/cost framework shown in Figure 11.2 (Charness & Boot, 2016). It condenses many of the factors mentioned in other models such as the Universal Theory of Adoption and Use of Technology (Venkatesh, Thong, & Xu, 2012) or the Senior Technology Adoption Model (Chen & Chan, 2014) into perceived costs and benefits.

This framework notes that for successful interaction there must be a balance between the demands of a technological system and the capabilities of the intended user. As can be seen, many factors can influence successful technology adoption and use. Broad classes of factors include user attitudes and motivation, self-efficacy, perceptual, cognitive, and psychomotor abilities, and demanding characteristics of the technology system such as hardware and software interfaces, complexity as well as available support and economic cost. In deciding whether to adopt and then use a system, the user weighs costs – perceived mismatches between user capabilities and system demands – and benefits – what

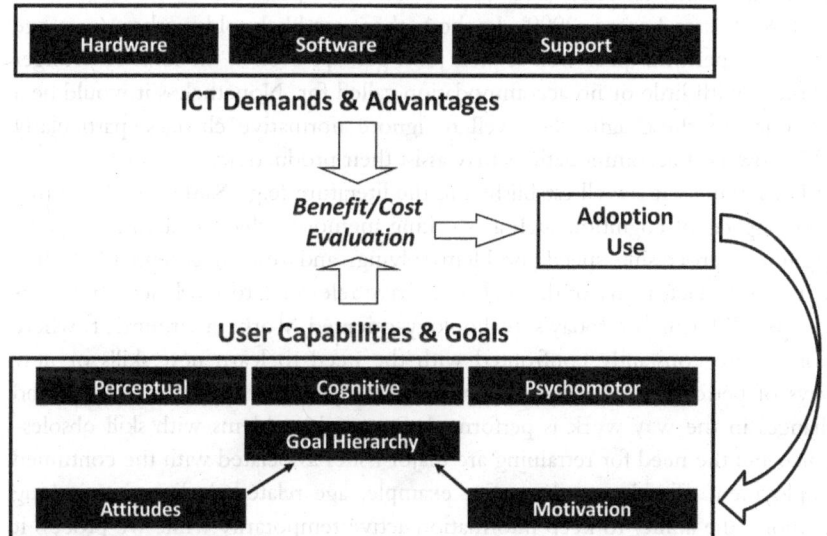

FIGURE 11.2 Technology adoption and use framework.
Source: Adapted from Charness and Boot (2016).

goal the tool may help the user attain. Part of the reduced use of technology seen in older adults may be attributed to anxieties about and attitudes toward technology coupled with normative age-related declines in cognition that make using complex technology a more difficult task (Czaja et al., 2006). Another contributing factor may be the age-related perceptual and psychomotor changes that make interaction with such systems more challenging than in earlier years (e.g., night driving as a function of changes in vision).

Age-Related Changes Constraining Work Performance

Decades of research on cognitive aging have provided useful information, including quantitative estimates (e.g., Jastrzembski & Charness, 2007; Verhaeghen, 2014) for how attention, memory, perception, and psychomotor abilities decline with age. Those normative age-related changes appear to have expected impacts on activities such as job-related training performance (Kubeck, Delp, Haslett, & McDaniel, 1996). However, caution must be exercised when generalizing from laboratory-type studies to predict performance on real world tasks. Aging is associated with a high degree of variability; people age differently so reliance on group averages may be misleading. Also, studies that examine age-related changes in basic abilities such as working memory or speed of processing do not account for contextual variables, such as experience with a task or the use of compensatory strategies (e.g., in typing: Bosman, 1993, Salthouse, 1984). The human brain is remarkably adaptive, with older adults recruiting additional brain areas to maintain high performance levels on tasks (Park & Reuter-Lorenz, 2009). In short, there are likely old workers (e.g., age 70+) who perform quite well at their jobs, perhaps even at the level of younger workers, with little or no accommodation called for. Nonetheless it would be a disservice to those aging less well to ignore normative changes, particularly when low-cost accommodations may assist their productivity.

For instance, it is well established in the literature (e.g., Salthouse, 2010) that many aspects of cognition such as working memory, selective attention, spatial cognition, processing speed, problem solving, and reasoning tend to decline with age. In fact, many of these changes have relevance to work activities. This is especially true in today's technology-oriented work environment where workers are constantly confronted with the need to learn new skills or new ways of performing jobs to keep pace with developments in technology and changes in the way work is performed. Potential problems with skill obsolescence and the need for retraining are major issues associated with the continued employment of older workers. For example, age-related declines in working memory, the ability to keep information active temporarily while we process it or until we use it, may make it difficult for older people to learn new concepts or skills or recall complex multi-step operational procedures. Declines in attention capacity may make it difficult for an older person to perform concurrent activities or switch attention between competing displays of information, an ability crucial for air traffic controllers. Older adults may also have problems selecting task targets or integrating information from crowded or complex displays or multiple information sources. In addition, because older people tend to process information at a slower rate, highly paced work may also be unsuitable for older workers or it may take older workers longer to learn new skills. However, while these changes tend to occur with age it is important to recognize that many declines in abilities have limited impact on real-world task performance and that older workers are willing and able to learn new tasks and skills. In fact, studies (e.g., Czaja & Sharit, 1998; Czaja, Sharit, Ownby, Roth, & Nair, 2001; Sharit et al., 2004) have shown that older adults are quite willing and able to learn technology-based work tasks. However, as discussed later in this chapter, it is important that they are provided with access to training programs and that training programs are designed to accommodate the learning styles of older adults.

Chronic health conditions increase strikingly with age. For instance, arthritis prevalence is about 50 percent for those age 65+ years (Federal Interagency Forum on Aging-Related Statistics, 2016). Thus, aging is also associated with changes in motor skills, including slower response times, declines in the ability to maintain continuous movements, disruptions in coordination, loss of flexibility, and greater variability in movement (Fisk et al., 2009). These changes in motor skills may make it difficult for older people to perform tasks, such as assembly work that requires small manipulation, or to use input devices, such as a mouse or keyboard.

Older adults also tend to have reduced strength and endurance. Generally, with age there is a gradual loss of muscle mass and muscles become weaker. Cardio capacity and the time it takes to repair muscular damage also declines with age (National Research Council (2004)). Clearly there is a great deal of variability in muscle groups, in types of muscular performance, and between individuals. However, in general, older adults are less willing and able to perform physically demanding jobs. See Peng, Jex, and Wang (Chapter 10, this volume) for details about occupational health issues.

A useful framework for intervening to improve productivity at work is a Rehabilitate, Augment, Substitute (RAS) one. If someone lacks a skill that would enable them to employ a new tool, or loses an existing one due to an injury or disease, offering training to help them acquire or re-acquire the skill would be a useful strategy. If that is not feasible, augment their abilities. For instance, at age 45, most people lose the ability to focus on near objects. However, it is easy to provide them with lenses to augment their ability to focus. If augmentation is not feasible, provide a tool that substitutes for the failed function. For example, if someone loses hearing because of damage to hair cells in the cochlea, a cochlear implant may substitute for missing hair cells and provide some hearing functionality.

In summary, there are many age-related changes in abilities that have relevance to work. However, as we illustrate throughout this chapter, many age-related changes in abilities can be compensated for through training and good design practices. Unfortunately, many designers of technology and interfaces have not considered the needs and preferences of older people. Furthermore, common myths that older people are less productive, and less able and less willing to work are not supported in the literature. In 2017, about 74 percent of American adults had the intention to work past the usual (age 65) retirement age (Gallup's Economy and Personal Finance Survey, 2017), though mostly in part-time work, and, as mentioned earlier, there is very limited evidence to suggest that work performance declines with age.

Findings and Principles for Training, Retraining, and Instruction

The steady influx of technology into work environments and the continual changes in technology, such as new versions of a software application or new forms of technology (i.e., the tablet versus the standalone PC) means that workers of all ages will constantly have to engage in learning activities to keep pace with job demands. Thus, as mentioned earlier, training is an essential component of today's workplace and is essential to the future growth of the economy. Equally important given the economic constraints faced by many organizations is ensuring that training programs are well designed, effective and match the needs and abilities of the training population. Issues with skill obsolescence and training are especially significant for older workers, who, as noted above, lag in technology adoption, and data suggest that employers invest less in training older workers as compared with younger workers (Czaja & Sharit, 2009; Olson and Jeske, Chapter 8 this volume). Thus, the design of training, retraining and instructional materials is pertinent for this population, especially those who had previously been in low skilled occupations and trying to gain re-entry into the labor force. Our work has shown (Lee, Czaja & Sharit, 2009) that these older adults perceive lack of technology skills as a major barrier to procuring employment. In this section, we will discuss what is known about training and older adults and provide some general guidelines for the design of training and instructional programs to accommodate older workers.

As discussed above there are some normative age-related changes in abilities that have relevance to learning and training, such as age-related declines in cognitive abilities and sensory/perceptual processes. With respect to cognition, age-related changes in speed of processing and in working memory play extremely important roles in learning and skill acquisition. We know for example, that older adults process information at a slower rate than younger people, which means that learning rates are slower for older adults. This implies that special attention needs to be given to the pacing of training. Declines in vision and audition also have implications for learning and training and the design of instruction materials. For example, multimedia instructions that have a speech component may be problematic for older adults if the speech rate is too rapid or speech is distorted by background noise or echo. The formatting of text such as font size is also an important consideration, as is the level and distribution of light in the training environment. Social factors may also influence how well older people learn. Older adults tend to prefer small as opposed to large group formats and learning with peers as opposed to mixed groups of older and younger adults. We found that people prefer to learn with others who are at the same skill level (Czaja, Lee, Branham, & Remis, 2012).

However, it is important to note that aging is associated with variability and there are vast inter-individual and intra-individual differences among older adults. With respect to inter-individual variability, workers in their 60s are typically different with respect to functional abilities from those in their 30s. Further, there may be differences among cohorts due to life experiences and historical events. Consider, for example, the vast developments and changes in telephone technology that have occurred over the last several decades. Inter-individual differences also reflect differences that occur within an age group; not all 65 year-olds are alike. Other individual differences are also important to consider. For example, people vary in terms of language, education, and skill level. The older population is becoming increasingly culturally and ethnically diverse and training may be challenging for those for whom English is not their first language.

Intra-individual differences refer to differences within an individual. For example, an individual experiences changes in their abilities over the course of time. Some of these changes reflect gains in abilities such as knowledge, while others reflect declines such as loss of visual acuity. Intra-individual differences can also be short term and due to factors such as stress or fatigue (Czaja & Sharit, 2009). Another important caveat is that aging is associated with plasticity. Older adults can learn and experience gains in functions and skills (National Academies of Science, Engineering, and Medicine, 2017). For example, we recently found that people in their eighth and ninth decade could learn to use a computer and software system (Czaja, Boot, Charness, Rogers, & Sharit, 2018). Older adults also bring a wealth of knowledge and experience to learning and training situations. This knowledge availability is often underutilized in training contexts.

With respect to training and older adults there have been meta-analyses that have focused specifically on job training (e.g., Kubeck, Delp, Haslett, & McDaniel, 1996; Callahan, Kiker & Cross, 2003). Overall, on average, the findings from these analyses that compare age groups show that older adults perform worse than younger people on training outcomes such as mastery of the training material. Typically, older workers also require more time to gain mastery of the training material, and need more practice/assistance. However, as pointed out earlier, this does not imply that older adults cannot learn new skills and job tasks.

Many studies have also focused on the ability of older people to learn to use new technologies (e.g., Charness, Schumann, & Boritz, 1992). These studies have also found age differences in learning, with differences favoring younger learners. However, findings also indicated that older people are receptive to and able to learn new technology applications; however, they typically learn at a slower pace and require more assistance and training. Other important findings from these studies are that factors other than age are important predictors of learning and training performance. These factors include cognitive abilities such as reasoning, processing speed and memory, as well as prior experience with technology systems. The findings from these training studies have important implications for the design of job training programs for older learners.

Before providing training guidelines it is important to realize that, to date, available data do not show clear training strategies by age interactions, indicating that a particular training format is not necessarily optimal for older adults (e.g., Callahan, Kiker & Cross, 2003); a wide variety of training formats and protocols are effective. The design of the training program should be based on the nature of the training tasks, the characteristics of the trainee population and the available resources. With these caveats in mind, we will proceed to a discussion of general guidelines for the design of training and instructional material for older adults. For a more complete discussion of these issues please see Czaja and Sharit (2013).

Clearly, one basic consideration given age-related changes in processing speed is the pace of and time allowed for training. Sufficient time must be provided for older adults to assimilate the training information and complete the practice exercises. With the advent of online training programs, it is now possible for learners to control the pace of training, which can be beneficial for older adults, assuming that they are able to effectively engage with the online program and that adequate support is provided. Issues associated with online learning will be discussed in more detail later in this section. Generally, self-paced training formats are preferred. In addition, it is advisable not to mix older and younger learners as younger people typically learn at a faster pace. Other important considerations are the provision of feedback and practice. The feedback regarding errors should allow the learner to understand how and why task performance was not correct. It is also important to be careful with the amount of information or feedback presented to a learner to avoid potential problems with information overload. Both positive and negative (though constructive) feedback should be provided during training. The timing of feedback is also important; it should not be delayed but timed to performance as much as possible.

Highlighting linkages between new training information and information that is already familiar is helpful in terms of explaining new concepts. Another effective training strategy is to increase the amount of practice and to provide backup or simple reminder materials that can be used outside of the training environment. The learner should also be actively involved in the learning process during training and trainees should be provided with and given practice on a wide variety of examples of a task or skill both during training and practice sessions. Training and support materials must be well designed and easy to use. Important things to consider are the size and contrast of text, pacing, amplitude and frequency of narration, organization of material, literacy demands, and technical difficulty level of the content. Training and assessment materials should always be pilot tested with a representative sample of trainees. The training environment should be free from distractions and excessive noise and the trainees' work areas should be set up using existing ergonomic guidelines. Lighting and temperature considerations are also important.

Special consideration needs to be given to e-learning formats given the increased use of online training programs within organizations. Currently there is not a solid evidence base regarding how to best design these programs for older learners. However, there are guidelines available for website design, as well as software and hardware interfaces (e.g., Fisk et al., 2009), which must be adhered to for online training programs. If these programs are used, it is essential to ensure that the trainees have the needed technical skills to access and use the programs and that they are provided with technical support.

Findings and Principles for Designing Supportive Work Environments

Most technological systems rely on hardware and software interfaces (see Figure 11.2) that should be designed to account for an older user's capabilities. For instance, a typical computer system has a keyboard and mouse as primary input devices, perhaps supplemented by a microphone for speech recognition, and a screen and speakers as output devices. A smartphone consolidates many of these functions by using a touch-sensitive screen instead of a mouse, a "software" keyboard in place of a hardware keyboard, and speech recognition, fitting into a more compact form factor, but running the risk of presenting visual information inefficiently to older users. Efficient use of such devices depends on the user's vision, hearing, and dexterity, all of which typically decline with age (Fisk et al., 2009). Next, we focus on addressing vision and hearing changes.

Vision Changes

The major normative change with age in vision is loss of ability to change the focus of the lens of the eye to see near objects: presbyopia (Schieber, 2006). Presbyopia typically occurs in the mid-40s and prompts most adults to obtain reading glasses or multifocal glasses if they already wear single lens glasses to correct near- or far-sightedness. Normal glasses might have been adequate for mid and far distance vision earlier in life, but now reading materials (e.g., newspapers, computer screens) are hard to see without additional correction. Often, traditional reading glasses are not adequate for mid-distance vision (e.g., 40–60 cm to the target object), a distance typical for computer monitor placement or a vehicle's instrument panel display. Special mid-distance computer glasses (or progressive lens glasses) may be a good solution.

Further, given changes in pupil size and in the optical media within the eye, less light is admitted to the back of the eye for transduction by the retina to neural impulses that travel to visual centers in the brain. A 65-year-old eye admits only about a third of the light that enters a young adult's eye. Thus, there is less light and correspondingly less contrast (e.g., for black print on a white background) available for older adults. Simply increasing light levels engenders other risks. Under high intensity light conditions, older adults are more susceptible to masking of significant visual details by glare because of greater diffusion of light through the eye (due to loss of transparency in the optical media).

Such changes require that designers pay close attention to the visual characteristics of work environments. For instance, print sizes smaller than 12 points should be avoided. An excellent source for design guidelines is the normative data collected in Japan at AIST: http://scdb.db.aist.go.jp/?lng=en. Good contrast needs to be maintained between text and background. Black on white or white on black text is optimal, though this contrast guideline is routinely violated on many websites. Although we don't deal here with promoting accessibility to digital information for those with non-normative visual and auditory impairments, there are excellent sources elsewhere (www.w3.org/TR/WCAG21/).

An attractive feature of computer-based reading is that it is possible to adjust text size to improve the legibility of print for older adults. However, users may not know how to magnify text and poor design of websites and browsers often make it very difficult to change font sizes or override default settings for text. What used to require special equipment (magnifying screens) can now be accomplished with software adjustments. However, few older adults are knowledgeable about how to access "accessibility" features built into many modern operating systems.

Hearing Changes

As we age, hair cells in the inner ear responsible for transducing sound may cease functioning, and conduction from the outer ear through the vestibular apparatus to those hair cells may also be diminished. There can also be central loss of brain cells that process auditory information (Wingfield & Lash, 2016). These losses are attributable both to lifelong exposure to noise in the environment, as well as to normative aging processes affecting the pathways to the brain (e.g., arthritic stiffening in the bones conducting sound from the outer to inner ear). Men are generally more affected than women. The result is that we become impaired at detecting sounds, particularly high frequency (high pitched) ones. Such changes negatively impact speech perception, particularly in men by their mid- to late-50s. Parallel to the case for vision, simply raising the intensity of sounds may not adequately compensate for hearing loss. Older adults are also more susceptible to masking by neighboring sound frequencies. As a result, picking out voices in noisy environments becomes particularly challenging. Although hearing aids can help hearing-impaired listeners, current versions generally boost both signal and background noise making them less effective in noisy environments.

One advantage of the shift from manufacturing to office work is that work environments have undoubtedly become quieter and hence more hospitable to those with normative age-related hearing loss. Nevertheless, attention to providing quieter work spaces by soundproofing work environments, or providing tools that might mitigate noise sources, such as noise-canceling headphones or earbuds, could benefit all workers, though differentially aid older workers.

Particularly for small electronic devices, warning signals are sometimes generated within frequency ranges that are difficult to perceive by older listeners even in quiet environments. Important signals should be kept in a narrow frequency band (around 1000 Hz) and at a reasonable intensity (e.g., 65+ decibels) to ensure audibility.

Consequences for Technology Use

When age-related impairments in vision and hearing are accompanied by modest changes in cognition and dexterity, problems can arise with typical computer input and output devices. A good example is the use of a computer mouse. A subset of older users, particularly novice users, have difficulty controlling cursor movement on a screen with movement of a mouse (Smith, Sharit, & Czaja, 1999) as in the case of easily acquiring small targets on a screen, or carrying out dragging and dropping operations. Double-clicking is often difficult because older adults have difficulty keeping the mouse from moving between clicks and thus the second click does not register as the second half of a double-click. One solution is to change the default parameters for the mouse (Worden, Walker, Bharat, & Hudson, 1997). Another strategy is to provide a different input device, such as a trackball or a touch screen device, although the choice of device also depends on the type of task (Rogers, Fisk, McLaughlin, & Pak, 2005).

On the other hand, some technological advances, such as the use of synthetic speech for output, may differentially handicap older workers who already have minor problems with normal speech perception (Roring, Hines, & Charness, 2007). By designing speech synthesis from databases composed of human-generated phonemes, words, and phrases, speech processing efficiency may be enhanced.

Some older adults are unfamiliar with a keyboard or are relatively unskilled at typing. A potential solution is to make use of speech recognition software, given that it seems to be equally effective for different age groups (Jastrzembski, Charness, Holley, & Feddon, 2005; Kalasky, Czaja, Sharit, & Nair, 1999). Although, this software has improved, there may still be some limitations. For example, it may not function well for people with foreign language accents.

Advances in technology can compensate for age-related changes in older workers, although thoughtful design and choice of appropriate devices and default settings is necessary. For instance, many users may not be aware of accessibility options available in popular computer operating systems that can increase legibility of text and icons, so providing that information as part of training is important.

The Future of Work

Many writers have envisioned scenarios where humans lead lives of leisure with low-cost robots providing goods and services to the entire human population. Recent strides in artificial intelligence, particularly that using pattern-based "unsupervised" learning from "big data," have raised the specter of machines replacing not just "physical," but also "knowledge" workers (Frey & Osborne, 2013). Self-driving vehicles, for instance, could easily replace thousands of professional (truck, taxi) driving jobs. One of the tasks used in prior older-worker experiments by our group, the Ryder truck task of travel data entry, can be totally automated using software and GPS-tracking of vehicles. A shrinking workforce is certainly a possibility (think of job loss during the recent Great Recession), but complete replacement of humans with subsequent endless leisure remains an elusive prospect. Someone (or some thing?) will still have to develop the software for and maintain (provide technical support for) robotic workers, at least in the short-term and we are still some way from having autonomous robots do other than "three-d" (dull, dirty, dangerous) work. But, at least for the next decade or two, the long-term employment shift from physically-demanding to mentally-demanding work is likely to continue. How will this affect employment prospects for older workers?

Notably, older workers tend to keep their jobs relative to younger (unskilled) ones during business cycle downturns (Rix, 2015). However, if they do lose their jobs, older workers take much longer to become re-employed, and suffer from under-employment. The US labor force in 2024 is projected to be comprised of an increasing number and percentage of older workers relative to other age cohorts (Toossi, 2016). So, an aging workforce is likely to be a reality for some time to come. Further, if current (circa 2018) job growth continues, older adults no longer in the labor force may become an important resource to tap to fill developing labor shortages, although only if they have relevant skill sets. Job training and retraining will continue to be necessary for those wanting to prolong the role of older worker.

The future of work over the next few decades will undoubtedly depend on the business cycle, much as it has in the past. That is, demand for and supply of labor will dictate how employers and employees respond to their roles for improving a firm's productivity balanced against managing quality of life for owners and employees alike. A safe bet is that things will look rather like they do today, with somewhat greater demands for learning and training to manage and integrate new technology into workflow processes.

Directions for Future Research

Societal challenges typically drive research-funding agendas. Today's challenges range from work productivity to income inequality to climate change. A recent report (National Academies of Science, Engineering, and Medicine, 2017) focuses on how technology may change work. Given the importance of work productivity to a very competitive job environment, future research should probably focus on improving our understanding of productivity drivers including how technology can contribute in the context of a RAS framework. Although productivity and age are generally found to be uncorrelated when the definition of productivity is work performance (output), the macro-relationship is likely to be negative when an economic definition is used: output/worker cost. Worker salary rises with age and the peak period for salary (measured cross-sectionally) is typically age 45–54, so economic productivity probably declines significantly with age.

Thus, from the standpoint of the productivity of the economy, the following questions might be considered. First, how do we invest more efficiently (training and equipment) to promote increases in human capital (skills, knowledge, and experience) to improve productivity, particularly at older ages. Second, could changes in compensation packages improve productivity. For instance, firms might need to contemplate a rising then falling salary pattern with worker age, like the inverted J-shaped function between age and peak performance described by Simonton (1988).

To address the first challenge we need to develop better measures of work performance, moving away from traditional ones such as supervisor and peer ratings, and simple output measures (e.g., items processed per unit of time, such as pages typed per hour). Why is this necessary? Feedback is the key to improving performance, as decades of research on expert performance has demonstrated (Ericsson, Hoffman, Kozblet & Williams, in press). Without better performance measures it will be difficult to assess whether interventions to improve productivity are effective. This task is going to be quite challenging considering the changing nature of work (from physical to mental) and the paucity of quality measures. An employee of any age coming up with one great idea can literally change the world. Think of the development of communication protocols such as TCP/IP, HTML, and the growth of the internet, or the idea of using cell broadcast technology to communicate by voice, and later, integrating email and a camera into a mobile phone.

A related challenge is the need to understand best practices to train and educate older workers because the empirical base for recommendations is thin: e.g., absence of an age by training method interaction. Also, when considering improving human capital, employers need to be alert to lifespan changes for employees, particularly assumption of a later-life caregiving role. How can we accommodate caregiving responsibilities of older workers? What are the best practices for providing flexible working hours or telework? Recent surveys suggest that different age cohorts experience different family pressures (Huffman, Culbertson, Henning & Goh, 2013).

Teamwork is also an increasingly important feature of work settings, yet we have relatively few studies of how to form effective teams that bridge intergenerational differences in knowledge and skills. Although the importance of mentoring is universally acknowledged, little is known about how knowledge transfer, that traditionally moved from older to younger generations, can become more bidirectional. For instance, although not in every case, knowledge about new technology often flows from younger to older generations. Finally, we need to remember that our workforce is becoming increasingly diverse and thus when designing training and job environments we need to broaden our conceptualization of "the worker."

Implications for Practice

Beyond the guidelines offered earlier in the chapter for accommodating normative changes with age, there is a need to consider how to integrate those past traditional retirement ages (e.g., 67+ years old in the US) into the labor force. For example, if the need for labor expands rapidly over coming years as part of a long-delayed robust recovery from the Great Recession, there will be a need to support the re-entry of older retired workers. For instance, particularly in industries with unique, aging equipment (manufacturing facilities), only older workers may have the expertise to maintain outdated equipment. When they retire, they take their knowledge with them. Offering them part-time work may be one way to attract them. Further, there are other older adults whose financial situation requires re-entry, and careful training, particularly with respect to technology skills, will be necessary.

Technology offers great promise for helping with many of these challenges, if it is well designed. Think of the option of remotely monitoring someone you are caring for over the internet either directly by checking in with a videocall, after being alerted of a problem by text message from a smart home equipped with sensors and clever algorithms. For an older employee needing to come up to speed with a new work process, consider the benefit of having instant access to online training opportunities, particularly to systems with intelligent tutoring interfaces that can adapt the training in real-time based on learner needs. Or consider how we all benefit from search engines that can provide work-related information almost instantly, assuming we have the knowledge and training to formulate efficient queries.

In summary, there are challenges to providing safe, supportive working environments for those who will be remaining in the workforce long past traditional retirement ages, or those returning after a traditional retirement. However, there are many opportunities to harness technology to support aging workers. There are even more opportunities for researchers to help design and provide training for those work environments, through both basic research on human performance changes with age, and through applied work shaping new tools and environments for better usability. Such innovations should benefit all age groups, but may be of particular value to aging workers.

References

Anderson, M., & Perrin, A. (2017). Technology use among seniors. Pew Research Center, May 2017, "Tech Adoption Climbs Among Older Adults," http://assets.pewresearch.org/wp-content/uploads/sites/14/2017/05/16170850/PI_2017.05.17_Older-Americans-Tech_FINAL.pdf (accessed September 20, 2017).

Bosman, E. A. (1993). Age-related differences in motoric aspects of transcription typing skill. *Psychology and Aging, 8*, 87–102.

Bouma, H. (1992). *Gerontechnology: Making technology relevant for the elderly*. In H. Bouma & J. A. M. Graafmans (Eds.). *Gerontechnology* (pp. 1–5). Amsterdam: IOS Press.

Callahan, J. S., Kiker, D. S., & Cross, T. (2003). Does method matter? A meta-analysis of the effects of training method on older learner training performance. *Journal of Management, 29*, 663–680.

Charness, N., & Boot, W. R. (2016). Technology, gaming, and social networking. In K. W. Schaie & S. L. Willis (Eds.). *The handbook of the psychology of aging* (8th Ed., Chapter 20, pp. 390–407). London, UK: Academic Press/Elsevier.

Charness, N., Kelley, C. L., Bosman, E. A., & Mottram, M. (2001). Word processing training and retraining: Effects of adult age, experience, and interface. *Psychology and Aging, 16*, 110–127.

Charness, N., Schumann, C. E., & Boritz, G. M. (1992). Training older adults in word processing: Effects of age, training technique, and computer anxiety. *International Journal of Technology and Aging, 5*, 79–106.

Chen, K., & Chan, A. H. S. (2014). Gerontechnology acceptance by elderly Hong Kong Chinese: A senior technology acceptance model (STAM). *Ergonomics, 57*(5), 635–652.

Czaja, S. J., & Sharit, J. (1998). Ability-performance relationships as a function of age and task experience for a data entry task. *Journal of Experimental Psychology: Applied, 4*, 332–351.

Czaja, S. J., & Sharit, J. (Eds.) (2009). *Aging and work: Issues and implications in a changing landscape*. Baltimore, MD: Johns Hopkins University Press.

Czaja, S. J., & Sharit, J. (2013). *Designing training and instructional programs for older adults*. London: CRC Press, Taylor & Francis Group.

Czaja, S. J., Boot, W. R., Charness, N., Rogers, W. A., & Sharit, J. (2018). Improving social support for older adults through technology: Findings from the PRISM randomized controlled trial. *The Gerontologist, 58*, 467–477.

Czaja, S. J., Charness, N., Fisk, A. D., Hertzog, C., Nair, S. N., Rogers, W. A., & Sharit, J. (2006). Factors predicting the use of technology: Findings from the Center for Research and Education on Aging and Technology Enhancement (CREATE). *Psychology and Aging, 21*, 333–352.

Czaja, S. J., Lee, C. C., Branham, J., & Remis, P. (2012). OASIS connections: Results from an evaluation study. *The Gerontologist, 52*, 712–721. doi: 10.1093/geront/gns004.

Czaja, S. J., Sharit, J., Ownby, R., Roth, D., & Nair, S. (2001). Examining age differences in performance of a complex information search and retrieval task. *Psychology and Aging, 16*, 564–579.

Ericsson, K. A., Hoffman, R., Kozbelt, A., & Williams, M. (Eds.) (in press). *Cambridge handbook on expertise and expert performance* (2nd Ed.). Cambridge, UK: Cambridge University Press.

Federal Interagency Forum on Aging-Related Statistics (2016). Older Americans 2016: Key indicators of well-being. Federal Interagency Forum on Aging-Related Statistics. Washington, DC: US Government Printing Office. August 2016. https://agingstats.gov/docs/LatestReport/Older-Americans-2016-Key-Indicators-of-WellBeing.pdf (accessed September 23, 2017).

Fisk, A. D., Rogers, W. A., Charness, N., Czaja, S. J., & Sharit, J. (2009). *Designing for older adults: Principles and creative human factors approaches* (2nd Ed.). Boca Raton: CRC Press.

Frey, C. B., & Osborne, M. A. (2013). The future of employment: How susceptible are jobs to computerization? www.oxfordmartin.ox.ac.uk/downloads/academic/The_Future_of_Employment.pdf (accessed September 23, 2017).

Gallup's Economy and Personal Finance Survey (2017). Most U.S. employed adults plan to work past retirement age. http://news.gallup.com/poll/210044/employed-adults-plan-work-past-retirement-age.aspx (accessed September 23, 2017).

Henkens, K., van Dalen, H., Ekerdt, D. J., Hershey, D. A., Hyde, M., Radl, J., van Solinge, H., Wang, M., & Zacher, H. (2017). What we need to know about retirement: Pressing issues for the coming decade. *Gerontologist*, doi:10.1093/geront/gnx095.

Huffman, A., Culbertson, S. S., Henning, J. B., & Goh, A. (2013). Work-family conflict across the lifespan. *Journal of Managerial Psychology, 28*, 761–780. https://doi.org/10.1108/JMP-07-2013-0220.

Jastrzembski, T. S., & Charness, N. (2007). The Model Human Processor and the older adult: Parameter estimation and validation within a mobile phone task. *Journal of Experimental Psychology: Applied, 13*, 224–248. DOI: 10.1037/1076-898X.13.4.224.

Jastrzembski, T., Charness, N., Holley, P., & Feddon, J. (2005). Aging and input devices: Voice recognition is slower yet more acceptable than a lightpen. *Proceedings of the 49th Annual Meeting of the Human Factors and Ergonomics Society*. Orlando, FL.

Kalasky, M. A., Czaja, S. J., Sharit, J., & Nair, S. N. (1999). "Is speech technology robust for older populations?" *Proceedings of the 43rd Annual Meeting of the Human Factors and Ergonomics Society*. Santa Monica, CA.

Krampe, R. T., & Charness, N. (2018). Aging and expertise. In K. A. Ericsson, R. Hoffman, A. Kozbelt, & M. Williams (Eds.). *Cambridge handbook on expertise and expert performance* (2nd Ed.). Cambridge, UK: Cambridge University Press.

Kubeck, J. E., Delp, N. D., Haslett, T. K., & McDaniel, M. A. (1996). Does job-related training performance decline with age? *Psychology and Aging, 11*, 92–107.

Kwon, S. (Ed.) (2016). *Gerontechnology: Research, practice, and principles in the field of technology and aging*. New York: Springer. ISBN: 978-0-8261-2888-1.

Lee, C., Czaja, S. J., & Sharit, J. (2009). Training older workers for a technology-based jobs. *Educational Gerontology, 35*, 15–31.

Nair, S. N., Czaja, S. J., & Sharit, J. (2007). A multilevel modeling approach to examining individual differences in skill acquisition for a computer-based task. *Journal of Gerontology: Psychological Science, 62B*, 85–96.

National Academies of Sciences, Engineering, and Medicine (2017). *Information technology and the U.S. workforce: where are we and where do we go from here?* Washington, DC: The National Academies Press. doi:10.17226/24649.

National Research Council (2004). *Health and safety needs of older workers.* Committee on the Health and Safety Needs of Older Workers. D. H. Wegman & J. P. McGee (Eds.), Division of Behavioral and Social Sciences and Education. Washington, DC: The National Academies Press.

Ng, T. W. H., & Feldman, D. C. (2008). The relationship of age to ten dimensions of job performance. *Journal of Applied Psychology, 93*, 392–423.

Park, D. C., & Reuter-Lorenz, P. (2009). The adaptive brain: Aging and neural scaffolding. *Annual Review of Psychology, 60*, 173–196. 10.1146/annurev.psych.59.103006.093656.

Rix, S. (2015). Long-term unemployment: Greater risks and consequences for older workers. Fact Sheet 319, February 2015. AARP Public Policy Institute. www.aarp.org/content/dam/aarp/ppi/2015-2/AARP953_LongTermUnemployment_FSFeb2v1.pdf (accessed September 24, 2017).

Rogers, W. A., Fisk, A. D., McLaughlin, A. C., & Pak, R. (2005). Touch a screen or turn a knob: Choosing the best device for the job. *Human Factors, 47*, 271–288. https://doi.org/10.1518/0018720054679452.

Roring, R. W., Hines, F. G., & Charness, N. (2007). Age differences in identifying words in synthetic speech. *Human Factors, 49*, 25–31.

Salthouse, T. A. (1984). Effects of age and skill in typing. *Journal of Experimental Psychology: General, 13*, 345–371.

Salthouse, T. A. (2010). *Major issues in cognitive aging.* Oxford: Oxford University Press.

Salthouse, T. A. (2012). Consequences of age-related cognitive declines. *Annual Review of Psychology, 63*, 201–226.

Schieber, F. (2006). Vision and aging. In J. E. Birren & K. W. Schaie (Eds.), *Handbook of the psychology of aging* (6th ed., pp. 129–162). Amsterdam: Elsevier Academic Press.

Sharit, J., Czaja, S. J., Hernandez, M., Yang, Y., Perdomo, D., Lewis, J. E., Lee, C. C., & Nair, S. (2004). An evaluation of performance by older persons on a simulated telecommuting task. *Journal of Gerontology: Psychological Sciences, 59B*, 305–316.

Simonton, D. K. (1988). Age and outstanding achievement: What do we know after a century of research? *Psychological Bulletin, 104*, 251–267.

Sinclair, D., Watson, J., & Beach, B. (2013). Working longer: An EU perspective. www.ilcuk.org.uk/files/Working_longer_an_EU_perspective.pdf (accessed February 6, 2018).

Smith, M. W., Sharit, J., & Czaja, S. J. (1999). Aging, motor control, and the performance of computer mouse tasks. *Human Factors, 41*, 389–396.

Toossi, M. (2016, December). Labor force projections to 2024: the labor force is growing, but slowly. *Monthly Labor Review*, U.S. Bureau of Labor Statistics, https://doi.org/10.21916/mlr.2015.48.

Venkatesh, V., Thong, J. Y. L., & Xu, X. (2012). Consumer acceptance and use of information technology: Extending the unified theory of acceptance and use of technology. *MIS Quarterly, 36*, 157–178.

Verhaeghen, P. (2014). *The elements of cognitive aging: Meta-analyses of age-related differences in processing speed and their consequences.* New York: Oxford University Press.

Wingfield, A., & Lash, A. (2016). Audition and language comprehension in adult aging: Stability in the face of change. In K. W. Schaie & S. L. Willis (Eds.), *The handbook of the psychology of aging* (8th ed., pp. 166–205). London, UK: Academic Press/Elsevier.

Worden, A., Walker, N., Bharat, K., & Hudson, S. (1997). Making computers easier for older adults to use: Area cursors and sticky icons. In S. Pemberton (Ed.), *Conference on Human Factors in Computing Systems – Proceedings* (pp. 266–271). ACM.

12

AGE AND WORK–FAMILY ISSUES

Reed J. Bramble, Emma K. Duerk, and Boris B. Baltes

This chapter explores work–family issues that are relevant to aging workers. As the population ages, the workforce itself is also aging, making it important to explore work–family issues across the lifespan. A review of the literature suggests that work–family conflict does differ across the lifespan but is more related to life stages then just chronological age. Furthermore, and perhaps more importantly, older and younger workers appear to differ in both the priorities they assign to work and family, as well as in their use of coping behaviors to help balance the two domains. The first section of this chapter will focus on investigating the relationship between age and work–family conflict. The second section will highlight lifespan approaches to work–family balance. The final section will focus on work–family related interventions for older workers.

The Relationship Between Age and Work–Family Conflict

When exploring the variables of age and work–family conflict, researchers have generally found that these two variables are related in either a non-linear or negative linear fashion (Huffman, Culbertson, Henning, & Goh, 2013; Ng & Feldman, 2012). If one considers the linear relationship, it appears that levels of work–family conflict tend to be higher at younger ages and then decrease over time. In a meta-analysis conducted by Ng and Feldman (2012), the authors found that age was very weakly correlated with family–work conflict, family–work enrichment, and work–family conflict. Further, age was not significantly related to work–family enrichment or perceptions of work–family balance. These findings indicate that the stereotype that older workers may experience more work–family conflict as a result of greater investment in their family and community and as such "don't have their heart in their work" or they "don't have their head in the game" does not seem to be supported by the extant literature (Ng & Feldman, 2012). If one considers a non-linear relationship, work–family conflict seems to exhibit an inverted U relationship with age whereas middle age individuals report the highest levels of work–family conflict (Allen & Finkelstein, 2014). Regardless of age, employees can and do experience work–family issues. Given this understanding it is important to note that all people, regardless of age or life/career stage, report work–life balance as one of their main concerns in life (Darcy, McCarthy, Hill, & Grady, 2012). When age differences are examined in the work–family domain, the life stage model has often been used to explain these discrepancies and better understand the potential factors influencing work–family conflict.

Life and Career Stages

The demands associated with both early family life and early career roles are often substantial and unpredictable, resulting in a greater susceptibility to work–family conflict. That being said, the needs of both younger and older individuals are often seen to be different from one another due to the idiosyncrasies of their career or life stages. As individuals continue to age and remain in the workforce for increasingly longer careers, this continues to impact the workforce as a whole. Subsequently, the aging of the workforce will likely alter the way organizations and individual employees approach work–family issues. Many researchers adopt a life-stages approach to explain the relationship between age and work–family conflict. This approach relies primarily on the developmental stages that concern criteria related to family size and the developmental age of the oldest child.

There have been multiple studies examining the association between both individual developmental stages and family developmental stages and their association with work–family demands (e.g., Darcy, McCarthy, Hill & Grady, 2012; Keith & Schafer, 1991; Schnittger & Bird, 1990). These studies ultimately indicate that the association between these factors can lead to potential work–family conflict. The model of work–family conflict through life-cycle stages refers to the variations in work and family role demands encountered throughout the lifespan (Aldous, 1978). It should be disclosed that life-cycle stages are not inherently bound to one's chronological age (although they are correlated with age), but are distinctive role structures that separate them from other periods (Baltes & Young, 2007). Given this lack of perfect covariation between the life stages models and age, this life stage model may help to additionally explain some issues that arise between work and family demands over the course of time.

The most commonly used conceptualization of the life-stages model was first presented by Duval and Hill (1948). The researchers proposed a model that revolves around a unique categorization system that is based on several criteria, including family size, the developmental age of the oldest child, and the work status of the family breadwinners (Hill, 1986). The family size construct is further divided into five distinct categories: (1) stable stage, childless; (2) expanding stage, childbearing; (3) stable stage, childrearing; (4) contracting stage, launching; (5) stable stage, empty nest. From these stages and with the inclusion of children, as the oldest child's development age increases, new stages arise in the expanding and stable childbearing stages of family size categories, which are as follows: (1) family with preschool children; (2) family with school-age children; (3) family with adolescents; (4) family with young adults. Finally, work status of the breadwinners additionally generates two additional stages, this time in the stable empty nest stage: (1) family in the middle years; (2) family in the retirement phase. Using the criteria explained above an individual can advance through eight mutually exclusive categories of development:

(1) Establishment stage (childless, newly married).
(2) First parenthood (family with infant to 3 years).
(3) Family with preschool children (oldest child 3–6 years of age).
(4) Family with school children (oldest child 6–12 years of age).
(5) Family with adolescents (oldest child 13–20 years of age).
(6) Family as launching center (children begin to leave the home).
(7) Family in middle years (postparental empty nest).
(8) Family in retirement (breadwinners in retirement).

When focusing on work–family conflict that may arise during the life stages, Higgins, Duxbury, and Lee (1994) found that reported levels of work–family conflict are shown to increase as an individual enters into the marriage stage and/or starts having children. Additional research has demonstrated that the age of the youngest child also has an impact on work–family conflict, such that as the youngest child grows older and the individual/family progresses through the proposed stages, there is an increase in work–family conflict. Further, the majority of job strain models (i.e., Karasek, 1979) would provide support for the theory that as the youngest child gets older the experience of work–family conflict should decrease. This is due to the fact that job strain models posit that when employees experience a lack of control over stressors, their experienced stress will increase. Therefore, given the lack of control that corresponds with the demands of younger children (e.g., Bass et al., 2009; Hochschild, 2003), there is no surprise that parents in these life stages generally report the highest level of work–family conflict compared to their counterparts.

Furthermore, research conducted by Allen and Finkelstein (2014) supports the idea that work–family conflict has a slightly negative relationship with age, as well as the family stages portion of the life stage model relating to work–family conflict. Interestingly, the researchers also found that family stage is not a good proxy for age, given individual differences (e.g., gender) and specific family situations (e.g., parents with teens or empty nesters). More specifically, life stage, gender, and age are uniquely related to work–family conflict and each of these factors contributes uniquely to work–family conflict above and beyond chronological age alone.

It should also be noted that the final life stage that involves retirement and post-retirement can occur under very different circumstances and may produce differences in work–family outcomes. A wide variety of factors can influence whether or not an individual retires in a timely fashion, including macro-economic, sociocultural, and organizational determinants (for review, see Fisher, Chaffee, & Sonnega, 2016). Employees with lower socioeconomic status may be required to work beyond expected retirement age, and may also be less able to provide financial support to meet family-related demands. The retirement context for these individuals is also more sensitive to factors beyond individual control, such as changes to government programs, employee benefits, and organizational staffing. Lastly, the actual process of retirement can differ between individuals, with some individuals retiring abruptly and others engaging in phased retirement or bridge employment (Wang, Adams, Beehr, & Shultz, 2009). In sum, transitioning to retirement and post-retirement does not carry with it an inherent increase in the capability to meet work–family demands.

Additionally, the authors discovered that while age tends to relate to work–family conflict in a monotonic, linear fashion, life stages exhibited an inverted-U relationship such that those on the ends of the continuum (i.e., family establishment and empty nesters) reported the least work–family conflict. However, one limitation with the current life-stages model is that it fails to account for unique individual/family situations (i.e., those with 'eldercare', or grandparents with childcare) and as such the model does not relate to all working individuals and may not explain the full range of work–family conflict across the lifespan. The following section aims to explain the caregiving responsibilities of older workers and provides an overview of the recent research that has been conducted on this topic as it relates to age and work–family conflict.

Eldercare and Caring for Grandchildren

Eldercare is defined as the care of elderly individuals (i.e., those who are 65 years or older). It comprises a wide range of responsibilities. These tasks could either be very simple in nature, such as grocery shopping for an elderly individual, or more complex, such as housing an elderly individual or providing all transportation for that person. It is projected that by 2035, 20 percent of the population will be comprised of individuals 65 and older and the population will remain this high until 2050 (Albright, 2012). Given the steady increase of elderly individuals, many of whom need some form of daily assistance, it is likely that the number of working adults attempting to balance careers and eldercare responsibilities has also increased. As mentioned in Dugan and colleagues (2016), two-thirds of older adults who receive eldercare at home receive all their care from family members. Further, 57 percent of family caregivers reported that they were employed either part or full time, 11 percent and 46 percent respectively. While the majority of research around balancing caregiving tasks and work responsibilities focuses on childcare, there is a growing body of literature centering on achieving work–family balance in the face of eldercare demands as well. The purpose of the following section is to provide a high-level overview of current eldercare research.

Over the past decade, there has been an increase in work–family research focusing on the impact of eldercare demands. For instance, a study conducted by Shoptaugh, Phelps, and Visio (2004) looked at a sample of employed nurses and found that dissatisfaction with eldercare responsibilities arose when it interrupted the caregivers work day or required the caregiver to leave work to provide assistance. This inter-domain conflict resulted in increased absences and greater turnover intention. Further, for this sample, employees providing eldercare were not significantly different in their levels of job satisfaction or organizational commitment than those employees without such responsibilities. Lastly, the majority of employees expressed interest in employer-sponsored eldercare support.

Another important study found that manufacturing employees over the age of 45 were more likely than younger employees to report taking on eldercare responsibilities (Dugan et al., 2016). Further, after controlling for potential differentiating factors (i.e., sociodemographic characteristics and competing demands) it was shown that eldercare demands were linked to both work–family conflict and depressive symptoms, such that family–work conflict was shown to result from personal care demands while depressive symptoms were more likely to come from more frequently occurring eldercare responsibilities. It is important to note that more frequently occurring eldercare responsibilities were those that took up five or more hours a week. Lastly, these more frequently occurring eldercare responsibilities were also shown to have a relationship with greater family interfering with work conflict, when compared with no eldercare responsibilities.

Interestingly, there is also a portion of older workers who have childcare responsibilities (Allen & Shockley, 2012). For instance, there is a rising percentage of older working adults who find themselves in situations that demand the care of grandchildren. This would be older working individuals who either assist in childcare responsibilities or those who fully take on childcare responsibilities for their grandchildren or younger individuals in their personal lives. Older adults may care for grandchildren under a "three-generation family" structure (i.e., both parents and grandchildren living in the household) or a "skipped-generation family" structure (i.e., grandchildren living in the home without parents; Wang & Marcotte, 2007). There is a range of research that demonstrates instances when older employees take on the responsibilities of their grandchildren, and is mostly done by grandmothers in times of crisis (Pebley & Rudkin, 1999). In addition, research has shown that caring for grandchildren has an impact on health outcomes (Copen, 2006; Wang & Marcotte, 2007). Care for grandchildren may prompt an older adult to remain in the workplace or leave retirement in order to fulfill the financial need associated with caregiving; these factors are not often considered in organizational supports or benefits (Copen, 2006).

Lastly, older workers may also fit into the "sandwich generation" (i.e., individuals that have simultaneous caregiving responsibilities for recipients both older and younger than themselves; for review, see Duxbury & Dole, 2015). Individuals in this position are at greater risk for negative outcomes, including increased levels of work–family conflict and job burnout, as well as decreased levels of health and well-being (Pines, Neal, Hammer, & Icekson, 2011; Rubin & White-Means, 2009; Tement & Korunka, 2015). Caregivers in the sandwich generation are also significantly more likely to engage in poor lifestyle habits and unhealthy behaviors (e.g., poor diet, neglecting to exercise, smoking cigarettes) that could be particularly detrimental in older age (Chassin, Macy, Seo, Presson, & Sherman, 2010). There is also evidence for compounding effects of caregiving, such that the responsibility for a greater number of care recipients is associated with greater family-to-work conflict, poorer relationship quality, greater stress, and poorer psychological functioning (DePasquale et al., 2014). While workers nearing retirement are less likely to be members of the sandwich generation, the relative effects of the caregiving demands suggest that employers should be especially attentive to older employees who fit this definition.

In summary, a number of studies now appear to support the idea that work–family conflict has an inverted-U relationship with life-stages (and to some extent chronological age) as demonstrated by Allen and Finkelstein (2014). Specifically, the youngest and oldest workers have the fewest conflicts, such that work–family conflict increases during the first years, and then begins to decrease throughout the remaining working years (Huffman et al., 2013). However, we should point out that eldercare, and care for grandchildren, could change the life stages model for many individuals and change this inverted-U relationship. Specifically, the decrease in work family conflict for older workers may not occur if these extra responsibilities increase for the older working populations as a whole.

Coping Strategies of Older Adults

In addition to life circumstances and caregiving responsibilities, coping strategies employed by older workers may also serve to explain the apparent decrease in work–family conflict for older workers. For example, the theory of selection, optimization, and compensation (SOC) assumes that older adults are able to cope with resource loss by selecting goals pertinent to an individual within the domain of interest, reframing goal structures to align with needs, and emphasizing existing resources that will compensate for those lost (Baltes, 1997; Baltes & Baltes, 1990; Freund & Baltes, 2002). This coping strategy affords older adults the opportunity to increase one's resources, maintain functioning in the face of obstacles, and avoid future resource loss. Employing a SOC strategy would be appropriate in the work–family context – for example, goal selection can be applied to the work–family domain both as elective selection (e.g., an individual prefers/chooses to engage in more family-relevant goals as opposed to work-relevant goals) as well as loss-based selection (e.g., loss of physical/cognitive resources makes working more cumbersome, prompting an emphasis on family-relevant goals). Additionally, older adults may choose to compensate for loss of resources by restructuring their job role or transitioning to a different role (Baltes & Heydens-Gahir, 2003).

The reprioritization of goals within the work and family domains should theoretically reduce inter-domain conflict. Accordingly, empirical research demonstrates that older adults employ SOC coping strategies to a greater extent than their younger counterparts (Urry & Gross, 2010). In turn, SOC strategies have been shown to reduce stressors in the work and family domains and minimize work–family conflict (Baltes & Heydens-Gahir, 2003; Blanchard-Fields, 2007; Urry & Gross, 2010; Young, Baltes, & Pratt, 2007). Lastly, SOC strategies appear to have spousal crossover effects on work–family conflict, such that a spouse's use of SOC strategies provided incremental variance in reducing work–family conflict above a person's own use of SOC strategies (Wynne, 2017).

In summary, the increased use of SOC coping strategies in older adults may explain the decrease in reported work–family conflict seen in older workers. The realignment of goals with changing needs and resources, paired with the allotment of energy towards goal pursuit that is suitable given an individual's domain-specific means and preferences, allows older workers to mitigate spillover across domain boundaries.

Outside of life circumstances and coping strategies, there are several theories of aging and work that suggest work–family balance is an especially important issue for older workers. The following sections will outline the theoretical bases for changes in adult behavior and motivation as retirement nears. Additionally, we will discuss implications in the context of work–family research.

Lifespan Approaches to Work–Family Balance

Despite the evidence that work–family conflict tends to decrease for older workers, the findings do not imply that work–family balance is unimportant to older adults. While life stage shifts are likely responsible for a part of the decrease in work–family conflict, relying solely on this explanation discounts the idea that older adults may play a role in affecting their own work–family balance. For example, a reduction in conflict may be a result of individuals placing additional time and resources into the maintenance of work–family balance. Evidence suggests that work–family balance could be especially important to older adults. Perceptions of work–family conflict have been previously associated with a desire to retire early (Raymo & Sweeney, 2006). Additionally, if older adults experience a characteristic motivational shift away from work responsibilities, the negative repercussions of work–family conflict are often substantially worse for these individuals (Bagger & Li, 2012; Carr, Boyar, & Gregory, 2008). The following section will outline three theories of aging and work that suggest a heightened importance of work–family balance for older adults: (1) socioemotional selectivity theory, (2) theory of work motivation for older workers, and (3) theory of work centrality and identity.

Socioemotional Selectivity Theory

Socioemotional selectivity theory (SST; Carstensen, 1991) postulates that individuals have an inherent awareness of time and will adjust behavior in accordance with the shortened time horizons associated with aging. Domain-relevant goals are contextualized with a certain time horizon in mind – therefore, goal pursuit is contingent on the perceived amount of time remaining to achieve a particular goal. Carstensen (1992) provides commentary on the changing nature of social relationships with age, such that the investment of time and energy in social interaction involves a cost–benefit analysis and a comparison of social alternatives. Owing to a decreased time horizon (also known as *future time perspective*, or FTP), the fostering of new relationships may not be worth the time investment relative to already existing, emotionally close relationships (e.g., family members). A constrained FTP is also thought to favor striving towards short-term emotion-regulation goals (e.g., positive mood regulation and focus on psychological well-being) as opposed to long-term knowledge acquisition goals (e.g., developing skills, seeking out novel experiences).

Applied to the work–family domain, SST suggests that FTP should diminish as individuals age, thereby influencing older adults to invest greater time and energy into family relationships as opposed to work. This shift in emphasis from work to family, combined with a greater incentive to foster a more positive outlook, ought to result in an increased emphasis on work–family balance. Indeed, Treadway et al. (2011) discovered that FTP was a moderator of the relationship between work–family conflict and organizational commitment, such that individuals with a more constrained FTP responded to work–family spillover with a reduced commitment to their work. Similarly, multiple empirical studies have found that decreases in FTP correspond with decreases in individual motivation to continue working (Garcia, Milkovits, & Bordia, 2014; Kooij, Bal, & Kanfer, 2014). These authors utilize SST in an effort to explain the finding, suggesting that as family interaction increases in importance and salience, the consequences of work–family conflict also increase in salience and prompt older adults to avoid such conflict.

Taken together, the diminishing future time perspective that is characteristic of the aging process is a potential driver towards an increased focus on work–family balance in one's life. As older adults perceive less time remaining in their careers, they experience a shift towards more immediate emotion-regulation goals and rely on familiar relationships for social interaction. These processes likely result in an emotional distancing from the work domain and a greater desire to achieve equilibrium between work and family domains.

Theory of Work Motivation for Older Workers

While perceived time remaining is a substantial factor in work motivation, researchers have begun to assess the role of additional motivations for individuals to continue working late into their adult lives (Kooij, De Lange, Jansen, & Dikkers, 2008; Kooij et al., 2011; Rudolph, Baltes, & Zabel, 2013; Thrasher, Zabel, Wynne, & Baltes, 2016). Kooij and colleagues (2008) acknowledged that while individuals may share a similar chronological age, their life circumstances and subjective perceptions of those circumstances may influence one individual to continue working while prompting another to opt for retirement. When contemplating retirement, older workers not only factor in chronological age, but also their health, work ability, career stage, tenure, family situation, and self-perception into their decision to remain working (De Lange et al., 2006; Sterns & Doverspike, 1989). Specifically, these factors are thought to influence one's desire to learn and develop new skills (i.e., *growth motive*), motivation to engage in social relationship-building (i.e., *social motive*), and inclination to retain existing resources and avoid loss (i.e., *security motive*; Kooij et al., 2011; Rudolph et al., 2013).

In the work–family context, it is expected that decreases in the growth and social motives, along with an increase in one component of the security motive (i.e., need for autonomy) should signal a shift in one's focus from work to family, as well as a corresponding shift in the importance of work–family balance. Consistent with this notion, a meta-analysis of age and work-related motives conducted by Kooij and colleagues (2011) found negative relationships between age and growth and social motives. Furthermore, this meta-analysis also found an increase in need for autonomy for older individuals.

Additionally, it has been found that decreases in FTP were associated with a decreased focus on promotion and growth, as well as a depleted motivation to remain working (Kooij, Bal & Kanfer, 2014). While the relationship between these specific work motives and work–family conflict has yet to be assessed, a strong theoretical foundation and empirical evidence in the work domain suggest that age-related changes in motives could be an additional determinant in the relationship between work–family conflict and age (Thrasher et al., 2016). It is likely that as individuals perceive less opportunity to benefit from growth-related strategies at work, they will gravitate towards familial relationships and close friendships that will aid in their emotion-regulatory goals. Taken together, while older adults may experience less work–family conflict overall, they may also place an increased emphasis on inter-domain balance and be less willing to tolerate the negative aspects of work–family conflict.

Work Centrality and Identification with Work

Another factor that plays a role in an individual's tolerance for conflict is their identification with work (i.e., *work centrality*), which is the general degree of importance that one places on work in their lives relative to other life domains. The concept of work centrality is based on the notion that work is an integral component of our self-identity and a source upon which we draw for meaning in our lives (Baltes, Rudolph, & Bal, 2012; Meaning of Work International Research Team, MOWIRT, 1987). Across national cultures, one's work identity is thought to be central to how people define themselves as individuals (e.g., Arvey, Harpaz, & Liao, 2004) and many people state that they would have a desire to work in the absence of financial need (MOWIRT, 1987). Nonetheless, the meaning individuals place on work in their lives is dependent on the choices and experiences of individuals, as well as the work and family domains they operate within (Snir & Harpaz, 2002). In the development of the Meaning of Work for Older Workers model (MOWFOW), Baltes and colleagues (2012) outline how the contributing components to one's work centrality may be dynamic across the lifespan and contingent on individual needs and desires.

Consistent with previously described theories, a progression away from work centrality and towards family centrality is expected for older workers nearing retirement, indicating a potentially greater need for work-family balance. In the work–family literature, studies have found that a lower work centrality is indeed associated with lower levels of work–family conflict – however, if those with low work centrality do experience work–family conflict, the negative repercussions of conflict are significantly worse (Bagger & Li, 2012; Carr et al., 2008).

Furthermore, there is indirect evidence that age is likely negatively related to work centrality. The importance of financial gain declines with age due to less financial obligation consistent with earlier life stages (children, mortgages, etc.; Loi & Shultz, 2007). Additionally, older employees tend to pay greater attention to their private lives (and especially to their committed familial relationships) when compared with younger employees (Evans & Bartolomé, 1984). Given the number of factors contributing to the meaning of work for older workers, Baltes et al. (2012) call for additional research assessing both work and family centrality in the aging context.

In summary, it is probable that older workers tend to possess a lesser degree of work centrality, which in turn translates to a greater need for inter-domain balance. Interwoven through several of the theories presented is a greater importance placed on the family domain relative to the work domain for older adults, which is both theoretically and empirically shown to be a negative correlate of work–family conflict. However, particular attention should be paid to older workers who, despite experiencing a motivational shift from work to family centrality, continue to experience work–family conflict and its exacerbated effects.

Directions for Future Research

Despite the effectiveness and prevalence of the interventions covered in the previous section, there is a general paucity of research testing the efficacy of interventions or offering alternatives to accepted practice. The following section will outline two types of interventions that deserve greater attention from organizational researchers: dependent care support and training related to selection, optimization, and compensation.

Dependent Care Supports

Dependent care supports (i.e., any services that consider the current or impending needs of dependents) may be particularly helpful for older workers engaging in eldercare. Older adults are more likely to benefit from eldercare support than other forms of dependents (Baltes & Young, 2007; Dellmann-Jenkins, Bennett, & Brahce, 1994). That being said, eldercare supports are relatively rare (Lockwood, 2003), and employers historically tend to view eldercare as a personal issue that is not of organizational concern (Marshall, Matthews & Rosenthal, 1993). Moreover, there is not consistent evidence that these kinds of interventions are effective (Hammer, Demsky, Kossek, & Bray, 2016), and employers are more likely to invest in scheduling and flextime initiatives that seemingly appear to have more tangible benefits (Baltes & Young, 2007). However, some studies have shown that the use of eldercare leave was associated with reduced levels of work–family conflict (Breaugh & Frye, 2008) and higher retention (Pavalko & Henderson, 2006). Scholars have also put forth eldercare support groups and forms of adult day care as viable intervention options, although these topics have not been investigated in the literature (Dellmann-Jenkins et al., 1994; Guberman & Maheu, 1999). While lack of validation of interventions is an issue across the work–family domain (Hammer et al., 2016), continued research on these types of interventions would provide a clearer illustration of how they can benefit the older worker.

Selection, Optimization, and Compensation Training

Providing employees with training on SOC strategies would serve as an effective work–family intervention, as they have been shown to reduce stressors in the work and family domains and minimize work–family conflict (Baltes &

Heydens-Gahir, 2003; Blanchard-Fields, 2007; Urry & Gross, 2010). Recent evidence suggests that SOC interventions can be effective. Müller and colleagues (2016) implemented a randomized controlled SOC training among a sample of hospital nurses, finding that the intervention was associated with enhanced mental well-being. While samples of older adults exhibit greater use of SOC coping strategies than their younger counterparts (Urry & Gross, 2010), it is possible that the use of SOC strategies have helped older adults to remain working, thereby allowing them availability for such research samples. Therefore, SOC strategies may be a key component to retaining older workers in late career. The realignment of goals with changing needs and resources, paired with the allotment of energy towards goal pursuit that is suitable given an individual's domain-specific means and preferences, would allow older workers to mitigate spillover across domain boundaries and continue working. However, additional studies demonstrating the effectiveness of SOC interventions for older workers are needed to bolster this conclusion.

Implications for Practice

While work–family balance is an important indicator of well-being for all individuals, theory suggests that balance is particularly critical for employees nearing retirement age. Given the importance of work–family balance for older workers, several interventions can be implemented into organizational practice in order to better serve the aging workforce, including flexible work arrangement and telework.

Flexible Work Arrangements

A very common form of work–family support is flexible scheduling, which provides employees with greater control over the circumstances under which their work is conducted. These practices enable employees to free up the structure of the work day to accommodate family demands (Rau, 2003). Flexible work arrangements have been previously associated with employee well-being and work–family conflict (e.g., Grzywacz, Carlson, & Shulkin, 2008; Grzywacz, Casey, & Jones, 2007; Jang, 2009). Given that older adults may place a greater premium on work–family balance, flexible work arrangements may be particularly desirable in late career. Schedule flexibility has been shown to influence older employees' decisions to remain working versus retiring (Pavalko & Henderson, 2006; Shacklock, Brunetto, & Nelson, 2009).

Additionally, as older workers are more likely than their younger counterparts to have eldercare and health responsibilities, flextime may facilitate work–family balance in the face of increasing family and personal demands (Calvano, 2013; Dembe, Dugan, Mutschler, & Piktialis, 2008; Kim, Ingersoll-Dayton, & Kwak, 2013; Zacher & Schulz, 2015). For instance, Rudolph and Baltes (2017) discovered that both the availability and use of flexible work arrangements was positively associated with work engagement in older adults, particularly in employees with lower functional health.

Telework and Flexibility Fit

A similar practice to flexible scheduling is telework, which allows individuals the option to work from a remote location. While remote work opportunities are generally perceived as desirable across age groups, it may be most suitable for older workers with increasing family demands and eldercare responsibilities. Indeed, research has shown that telework helps individuals to manage eldercare demands (Major, Verive, & Joice, 2008). While the evaluation of telework programs on work–family outcomes still needs to gather additional scientific evidence, there have been some positive examples of interventions for older workers. For instance, the CVS Snowbird Program (Pitt-Catsouphes, Matz-Costa, & Besen, 2009) allowed older employees to transfer to an alternative geographical location for a few months during the year, thereby increasing the retention rate of older workers. Telework and the CVS Snowbird Program are both examples of *flexibility fit* (i.e., the extent to which employees believe their flexibility needs are being met; Pitt-Catsouphes et al., 2009). Flexibility fit has been empirically associated with work engagement, work overload, health, and satisfaction with work–family balance (Pitt-Catsouphes et al., 2009). The fit between personal needs and work supports may be a critical indicator for older adults that likely require more flexibility in order to achieve adequate work–life balance.

Conclusion

In conclusion, the research evidence demonstrates that work–family conflict does have a life course. Specifically, the relationship between reported levels of work–family conflict and age seems to be most dependent on an individual's lifestage and is one that demonstrates an inverted-U shape, with younger and older workers reporting the lowest levels of work–family conflict. However, increasing amounts of eldercare and care of grandchildren may bend this inverted-U upward and the reported levels of work–family conflict could increase in older workers. Furthermore, and perhaps more importantly, the priorities given to work versus family change as an employee ages. As pointed out earlier, multiple lifespan theories would suggest that work centrality decreases, and family centrality increases with age. This results in older workers putting a greater emphasis on achieving work–family balance. With this in mind, we explored several types of interventions that would be helpful for organizations in recruiting and retaining older workers. Most of these focus on allowing older workers to continue working while maintaining work–family balance.

References

Albright, V. A. (2012). Workforce demographics in the United States. In J. W. Hedge & W. C. Borman (Eds.), *The Oxford handbook of work and aging* (pp. 33–59). New York: Oxford University Press.

Aldous, J. (1978). *Family careers: Developmental change in families*. New York: Wiley.

Allen, T. D., & Finkelstein, L. M. (2014). Work–family conflict among members of full-time dual-earner couples: An examination of family life stage, gender, and age. *Journal of Occupational Health Psychology, 19*, 376–384.

Allen, T. D., & Shockley, K. M. (2012). Older workers and work–family issues. In J. W. Hedge & W. C. Borman (Eds.), *The Oxford handbook of work and aging* (pp. 520–537). New York: Oxford University Press.

Arvey, R. D., Harpaz, I., & Liao, H. (2004). Work centrality and post-award work behavior of lottery winners. *The Journal of Psychology, 138*, 404–420.

Bagger, J., & Li, A. (2012). Being important matters: The impact of work and family centralities on the family-to-work conflict–satisfaction relationship. *Human Relations, 65*, 473–500.

Baltes, P. B. (1997). On the incomplete architecture of human ontogeny: Selection, optimization, and compensation as foundation of developmental theory. *American Psychologist, 52*, 366–380.

Baltes, P. B., & Baltes, M. M. (1990). Psychological perspectives on successful aging: The model of selective optimization with compensation. In P. B. Baltes & M. M. Baltes (Eds.), *Successful aging: Perspectives from the behavioral sciences* (pp. 1–34). New York: Cambridge University Press.

Baltes, B. B., & Heydens-Gahir, H. A. (2003). Reduction of work-family conflict through the use of selection, optimization, and compensation behaviors. *Journal of Applied Psychology, 88*, 1005–1018.

Baltes, B. B., & Young, L. M. (2007). Aging and work/family issues. In K. S. Shultz & G. A. Adams (Eds.), *Aging and work in the 21st century* (pp. 251–275). New York: Psychology Press.

Baltes, B. B., Rudolph, C. W., & Bal, A. C. (2012). A review of aging theories and modern work perspectives. In J. W. Hedge & W. C. Borman (Eds.), *The Oxford handbook of work and aging* (pp. 117–136). New York: Oxford University Press.

Bass, B. L., Butler, A. B., Grzywacz, J. G., & Linney, K. D. (2009). Do job demands undermine parenting? A daily analysis of spillover and crossover effects. *Family Relations, 58*, 201–215.

Blanchard-Fields, F. (2007). Everyday problem solving and emotion: An adult developmental perspective. *Current Directions in Psychological Science, 16*, 26–31.

Breaugh, J. A., & Frye, N. K. (2008). Work–family conflict: The importance of family-friendly employment practices and family-supportive supervisors. *Journal of Business and Psychology, 22*, 345–353.

Calvano, L. (2013). Tug of war: Caring for our elders while remaining productive at work. *The Academy of Management Perspectives, 27*, 204–218.

Carr, J. C., Boyar, S. L., & Gregory, B. T. (2008). The moderating effect of work-family centrality on work-family conflict, organizational attitudes, and turnover behavior. *Journal of Management, 34*, 244–262.

Carstensen, L. L. (1991). Selectivity theory: Social activity in life-span context. *Annual Review of Gerontology and Geriatrics, 11*, 195–217.

Carstensen, L. L. (1992). Social and emotional patterns in adulthood: Support for socioemotional selectivity theory. *Psychology and Aging, 7*, 331–338.

Chassin, L., Macy, J. T., Seo, D. C., Presson, C. C., & Sherman, S. J. (2010). The association between membership in the sandwich generation and health behaviors: A longitudinal study. *Journal of Applied Developmental Psychology, 31*, 38–46.

Copen, C. E. (2006). Welfare reform: Challenges for grandparents raising grandchildren. *Journal of Aging & Social Policy, 18*, 193–209.

Darcy, C., McCarthy, A., Hill, J., & Grady, G. (2012). Work–life balance: One size fits all? An exploratory analysis of the differential effects of career stage. *European Management Journal, 30*, 111–120.

De Lange, A. H., Taris, T. W., Jansen, P., Smulders, P., Houtman, I., & Kompier, M. (2006). Age as a factor in the relation between work and mental health: Results from the longitudinal TAS survey. *Occupational Health Psychology: European Perspectives on Research, Education and Practice, 1*, 21–45.

Dellmann-Jenkins, M., Bennett, J. M., & Brahce, C. I. (1994). Shaping the corporate response to workers with elder care commitments: Considerations for gerontologists. *Educational Gerontology: An International Quarterly, 20*, 395–405.

Dembe, A. E., Dugan, E., Mutschler, P., & Piktialis, D. (2008). Employer perceptions of elder care assistance programs. *Journal of Workplace Behavioral Health, 23*, 359–379.

DePasquale, N., Davis, K. D., Zarit, S. H., Moen, P., Hammer, L. B., & Almeida, D. M. (2014). Combining formal and informal caregiving roles: The psychosocial implications of double-and triple-duty care. *Journals of Gerontology Series B: Psychological Sciences and Social Sciences, 71*, 201–211.

Dugan, A. G., Fortinsky, R. H., Barnes-Farrell, J. L., Kenny, A. M., Robison, J. T., Warren, N., & Cherniack, M. G. (2016). Associations of eldercare and competing demands with health and work outcomes among manufacturing workers. *Community, Work & Family, 19*, 569–587.

Duval, E. M., & Hill, R. L. (1948). *Report of the committee on the dynamics of family interaction*. Washington, DC: National Conference on Family Life.

Duxbury, L., & Dole, G. (2015). Squeezed in the middle: Balancing paid employment, childcare and eldercare. In R. J. Burke, K. M., Page, & C. L. Cooper (Eds.), *Flourishing in life, work and careers: Individual wellbeing and career experiences* (pp. 141–166). Cheltenham: Edward Elgar Publishing.

Evans, P., & Bartolomé, F. (1984). The changing pictures of the relationship between career and family. *Journal of Organizational Behavior, 5*, 9–21.

Fisher, G. G., Chaffee, D. S., & Sonnega, A. (2016). Retirement timing: A review and recommendations for future research. *Work, Aging and Retirement, 2*, 230–261.

Freund, A. M., & Baltes, P. B. (2002). Life-management strategies of selection, optimization, and compensation: Measurement by self-report and construct validity. *Journal of Personality and Social Psychology, 82*, 642–662.

Garcia, P. R. J. M., Milkovits, M., & Bordia, P. (2014). The impact of work–family conflict late-career workers' intentions to continue paid employment: A social cognitive career theory approach. *Journal of Career Assessment, 22*, 682–699.

Grzywacz, J. G., Carlson, D. S., & Shulkin, S. (2008). Schedule flexibility and stress: Linking formal flexible arrangements and perceived flexibility to employee health. *Community, Work and Family, 11*, 199–214.

Grzywacz, J. G., Casey, P. R., & Jones, F. A. (2007). The effects of workplace flexibility on health behaviors: A cross-sectional and longitudinal analysis. *Journal of Occupational and Environmental Medicine, 49*, 1302–1309.

Guberman, N., & Maheu, P. (1999). Combining employment and caregiving: An intricate juggling act. *Canadian Journal on Aging, 18*, 84–106.

Hammer, L. B., Demsky, C. A., Kossek, E. E., & Bray, J. W. (2016). Work–family intervention research. In T. D. Allen & L. T. Eby (Eds.), *The Oxford handbook of work and family* (pp. 349–361). New York: Oxford University Press.

Hill, R. (1986). Life cycle stages for types of single parent families: Of family development theory. *Family Relations, 35*, 19–29.

Higgins, C., Duxbury, L., & Lee, C. (1994). Impact of life-cycle stage and gender on the ability to balance work and family responsibilities. *Family Relations, 43*, 144–150.

Hochschild, A. (2003). Marriage, family, and economics: The time bind: When work becomes home and home becomes work. In J. M. Henslin (Ed.), *Down to earth sociology: Introductory readings* (pp. 379–389). New York: Free Press.

Huffman, A., Culbertson, S., Henning, J., & Goh, A. (2013). Work-family conflict across the lifespan. *Journal of Managerial Psychology, 28*, 761–780.

Jang, S. J. (2009). The relationships of flexible work schedules, workplace support, supervisory support, work-life balance, and the well-being of working parents. *Journal of Social Service Research, 35*, 93–104.

Karasek, R. (1979). Job demands, job decision latitude and mental strain: Implications for job redesign. *Administrative Science Quarterly, 24*, 285–307.

Keith, P., & Schafer, R. (1991). *Relationships and wellbeing over the life stages*. New York: Praeger.

Kim, J., Ingersoll-Dayton, B., & Kwak, M. (2013). Balancing eldercare and employment: The role of work interruptions and supportive employers. *Journal of Applied Gerontology, 32*, 347–369.

Kooij, D. T., Bal, P. M., & Kanfer, R. (2014). Future time perspective and promotion focus as determinants of intraindividual change in work motivation. *Psychology and Aging, 29*, 319–328.

Kooij, D., De Lange, A., Jansen, P., & Dikkers, J. (2008). Older workers' motivation to continue to work: Five meanings of age: A conceptual review. *Journal of Managerial Psychology, 23*, 364–394.

Kooij, D. T., De Lange, A. H., Jansen, P. G., Kanfer, R., & Dikkers, J. S. (2011). Age and work-related motives: Results of a meta-analysis. *Journal of Organizational Behavior, 32*, 197–225.

Lockwood, N. R. (2003). *The aging workforce: The reality of the impact of older workers and eldercare in the workplace*. SHRM Research Department.

Loi, J. L. P., & Shultz, K. S. (2007). Why older adults seek employment: Differing motivations among subgroups. *Journal of Applied Gerontology, 26*, 274–289.

Major, D. A., Verive, J. M., & Joice, W. (2008). Telework as a dependent care solution: Examining current practice to improve telework management strategies. *The Psychologist-Manager Journal, 11*, 65–91.

Marshall, V. W., Matthews, S. H., & Rosenthal, C. J. (1993). Elusiveness of family life: A challenge for the sociology of aging. *Annual Review of Gerontology and Geriatrics, 13*(1), 39–72.

Meaning of Work International Research Team (MOWIRT) (1987). *The meaning of working*. London, UK: Academic Press.

Müller, A., Heiden, B., Herbig, B., Poppe, F., & Angerer, P. (2016). Improving well-being at work: A randomized controlled intervention based on selection, optimization, and compensation. *Journal of Occupational Health Psychology, 21*, 169–181.

Ng, T. W., & Feldman, D. C. (2012). Evaluating six common stereotypes about older workers with meta-analytical data. *Personnel Psychology, 65*, 821–858.

Pavalko, E. K., & Henderson, K. A. (2006). Combining care work and paid work: Do workplace policies make a difference? *Research on Aging, 28*, 359–374.

Pebley, A. R., & Rudkin, L. L. (1999). Grandparents caring for grandchildren: What do we know? *Journal of Family Issues, 20*, 218–242.

Pines, A. M., Neal, M. B., Hammer, L. B., & Icekson, T. (2011). Job burnout and couple burnout in dual-earner couples in the sandwiched generation. *Social Psychology Quarterly, 74*, 361–386.

Pitt-Catsouphes, M., Matz-Costa, C., & Besen, E. (2009). Workplace flexibility: Findings from the age & generations study. *Sloan Center on Aging & Work: Issue Brief, 19*, 1–21.

Rau, B. (2003). Flexible work arrangements. In E. Kossek & M. Pitt-Catsouphes (Eds.), *Work and family encyclopedia*. Chestnut Hill, MA: Sloan Work and Family Research Center.

Raymo, J. M., & Sweeney, M. M. (2006). Work-family conflict and retirement preferences. *The Journals of Gerontology: Series B, 61*, 161–169.

Rubin, R. M., & White-Means, S. I. (2009). Informal caregiving: Dilemmas of sandwiched caregivers. *Journal of Family and Economic Issues, 30*, 252–267.

Rudolph, C. W., & Baltes, B. B. (2017). Age and health jointly moderate the influence of flexible work arrangements on work engagement: Evidence from two empirical studies. *Journal of Occupational Health Psychology, 22*, 40–58.

Rudolph, C., Baltes, B. B., & Zabel, K. L. (2013). Age and work motives. In J. Field, R. J. Burke, & C. L. Cooper (Eds.), *The SAGE handbook of aging, work, and society* (pp. 118–140). SAGE.

Schnittger, M. H., & Bird, G. W. (1990). Coping among dual-career men and women across the family life cycle. *Family Relations*, 199–205.

Shacklock, K., Brunetto, Y., & Nelson, S. (2009). The different variables that affect older males' and females' intentions to continue working. *Asia Pacific Journal of Human Resources, 47*, 79–101.

Shoptaugh, C. F., Phelps, J. A., & Visio, M. E. (2004). Employee eldercare responsibilities: Should organizations care? *Journal of Business and Psychology, 19*, 179–196.

Snir, R., & Harpaz, I. (2002). Work-leisure relations: Leisure orientation and the meaning of work. *Journal of Leisure Research, 34*, 178–203.

Sterns, H. L., & Doverspike, D. (1989). Aging and the training and learning process. In I. L. Goldstein (Ed.), *Training and development in organizations: Frontiers of industrial and organizational psychology* (pp. 299–332). San Francisco, CA: Jossey-Bass.

Treadway, D. C., Duke, A. B., Perrewe, P. L., Breland, J. W., & Goodman, J. M. (2011). Time may change me: The impact of future time perspective on the relationship between work–family demands and employee commitment. *Journal of Applied Social Psychology, 41*, 1659–1679.

Tement, S., & Korunka, C. (2015). The moderating impact of types of caregiving on job demands, resources, and their relation to work-to-family conflict and enrichment. *Journal of Family Issues, 36*, 31–55.

Thrasher, G. R., Zabel, K., Wynne, K., & Baltes, B. B. (2016). The importance of workplace motives in understanding work-family issues for older workers. *Work, Aging and Retirement, 2*, 1–11.

Urry, H. L., & Gross, J. J. (2010). Emotion regulation in older age. *Current Directions in Psychological Science, 19*, 352–357.

Wang, M., Adams, G. A., Beehr, T. A., & Shultz, K. S. (2009). Bridge employment and retirement. In S. G. Baugh & S. E. Sullivan (Eds.), *Maintaining focus, energy, and options over the career* (pp. 135–157). Charlotte, NC: Information Age Publishing.

Wang, Y., & Marcotte, D. E. (2007). Golden years? The labor market effects of caring for grandchildren. *Journal of Marriage and Family, 69,* 1283–1296.

Wynne, K. T. (2017). Exploring crossover effects among working spouses through the lens of social cognitive theory: SOC and work-family conflict. Unpublished dissertation. Wayne State University.

Young, L. M., Baltes, B. B., & Pratt, A. K. (2007). Using selection, optimization, and compensation to reduce job/family stressors: Effective when it matters. *Journal of Business and Psychology, 21,* 511–539.

Zacher, H., & Schulz, H. (2015). Employees' eldercare demands, strain, and perceived support. *Journal of Managerial Psychology, 30,* 183–198.

13
RETIREMENT FROM THREE PERSPECTIVES

Individuals, Organizations, and Society

Minseo Kim and Terry A. Beehr

It has often been noted that retirement is an important issue for researchers in multiple fields (e.g., Beehr & Bennett, 2007; Shultz & Wang, 2011). The baby-boomer generation, a result of the large birth rate in many countries during an approximately 20-year period after World War II (Hatcher, 2003), made retirement an important research topic as that cohort approached retirement ages *en masse*. The present review and essay focuses mainly on the US, where the impending large retirement cohort is often considered a problem. It is interesting that it can be considered a current problem when there has been so much lead-time and knowledge about it that has been readily available for decades. Perhaps political leaders can be criticized for not enacting much-needed legislation about issues such as retirement funding until crises are near.

For example, in the US, President Reagan and Senator O'Neill worked together to reform the nation's social security program when its funding was becoming unsustainable 30 years ago, but the US may be approaching another such decision point as this is being written. Researchers might also be criticized, however, for similarly not looking very far ahead. As a somewhat personal example, the second author published a comprehensive review of retirement research and theory a few decades ago (Beehr, 1986). Tracking its citation rate, one can see that it was widely ignored by other researchers until the baby-boomer generation started to be considered a potential crisis to retirement funding. The Web of Science site (information obtained September 14, 2017) shows that the retirement review article was cited 22 times in the first ten years after its publication and 38 times in the 10 years after that. In the subsequent ten years, however, as people began to consider a potential retirement crisis looming, it received 107 citations. Perhaps, researchers are as prone as politicians to ignore issues until they start looming as potential crises. In any event, retirement has now caught our attention.

The baby-boomer generation has affected US life in many ways over the decades. After "burdening" or at least changing society, communities, and families in the form of large numbers of children requiring care, expanding sizes of schools, more teenage drivers, increased demand for specific forms of entertainment (e.g., young-adult oriented movies), an expanding workforce, and a host of other effects as they grew and matured, the baby-boomer generation now requires specific types of health care for older adults and consideration for how to fund increased numbers of retirees.

In addition, retirement itself is difficult to define, or, more precisely, perhaps it has many definitions. Scanning the research on retirement across several disciplines, it is operationally defined as receiving some kind of pension income, subjective self-reports that one is retired, voluntarily (or not) leaving the paid workforce after reaching an old age, changing jobs (often with reduction in hours or pay) after reaching an old age, and some combination of these. The widespread recognition that there is more than one definition or type of retirement, rather than simply being total withdrawal from the workforce at an old age, complicates the retirement studies (Shultz & Wang, 2011). This review takes a broad approach, considering retirement to have many legitimate definitions and forms.

Three Perspectives on Retirement

We take the position that retirements can affect and be affected by individuals, their organizations, and the larger society (Beehr & Bennett, 2007; Lee, Zikic, Noh, & Sargent, 2017). Regarding the individual "level," retirement has an inherently personal character. In countries such as the US, where mandatory retirement is mostly abolished by law, the decision to retire is officially an individual's decision (not the government's or the organization's), although other people may have influences on the decision (e.g., a spouse). Furthermore, retirement usually represents a major change in the person's life and probably her or his self-image, activities and use of time, and interpersonal contacts, as well as the responses of others to him or her. Organizations can try to affect who and how many people retire at a given time by, for example, offering retirement incentives to its older employees (Wang & Shultz, 2010). In addition, organizations often have some members whose loss would be especially detrimental because of the various skills and contributions of these individuals, but they can also have others whose loss would not make the organization less effective. It is not necessarily one group versus the other (employees who are viewed as more or less effective in their jobs) who retire at any one time, however.

From the societal perspective, larger or smaller proportions of retirees among a population are likely to affect the nature of life and of a society's institutions. This is due in part to the changes in the size of specific needs, such as need for eldercare facilities, for money to disburse in the form of government pensions, for more housing in a region where retires prefer to retire, and for public transportation that is user-friendly for retirees, for example. Of course, society can also affect who and how many people retire, with its cultural norms, the pattern of its government spending for pensions under what conditions and for what ages of workers, and so forth.

Individuals and Retirement

Why Individuals Retire – Predictors

As we noted in a review about a decade ago (Beehr & Bennett, 2007), one of the key research issues in retirement is *why* people retire. Variables offering answers include health, family situations, social pressure, workers' performance, subjective life expectancy, and financial resources (e.g., pensions, expected social security income, and early retirement incentives) (Wang & Wanberg, 2017). Working conditions such as decision authority, recognition, and physical and psychological job demands are also significant factors affecting retirement preferences/decisions (Carr et al., 2016). It can be difficult to study retirement at the individual level due to its predictors varying so widely.

Retirement is a process involving a series of decisions regarding timing and form of retirement rather than a single, one-time event. The decision to retire may be driven by three interconnected assessments of the work situation over time: imagining the possibility of a future retirement, assessing when it is time to let go of long-time jobs, and putting concrete plans for retirement into action at present (Feldman & Beehr, 2011). Furthermore, these stages could occur within a short time interval or over a period of years. Despite the time that can be involved in moving toward retirement decisions, many retirement studies are cross-sectional. They might gather data, for example, from retirees and ask for retrospective reports of factors that could predict the retirement decision, or they might measure future retirement plans and intentions about retirement behaviors that have not happened yet. Both approaches have inherent problems that are avoided with more difficult and costly data collections over a period of years (Fisher & Willis, 2013).

A study using five-year panel data on workers 57–79 years old addressed retirement issues by exploring possible associations between retirement intentions and actual retirement behavior. Retirement intentions, including making decisions about what age to retire, preference for a certain retirement age, and contemplating continuing working after becoming eligible for a pension, were all reflected in actual subsequent retirement behavior (Solem et al., 2016). Earlier work also showed an expectation–intention–action chain of retirement decisions: Expectations predicted intentions, and intentions subsequently predicted action (Prothero & Beach, 1984). Fortunately, results of both studies substantiate the use of retirement intentions as a proxy for actual retirement behavior.

Individuals' Forms of Retirement

Over time, research on retirement has made it increasingly clear that there are many forms or types of retirement, including partial retirement most easily identified by people formally retiring from one job but then working fewer hours per week in another job. Researchers often refer to the second job as a bridge job. Bridge employment is considered to be a transition into full retirement later on, but it may not work out that way (e.g., if the person dies before becoming fully retired), as we have noted previously (Beehr & Bennett, 2015). Bridge jobs as a form of partial retirement also include continued employment in the same career, but with a reduced time commitment for the same employer; in addition to retiring and then working part time for the same or a different employer, some bridge jobs include becoming self-employed part- or full-time.

In addition, retirees may engage in bridge employment in the same type of work or in entirely new work domains. Need for additional income can be a reason for obtaining bridge employment, but it often is not, because people work for more than one functional reason (e.g., obtaining sense of accomplishment or social contact). It has become clear over the last couple of decades of research that bridge employment is very common in the US; at least half of the older US workers with full-time career jobs take on bridge jobs before fully retiring (Bennett, Beehr, & Lepisto, 2016).

Effects of Retirement on the Individual's Family – Outcomes

Retirement decision-making is not always done entirely by the older employee alone; sometimes, for example, it is seen as a joint decision of a couple within the family context. Retirement for married women tends to occur within the context of their husbands' work and retirement behavior, while men are less likely to be influenced by their wives' retirement decisions (Wong & Hardy, 2009). However, if retirement were involuntary, the employment/retirement status of a partner plays a large role for retirement decisions among men (Radl & Himmelreicher, 2015).

Involvement in one's spouse's retirement decision may not be all positive, however; for both sexes, the retiring spouse tends to be less satisfied with his or her retirement if the spouse had a strong influence on the decision to retire (Szinovacz & Davey, 2005). Also, longitudinally, the happiness of one partner may be affected by the status of the other, because retirees are less satisfied if their spouse still works for pay. Simultaneous retirement can allow spouses to spend more time with each other, and either that is a good thing or the retired spouse thinks it would be a good thing. But of course spouses may be not be ready, as individuals, to retire at the same time. Ho and Raymo (2009) reported that about 40 percent of men and women expect to retire around the same time as their partner, despite the fact that the wives are usually younger and have less time in the workforce than their husbands. This last fact often means that the women would, on average, receive less money from their pensions than if they waited longer to retire. The positive view, however, is that retired couples can enjoy each other's company and may happily engage in activities together.

We did not find much new empirical research since our review over a decade ago (Beehr & Bennett, 2007) to update knowledge about the potential effects that retirement has on families. At that time we had reported evidence that it can have some benefits, even though the reports come from studies that seem to focus on marital conflict leading to dissatisfaction after retirement. For example, in a national survey, husbands noticed fewer "strong" arguments after their wives retired (Szinovacz & Schaffer, 2000), and husbands' retirements were followed by more calm discussions. Although these are good signs for retirement's effects on families (or at least on husbands and wives), some of these findings held only for couples in which one or both spouses were strongly committed to the marriage. Beehr and Bennett (2007) also reported a very specific finding that husbands who relax physiologically and have positive affect while talking to their wives were happier five years later in retirement. The same was not as true for wives, however (Kupperbusch, Levenson, & Ebling, 2003). Other recent reviews have also reported few empirical studies specifically on retirement and families in the last decade (Matthews & Fisher, 2013; Rauer & Jensen, 2016). We conclude, similar to them, that many of the existing empirical research results on this topic are inconsistent, and the relationship between family life and retirement is not clear. Potential relationships in need of more research include whether married people have more positive attitudes toward retirement, whether there is any relationship between family issues and seeking bridge employment, the degree to which division of labor on family chores changes very much after retirement, and whether either work–family enhancement or work–family conflict is related to decisions to retire.

Retirement and Individuals' Gender

Historically, men were greatly over-represented in samples used to study retirement effects (Beehr & Bennett, 2007). Because women comprise a large percentage of the modern workforce, it is important to know if they react in relation to retirement in the same way that men do. For instance, women's retirement timing is much more influenced than men's by family experiences. Women who have children living at home during preretirement years or who have ever been divorced intend to retire relatively late (Damman, Henkens, & Kalmijn, 2015), whereas women who are part of dual-earner couples are more likely to be retired earlier if their spouses are in poor health (Denaeghel, Mortelmans, & Borghgraef, 2011). Men are more likely to delay retirement if their spouse has poor health, which suggests women might take the role of care-taker more than men (similar results to Dentinger & Clarkberg, 2002; Talaga and

Beehr, 1995). Family responsibilities may also be a special reason why women would engage in bridge employment; that is, if they need employment for financial reasons but also feel care-taking obligations are a priority, a part-time job would make that more feasible. More research is needed in order to be certain of these possible gender differences, however.

Gender may interact with retirement planning. Overall, having retirement plans is related to being in better health, having more resources in general, and feeling fewer obligations (Devaney & Kim, 2003). Women, especially those without partners, are often disadvantaged regarding their living standards and tend to be less financially prepared for retirement than men (Noone, Alpass, & Stephens, 2010). Furthermore, women tend to focus on their retirement planning in the health and interpersonal/leisure areas (Petkoska & Earl, 2009); they also may be more health-conscious and relationship-conscious after retirement (e.g., Loe & Johnston, 2016). Men, on the other hand, set clearer financial goals for retirement; thus, the kind of retirement planning the sexes do may have different emphases (Wang & Shi, 2014). One study of Israeli working men approaching retirement also showed that they expected to have continuity of their lifestyle after retirement; they had anxiety linked to uncertainty before retiring, but a year after retiring, they generally decided their anxiety had been unwarranted (Nuttman-Shwartz, 2004). We note that research on one of the sexes only (e.g., Loe & Johnston, 2016; Nuttman-Shwartz, 2004) can only provide suggestive evidence about sex differences, however, because sex is a constant rather than a variable in such studies.

There is, of course, formal help available for people approaching retirement, so that if there are some average gender differences in preparedness, retirement planning or training can alleviate deficiencies. Many of the training programs focus on financial planning for older workers (e.g., Devaney & Kim, 2003), which could disproportionately aid women if it is true that they overlook this domain more than men. Such planning could include not only savings and investment, but also finding (bridge) employment.

Organizations and Retirement

At the organization level, questions include how the organization can affect employees' retirement decisions and how retirement affects the employing organization. Compared with our knowledge about retirement at the individual level, there is less research knowledge available regarding organizations and retirement (Beehr, 2014). In fact, some articles seem to classify almost any work-related variable as organizational, perhaps in order to find enough information to discuss. Examples include employees' career goal achievement and commitment, job involvement, job alternatives, and perceived pressure to retire (Bennett et al., 2016), as well as employees' say or influence about the timing of their retirement, choice to retire, and favorable conditions for exit

(Wong & Earl, 2009). However, most of these variables could be categorized as individual-level reactions to the job rather than something the organization is doing or something affecting the organization.

Organizational Influences on Retirement – Predictors

An organization's type of retirement plan is thought to be one factor in encouraging or discouraging turnover, and it also may be a factor in encouraging and discouraging retirement. In the US, there has been a large-scale change in retirement pension systems offered by organizations, from defined benefit to defined contribution plans (Quinn & Cahill, 2016). In defined benefit plans, organizations/employers "guarantee" to pay retirees a given stipend per month after they retire from the organization, whereas in defined contribution plans organizations "guarantee" to contribute a certain amount of money (usually per paycheck) to an account from which the employee can draw after retiring. In the US, the government has encouraged the use of defined contribution plans in recent decades by passing laws allowing money in retirement funds such as Individual Retirement Accounts (IRAs) to be tax-free until it is withdrawn. In addition, the experience of some organizations defaulting on their defined benefit plans during difficult economic times has probably prodded a move in the direction of defined contribution plans. With defined contribution plans, the money is invested, and the investment risk is borne by the individual instead of by the organization; that is, the organization promises little or nothing after making its contribution (no promise of a certain level of pension benefits in retirement, which would put the risk burden on the organization).

Regarding defined contribution plans, however, it is probably not widely known yet that some organizations have defaulted on them too. In the United Kingdom, for example, some employing organizations have taken "pension holidays" in which they went for a period without contributing money to their employees' defined contribution retirement accounts (de Thierry, Lam, Harcourt, Flynn, & Wood, 2014). This is often done on the grounds or rationalization that the money already invested is doing well in the stock market, and so there is little need for the organization to contribute constantly. Of course, this logic only spreads the risk to *both* parties if, during a stock market downturn, the organization invests more in these defined contribution accounts, a phenomenon that remains to be seen. Thus, with *either* defined benefit or defined contribution retirement plans, organizations can renege on their financial promises to their employees; fortunately however, this is not the norm for either form of organizational pension plan.

Reading the literature on retirement, we conclude that there has been at least an implicit belief that defined benefit plans might be best for the employee or retiree. They are also thought to help the organization deter turnover, because the employee is often paid very little when entering the organization at a young age but has not only the promise of wage increases over time, but the ultimate payoff of a pension by staying in the organization until old age. Thus, seniority payoff systems (including retirement pensions after workers become most senior and retire) may keep older workers in the organization. These retirement plans can make it harder to recruit older workers if that becomes a desirable practice, however, because they are tied to their current employer. Another issue about seniority pay systems keeping older workers in the organization longer is that the older workers are likely to become less effective workers than younger employees *on a cost basis* (this is not saying older workers necessarily perform worse). That is, if employees' pay increases consistently over time, their productivity also needs to increase over time, just to break even in terms of being as valuable to the organization as a younger and lower-paid employee.

Overall, the defined benefit plans might make employees more likely to retire if they feel the security of a steady pension income, whereas the defined contribution plan, psychologically, is likely to promote more uncertainty about payouts. In addition, if turnover of older employees is an event to be avoided, then the organization can embrace promotion-from-within policies, which suggests a promise of advancement and higher pay as employees age in place toward retirement (de Thierry et al., 2014). Competency-based rewards might also help encourage older employees to engage in forms of training, as they remain longer before leaving or retiring. This goes against many organizational practices of promoting training primarily for young employees, on the grounds that training older employees might not be justifiably financially. That is, the investment in training older employees would not pay off if the training is costly and if the older trainees retire too soon after receiving the training (Liu, Courtenay, & Valentine, 2011). It is often thought that older workers do not want to engage in training (e.g., review by Truxillo, Cadiz, & Hammer, 2015), but the organization may need to find ways to encourage their development if it wants them to delay retirement and remain productive employees into older ages (Liu et al., 2011). At a minimum, organizations can tactfully suggest ways for older workers to update their skills (Taneva, Arnold, & Nicolson, 2016).

One reason organizations might be changing to defined contribution plans is related to a view that they might be less risky to the organization (no need to guarantee future payouts). However, the change may also exemplify some organizations' common financial view that retirees with defined benefits, like employees in general, represent costs, and costs are of course to be minimized. In contrast to a finance view, the human resources management view is that employees are assets and tools to be managed and for the organization to benefit from. If the organization is not benefiting from older employees, it can offer retirement incentives, which often work in inducing older employees to retire (de Thierry et al., 2014). Of course, that must depend in part on the size and details of the incentive offer.

Lee et al.'s (2017) recent qualitative study of human resource managers inductively developed a typology consisting of four approaches that human resources departments, as agents of the organization, can take toward their employees' retirements or impending retirements: gatekeeping, improvising, orchestrating, and partnering. Gatekeeping is a kind of maintaining orientation in which organizations are relatively passive, mainly keeping track of retirement rates, taking replacement actions where appropriate, and keeping track of costs of these. Improvising is somewhat more reactive, where the organization keeps track of more specific variables such as skills needed in the organization and skills available in the (external) workforce. Orchestrating is more active still and includes a focus on formal retirement policy. It is more likely to include developing and using policies about workers retiring part-time or even retiring and returning (bridge employment) if there is an organizational need. Partnering is the most interactive, with older workers, their managers, and the human resources department interacting; it could be the most innovative and experimental, with each party capable of suggesting ways to deal with retirements. This typology can serve as a template for future research to determine what conditions lead organizations to adopt each stance toward retirements.

Retirees' Influence on Organizations – Outcomes

It is sometimes in the organization's interest to have either more or fewer retirees (i.e., a higher or lower rate of retirements during a given period of time). At times, retirements can be one somewhat painless way of downsizing (usually less painful to the parties than layoffs), but if there are labor shortages, keeping rather than losing older workers might be in the organization's interest. Some organizational policies, therefore, are likely to purposely encourage retirements, while others are likely to discourage them.

On the other hand, losing the most experienced employees can have another downside, especially if large numbers of employees retire in a short period of time, which can occur when baby-boomers retire. Besides simply replacing them, some institutional knowledge may slip away. For example, some of the most veteran employees are likely to have such very specific knowledge, such as historical reasons why the organization's processes are done the way they are, where to go for help when something goes wrong (where specific knowledge resides in the organization), and why one vendor's products are more reliable than another's. In principle, such organizational knowledge could be transferred to the remaining employees, but there is little research directly on this type of knowledge-transfer phenomenon (Burmeister & Deller, 2016).

The bridge employment phenomenon noted earlier (employees working for pay after retirement; Beehr & Bennett, 2015) is also a point of contact between organizations and employee retirements. There are many types of bridge employment, and some of them involve working for organizations. Retired employees can work for the same organization where they worked before retirement or for a different organization. Retired professors, for example, might teach courses for the same university or for a different institution, and some professors may decide to retire part-time, by teaching fewer classes for the same organization and receiving less pay, maybe simultaneously also drawing retirement pay (e.g., social security or defined contribution withdrawals) as they near the end of their working lives. These obviously have implications for the organization. If the organization has a need for the retirees' services, it can make the process of bridge employment in the same organization easier and more financially rewarding, for example, but if the organization does not have a need, it can decline to engage in such practices. Organizations can attempt to encourage senior employees to become bridge employees who stay, by offering flexible schedules, but offering them chances to mentor others or to obtain more training do not appear to be successful incentives (review by Beehr & Bennett, 2015).

A unique situation regarding bridge employment revolves around occupations in which retirement commonly occurs at younger ages; examples include military personnel and some public safety positions (Hill, Snell, & Sterns, 2015). After retiring from these occupations, many people obtain a bridge job in another organization. Because it is predictable that there will be "young" retirees from these occupations, organizations in certain industries seeking to fill part- and full-time positions might specifically recruit retirees from police and military organizations. Examples could include security firms or organizations in any industry looking for skills related to police and/or military jobs. Thus, organizations may actively seek to benefit from retirees from other organizations by employing them in bridge jobs.

Organizations have always been concerned about retirement of their employees, whether because of the cost of replacing them, because it might be a convenient way to downsize, because of a concern over how to fund retirements, or because keeping one's own or obtaining another organization's retirees as new employees can be useful. These situations have not been studied very intensively however, and future research is needed to inform us of the benefits and pitfalls of organizational practices related to these concerns.

Society and Retirement

By society, in relation to retirement, we mean the largest aggregate of people who live under relatively common conditions, laws, and cultures. In this section, we mainly discuss possible relationships of retirement trends within a country, using nation as the operational definition of society. Perhaps like any other generational cohort, large numbers of retires can affect demand for various products, in this case products (and services) that are desired by older people with leisure time, perhaps fewer skateboards and more three-wheel bicycles for example, or maybe a demand for health care specialists in health issues that are more common among older people. The society can also affect retirements and retirees with its policies toward older generations and retirees in general. There are generally unanswered (and maybe unanswerable) questions at the societal level, such as how much retirement is best for society, who should pay for people's retirements, what is the status of retirees in a society, and do people really need to retire?

This review focused especially on retirement factors in the US, but there are wide variations worldwide in some retirement variables, such as typical retirement ages, whether there is a mandatory retirement age, and the typical age or rate of aging in various countries (e.g., OECD, 2016; Taneva et al., 2016; Truxillo et al., 2015). In the United States, there are more retirees than ever before as the employees of the baby-boomer generation, born between 1946 and 1964, are expected to live as retirees for quite a few years (Beehr & Bennett, 2007). The percentage of people turning age 65 is now rapidly increasing (Quinn & Cahill, 2016). Even though 65 is no longer a universal mandatory retirement age in the US, aging of the population will almost inevitably result in more retirees living in the nation (this is not necessarily true, because people could instead work until they die, or they could leave the country when they retire).

Society's Influence on Retirement – Predictors

Society, in the form of its government, influences who and how many people will retire through its laws and policies. It can pass laws about the definition and ages of retirement, the availability and generosity or meagerness of pensions and retiree health care, and the general treatment of retirees versus others. Although many laws are based on cultural values, culture also includes less formalized influences. In the form of its culture, a society also influences the social situation of retirees by providing them with a higher or lower status and expectations for how they should behave, should cope, and should be treated by others.

In general, some Western societies may devalue old age, showing up in age discrimination at work for example (Schermuly, Deller, & Büsch, 2014), and, by extension, perhaps also generally devaluing retirees and retirement. Thus, there is some tendency for retirees to have a low status and less respect compared with those still in the workforce. Employees' self-perceived workability declines as they reach older ages (McGonagle, Fisher, Barnes-Farrell, & Grosch, 2015), although older employees in one recent qualitative study seemed to report their late career might be thriving as much as declining (Taneva et al., 2016). Self-perceptions of decline, however, predict withdrawal from the labor force, and for older employees, that often means retiring. Perceptions of lower ability may also mean the person has less value in society or lower status; if retirement is considered a sign of lower ability, then the retiree is likely to have lower status.

The status of retirement is relative however, and it can depend on a comparison status. We can see this by considering the older person who has a choice of identities or roles. Compared with working for pay, retirement tends to have a lower status, but compared with being unemployed, retirement has a higher status (e.g., Wetzel & Mahne, 2016). Thus, an older worker who is unemployed may choose to become retired instead, thereby increasing his or her status in society. Depending on a retiree's age and work history, and on a nation's retirement laws, the differences in these two societal roles might include more money (if some form of pension is available that pays more than available unemployment compensation) as well as higher status. Overall, it might make a better impression in one's culture to say, "I am a retired professor" than to say, "I am an unemployed professor," for example.

Effects of Retirement on Society – Outcomes

When people retire, they often lose resources (e.g., Wetzel & Mahne, 2016), and if we interpret resources broadly, they could include money (if retirement pay is less than employment pay), friends and social contacts (with co-workers), and authority and expertise (if these were held due to one's job status), among other things. Work can be a major source of someone's identity, sense of self-worth, and how he or she is treated by others in society. From an economic point of view, retirees can be considered a cost to society, because they are no longer contributing materially with their labor, but they are continuing to use society's resources. If they have amassed a large amount of money before retiring, they may seem to be using few of society's resources and contributing to society's economic engine if their money is spent locally or deposited in financial institutions that invest it in ways that drive a nation's economic growth. Nevertheless, the retiree is not needed for this purpose, only his or her money; the money is benefiting society more than the person.

If this discussion of the relationship between retirees and society seems grim, there are also favorable elements. Older workers who retire tend to experience their health as better (e.g., Eibich, 2015; Syse, Veenstra, Furunes, Mykletun, & Solem, 2017), perhaps especially their subjective view of their own health. This might be related to functional health. Poor health might have made it more difficult to function on some jobs, making small health issues seem more important, and health therefore seems to improve if one can function well in the role of a retiree. This has implications for national health care systems, such that encouraging retirement may delay older people's felt need for medical treatment.

We note, however, that widespread increases in automation, information technology, and service jobs, reported in the US Bureau of Labor Statistics data, result in substantially fewer jobs requiring physical exertion than existed decades ago (e.g., Church et al., 2011). The result is that physical vigor is less often a requirement for modern jobs. Nevertheless, older workers may use their seniority to move into different, less demanding jobs; this may remove an incentive to retire earlier (Gommans et al., 2016), and we can speculate that the trend toward older workers (and probably others) having less physically demanding jobs might also delay both retirement and health care actions.

In addition, the very definition of retirement is important in determining the favorability or unfavorability of retired life. Bridge employment, if we define it loosely, is exemplified by an older worker who works for pay after retiring from a long-held job (e.g., Beehr & Bennett, 2015). Society can encourage or discourage this status by its pension laws, such as allowing people of a certain age to receive government pensions while still working for pay (including limiting or not limiting the number of hours worked in conjunction with receiving a pension). If older citizens want to continue working but in a different job and with reduced hours, for example, they can be financially enabled to do so by some retirement pension laws. Being able to choose one's type of retirement status (e.g., fully retired or bridge employed), may result in more satisfactory retirements.

Income variability in the US in general has been widening in recent decades, but a society can affect disparity in retirees' incomes through its taxing and retirement pensions systems. For example, society, through government enacting laws, can choose to generally tax some sources (e.g., businesses, wealthy or poorer people, retirees or workers) more or less, and to disperse pension funds more or less generously. It can also make pension amounts variable, based on wealth and other income of retirees for example, thus allowing society to influence the disparities in wealth and income. The move toward defined contributions retirement plans in the US may have increased the disparity in retirement incomes, because wealthy and high income people tend to put much more money into these plans. These plans, encouraged by tax laws, greatly benefit wealthier workers, but for poorer workers, even those participating in defined contribution plans, the amount of money in their retirement plans is often negligible (e.g., Quinn & Cahill, 2016).

Regarding effects on retirement in general, at one extreme, if government were to tax very little, provide a great deal of money in pensions, and allow retirement pensions at young ages, it is more difficult for government to spend money on other desirable things. On the other hand, if it levies very high taxes, pays only small retirement pensions, and allows retirement pensions to be received only at very high ages, then older workers and retirees may suffer but other programs can be funded. There are many other scenarios possible for society, through government, to affect retirements.

The large shift in the US from defined benefits to defined contributions pension plans (e.g., de Thierry et al., 2014; Polivka & Baozhen, 2015; Quin & Cahill, 2016) has been spurred by government, for example by offering and promoting in various forms, tax-free retirement savings. This is likely attractive to many employers, because some of them have had trouble supporting their employees with traditional employer pensions after these employees retire, due to a number of circumstances (e.g., general economic downturns, specific company performance, and poor financial planning with retirement funds). As noted above, defined contribution plans might also play a role in widening income disparities among retirees however, because wealthier, higher income people have more money to contribute to these plans. Widening income gaps among workers may be especially likely to lead to widening income gaps among retirees under typical defined contributions plans. If this is considered a problem, a solution is for the government and retirement experts to exhort people to save more for their own retirements now that there are fewer defined benefits plans, but the fact is many people do not follow this advice. This could contribute to further widening of the gap between rich and poor retirees and return the US to a time before Social Security, wherein poverty and old age commonly went together (e.g., Quinn & Cahill, 2016).

Financial issues thus may vary greatly among retirees, but so do other important life issues. Retirees may desire to have widely varying retirement life styles; for example, some may want to spend more time with their families wherever they live, some may move to a warmer climate, some may live in a rural area and some an urban area, some may do extensive travelling, and others may engage in meaningful volunteer work or hobbies, for example. Society's or government's policies can affect the viability of different retirement styles and therefore the quality of retirees' lives. A one-size-fits-all retirement policy is unlikely to satisfy everyone equally (e.g., Noone, O'Loughlin, & Kendig, 2012). Government programs including medical care for retirees can be made more available in rural locales, tax breaks can be provided for certain volunteer work, transportation can be discounted for retirees, and housing can be subsidized for retirees in warmer locales, as examples.

Overall, the proportion of a society's people who are retired at any one time is likely to interact with other factors – such as who pays to support retirees, the social status of retirees, what retirees do (e.g., bridge employment and volunteerism) during their retired years, what their saving or spending/consumption patterns are, where they live, and their health care arrangements – to influence a multitude of societal variables. Such variables include political arguments, tax patterns, parts of the economy, and unequal political and economic pressures for various services in different geographical regions of the country. Because of these effects, society (in the form of government-enacted laws) responds by trying to encourage more or fewer people to retire.

Directions for Future Research

In this chapter we reviewed the retirement process, as well as its predictors and outcomes, from individual, organizational, and societal perspectives. Although publication of studies on retirement has been increasing rapidly and providing rich suggestions, multiple research questions still remain. For example, the existing literature on retirement covers many of the predictors affecting the (early) retirement decisions and actions at the individual level, but noticeably less attention has been given to society and especially organizational level predictors of retirement. Future research should investigate the potential factors that may influence the retirement process at more macro levels. It would also be important to examine how each variable at the three different levels can interact with each other in order to better understand the complex retirement planning and decision processes.

Older workers are increasingly accepting bridge jobs for various reasons, but we do not know the effects of bridge jobs on organizations and society. By addressing this research question, future studies can provide answers on why bridge jobs matter from a multi-level perspective. Although individual-level predictors of bridge employment are slowly becoming better understood, research regarding what organizational or societal factors make employees work in bridge jobs is still lacking. Organizations could create specially designed jobs for bridge workers or encourage job crafting behaviors by them as strategies to make employees approaching typical retirement ages remain in their career jobs, even if only part-time.

A recent study suggests that older workers initiate changes in their current jobs that allow them to adapt if their abilities have changed. This may help them adjust their job's demands and fulfill their old or changed motives, which leads them to stay healthy and age more successfully at work (Lichtenthaler, Lichtenthaler, Fischbach, & Fischbach, 2016). Because of their long work experience and job tenure, many older workers know their abilities and (future) work requirements. Therefore, individualized job crafting behaviors may help older workers continue working after reaching common retirement ages, modifying their jobs and motivation. Future research needs to pay attention to job crafting activities among aging employees and their effects on time to retirement and bridge employment decisions.

Retirement is accompanied by substantial changes in lifestyles, and many studies have shown accompanying retirement outcomes in terms of financial, physical, and psychological well-being. However, the influence of retirement on families, in particular, is still under-researched. Future research needs to examine the effect of retirement on one's spouse and family members, who can both affect and be affected by the employee's retirement.

At the societal level, the baby-boomer generation has become a focus and concern to some retirement researchers, often just because of its sheer size and potential to disrupt retirement funding and other issues for society. There are many commonly assumed features about that generation and how it is different from others, but there is little strong evidence for most of those assumptions (other than what its size will be). One recent study reported that work interfering with family life occurred less and family interfering with work occurred more for this generation than for later generations, and that the family being the most central part of life characterized boomers more than later generations (Bennett, Beehr, & Ivanitskaya, 2017). More research should be done to confirm this, but if these are indeed special features of the baby-boomer generation, we could speculate that this generation especially does not want work that interferes with the most important part of their lives – their families. Flexible work policies that some organizations already have in effect, such as policies allowing flexible schedules, part-time schedules, or working from home, might accommodate some older employees or bridge employees who want to focus more on family life than other generations do, on average. More research on these arrangements, specifically in relation to retirees, is needed. Because of the age of the boomers, we speculate that the concern for family may be as much a concern for their grandchildren as for their children, which could be different from younger generations. Research could address, for example, whether the retirees living near and providing care for grandchildren create a desire for flexible working arrangements.

Concluding Remarks

Causes and consequences of retirement are apparent at the individual, organizational and societal levels. It has been recognized for quite some time that many countries have a baby-boomer generation working its way toward old age and retirement, and its leading edge is now in the process of retiring. We noted in our (Beehr & Bennet) 2007 review that individuals were spending longer parts of their lives in retirement than previous generations did; this has been due to both longer life spans and earlier retirement ages, trends that occurred over a long period of decades. We note in closing, however, that the trend in the US toward retiring at earlier ages stopped some time ago and has actually reversed (Munnell, 2015), which will probably reduce the amount of ones' lives spent in retirement by a few years.

Researchers have increased their amount of study on retirement over the last decade or more, and so we are rapidly filling in the gaps to our knowledge about it. There are even new journals focusing on older employees and their retirement issues (e.g., *Work, Aging, & Retirement*), another sign of increased interest in the topic. One special issue that has increasingly caught researchers' interest is bridge employment, broadly defined as working for pay after retirement. Bridge employment is of practical importance for individuals who may wish to engage in it, organizations who might want to hire retirees into bridge jobs, and societies that may need more employees during times of high employment rates.

Finally, as we noted in 2007, predictions about retirement in the future are inherently difficult due to unforeseen events and conditions, such as economic depressions, major wars, disease epidemics, climate changes, or large-scale migrations. Nevertheless, we believe now that, somewhat ironically because little seems to have been done about it until the last minute, the major influence of the baby-boomer generation on retirement levels was slow-moving but inexorable, is now upon us, and is probably going to turn out to have been quite predictable.

References

Beehr, T. A. (1986). The process of retirement: A review and recommendations for future investigation. *Personnel Psychology, 39*, 31–55.

Beehr, T. A. (2014). To retire or not to retire: That is not the question. *Journal of Organizational Behavior, 35*, 1093–1108.

Beehr, T. A., & Bennett, M. M. (2007). Examining retirement from a multi-level perspective. In K. S. Shultz & Gary A. Adams (Eds.), *Aging and work in the 21st century* (pp. 288–302). Mahwah, NJ: Lawrence Erlbaum, Publishers.

Beehr, T. A., & Bennett, M. M. (2015). Working after retirement: Features of bridge employment and research directions. *Work, Aging, and Retirement, 1*, 112–128.

Bennett, M. M., Beehr, T. A., & Ivanitskaya, S. (2017). Work-family conflict: Differences across generations and life cycles. *Journal of Managerial Psychology, 32*, 314–332.

Bennett, M. M., Beehr, T. A., & Lepisto, L. R. (2016). A longitudinal study of work after retirement: Examining predictors of bridge employment, continued career employment, and retirement. *The International Journal of Aging and Human Development, 83*, 228–255.

Burmeister, A., & Deller, J. (2016). Knowledge retention from older and retiring workers: What do we know, and where do we go from here? *Work, Aging and Retirement, 2*, 87–104.

Carr, E., Hagger-Johnson, G., Head, J., Shelton, N., Stafford, M., Stansfeld, S., & Zaninotto, P. (2016). Working conditions as predictors of retirement intentions and exit from paid employment: A 10-year follow-up of the English longitudinal study of ageing. *European Journal of Ageing, 13*, 39–48.

Church, T. S., Thomas, D. M., Tudor-Locke, C., Katzmarzyk, P. T., Earnest, C. P., Rodarte, R. Q., ... & Bouchard, C. (2011, May 23). Trends over 5 decades in U.S. occupation-related physical activity and their associations with obesity. *PLOS One*.

Damman, M., Henkens, K., & Kalmijn, M. (2015). Women's retirement intentions and behavior: The role of childbearing and marital histories. *European Journal of Population, 31*, 339–363.

de Thierry, E., Lam, H., Harcourt, M., Flynn, M., & Wood, G. (2014). Defined benefit pension decline: The consequences for organizations and employees. *Employee Relations, 36*, 654–673.

Denaeghel, K., Mortelmans, D., & Borghgraef, A. (2011). Spousal influence on the retirement decisions of single-earner and dual-earner couples. *Advances in Life Course Research, 16*, 112–123.

Dentinger, E., & Clarkberg, M. (2002). Informal caregiving and retirement timing among men and women. *Journal of Family Issues, 23*, 857–879.

Devaney, S. A., & Kim, H. (2003). Older self-employed workers and planning for the future. *Journal of Consumer Affairs, 37*, 123–142.

Eibich, P. (2015). Understanding the effect of retirement on health: Mechanisms and heterogeneity. *Journal of Health Economics, 43*, 1–12.

Feldman, D. C., & Beehr, T. A. (2011). A three-phase model of retirement decision making. *American Psychologist, 66*, 193–203.

Fisher, G. G., & Willis, R. J. (2013). Research methods in retirement research. In M. Wang (Ed.), *The Oxford handbook of retirement* (Chapter 12, pp. 177–301). New York: Oxford University Press.

Gommans, F. G., Jansen, N. W., Mackey, M. G., Stynen, D., de Grip, A., & Kant, I. (2016). The impact of physical work demands on need for recovery, employment status, retirement intentions, and ability to extend working careers: A longitudinal study among older workers. *Journal of Occupational and Environmental Medicine, 58*, e140–e151.

Hatcher, C. B. (2003). The economics of the retirement decision. In G. A. Adams & T. A. Beehr (Eds.), *Retirement: Reasons, processes, and results* (pp. 136–158). New York: Springer.

Hill, S. C., Snell, A. F., & Sterns, H. L. (2015). Career influences in bridge employment among retired police officers. *International Journal of Aging and Human Development, 81*, 101–119.

Ho, J. H., & Raymo, J. M. (2009). Expectations and realization of joint retirement among dual-worker couples. *Research on Aging, 31*, 153–179.

Kupperbusch, C., Levenson, R. W., & Ebling, R. (2003). Predicting husbands' and wives' retirement satisfaction from the emotional qualities of marital interaction. *Journal of Social and Personal Relationships, 20*, 335–354.

Lee, M. D., Zikic, J., Noh, S., & Sargent, L. (2017). Human resource approaches to retirement: Gatekeeping, improvising, orchestrating, and partnering. *Human Resource Management. 56*, 455–477.

Lichtenthaler, P. W., Lichtenthaler, P. W., Fischbach, A., & Fischbach, A. (2016). Job crafting and motivation to continue working beyond retirement age. *Career Development International, 21*, 477–497.

Liu, S., Courtenay, B. C., & Valentine, T. (2011). Managing older worker training: A literature review and conceptual framework. *Educational Gerontology, 37*, 1040–1062.

Loe, M., & Johnston, D. K. (2016). Professional women "rebalancing" in retirement: Time, relationships, and body. *Journal of Women & Aging, 28*, 418–430.

Matthews, R. A., & Fisher, G. G. (2013). Family, work, and the retirement process: A review and new directions. In M. Wang (Ed.), *The Oxford handbook of retirement* (pp. 354–370). New York: Oxford University Press.

McGonagle, A. K., Fisher, G. G., Barnes-Farrell, J. L., & Grosch, J. W. (2015). Individual and work factors related to perceived work ability and labor force outcomes. *Journal of Applied Psychology, 100*, 376–398.

Munnell, A. H. (2015). The average retirement age – An update. *Issue in Brief*, Center for Retirement Research at Boston College, March 2015, Number 15–4, pp. 1–5. Retrieved online September 19, 2017: http://news.gallup.com/poll/168707/average-retirement-age-rises.aspx.

Noone, J., Alpass, F., & Stephens, C. (2010). Do men and women differ in their retirement planning? Testing a theoretical model of gendered pathways to retirement preparation. *Research on Aging, 32*, 715–738.

Noone, J., O'Loughlin, K., & Kendig, H. (2012). Socioeconomic, psychological and demographic determinants of Australian baby boomers' financial planning for retirement. *Australasian Journal on Ageing, 31*, 194–197.

Nuttman-Shwartz, O. (2004). Like a high wave: Adjustment to retirement. *The Gerontologist, 44*, 229–236.

OECD. (2016). Employment rate by age group: 55–64 years-old, Q3 2015. Retrieved February 5, 2018, from https://data.oecd.org/chart/4w26.

Petkoska, J., & Earl, J. K. (2009). Understanding the influence of demographic and psychological variables on retirement planning. *Psychology and Aging, 24*, 245–251.

Polivka, L., & Baozhen, L. (2015). The neoliberal political economy and erosion of retirement security. *The Gerontologist, 55*, 183–190.

Prothero, J., & Beach, L. R. (1984). Retirement decisions: Expectation, intention, and action. *Journal of Applied Social Psychology, 14*, 162–174.

Quinn, J. E., & Cahill, K. E. (2016). The new world of retirement income security in America. *American Psychologist, 71*, 321–333.

Radl, J., & Himmelreicher, R. K. (2015). The influence of marital status and spousal employment on retirement behavior in Germany and Spain. *Research on Aging, 37*, 361–387.

Rauer, A., & Jensen, J. F. (2016). These happy golden years? The role of retirement in marital quality. In J. Bookwala (Ed.), *Couple relationships in the middle and later years: Their nature, complexity, and role in health and illness* (pp. 157–176). Washington, DC: American Psychological Association.

Schermuly, C. C., Deller, J., & Büsch, V. (2014). A research note on age discrimination and the desire to retire: The mediating effect of psychological empowerment. *Research on Aging, 36*, 382–393.

Shultz, K. S., & Wang, M. (2011). Psychological perspectives on the changing nature of retirement. *American Psychologist, 66*, 170–179. doi: 10.1037/a0022411.

Solem, P. E., Syse, A., Furunes, T., Mykletun, R. J., De Lange, A., Schaufeli, W., & Ilmarinen, J. (2016). To leave or not to leave: Retirement intentions and retirement behaviour. *Ageing & Society, 36*, 259–281.

Syse, A., Veenstra, M., Furunes, T., Mykletun, R. J., & Solem, P. E. (2017). Changes in health and health behavior associated with retirement. *Journal of Aging and Health, 29*, 99–127.

Szinovacz, M. E., & Davey, A. (2005). Retirement and marital decision making: Effects on retirement satisfaction. *Journal of Marriage and Family, 67*, 387–398.

Szinovacz, M. E., & Schaffer, A. M. (2000). Effects of retirement on marital conflict tactics. *Journal of Family Issues, 21*, 367–389.

Talaga, J. A., & Beehr, T. A. (1995). Are there gender differences in predicting retirement? *Journal of Applied Psychology, 80*, 16–28.

Taneva, S. K., Arnold, J., & Nicolson, R. (2016). The experience of being an older worker in an organization: A qualitative analysis. *Work, Aging, and Retirement, 2*, 396–414.

Truxillo, D. M., Cadiz, D. M., & Hammer, L. B. (2015). Supporting the aging workforce: A review and recommendations for workplace intervention research. *Annual Review of Organizational Psychology and Organizational Behavior, 2*, 351–381.

Wang, M., & Shi, J. (2014). Psychological research on retirement. *Annual Review of Psychology, 65*, 209–233.

Wang, M., & Shultz, K. S. (2010). Employee retirement: A review and recommendations for future investigation. *Journal of Management, 36*, 172–206.

Wang, M., & Wanberg, C. R. (2017). 100 years of applied psychology research on individual careers: From career management to retirement. *Journal of Applied Psychology, 102*, 546–563.

Wetzel, M., & Mahne, K. (2016). Out of society? Retirement affects perceived social exclusion in Germany. *Zeitschrift Für Gerontologie und Geriatrie, 49*, 327–334.

Wong, J. Y., & Earl, J. K. (2009). Towards an integrated model of individual, psychosocial, and organizational predictors of retirement adjustment. *Journal of Vocational Behavior, 75*, 1–13.

Wong, J. D., & Hardy, M. A. (2009). Women's retirement expectations: How stable are they? *Journal of Gerontology: Social Sciences, 64B*, 77–86.

14
GLOBAL ISSUES IN WORK, AGING, AND RETIREMENT

Cort W. Rudolph, Justin Marcus, and Hannes Zacher

Population and workforce aging are global phenomena that accompany significant challenges and opportunities in most countries around the world (Chand & Tung, 2014; Phillips & Siu, 2012; Roberts, 2011). Given the global scope of such trends, the coming decades will be characterized by increasingly older and more age diverse workforces (Hertel & Zacher, 2018), both in developed countries (e.g., Albright, 2012; Skirbekk, Loichinger, & Barakat, 2012) and in developing countries (e.g., James, 2011; Peng, 2011). The goal of this chapter is to review and discuss research related to work, aging, and retirement from a global, international, and cross-cultural perspective. The majority of theories in this area focuses on the Western context, and were developed and tested mainly by researchers based in these countries (B. B. Baltes, Rudolph, & Bal, 2012; Rudolph, 2016; see also Hofstede, 1980). However, some empirical findings and best practice examples on work, aging, and retirement are also available from, or have explicitly been applied to, other world regions (e.g., Kinsella & Phillips, 2005; Kunze & Boehm, 2015; Peiro, Tordera, & Potocnik, 2013). Thus, taking a global perspective on work, aging, and retirement is consistent with repeated calls by researchers to focus not only on intraindividual age-related processes, but also on the broader social and cultural context surrounding worker aging and retirement, as well as macro-sociological questions (Hyde & Higgs, 2016; Phillipson, 2009).

As a theoretical organizing framework for this chapter, we use the lifespan developmental perspective (P. B. Baltes, 1987; P. B. Baltes, Reese, & Lipsitt, 1980). The lifespan perspective focuses on individual development over time within a given sociocultural and historical context, and is thus an ideal framework for examining contemporary and global issues in work, aging, and retirement (Lerner, Fisher, & Weinberg, 2000; Rudolph, 2016). After introducing the lifespan developmental perspective and theoretically integrating it with the chapter topic, we consider global issues in work, aging, and retirement through four more specific conceptual lenses. Specifically, we focus on (a) demography and workforce aging; (b) workforce health and wellbeing in the face of global population aging; (c) worker mobility in a global context; and (d) overarching global institutional issues in work, aging, and retirement.

Lifespan Developmental Perspective

The lifespan perspective emphasizes that individuals' development is influenced by and interacts with their sociocultural and historical context (P. B. Baltes, 1987; P. B. Baltes, Reese, & Lipsitt, 1980). This idea dates back to the 1930s, when Vygotsky (1978) first proposed that social interactions, social learning, and cultural influences play an important role in children's cognitive development (see Van der Veer, 1996, for a critical review). Building upon this view, Bronfenbrenner (1979) developed ecological systems theory, explaining how individuals' experiences and behaviors are shaped by different contexts. Specifically, Bronfenbrenner (1979) argued that individuals interact with five environmental systems (i.e., chronosystem, microsystem, mesosystem, exosystem, and macrosystem). The chronosystem involves people's experienced events and transitions over their life course, such as marriage. The microsystem includes social interactions with family members (i.e., the household level) and other direct social contacts, whereas the mesosystem involves interactions between different microsystems, such as family and work (see also Chapter 12 of this volume). The exosystem includes links between an individual's microsystem and contexts in which the individual does not play an active role (e.g., spouse's work situation). Most relevant for our topic is the macrosystem, which includes the overarching societal environment in which someone is embedded. The societal environment entails, for instance, individual socioeconomic status (how rich or poor one is), gender (one's biological sex and one's gender identity/expression), tribe (one's race, ethnicity, religion, nationality, and color), and societal socioeconomic status (whether one lives in a developed, developing, or less developed country). Moreover, it includes societal culture (e.g., the extent to which one's society is collectivistic or individualistic) and organizational culture (e.g., the extent to which one's workplace or work team is collectivistic or individualistic; see also Chao & Moon, 2005, for a theoretical review on links between demography and culture). In summary, Bronfenbrenner's (1979) theory speaks to the importance of societal, contextual, and cultural influences on the aging process.

Lifespan scholars have long acknowledged that individual development is not only a product of the context in which it takes place, but that individuals can also actively shape their own development and environmental contexts (Lerner & Busch-Rossnagel, 1981; see also Zacher, Hacker, & Frese, 2016). In the

1980s, Lerner and colleagues introduced the notion of developmental contextualism in their explanation of developmental systems theory. Briefly, developmental systems theory posits that the individual and the environment exist in a continuous state of interaction; in turn, such person–environment interactions impact changes in both the environment's characteristics and individuals' physiological and psychological characteristics (Featherman & Lerner, 1985; Ford & Lerner, 1992; Lerner, 1996; Lerner & Kauffman, 1985). Thus, from a developmental systems perspective, not only does the macrosystemic context shape individual characteristics, but individual decisions and actions themselves may also shape the macrosystemic context. As an example, motivational changes at the individual level, such as the motivation to work longer and past traditional retirement ages, in the aggregate, may lead to sociocultural (e.g., attitudes toward older workers) and economic changes (e.g., greater flexibility of businesses to accommodate older workers).

The lifespan developmental perspective provides a theoretical basis to study individuals' experiences and behavior over time and embedded within multiple layers of context (P. B. Baltes, 1987; P. B. Baltes, Lindenberger, & Staudinger, 2006; P. B. Baltes et al., 1980). Lifespan researchers not only focus on normative developmental trajectories, but also on how different personal and idiosyncratic factors (e.g., health problems) and contexts (e.g., culture) may modify these developmental trajectories. In a seminal article, Baltes (1987) outlined seven key propositions of the lifespan perspective, of which two are particularly relevant for a global perspective on work, aging, and retirement. Specifically, Baltes (1987) argued that development is embedded in a historical and sociocultural context, and that development is shaped by the interaction of normative and non-normative, as well as person and contextual influences (i.e., the "paradigm of contextualism"). Importantly, changes in the historical and sociocultural context may interact; for instance, attitudes toward older workers may improve over historical time in some cultures, but not others.

According to the proposition of historical and sociocultural embeddedness, individual development (ontogenesis) is not only influenced by biological factors (e.g., genetics), but also by historical context and sociocultural conditions (P. B. Baltes, 1987). For instance, Elder and Liker (1982) found that a historical event (i.e., the Great Depression) experienced in childhood interacted with social class in influencing women's well-being over time. Similarly, Nesselroade and Baltes (1974) showed that individual age-related factors interacted with the historical context in predicting changes in adolescents' personality. Thus, this proposition suggests that macrosystems may not only influence absolute levels in psychological variables of interest, but also how these variables develop across a person's lifespan.

The paradigm of contextualism assumes that individuals process, react to, and act upon (i) normative age-graded, (ii) contextual normative, (iii) normative history-graded, and (iv) non-normative influences that interact and co-determine development (P. B. Baltes, 1987). Normative age-graded influences include person and contextual influences that most people encounter as they age. For instance, on average, people experience declining physical strength as they transition from young to older adulthood. While it is assumed that these biological changes are similar across macrosystems, normative trajectories may be modified by the societal context. Next, contextual normative influences include common socialization events in a given culture, such as the influence of school entry or retirement on people's experiences and behavior. These contextual normative influences may vary across macrosystems. For instance, retirement policies in African countries differ substantially from those in most Western countries (Darkwa & Mazibuko, 2002). Normative history-graded influences include person and contextual factors that are linked to a specific chronological period. For instance, the well-being of people born during economically difficult times may develop differently compared with the well-being of those born during more prosperous times (Elder & Liker, 1982). Finally, non-normative influences include person and contextual determinants of development that are idiosyncratic in the population and whose manifestations are unique to each individual (e.g., career changes, job loss, accidents).

In summary, the lifespan developmental perspective and earlier related theories suggest that individuals' aging process, as well as the processes of aging at work and retirement, are influenced by the macrosystemic context in which they occur. Thus, various societal, organizational, and contextual cultural factors may influence both absolute levels and the form of age-related trajectories of psychological variables. The notion of developmental contextualism suggests that, as individuals' age, they are not only influenced by their macrosystemic context, but they may also influence their development and the context in which they are embedded.

Global Demographic Trends in Population and Workforce Aging and Age Diversity

Three key factors contributing to population and workforce aging are continuously low or declining fertility rates, steady increases in life expectancy, and the aging of the large post-World War II baby boomer cohorts (Hertel & Zacher, 2018). The decline in fertility rates – which is largely due to cultural and political changes, such as the introduction of birth control in the 1960s or China's one-child policy – is particularly impactful, as the parents of tomorrow's children are never born in the first place. That is, if a population stops growing, population aging starts and cannot be reversed.

The global average life expectancy has increased from 48 years in 1950 to 68 years in 2010 (Roberts, 2011), and it is expected to further increase to 76 years in 2050 and 81 years in 2100 (Bloom, 2011). To visualize this phenomenon, Figure 14.1 depicts global population age distributions in 2017 versus projections in 2050. Indeed, people aged 65 and older are expected to represent almost a fifth of the global population by 2050 (He, Goodkind, & Kowal, 2016). While people in developed countries have the highest life expectancy (e.g., currently 79 years in the United States), the greatest relative increases in life expectancy are predicted in African and Asian countries. As a consequence, more than 60 percent of people aged 65 years and older now live in developing countries (Phillips & Siu, 2012), with a projected increase to 80 percent by 2050 (United Nations, 2013). Driving these developments are improvements in health care, nutrition, lifestyles, safety, technologies, and workplaces.

On the basis of data and population projections from the United States Census Bureau, recent work by He et al. (2016) updates the global population projections offered by Kinsella and He (2009) and reviewed in the work and aging literature by Phillips and Siu (2012). Several key areas of relevance to the study of work and aging are offered by He et al. (2016), namely the dynamics in population aging, their impact on health, and how these changes influence work and retirement. We review highlights of this work here to set the stage for a differentiated discussion of specific topics in work, aging, and retirement that have a global reach.

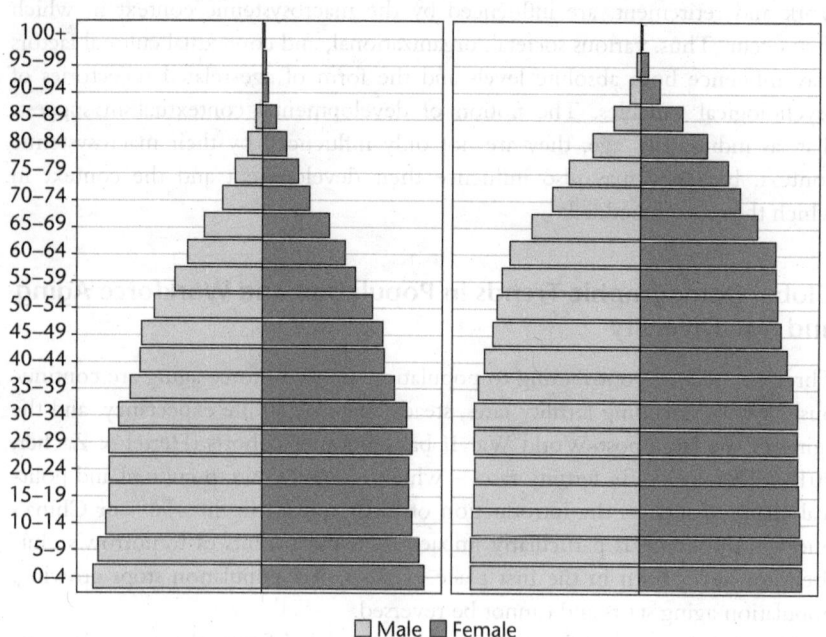

FIGURE 14.1 Global population age distribution in 2017 versus projections for 2050.

Population Growth

He et al. (2016) suggest that, in 2015, 8.5 percent of the world's population was aged 65 and over (~617 million people). This group is projected to increase by an average of 27 million people per year over the next 35 years, to 1.6 billion by 2050 (16.7 percent of the world's population). While the world population *at large* is aging, the oldest segment of the population itself is also aging at an unprecedented rate, largely due to increases in life expectancy at older ages across the past century. For example, in the United States, life expectancy from 65 years onward was 11.90 years in 1900, and 19.10 years in 2010; from 80 years onward it was 5.30 and 9.10 years, respectively, across the same time span (see Arias, 2014; United Nations, 2013). In certain regions, especially Asia and Latin America, the population of those aged 80 years and older is expected to increase fourfold in the next 35 years. He et al. (2016) note that, in some countries, the "oldest old" (those aged 85 and older) are growing faster than relatively younger segments of the population. For example, United States census data showed that the number of oldest old tripled between 1980 to 2010, compared with a doubling of the population aged 65 to 89 (He & Muenchrath, 2011). During the same period, the number of centenarians in the United States increased by 65.8 percent (Meyer, 2012).

He et al. (2016) suggest that declining fertility levels have been an important catalyst for population aging. As of 2015, the total fertility rate (i.e., the average number of children that would be born to a woman over her lifetime if she were to experience the same fertility rate throughout her lifetime, and she were to survive until the end of her reproductive life) was near or below the replacement level (i.e., the fertility rate at which enough babies are born to sustain population levels; ~2.33 children per woman) across all global regions, except for Africa.

In population demography, dependency ratios are a measure of the "pressure" on the workforce-aged population (Gerland et al., 2014). Dependency ratios are computed as the ratio of those not in the labor force (i.e., the 'dependent' population: youths from birth to 14 years and adults aged 65 and over) and those typically in the labor force (the 'productive' population: those aged 15 to 64). Global projections by He et al. (2016) of the dependency level in 2050 are similar to the level observed in 2015. However, given projected age demographic shifts, the age composition of the dependent population is predicted to increase. Indeed, the share associated with the older population is expected to nearly double, from 20 percent (approximately two dependents for every ten workers) in 2015 to 38 percent by 2050 (approximately two dependents for every five workers). Even more dramatic changes in this ratio are projected in certain countries: for example, in Japan the dependency ratio in 2014 was 40 percent (Japanese Ministry of Internal Affairs and Communication, n.d.; double the global average for 2015), and is projected to increase to 60 percent by 2036 and to nearly 80 percent by 2060 (National Institute of Population and Social Security Research, 2012).

Health and Aging

According to He et al. (2016), global life expectancy at birth reached 68.6 years in 2015 and is projected to increase to 76.2 years by 2050. Despite such gains, regions and countries vary drastically, with current life expectancy exceeding 80 years in over 20 countries (e.g., Japan – 2015: 84.70 years, 2050: 91.60 years) but less than 60 years in almost 30 countries (e.g., South Africa – 2015: 49.70 years; 2050: 63.20 years). There is also considerable cross-societal variability in *remaining* life expectancy. Whereas in several countries (e.g., Singapore, Switzerland, Australia), both men and women at age 65 can expect to live for 20 and 25 additional years, respectively, in poorer countries such individuals may expect to live only an additional 12 and 13 years, respectively (e.g., Afghanistan, Somalia, Burkina-Faso).

While life expectancy projections suggest that people may live longer, what quality of life do people experience at older ages? To this end, He et al. (2016) offer data from the World Health Organization's (WHO) healthy life expectancy (HALE) index, operationalized as the average number of years that a person can expect to live in 'full health' by taking into account "years lived in less than full health due to disease and/or injury" (WHO, 2012). Thus, beyond life expectancy as an index of population mortality, HALE takes into account both the mortality *and* morbidity of individuals. For example, among European countries in 2012 (European Commission, 2014, Figure 4–4), French women had the longest life expectancy at age 65 of 23.4 years. However, Norway had the longest *healthy* life expectancy for women; Norwegian women at age 65 were expected to live another 16 years without activity limitations, whereas French women at age 65 were expected to live less than 10 years without such limitations. On the contrary, certain Eastern European countries had relatively short HALE. For example, in Latvia and Estonia, both men and women aged 65 years were expected to live only about five years without activity limitations, whereas in Slovakia, both men and women could only expect to live about three years without activity limitations.

Healthcare

Increasing longevity brings associated changes to health care. Older people have different health care needs than younger people because chronic conditions and disabilities tend to increase with older age. For example, it is estimated that between 25 and 30 percent of the global population aged 85 or older have dementia (WHO, 2011). Projected increases in rates of growth of dementia associated with population aging between 2010 and 2050 are notable, with a much more dramatic increase assumed to occur in low- and middle-income countries (Alzheimer's Disease International, 2010). It is estimated that at least 80 percent of people age 65 and older have at least one chronic health condition (e.g., heart disease, diabetes, or arthritis; see He, Sengupta, Velkoff, & DeBarros,

2005). The rate of having multiple chronic illnesses is higher in older populations (US Department of Health and Human Services, 2010). Beyond their toll on individual quality of life, chronic conditions have a substantial economic impact, accounting for an estimated 75 percent of total healthcare expenditure in the United States (Centers for Disease Control and Prevention, 2010). Globally, the economic impact of five leading chronic diseases (cancer, diabetes, mental illness, heart disease, and respiratory diseases) could reach $47 trillion by 2030 (Bloom et al., 2011). There are notable income-graded disparities in global mortality risks associated with chronic disease, with those in lower income countries far more likely to die from communicable, maternal, perinatal, and nutritional conditions (Mathers et al., 2003).

Older adults are not universally covered by pensions or long-term care insurance. Indeed, He et al. (2016) suggest that unpaid caregiving (e.g., by family members and/or friends) remains the main source of long-term care worldwide. As of 2015, about 34 million Americans reported having provided unpaid care to an adult age 50 or older over the past year (National Alliance for Caregiving, 2015). In 2013, the economic value of informal caregiving in the United States was estimated to be $470 billion dollars, which outpaces the value of paid home care and total Medicaid spending in the same year (Feinberg, Reinhard, Choula, & Houser, 2015).

Caregivers – who are still mostly female – must balance multiple life roles (e.g., work, family), and caregiving responsibilities represent a significant time burden, leading many caregivers to shift to part-time work or even exit paid employment. Fisher et al. (2011) report that caregivers of people with dementia report spending an average of 9 hours per day offering care and assistance. Given the significant time commitment, caregiving responsibilities and resulting demands have important consequences for both the wellbeing and work outcomes of current members of the workforce. To this end, researchers have begun adopting a lifespan perspective on work–family balance issues (see also Chapter 12 of this volume). For example, Thrasher, Zabel, Wynne, and Baltes (2016) offer a lifespan-based perspective on aging and work–family conflict that is based upon an integration of both role theories and research concerning dynamics in work motives over time. Considering global issues, Thrasher et al. (2016) called for increased research attention to be paid to cultural differences in how work motives and the aging process influence the work–family conflict.

Finally, the increase of older people and the associated increase in chronic disease burden will give way to new employment opportunities related to professional caregiving, development of new technologies, and service provision (Knickman & Snell, 2002; Phillips & Siu, 2012). In the United States, the number of jobs for home healthcare professionals (e.g., home health aides) is projected to increase by as much as 40 percent by 2024 (Bureau of Labor Statistics, 2017). Similar trends are projected in developing countries, such as China and India (Shobert, 2016). Likewise, longstanding warnings regarding global nursing shortages (Oulton, 2006) are mirrored in patterns in the geriatric healthcare workforce. For example, the number of geriatricians practicing in family and internal medicine in the United States decreased by approximately 23 percent from 1996 to 2010 (Geriatrics Workforce Policy Studies Center, 2011). This decrease has also been noted globally, leading the WHO (n.d.) to call for all primary care physicians to be trained in geriatrics. One explanation for this decline is that those who pursue aging sciences may face certain barriers and stigmas associated with ageism (Pimental, 2017).

Work and Retirement

With the decline of traditional retirement models (e.g., the shift from defined benefit to defined contribution; see Munnell, 2006), and the extension of qualifying or statutory retirement ages across many OECD countries, it should come as no surprise that labor force participation among older adults continues to rise across such countries (see also Chapter 13 of this volume). According to Sterns (2010), older adults plan to remain in the workforce for a variety of reasons, including concerns regarding maintaining healthcare benefits and income, and the desire to remain active and engaged. He et al. (2016) suggest that labor force participation rates among older adults are far higher in low-income countries. For example, in 2012, labor force participation rates for those aged 65 and older in Zambia were as high as 71.20 percent and 52.20 percent for men and women respectively, which stands in stark contrast to other countries, such as Italy, where the same rates were 6.2 percent and 1.2 percent, respectively.

Once older workers do decide to retire, expectations of retirement differ by country (He et al., 2016). For example, in Poland only 15 percent of respondents suggested that they are confident in their ability to fully retire with a lifestyle considered comfortable, compared with 77 percent in Canada (Aegon, 2013). There are also notable cross-national differences surrounding plans to work after retirement. For example, Aegon (2013) suggests that when asked how they envision their transition to retirement, 24 percent of Japanese respondents and 49 percent of French respondents suggested that they would immediately stop working altogether and enter full retirement.

Beyond cross-national differences, the employer or organization (i.e., representing the demand side of labor market) also matters in the work trajectories of older workers. Top managers in particular have an outsized influence on such normative organizational considerations (Finkelstein, Hambrick, & Cannella, 2008). In particular, top managers' age equality norms (the extent to which top managers believe older versus younger workers ought to be treated fairly versus preferences given to younger workers) and retirement age norms (top managers' beliefs about when older workers should retire from work) have been found to predict age-related organizational recruitment and retention policies (Mulders, Henkens, & Schippers, 2017; see also Chapter 2 of this volume). Organizations with top managers who believe in age equality are more likely to recruit older workers and encourage them to work until the normal retirement age; organizations with top managers who believe in older workers retiring at later ages are more likely to recruit retirees and encourage workers to work beyond the normal retirement age (Mulders et al., 2017).

Similarly, organizational characteristics, job requirements, and institutional factors are also important considerations. Organizations with higher proportions of older workers, remuneration systems tied strongly to seniority, influential labor unions, and/or in industries where training requirements are high, are more likely to accommodate, develop, and offer exit strategies for older workers (van Dalen, Henkens, & Wang, 2015). Thus, workforce aging can be seen as not just an influential source of national but also organizational human resources (HR) policy. Leadership, organizational age diversity (see Chapter 3 of this volume), job factors, and institutional characteristics such as compensation schemes and union presence all matter for work, aging and retirement.

We next consider some specific areas in which these more macro trends influence phenomena related to work, aging, and retirement. In particular, we consider first how differences in life expectancies and cultural values across societies may lead to different definitions of who is considered "old" and what characterizes an "older worker" (Cleveland & Hanscom, 2017; Kinsella & Phillips, 2005). Then, we consider impacts on retirement, including changes in retirement entry ages, actual retirement ages, as well as increased flexibility in retirement entry in different countries (Peiro et al., 2013). Finally, we discuss international poverty risk for older workers (Alcover, Topa, Parry, Fraccaroli, & Depolo, 2014).

Work-Relevant Consequences of Global Demographic Trends

(Re)defining Age

What is considered "old?" Who is an "older worker?" Much attention has been paid to these questions over recent decades (Kinsella & Phillips, 2005), with researchers noting that chronological age itself is an "empty" variable and a mere proxy for time-related processes that can influence human development (Birren, 1999; Lawrence, 1997).

A recent review of alternative age conceptualizations by Cleveland and Hanscom (2017) suggests great variety in the ways in which researchers have alternatively construed age (e.g., biological, functional, social, subjective, and physical). However, less research has attempted to disentangle various age conceptualizations from the actual psycho-socio-physical processes that they are said to represent (i.e., those that actually covary with one's chronological age by virtue of prototypical patterns of human development). This represents a significant gap in our understanding of the nature and operation of such constructs, which future research must attempt to fill.

The answer to the first question posed above, "Who is considered 'old'?" is not simple, as it is qualified by both age and cultural boundaries. To the former point, relatively younger people tend to think of older age beginning at a younger threshold age than relatively older people (US Trust, 2017). Importantly, for individuals, such beliefs have been linked to declining cognitive functioning over time via the process of stereotype embodiment (i.e., via so-called *self-relevance* effects, see Levy, Zonderman, Slade, & Ferrucci, 2012). To the latter point, societal, contextual, and organizational cultural norms dictate who is "young" or "old." For example, there are notable country-level differences in what is considered to be "old age," in particular the age at which people become "old." Consider, for example, data from the *Generations of Talent* study (GOT; Pitt-Catsouphes & Sarkisian, 2010), which is a large scale (N = 11,298), publicly available, multinational (representing 11 countries) study of age and work processes conducted by the Sloan Center on Aging and Work. GOT includes questions about the age at which men and women can be considered "old." To illustrate variability in such perceptions, Figure 14.2 depicts average responses to these questions across each of the 11 countries represented in the GOT database. As shown, there is clear country-dependent variability in perceptions of the threshold for old age. In the United States, old age is perceived to begin at 69.17 and 68.64 for women and men, respectively, whereas in Japan, these ages are 41.77 and 42.97 respectively. Subtle gender differences noted here may reflect a form of intersectionality that has been posited to be of

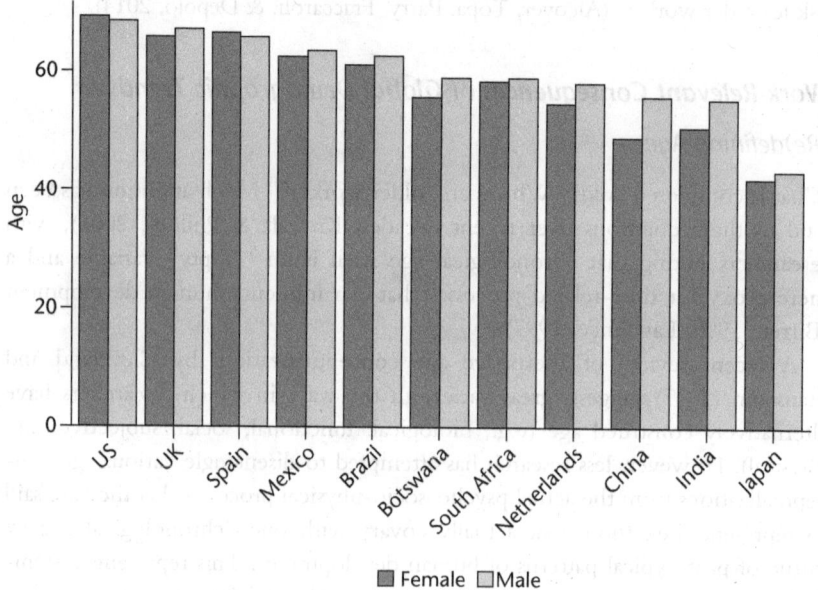

FIGURE 14.2 Average age at which people are considered "old" across 11 countries.

importance for understanding how we make sense of age (see Marcus & Fritzsche, 2015). More research is needed to unpack "why" such cross-national differences are observed, and what implications such differences have for various work outcomes and processes (e.g., age stereotyping, prejudice, and discrimination at work; see Chapter 4 of this volume).

To a large extent, these norms reflect how we have constructed age as a meaningful concept for organizing social processes and systems (Fineman, 2011). Public policy both reflects and reinforces these cultural norms. In the United States, for example, the Age Discrimination in Employment Act (ADEA) protects workers aged 40 and over from employment discrimination, subsequently the criterion of "aged 40 and over" is often used by researchers to justify characterizing their samples of "older workers" (e.g., Kooij, De Lange, Jansen, & Dikkers, 2008; Ng & Feldman, 2008). Indeed, as suggested by McCarthy, Heraty, Cross, and Cleveland (2014, p. 376), because research has rarely offered explicit definitions to guide what is "older," researchers in different countries tend to rely on the "dominant policy age markers" (e.g., age of pension eligibility; age associated with protective employment legislation) in the respective country/context of their research.

Social institutions reinforce these cultural norms. Notable shifts in retirement age and the relaxing of mandatory retirement and pension eligibility requirements, along with the extension of working lives across various countries are redefining not only the institution of retirement, but what it means to be "old" itself (Henkens et al., 2017). Notable increases in health and longevity discussed previously are calling into question existing criteria for establishing what it means to be "old." For example, citing increases in healthy function at old age that has occurred over time, a recent report from a joint committee of Japanese gerontologists and geriatricians has called for redefining the legal criterion for "older" from 65 to 75 years of age in Japan (Ouchi et al., 2017). Future policy research must address the broad-reaching implications of such shifts (see also Chapter 5 of this volume).

Additionally, culture affects not only how age is construed and contracted, but also attitudes towards aging. For example, a meta-analysis by North and Fiske (2015), found that attitudes towards aging were more negative in Eastern as compared with Western societal cultures. Considering the role of culture and population dynamics, North and Fiske (2015) reported that country-level increases in population aging predicted negative attitudes toward older people, even when controlling for industrialization over the same time period. The answer to the second question posed, "Who is an 'older worker?'" is equally challenging. Recent work by McCarthy et al. (2014) surveyed over 400 organizational decision makers to determine how they defined "older workers" in terms of chronological age, and to identify the basis for such definitions. With respect to the former, findings suggest workers are considered as 'older' at a younger age than might be expected, with quite a bit of variability around this estimate. Respondents reported that "older" workers could range anywhere from 28 to 75 years of age (median = 55.00 years; $M = 52.40$ years, $SD = 6.95$ years). Regarding the latter, organizational decision makers rely on different factors associated with organizational context to decide if workers are "older," including assumptions related to their tenure, participation in retirement planning, career stage, and organizational/industry age norms. As the workforce continues to age, definitions of what is means to be an older worker are likely to shift; more research is required to flesh out the implications of these meanings.

(Re)defining Retirement

Population aging trends have bearing on how we define retirement (see also Chapter 13 of this volume). Indeed, qualifying retirement entry ages, actual retirement ages, as well the (increased) flexibility in retirement entry vary across countries (for a review, see Peiro et al., 2013). Likewise, as outlined by Alcover et al. (2014), we have also witnessed a notable global trend in flexible retirement via bridge employment. The lifespan perspective adopts the notion that successful development requires certain changes in the allocation of resources. To this end, P. B. Baltes (1997, p. 370) suggests:

> In childhood, the primary allocation is directed toward growth; during adulthood, the predominant allocation is toward maintenance and recovery (resilience). In old age, more and more resources are directed toward regulation or management of loss. Such a characterization of the life span, of course, is an oversimplification, as individual, functional (domain), contextual, and historical differences need to be taken into account. The life span script is about relative probability and prevalence.

In this tradition, recent research has focused on resource-based and dynamic models of retirement transitions and adjustment (see Wang, 2007) in various societal contexts. For example, Yeung and Zhou (2017) examined the influence of pre-retirement planning activities on tangible, mental and social resources, and how such resources influence both psychological and physical well-being using a three-wave longitudinal study of pre and post-retirees in Hong Kong. Consistent with resource-based theories of retirement adjustment, retirees who participated in more preparatory activities before retirement acquired greater resources, which contributed to positive changes in post-retirement well-being (physical and psychological well-being, psychological distress, and life satisfaction) one year after their actual retirement. In a similar study, Topa, Jiménez, Valero, and Ovejero (2017) investigated the relative influence of resource losses versus gains explaining well-being (life satisfaction and subjective health complaints) in the transition to retirement, using a two-wave panel design among

Spanish workers/retirees. Interestingly, losses in resources at Time 1, but not gains in resources, were significant predictors of Time 2 life satisfaction and health complaints.

The lifespan perspective has also adopted the premise that human development is defined by an "incomplete architecture" (P. B. Baltes, 1997). Regarding the influence of culture on the aging process, P. B. Baltes (1997) suggests that there is an inherent interaction between these two forces, likewise conditioned by decreasing functioning that is associated with older age. On the one hand, the need for culture to support aging increases with age; on the other hand, the relative effectiveness of psychological, social, material, and cultural interventions decreases with age (P. B. Baltes, 1997). For lifespan theorists, culture is understood as, "... the entirety of psychological, social, material, and symbolic (knowledge-based) resources that humans have generated over the millennia, and which as they are transmitted across generations, make human development possible as we know it today" (P. B. Baltes, 1997, p. 368).

One relevant embodiment of this idea comes from research concerning poverty risk among older adults, resulting from a lack of social infrastructure to support aging populations in developing countries. Globally, poverty risk is higher for older people than for younger people. Across OECD countries, the poverty rates among those aged 75 and over is approximately 15 percent, which is about 3.5 percent higher than among those aged 66 to 75 years (OECD, 2015). However, the poverty risk rate varies greatly across countries. For example, in the European Union, Zaidi (2010) reports that at much as 51 percent of the population of Latvia aged 65 and over is at risk of poverty, compared with a low of 4 percent in Hungary, and 20 percent across all European Union countries. Even higher rates of poverty risk among those aged 65 and over are noted in Ghana (64.1 percent), Nicaragua (66 percent), and Honduras (69.9 percent; see Barrientos, Gorman, & Heslop, 2003).

Cross-Cultural and Cross-National Considerations for an Aging Workforce

Pivotal to the lifespan perspective is the continuous interplay between the individual and their sociocultural environment. From a macrosystemic perspective, this environment includes demography (age, gender, tribe, and socioeconomic status), societal culture, and organizational culture. This confluence of factors is well elucidated by Chao and Moon's (2005) cultural mosaic theory, whereby societal culture represents geographic elements of the cultural mosaic, organizational culture represents associative elements, demography itself is viewed as an independent cultural mosaic tile, and individual differences give rise to cultural variations at the most micro level of analysis. There has been little research directed toward understanding the intertwined effects of these various elements on outcomes related to the aging workforce (Posthuma & Campion, 2009), with existing evidence focusing on the societal element of culture. Beyond cross-cultural issues, transnational issues arise when considering the mobility of an aging workforce in a global context. The following subsections address the research related to these issues, with the aim of identifying areas for future research.

Cross-Cultural Issues

Recent scholarship has demonstrated the role of societal-level age stereotypes for age-based outcomes (e.g., Shiu, Hassan, & Parry, 2015). Although there exists variation in stereotype magnitude among societies (Shiu et al., 2015), evidence indicates the content of societal-level age stereotypes to be stable across culture and time (Marcus & Sabuncu, 2016). Given prevalent assumptions that Eastern cultures honor and respect older adults and thus ought to be less ageist (see Palmore & Maeda, 1985), these results are, at first glance, counterintuitive. Research, however, is consistent with the culture hypothesis, namely that Easterners show more positive judgments about older people, but that their personal opinions may differ. Specifically, Vauclair, Hanke, Huang, and Abrams (2017) found that although respondents in a Taiwanese sample expressed greater admiration for and viewed older adults as more competent relative to a sample from the United Kingdom, Taiwanese respondents also viewed older adults with greater contempt and envy, scored higher on direct and indirect measures of prejudice, and had fewer intergenerational friendships.

Thus, cultural stereotypes of older adults, even when positive, may not indicate less ageism against older adults. Individuals from each cultural context internalize cultural values with age; older adults have been found to show greater endorsement of normative societal cultural values and exhibit personality traits more consistent with dominant cultural values vis-à-vis younger adults (Fung, 2013). In particular, it has been shown that any explanation for ageism accounted for by cultural stereotypes must also take into account in-group favoritism effects. Explanations that consider both in-group favoritism and cultural stereotypes have been found to be the most predictive of attributions related to innovation, change, and performance of members of different age groups (McNamara, Pitt-Catsouphes, Sarkisian, Besen, & Kidahashi, 2016).

Despite evidence examining links between culture and age-based outcomes, there has been little theoretical advancement regarding the exact ways by which culture (e.g., at the societal, organizational, or individual levels), might influence work outcomes for an aging workforce. Existing research views culture as broad "East–West" distinctions, with little attention paid to the possible ways by which organizational culture or individual differences in cultural values might affect work outcomes for older workers. Toward that end, one recent theoretical framework to advance understanding of the confluence of culture and age is the Cultural Anchors of Ageism (CAA; Marcus & Fritzsche, 2016).

Drawing on social identity theory (Brewer, 1991; Turner, 1985), the CAA posits that psychological dimensions of culture relating to the formation and permeability of in- and out-groups are most relevant to age-based outcomes. According to the CAA, there are two psychological cultural dimensions of relevance. Collectivism–individualism focuses on the role of individuals and groups in social relationships and deals with the relative permeability of group boundaries. Tightness–looseness focuses on the relative importance of rules versus relationships in behavioral control and deals with the degree to which deviances from group norms are permissible (Marcus & Fritzsche, 2016). The CAA also posits a societal quadrant, whereby societies that are both collectivistic (strict in- and out-group distinctions) and tight (deviances from group norms are sanctioned) are considered to have the most potential for discrimination against older workers, and vice versa for societies that are both individualistic (flexible group boundaries) and loose (tolerance for individual behavioral deviances from the norm). The CAA provides a roadmap for understanding the role of societal culture on work outcomes related to the aging workforce and the extent to which older workers may face challenges based on societal culture. Indeed, with tight and collectivistic societies (with exceptions, most Asian and African societies) being the most likely to present challenges for older workers (e.g., job entry, promotion, and retention), future research disentangling the influences of culture from other macrosystemic factors on work outcomes for a globally aging population may be fruitful.

The CAA also posits the role of organizational culture and individual differences on age-based outcomes, with institutional collectivism (see Gelfand, Bhawuk, Nishii, & Bechtold, 2004) and organizational tightness–looseness being the organizational cultural equivalent of psychological dimensions of relevance, and felt accountability being the individual equivalent (Gelfand, Nishii, & Raver, 2006). Institutional collectivism and organizational tightness–looseness are expected to affect age-based work outcomes in the same way as their societal counterparts, with the expected result that older workers will face the most barriers to mobility in organizationally collectivistic and tight settings.

From an individual perspective, persons high on felt accountability are expected to hold cultural values most related to collectivism and tightness; individuals high on these values are thus expected to discriminate the most against older workers (Gelfand et al., 2006). Older workers who themselves are higher on these values may also be expected to experience more challenges related to global mobility. An older worker who has high need for security may find transitioning to a different job or career in later life to be more adversarial than one who has relatively low need for security (see also Chapter 9 of this volume). Finally, societal, organizational, and individual levels of culture are expected to interact and influence work outcomes, such that barriers to global mobility for an older workforce may be expected to be highest when both the host society and the organization/individual hold values that are collectivistic and tight. Indeed, the interactive effects of levels of culture (collectivism–individualism) have been meta-analytically shown to impact important work outcomes such as cooperation and performance (Marcus & Le, 2013; see also Chapter 6 of this volume).

Cross-National Issues

Beyond the role of culture, the mobility of an aging workforce in the global context acknowledges the role of structural cross-national issues. A useful framework for addressing such career mobility challenges for an aging workforce is the notion of Protean and boundaryless careers, whereby careers are seen as cyclical, lateral, and individualistic (Mirvis & Hall, 1996). Modern careers unfold across multiple employment settings within and across industries, and work becomes transportable across geographic and structural boundaries (Arthur & Rousseau, 1996). Baruch and Reis (2016) provide a typology suggesting that careers may be conceptualized as both local–global (i.e., a global career transcends national borders while a local one does not), and traditional–boundaryless (a traditional career is lived along a single path while a boundaryless one entails shifts across industries or sectors). Hence, careers may span the continuum from local and traditional to global and boundaryless (Baruch & Reis, 2016).

The latter provides particular challenges to an aging workforce. Ageism against older workers has been found to be prevalent across all European countries (Abrams & Swift, 2012); the magnitude of ageism has been found to vary across even culturally similar countries such as Germany (more age discrimination) and Norway (less age discrimination; Busch, Dahl, & Dittrich, 2004). Thus, given employer age prejudices, older workers are likely to find it the most difficult to cross national borders and engage in global careers (Baruch & Reis, 2016). Because of the nature of old age stereotypes, older female workers may be less likely to engage in global careers (Baruch & Reis, 2016; Marcus & Fritzsche, 2015; see also Chapter 9 of this volume).

Although overall worker mobility across national borders is low as a percentage of the population, and data on global worker mobility are scarce (Willekens, Massey, Raymer, & Beauchemin, 2016), the prevailing evidence indicates more not less migration for women of all ages (Wilson, 2002). This is driven by economic necessity, whereby women from poorer and economically disadvantaged countries work as blue-collar immigrants, often in domestic or care giving jobs, in richer countries (Wilson, 2002). Thus, any analysis of older worker mobility across national borders must take socioeconomic status into account, particularly when considering migration from less to more industrialized economies.

Despite widespread societal prevalence of ageism, older workers have been found to view their late careers more in terms of development than decline, emphasizing positive perceptions of themselves and benefits of age-related changes (Taneva, Arnold, & Nicolson, 2016). From a lifespan perspective, older workers have a more limited sense of future time, giving greater emphasis to emotional meaning and life satisfaction, placing priority on relationships and existing skill development (Carstensen, 2006). Older workers in jobs that have more complexity and control perceive greater remaining opportunities in their occupational future (Zacher & Frese, 2009). Although lower socioeconomic status older workers, driven by financial need, may be more likely to cross borders and engage in global careers, higher socioeconomic status older workers, occupying jobs greater in complexity and control, may be more likely to engage in boundaryless careers. More research is needed to disentangle the effects of socioeconomic status, job type, and age on global worker mobility.

Conversely, more evidence exists regarding the global-boundaryless careers and individual differences. Using a selection, optimization, and compensation (SOC) framework, Unson and Richardson (2012) found that older workers who had stronger familial and work support networks, or who held flexible attitudes to change, optimism, and a concern to make the most of their remaining careers, were the most likely to transition into a new career (see also Chapter 7 of this volume). Evidence indicates that older workers who attempt to transition into new careers face more difficulty in finding jobs, compared with those who make within-career transitions. Such effects are exacerbated by rater ageism and situational stereotype salience (Fritzsche & Marcus, 2013).

Overall, there exists more theory than hard evidence on cross-cultural and cross-national considerations related to global issues in work and aging. More research is needed at the micro levels of culture, including organizational cultures and individual cultural values. Research is also needed to gain a better understanding of the challenges of emigration for older workers. Finally, more research is needed to identify specific features of organizations and jobs that may make late life career transitions more or less challenging for older workers (see also Chapter 9 of this volume).

Institutional Considerations and Global Issues in Work, Aging, and Retirement

We next examine global issues in work, aging, and retirement from an institutional perspective that integrates elements of lifespan developmental theory. Boundaryless and global careers can be facilitated by organizational and national policies and practices (Baruch & Reis, 2016). We consider policies and national, organizational, and other (non-governmental organizations) institutions that may address the challenges of an aging workforce.

National Policies

Recommendations from the policy literature for addressing the aging workforce include encouraging older people to stay in the labor market, increasing the retirement age, promoting self-funded retirement, reducing entitlements to contain fiscal costs, and the introduction of consumer-directed care in the provision of aged care services (Phillips & O'Loughlin, 2017). At a macro level, governments can address the growing demographic deficit either by offering policies that encourage childbearing (such as including affordable childcare, parental leave, financial transfers, and tax provisions), by increasing immigration, or by changing dependency ratios and increasing the retirement age (Harper, 2014). None of these potential prescriptions are without pitfalls.

Financial incentives and tax provisions either raise the tax burden on currently working-age populations or raise the deficit to burden future working-age populations. Raising the retirement age raises questions of intergenerational responsibility and equity – at what point are individuals expected to begin to benefit from the social care system after putting in a lifetime of labor? Immigration from young and populous countries, primarily in South Asia and Africa, although providing a rich potential pool of young talent for aging industrialized societies, causes social tension and backlashes to increased demographic diversity (Kulik, Ryan, Harper, & George, 2014). More pointedly, immigration is only a short-term solution, and is unsustainable in the long run. Analyses of migrant flows in recent decades in developed countries have found little evidence for the "rejuvenating" effect of immigration, because immigrant populations tend to adapt to host country fertility and mortality levels in the long-term (United Nations, 2001). Moreover, the volume of immigration needed to offset population aging in the long term is projected to be upwards of 30 percent in most developed countries, such as France and Germany, thereby making the potential social and political costs the immigration solution provides unfeasible (United Nations, 2001).

Similarly, pronatalistic policies favoring marriage and childbirth have not been found to be effective counters to population aging, with the evidence indicating that the net effect of family-redistribution policies is uncertain and minimal at best (Demeny, 2011). Aggressive forms of such policies such as rewards that disproportionately favor large families are no longer acceptable, and less aggressive "children-friendly" policies such as monetary transfers to parents of children and fully subsidized education are not fiscally sustainable in the long-term for welfare states already overburdened by an aging population (Demeny, 2011). When comparing all of these potential solutions, increases in the retirement age to age 75 have been found to be the most effective potential solution (United Nations, 2001). That being said, there is little to no research on potential workforce reactions to such an advanced retirement age (i.e., older worker reactions to possibly having to work longer; younger worker reactions to being denied retirement benefits a decade or even two decades past their forefathers' eras). This underscores the need for research linking national policy to outcomes for both older and younger workers.

Governments are also burdened by the growing need for eldercare services (Harper, 2014). Governments can adopt a variety of policies focused on public–private partnerships to ease societal and fiscal burdens on eldercare. For example, New Zealand introduced legislation in 2008 that provided employees responsible for the care of any person and who had worked for the same employer for at least six months with the right to request flexible working arrangements (Alpass, Keeling, Allen, Stevenson, & Stephens, 2017). Evidence indicates that flexible working arrangements were important for caregiver mental health (Alpass et al., 2017). Similarly, Germany introduced a long-term care insurance system, allowing working caregivers to reduce their working hours up to a minimum of 15 hours per week for up to two years (Kodate & Timonen, 2017). Public–private eldercare/long-term care policies have also been implemented in Japan, Korea, Taiwan, and Singapore (e.g., the "Silver Support Scheme," see Kodate & Timonen, 2017). Research remains inconclusive as to the relative efficacy of any of these long-term care insurance policies on age-based work and life outcomes (Kodate & Timonen, 2017).

Organizational Policies

There exists more evidence on the efficacy of organizational policies in relation to age-based work outcomes. From a worker perspective, research indicates that the forms of organizational support desired by older workers include work meaningfulness, social cohesion, knowledge transfer, feedback from direct supervisors, and procedural justice (see Taneva et al., 2016). Moreover, actual and perceived organizational support seem to constitute important psychosocial resources for employed caregivers that impact their wellbeing and participation in employment (Zacher, Rudolph, & Reinicke, 2017). These findings are consistent with research from the lifespan perspective indicating that older workers are more centered on emotional and relational development (Carstensen, 2006), and on their emphasis on internal as opposed to external motives and rewards (Kooij, De Lange, Jansen, Kanfer, & Dikkers, 2011).

For organizations, ageism against older workers has been found to be closely associated with discriminatory selection practices and a lack of organizational support for development (Jones et al., 2017; see also Chapter 4 of this volume). However, age-inclusive Human Resources (HR) practices have been found to positively impact the organizational age diversity climate. Organizations implementing such age-inclusive HR practices have shown greater social cohesion, reduced collective turnover intentions, and enhanced firm performance (Boehm, Kunze, & Bruch, 2014). Cross-societal research from both the United Kingdom and Hong Kong supports this view, with anti-age discrimination policies having positive influences on views toward older workers (Chiu, Chan, Snape, & Redman, 2001). Indeed, the importance of enabling a non-age discriminatory organizational environment has been posited to be essential for older worker mobility (Baruch & Reis, 2016). Conversely, increasing the age diversity of the organization has been found to be positively related to organizational age discrimination climate (Kunze, Boehm, & Bruch, 2011). This perhaps speaks to the exacerbated potential for intergenerational conflict when organizational members of diverse age groups work together (Rudolph & Zacher, 2015).

Other (Non-Governmental Organizations) Institutional Influences

There is a wealth of research on the role of non-governmental organizations (NGOs) in global issues facing an aging workforce, which have played significant roles in shaping governmental policy. For example, the Madrid International Plan of Action on Aging influenced governmental policy toward the aging workforce across industrialized countries; the United Nations Department for Economic and Social Affairs' World Economic Survey 2007 similarly shaped international policy regarding older workers (Phillips & Siu, 2012). Efforts made on behalf of older persons by NGOs (e.g., Phillips & Siu, 2012) have resulted in global awareness in and implementation of policies related to the active participation and development of older workers in the global economy (see also Chapter 8 of this volume), equitable employment and hiring practices toward older workers (see also Chapter 2 of this volume), and the advancing of health and well-being into old age (see also Chapter 10 of this volume).

Hence, it may be posited that although NGOs do not shape policy regarding older workers in the same fashion that national and organizational actors do, they are instrumental in the shaping of policy discussions and outcomes. NGOs play an important, albeit advisory institutional role in the shaping of policy regarding a global and aging workforce. Academic research is lacking with regard to the efficacy of NGO actions on age-based work outcomes. Even at the organizational level of analysis, little to no research examines such contextual factors. There is thus much room for exploration in the confluence of institutional policy and age-based work outcomes, and especially as it concerns a lifespan perspective.

Discussion

In this chapter, we sought to review and discuss research related to work, aging, and retirement from a global, international, and cross-cultural perspective. With the lifespan developmental perspective as an organizing theoretical framework, we considered global issues in work, aging, and retirement through four conceptual lenses: (a) demography and workforce aging; (b) workforce health and well-being in the face of global population aging; (c) worker mobility in a global context; and (d) overarching institutional issues. Our sincere hope is that this review and accompanying recommendations inspire future researchers to consider work, aging, and retirement from a global perspective.

Directions for Future Research

Demography and Workforce Aging

Given rapid global population aging in some parts of the world (e.g., Western Europe and East Asia versus Latin American and Africa; He et al., 2016), norms regarding what is or is not old age are bound to change differentially across societies, with concomitant differences in the definition of old age itself across societies. Even within societies, members of different birth cohorts may have different definitions of old age, with people born in the late 20th century potentially having a different definition of "old age" (e.g., 50+) as opposed to people born in the early 21st century, and who come of age in an overall older society with far more septua-, octo-, and nonagenarians. Thus, future research should investigate differences in normative standards of old age across societal and temporal boundaries in order to best operationalize age itself, and to derive ecologically valid definitions of "older workers."

Similarly, further research is needed on optimal retirement ages given differences in national aging profiles. For example, would mandating 75 years as the age of retirement in advanced economies (United Nations, 2001) be politically or socially feasible? What factors would lead to increases in the retirement age within countries, and what effect would potential disparities in the retirement age across countries have on the future work and retirement plans of workers? How would such differences affect worker mobility in a global context? Future policy research must be able to incorporate the potential broad-reaching implications of such shifts.

Health and Well-Being

Differences in mortality and morbidity across countries (WHO, 2012) drive differences in the quality of life that older individuals may expect to experience in different societal environments. Within societies, women have been found to experience significantly better quality of life into older age than men (European Commission, 2014). Such quality of life differences and resultant differences in activity limitations imply demographic and societal differences in the psychological and physical consequences of old age. Research is thus needed to investigate potential country-level effects of such disparities on populations of older adults and workers.

Older people also have different health care needs from younger people; the rate of having multiple chronic illnesses is higher in older populations (US Department of Health and Human Services, 2010; see also Chapter 10 of this volume). Therefore, an aging population will create new burdens on employed caregivers (i.e., typically female family members). Future research on work–family balance issues given increases in caregiving is thus needed. To this end, incorporating a lifespan developmental perspective by considering role theories and changes in work motives over time (see Thrasher et al., 2016) may be fruitful. Cross-cultural differences (e.g., caregiving and work–family balance in collectivistic versus individualistic societies) need also be considered to build nuance as to how such new work–family balance issues resultant of aging populations play out differently across global contexts.

Worker Mobility

From an individual perspective, more research needs to be conducted on experiences of, motivations for, and consequences for career-change in later life (see also Chapter 9 of this volume). Given that modern careers are Protean and boundaryless (Arthur & Rousseau, 1996), career-change in late life, both within and especially between career trajectories, remains an understudied topic. Although some experimental research exists regarding the consequences of old age for career changers (Fritzsche & Marcus, 2013), the field lacks systematic and widespread data on job incumbents regarding this topic. One potentially fruitful and especially understudied avenue of such research arises when one also considers cross-national and cross-cultural differences; these latter factors have not been studied with regard to worker mobility in old age.

There is also much potential for future research in this area when one considers the demand (organizational) side of the equation. For example, although organizational factors such as job and industry type, organizational size, leader characteristics, and labor union presence have been previously linked to support for worker mobility in late life (Mulders et al., 2017; van Dalen et al., 2015), research on this topic remains embedded in a top-down organizational paradigm. That is, research is need that considers the worker and job incumbent/job applicant side of the worker mobility in late life question, with regards to these and other potentially relevant organizational factors. Additionally, the potential moderating role of cross-cultural influences on these relations, both in terms of organizational and societal cultures, has been neglected.

Cross-Cultural and Institutional Factors

Perhaps most lacking is the role of cross-cultural and overarching institutional factors (e.g., the role of state or NGO actors) when one considers global issues in work, aging, and retirement. Reflecting the relatively more micro orientation of most age-in-the-workplace researchers, there is a dearth of data on older workers at higher levels of analyses, particularly at the firm or country level. Similarly, academic research is lacking in to the efficacy of NGO actions on age-based work outcomes. On a national level, research remains inconclusive as to the relative efficacy of long-term care insurance policies on age-based work and life outcomes (Kodate & Timonen, 2017). Moreover, we know little about potential workforce reactions to increases in the retirement age, to potentially even up to age 75, thereby underscoring the need once again for research linking national policy to outcomes for both older and younger workers.

Practical Implications

Demography and Workforce Aging

Unprecedented population aging, both in developing economies and especially in developed economies, will present new challenges for governmental and business decision-makers. The needs of an older workforce are different from the needs of a younger one. For example, older workers are likely to consider pension plans and insurance options much more so than younger workers, who conversely may be more likely to focus on childcare and family-related services such as help with tuition costs. Thus, employers may need to rethink and restructure their benefits and rewards systems in order to meet the needs of an aging workforce. Governments, meanwhile, may need to fashion tax and benefits policies that best serve the needs of an aging workforce while maintaining fiscal equilibrium, given also the needs of the younger tax-paying body public. This is no easy challenge, and may well require concerted efforts at the regional (e.g. European Union) or broader international (e.g., United Nations, WHO) level in order to face mutually shared challenges brought about by the graying population.

Health and Well-Being

The aging workforce also means more expenditures on healthcare. From a governmental perspective, this will imply that more tax dollars must be spent on healthcare costs relative to other tax dollars on other things, such as infrastructure. Meeting such a challenge will be no easy task, again in light of the need to maintain fiscal solvency and equilibrium given the needs of other, particularly younger, members of the tax-paying body public. Thus, governments may be forced to rethink priorities in order to deal with rising healthcare costs (e.g., less spending on military budgets). On the other hand, governments may also need to start working more closely and in concert with NGOs who may be able to help alleviate some of the cost burden, for example via the offering of hospital and clinical care treatment to older persons of limited pecuniary means.

Likewise, employers will also need to pay more attention to health benefits and other services that may benefit an aging workforce. Offering flexible work schedules, work-from-home regimes, and even on-site care centers may be of much value to older workers, and especially older female workers, who still bear the brunt of the burden when it comes to caregiving for aging partners or other family members.

Furthermore, from a job-seeker perspective, new employment opportunities related to professional caregiving, development of new technologies, and service provision (Knickman & Snell, 2002; Phillips & Siu, 2012) will mean new avenues for professional success (see also Chapter 11 of this volume). Younger adults may thus consider healthcare-related professions as a promising new career path, especially so in the developed world. From a global perspective, this may likely mean a further "brain drain" of the best and brightest doctors and nurses in the developing world to the developed one, thereby exacerbating such immigration trends that are already underway today.

Worker Mobility

As an increasing number of older workers seek to change careers in the Protean and boundaryless professional world of the 21st century, employers increasingly wrestle with considerations related to the employment of older workers. Organizations may need to focus on training and development programs (see Chapter 8 of this volume), especially remedial job training for retirees, or perhaps for older workers changing from one field to another, given the knowledge intensity levels that are needed in the job at hand (see van Dalen et al., 2015). On the plus side, organizations with older employee profiles are more likely to hire and accommodate older workers (van Dalen et al., 2015), so it may be the case that age discrimination in the hiring of older job applicants will decrease. Of course, that may not necessarily hold true for all older workers, given the theory indicating that women are likely to suffer more negative age discrimination (Marcus & Fritzsche, 2015). Hence, organizations may need to consider especially demographic and other potential cross-cultural differences between older workers instead of treating them as a uniform group, and thereby to fashion training and development programs and hiring policies to best meet the needs of diverse types of older workers and older job seekers.

Cross-Cultural and Institutional Considerations

Given cross-cultural and other institutional differences between countries, industries, and even organizations, a truly global view of work, aging, and retirement will need to take such differences into account. Specific organizational policies regarding training, development, and the general management of the aging workforce may need to be developed for workers from different cultural backgrounds (see Chapter 8 of this volume). For example, members of more individualistic cultures may place a priority on personal choice and thereby value the greatest variety of training programs possible within an organization, whereas members of more collectivistic cultures may place a priority on group cohesion and thereby value a variety of training programs that are geared toward the greatest number of fellow organizational members. In other words, multinational organizations may be best served by tailoring benefits and employee services for older and younger workers in light of cultural nuances within each particular nation. Similarly, organizations located in different industries may have uniquely different considerations as to these. For example, organizations in knowledge-intensive tech industries may need to invest more resources in the development process and thereby offer more training opportunities for older workers, whereas organizations in industries typified by manual labor may need to invest more resources in the accommodation of older workers, such as reducing workloads or working hours for older employees.

Conclusion

Research and practice related to work, aging, and retirement is often only discussed from the perspective of the individual and from the perspective of Western developed countries. In this final chapter, we aimed to broaden this narrow focus by adopting a global, international, and cross-cultural standpoint and by focusing on the multiple layers of sociocultural context surrounding aging and older workers. Populations and workforces are aging rapidly around the globe, and these developments have important implications for worker health and well-being, informal caregiving and work–family balance, as well as career mobility in a changing world of work. We hope our chapter inspires researchers and practitioners interested in work, aging, and retirement to "think global" and take contextual factors into account.

Acknowledgment

The authors would like to thank Rachel S. Rauvola for her assistance in the preparation of this manuscript.

References

Abrams, D., & Swift, H. J. (2012). Ageism doesn't work. *Public Policy & Aging Report*, *22*(3), 3–8. doi:0.1093/ppar/22.3.3.

Aegon (2013). *The changing face of retirement: The Aegon retirement readiness survey 2013*. The Hague, the Netherlands: Aegon and the Transamerica Center for Retirement Studies.

Albright, V. A. (2012). Workforce demographics in the United States: Occupational trends, work rates, and retirement projections in the United States. In J. W. Hedge & W. C. Borman (Eds.), *The Oxford handbook of work and aging* (pp. 33–59). New York: Oxford University Press.

Alcover, C.-M., Topa, G., Parry, E., Fraccaroli, F., & Depolo, M. (2014). *Bridge employment: A research handbook*. London, UK: Routledge.

Alpass, F., Keeling, S., Allen, J., Stevenson, B., & Stephens, C. (2017). Reconciling work and caregiving responsibilities among older workers in New Zealand. *Journal of Cross Cultural Gerontology*. Advance online publication. doi:10.1007/s10823-017-9327-3.

Alzheimer's Disease International (2010). *World Alzheimer report*. Retrieved from www.alz.co.uk/research/files/WorldAlzheimerReport2010.pdf.

Arias, E. (2014). *United States life tables: 2010*. National Vital Statistics Reports (63/7). Hyattsville, MD: National Center for Health Statistics.

Arthur, M. B., & Rousseau, D. M. (1996). Introduction: The boundaryless career as a new employment principle. In M. B. Arthur & D. M. Rousseau (Eds.), *The boundaryless career: A new employment principle for a new organizational era* (pp. 3–20). New York: Oxford University Press.

Baltes, P. B. (1997). On the incomplete architecture of human ontogeny: Selection, optimization, and compensation as foundation of developmental theory. *American Psychologist, 52*, 366–380. doi:10.1037/0003-066x.52.4.366.

Baltes, P. B. (1987). Theoretical propositions of life-span developmental psychology: On the dynamics between growth and decline. *Developmental Psychology, 23*, 611–626. doi:10.1037/0012-1649.23.5.611.

Baltes, P. B., Lindenberger, U., & Staudinger, U. M. (2006). Lifespan theory in developmental psychology. In W. Damon & R. M. Lerner (Eds.), *Handbook of child psychology: Vol. 1. Theoretical models of human development* (6th ed., pp. 569–664). New York: Wiley.

Baltes, P. B., Reese, H. W., & Lipsitt, L. P. (1980). Life-span developmental psychology. *Annual Review of Psychology, 31*, 65–110. doi:10.1146/annurev.ps.31.020180.000433.

Baltes, B. B., Rudolph, C. W., & Bal, A. C. (2012). A review of aging theories and modern work perspectives. In J. W. Hedge & W. C. Borman (Eds.), *The Oxford handbook of work and aging* (pp. 117–136). New York: Oxford University Press.

Barrientos, A., Gorman, M., & Heslop, A. (2003). Old age poverty in developing countries: Contributions and dependence in later life. *World Development, 31*, 555–570. doi:10.1016/s0305-750x(02)00211-5.

Baruch, Y., & Reis, C. (2016). How global are boundaryless careers and how boundaryless are global careers? Challenges and a theoretical perspective. *Thunderbird International Business Review, 58*, 13–27. doi:10.1002/tie.21712.

Birren, J. E. (1999). Theories of aging: A personal perspective. In V. L. Bengtson & K. W. Schaie (Eds.), *Handbook of theories of aging* (pp. 459–471). New York: Springer.

Bloom, D. E. (2011). 7 billion and counting. *Science, 333*, 562–569. doi:10.1126/science.1209290.

Bloom, D. E., Cafiero, E. T., Jané-Llopis, E., Abrahams-Gessel, S., Bloom, L. R., Fathima, S., … Weinstein, C. (2011). The global economic burden of noncommunicable diseases. Geneva: World Economic Forum. Retrieved from www3.weforum.org/docs/WEF_Harvard_HE_GlobalEconomicBurdenNonCommunicableDiseases_2011.p df.

Boehm, S. A., Kunze, F., & Bruch, H. (2014). Spotlight on age diversity climate: The impact of age-inclusive HR practices on firm-level outcomes. *Personnel Psychology, 67*, 667–704. doi:10.1111/peps.12047.

Brewer, M. B. (1991). The social self: On being the same and different at the same time. *Personality and Social Psychology Bulletin, 17*, 475–482. doi:10.1177/0146167291175001.

Bronfenbrenner, U. (1979). *The ecology of human development: Experiments by nature and design*. Cambridge, MA: Harvard University Press.

Bureau of Labor Statistics (2017). Occupations with the most job growth. Retrieved from www.bls.gov/emp/ep_table_104.htm.

Busch, V., Dahl, S.-A., & Dittrich, A. V. (2004). Age discrimination in hiring decisions: A comparison of Germany and Norway. *Working Paper, 75*.

Carstensen, L. L. (2006). The influence of a sense of time on human development. *Science, 312*, 1913–1915. doi:10.1126/science.1127488.

Centers for Disease Control and Prevention (2010). Chronic diseases: The power to prevent, the call to control. Retrieved from www.cdc.gov/chronicdisease/pdf/2009-power-of-prevention.pdf.

Chand, M., & Tung, R. L. (2014). The aging of the world's population and its effects on global business. *Academy of Management Perspectives, 28*, 409–429. doi:10.5465/amp.2012.0070.

Chao, G. T., & Moon, H. (2005). The cultural mosaic: A metatheory for understanding the complexity of culture. *Journal of Applied Psychology, 90*, 1128–1140. doi:10.1037/0021-9010.90.6.1128.

Chiu, W. C. K., Chan, A. W., Snape, E., & Redman, T. (2001). Age stereotypes and discriminatory attitudes towards older workers: An East–West comparison. *Human Relations, 54*, 629–661. doi:10.1177/0018726701545004.

Cleveland, J. N., & Hanscom, M. (2017). What is old at work? Moving past chronological age. In E. Parry & J. McCarthy (Eds.), *The Palgrave handbook of age diversity and work* (pp. 17–46). London, UK: Palgrave Macmillan.

Darkwa, O. K., & Mazibuko, F. N. M. (2002). Population aging and its impact on elderly welfare in Africa. *International Journal of Aging and Human Development, 54*, 107–123. doi:10.2190/xtqg-6dxd-9xwe-9x85.

Demeny, P. (2011). Population policy and the demographic transition: Performance, prospects, and options. *Population and Development Review, 37*, 249–274. doi:10.1111/j.1728-4457.2011.00386.x.

Elder, G. H., & Liker, J. K. (1982). Hard times in women's lives: Historical influences across forty years. *American Journal of Sociology, 88*, 241–269. doi:10.1086/227670.

European Commission (2014). Eurostat. Retrieved from http://ec.europa.eu/eurostat/data/database.

Featherman, D. L., & Lerner, R. M. (1985). Ontogenesis and sociogenesis: Problems for theory and research about development and socialization across the lifespan. *American Sociological Review, 50*, 659–676. doi:10.2307/2095380.

Feinberg, L., Reinhard, S. C., Choula, R., & Houser, A. (2015). Valuing the invaluable: 2015 update: Undeniable progress, but big gaps remain. *Washington, DC: AARP Public Policy Institute, 51*, 1–28. Retrieved from www.aarp.org/content/dam/aarp/ppi/2015/valuing-the-invaluable-2015-update-new.pdf.

Fineman, S. (2011). *Organizing age.* New York: Oxford University Press.

Finkelstein, S., Hambrick, D. C., & Cannella, A. A. (2008). *Strategic leadership: Theory and research on executives, top management teams, and boards.* Oxford, UK: Oxford University Press.

Fisher, G. G., Franks, M. M., Plassman, B. L., Brown, S. L., Potter, G. G., Llewellyn, D., ... Langa, K. M. (2011). Caring for individuals with dementia and cognitive impairment, not dementia: Findings from the aging, demographics, and memory study. *Journal of the American Geriatrics Society, 59*, 488–494. doi:10.1111/j.1532-5415.2010.03304.x.

Ford, D. H., & Lerner, R. M. (1992). *Developmental systems theory: An integrative approach.* Thousand Oaks, CA: Sage.

Fritzsche, B. A., & Marcus, J. (2013). The senior discount: Biases against older career changers. *Journal of Applied Social Psychology, 43*, 350–362. doi:10.1111/j.1559-1816.2012.01004.x.

Fung, H. H. (2013). Aging in culture. *The Gerontologist, 53*, 369–377. doi:10.1093/geront/gnt024.

Gelfand, M. J., Bhawuk, D. P. S., Nishii, L. S., & Bechtold, D. J. (2004). Individualism and collectivism. In R. J. House, P. J. Hanges, M. Javidan, P. W. Dorfman, & V. Gupta. (Eds.), *Culture, leadership, and organizations: The GLOBE study of 62 societies* (pp. 438–502). Thousand Oaks, CA: Sage.

Gelfand, M. J., Nishii, L. H., & Raver, J. L. (2006). On the nature and importance of cultural tightness–looseness. *Journal of Applied Psychology, 91*, 1225–1244. doi:10.1037/0021-9010.91.6.1225.

Geriatrics Workforce Policy Studies Center (2011). Comparison of number of certificates awarded to number of active certificates in geriatric medicine (internal & family medicine). Retrieved from www.americangeriatrics.org/files/documents/gwps/Figure%201_3.pdf.

Gerland, P., Raftery, A. E., Ševčíková, H., Li, N., Gu, D., Spoorenberg, T., ... Wilmoth, J. (2014). World population stabilization unlikely this century. *Science, 346*, 234–237. doi:10.1126/science.1257469.

Harper, S. (2014). Economic and social implications of aging societies. *Science, 346*, 587–591. doi:10.1126/science.1254405.

He, W., & Muenchrath, M. N. (2011). *90+ in the United States: 2006–2008*. American Community Survey Reports (ACS-17), US Census Bureau. Washington, DC: US Government Printing Office.

He, W., Goodkind, D. E., & Kowal, P. (2016). *An aging world: 2015*. International Population Reports (P95/09–1). Washington, DC: US Government Printing Office.

He, W., Sengupta, M., Velkoff, V. A., & DeBarros, K. A. (2005). *U.S. Census Bureau Current Population Reports, P23–209*. Washington, DC: Government Printing Office. Retrieved from www.census.gov/prod/.

Henkens, K., van Dalen, H. P., Ekerdt, D. J., Hershey, D. A., Hyde, M., Radl, J., ... Zacher, H. (2017). What we need to know about retirement: Pressing issues for the coming decade. *The Gerontologist*. Advance online publication. doi:10.1093/geront/gnx095.

Hertel, G., & Zacher, H. (2018). Managing the aging workforce. In D. S. Ones, N. Anderson, C. Viswesvaran, & H. K. Sinangil (Eds.), *The SAGE handbook of industrial, work and organizational Psychology* (Vol. 3, pp. 396–428). New York: Sage.

Hofstede, G. (1980). Motivation, leadership, and organization: Do American theories apply abroad? *Organizational Dynamics, 9*, 42–63. doi:10.1016/0090-2616(80)90013-3.

Hyde, M., & Higgs, P. (2016). *Ageing and globalisation*. Bristol, UK: Policy Press.

James, K. S. (2011). India's demographic change: Opportunities and challenges. *Science, 333*, 576–580. doi:10.1126/science.1207969.

Japanese Ministry of Internal Affairs and Communication (n.d.) *Japan statistical yearbook, chapter 2: Population and households*. Retrieved from www.stat.go.jp/english/data/nenkan/1431-02.htm.

Jones, K. P., Sabat, I. E., King, E. B., Ahmad, A., McCausland, T. C., & Chen, T. (2017). Isms and schisms: A meta-analysis of the prejudice–discrimination relationship across racism, sexism, and ageism. *Journal of Organizational Behavior, 38*, 1076–1110. doi:10.1002/job.2187.

Kinsella, K., & He, W. (2009). *An aging world: 2008*. International Population Reports (P95/09–1). Washington, DC: US Government Printing Office.

Kinsella, K. G., & Phillips, D. R. (2005). Global aging: The challenge of success. *Population Bulletin, 60*, 5–42.

Knickman, J. R., & Snell, E. K. (2002). The 2030 problem: Caring for aging baby boomers. *Health Services Research, 37*, 849–884. doi:10.1034/j.1600-0560.2002.56.x.

Kodate, N., & Timonen, V. (2017). Bringing the family in through the back door: The stealthy expansion of family care in Asian and European long-term care policy. *Journal of Cross Cultural Gerontology, 32*, 291–301. doi:10.1007/s10823-017-9325-5.

Kooij, D., De Lange, A., Jansen, P., & Dikkers, J. (2008). Older workers' motivation to continue to work: Five meanings of age: A conceptual review. *Journal of Managerial Psychology, 23*, 364–394. doi:10.1108/02683940810869015.

Kooij, D., De Lange, A. H., Jansen, P. G. W., Kanfer, R., & Dikkers, J. S. E. (2011). Age and work-related motives. *Journal of Organizational Behavior, 32*, 192–225. doi:10.1002/job.665.

Kulik, C. T., Ryan, S., Harper, S., & George, G. (2014). From the editors: Aging populations and management. *Academy of Management Journal, 57*, 929–935. doi:10.5465/amj.2014.4004.

Kunze, F., & Boehm, S. (2015). Age diversity and global teamwork: A future agenda for researchers and practitioners. In L. M. Finkelstein, D. M. Truxillo, F. Fraccaroli, & R. Kanfer (Eds.), *Facing the challenges of a multi-age workforce: A use-inspired approach* (pp. 27–49). New York: Routledge.

Kunze, F., Boehm, S. A., & Bruch, H. (2011). Age diversity, age discrimination climate and performance consequences – a cross-organizational study. *Journal of Organizational Behavior, 32*, 264–290. doi:10.1002/job.698.

Lawrence, B. S. (1997). The black box of organizational demography. *Organization Science, 8*, 1–22. doi:10.1287/orsc.8.1.1.

Lerner, R. M. (1996). Relative plasticity, integration, temporality, and diversity in human development: A developmental contextual perspective about theory, process, and method. *Developmental Psychology, 32*, 781–786. doi:10.1037/0012-1649.32.4.781.

Lerner, R. M., & Busch-Rossnagel, N. A. (1981). *Individuals as producers of their development: A life-span perspective.* New York: Academic Press.

Lerner, R. M., & Kauffman, M. B. (1985). The concept of development in contextualism. *Developmental Review, 5*, 309–333. doi:10.1016/0273-2297(85)90016-4.

Lerner, R. M., Fisher, C. B., & Weinberg, R. A. (2000). Applying developmental science in the 21st century: International scholarship for our times. *International Journal of Behavioral Development, 24*, 24–29. doi:10.1080/016502500383430.

Levy, B. R., Zonderman, A. B., Slade, M. D., & Ferrucci, L. (2012). Memory shaped by age stereotypes over time. *Journals of Gerontology: Series B, 67*, 432–436. doi:10.1093/geronb/gbr120.

Marcus, J., & Fritzsche, B. A. (2015). One size doesn't fit all: Toward a theory on the intersectional salience of ageism at work. *Organizational Psychology Review, 5*, 168–188. doi:10.1177/2041386614556015.

Marcus, J., & Fritzsche, B. A. (2016). The cultural anchors of age discrimination in the workplace: A multilevel framework. *Work, Aging and Retirement, 2*, 217–229. doi:10.1093/workar/waw007.

Marcus, J., & Le, H. (2013). Interactive effects of levels of individualism–collectivism on cooperation: A meta-analysis. *Journal of Organizational Behavior, 34*, 813–834. doi:10.1002/job.1875.

Marcus, J., & Sabuncu, N. (2016). "Old oxen cannot plow": Stereotype themes of older adults in Turkish folklore. *The Gerontologist, 56*, 1007–1022. doi:10.1093/geront/gnv108.

Mathers, C. D, Bernard, C., Iburg, K. M., Inoue, M., Ma Fat, D., Shibuya, K., ... Tomijima, N. (2003). The global burden of disease in 2002: Data sources, methods and results. GPE Discussion Paper No. 54. Geneva: World Health Organization. Retrieved from www.who.int/healthinfo/paper54.pdf.

McCarthy, J., Heraty, N., Cross, C., & Cleveland, J. N. (2014). Who is considered an 'older worker'? Extending our conceptualisation of 'older' from an organisational decision maker perspective. *Human Resource Management Journal, 24*, 374–393. doi:10.1111/1748-8583.12041.

McNamara, T. K., Pitt-Catsouphes, M., Sarkisian, N., Besen, E., & Kidahashi, M. (2016). Age bias in the workplace: Cultural stereotypes and in-group favoritism. *The International Journal of Aging and Human Development, 83*, 156–183. doi:10.1177/0091415016648708.

Meyer, J. (2012). *Centenarians: 2010.* 2010 Census Special Reports (C2010SR-03), US Census Bureau. Washington, DC: US Government Printing Office.

Mirvis, P. H., & Hall, D. T. (1996). Psychological success and the boundaryless career. In M. B. Arthur & D. M. Rousseau (Eds.), *The boundaryless career: A new employment principle for a new organizational era* (pp. 237–255). New York: Oxford University Press.

Mulders, J. P., Henkens, K., & Schippers, J. (2017). European top managers' age-related workplace norms and their organizations' recruitment and retention practices regarding older workers. *The Gerontologist*, *57*, 857–866. doi:10.1093/geront/gnw076.

Munnell, A. (2006). Employer-sponsored plans: The shift from defined benefit to defined contribution. In G. L. Clark, A. Munnell, and M. Orszag (Eds.) *The Oxford handbook of pensions and retirement income* (pp. 359–380). Oxford, UK: Oxford University Press.

National Alliance for Caregiving (2015). Caregiving in the US 2015. Retrieved from www.caregiving.org/caregiving2015.

National Institute of Population and Social Security Research (2012). Population projections for Japan: 2011 to 2060, tables 1–4. Retrieved from www.ipss.go.jp/site-ad/index_english/esuikei/ppfj2012.pdf.

Nesselroade, J. R., & Baltes, P. B. (1974). Adolescent personality development and historical change: 1970–1972. *Monographs of the Society for Research in Child Development*, *39* (1), 1–80. doi:10.2307/1165824.

Ng, T. W. H., & Feldman, D. C. (2008). The relationship of age to ten dimensions of job performance. *Journal of Applied Psychology*, *93*, 392–423. doi:10.1037/0021-9010.93.2.392.

North, M. S., & Fiske, S. T. (2015). Modern attitudes toward older adults in the aging world: A cross-cultural meta-analysis. *Psychological Bulletin*, *141*, 993–1022. doi:10.1037/a0039469.

OECD (2015). *Pensions at a glance 2015: OECD and G20 indicators*. OECD Publishing.

Ouchi, Y., Rakugi, H., Arai, H., Akishita, M., Ito, H., Toba, K., & Kai, I. (2017). Redefining the elderly as aged 75 years and older: Proposal from the Joint Committee of Japan Gerontological Society and the Japan Geriatrics Society. *Geriatrics & Gerontology International*. Advance online publication. doi:10.1111/ggi.13118.

Oulton, J. A. (2006). The global nursing shortage: An overview of issues and actions. *Policy, Politics, & Nursing Practice*, *7*, 34S–39S. doi:10.1177/1527154406293968.

Palmore, E. B., & Maeda, D. (1985). *The honorable elders revised: A revised cross-cultural analysis of aging in Japan*. Durham, NC: Duke University Press.

Peiro, J. M., Tordera, N., & Potocnik, K. (2013). Retirement practices in different countries. In M. Wang (Ed.), *The Oxford handbook of retirement* (pp. 510–540). New York: Oxford University Press.

Peng, X. (2011). China's demographic history and future challenges. *Science*, *333*, 581–587. doi:10.1126/science.1209396.

Phillips, D. R., & Siu, O. (2012). Global aging and aging workers. In J. W. Hedge & W. C. Borman (Eds.), *The Oxford handbook of work and aging* (pp. 11–32). New York: Oxford University Press.

Phillips, J., & O'Loughlin, K. (2017). Older workers and caregiving in a global context. *Journal of Cross Cultural Gerontology*, *32*, 283–289. doi:10.1007/s10823-017-9328-2.

Phillipson, C. (2009). Reconstructing theories of aging: The impact of globalization on critical gerontology. In V. L. Bengtson, D. Gans, N. M. Putney, & M. Silverstein (Eds.), *Handbook of theories of aging* (pp. 615–628). New York: Springer.

Pimental, N. (2017). Aging studies faces low enrollment due to stigmas surrounding field. *The Ithacan*. Retrieved from https://theithacan.org/news/students-disinterested-in-studying-aging-studies/.

Pitt-Catsouphes, M, and Sarkisian, N. (2010). *Generations of talent study*. Ann Arbor, MI: Inter-University Consortium for Political and Social Research [ICPSR35034-v1.]. doi: 10.3886/ICPSR35034.v1.

Posthuma, R. A., & Campion, M. A. (2009). Age stereotypes in the workplace: Common stereotypes, moderators, and future research directions. *Journal of Management, 35,* 158–188. doi:10.1177/0149206308318617.

Roberts, L. (2011). 9 Billion? *Science, 333,* 540–543. doi:10.1126/science.333.6042.540.

Rudolph, C. W. (2016). Lifespan developmental perspectives on working: A literature review of motivational theories. *Work, Aging and Retirement, 2,* 130–158. doi:10.1093/workar/waw012.

Rudolph, C. W., & Zacher, H. (2015). Intergenerational perceptions and conflicts in multi-age and multigenerational work environments. In L. M. Finkelstein, D. M. Truxillo, F. Fraccaroli, & R. Kanfer (Eds.), *Facing the challenges of a multi-age workforce* (pp. 253–282). New York: Routledge.

Shiu, E., Hassan, L. M., & Parry, S. (2015). The moderating effects of national age stereotyping on the relations between job satisfaction and its determinants: A study of older workers across 26 countries. *British Journal of Management, 26,* 255–272. doi:10.1111/1467-8551.12091.

Shobert, B. (2016). China, India's aging crises are huge expansion opportunities for U.S. home healthcare firms. *Forbes.* Retrieved from www.forbes.com/sites/benjaminshobert/2016/10/18/the-key-for-u-s-home-healthcare-companies-is-overseas-expansion/2/#289aa1976dba.

Skirbekk, V., Loichinger, E., & Barakat, B. F. (2012). The aging of the workforce in European countries: Demographic trends, retirement projections, and retirement policies. In J. W. Hedge & W. C. Borman (Eds.), *The Oxford handbook of work and aging* (pp. 60–79). New York: Oxford University Press.

Sterns, H. L. (2010). New and old thoughts about aging and work in the present and future. *The Gerontologist, 50,* 568–571. doi:10.1093/geront/gnq044.

Taneva, S. K., Arnold, J., & Nicolson, R. (2016). The experience of being an older worker in an organization: A qualitative analysis. *Work, Aging and Retirement, 2,* 396–414. doi:10.1093/workar/waw011.

Thrasher, G. R., Zabel, K., Wynne, K., & Baltes, B. B. (2016). The importance of workplace motives in understanding work–family issues for older workers. *Work, Aging and Retirement, 2,* 1–11. doi:10.1093/workar/wav021.

Topa, G., Jiménez, I., Valero, E., & Ovejero, A. (2017). Resource loss and gain, life satisfaction, and health among retirees in Spain: Mediation of social support. *Journal of Aging and Health, 29,* 415–436. doi:10.1177/0898264316635589.

Turner, J. C. (1985). Social categorization and the self-concept: A social-cognitive theory of group behavior. In E. J. Lawler (Ed.), *Advances in group processes* (vol. 2, pp. 77–122). Greenwich, CN: JAI.

United Nations (2001). *Replacement migration: Is it a solution to declining and ageing populations?* New York: United Nations. Retrieved from www.un.org/esa/population/publications/migration/migration.htm.

United Nations (2013). *World population ageing 2013.* New York: United Nations. Retrieved from www.un.org/en/development/desa/population/publications/pdf/ageing/WorldPopulationAgeing2013.pdf.

Unson, C., & Richardson, M. (2012). Insights into the experience of older workers and change: Through the lens of selection, optimization, and compensation. *The Gerontologist, 53,* 484–494. doi:10.1093/geront/gns095.

US Department of Health and Human Services (2010). *Multiple chronic conditions: A strategic framework: Optimum health and quality of life for individuals with multiple chronic conditions.* Washington, DC: US Department of Health and Human Services. Retrieved from www.hhs.gov/sites/default/files/ash/initiatives/mcc/mcc_framework.pdf.

US Trust (2017). *2017 insights on wealth and worth*. Retrieved from www.ustrust.com/ust/pages/insights-on-wealth-and-worth-2017.aspx.

van Dalen, H. P., Henkens, K., & Wang, M. (2015). Recharging or retiring older workers? Uncovering the age-based strategies of European employers. *The Gerontologist, 55*, 814–824. doi:10.1093/geront/gnu048.

Van der Veer, R. (1996). The concept of culture in Vygotsky's thinking. *Culture & Psychology, 2*, 247–263. doi:10.1177/1354067x9600200302.

Vauclair, C.-M., Hanke, K., Huang, L.-L., & Abrams, D. (2017). Are Asian cultures really less ageist than Western ones? It depends on the questions asked. *International Journal of Psychology, 52*, 136–144. doi:10.1002/ijop. 12292.

Vygotsky, L. S. (1978). *Mind in society: The development of higher psychological processes*. Cambridge, MA: Harvard University Press.

Wang, M. (2007). Profiling retirees in the retirement transition and adjustment process: Examining the longitudinal change patterns of retirees' psychological well-being. *Journal of Applied Psychology, 92*, 455–474. doi:10.1037/0021-9010.92.2.455.

Willekens, F., Massey, D., Raymer, J., & Beauchemin, C. (2016). International migration under the microscope. *Science, 352*, 897–899. doi:10.1126/science.aaf6545.

Wilson, G. (2002). Globalisation and older people: Effects of markets and migration. *Ageing & Society, 22*, 647–663. doi:10.1017/s0144686x02008747.

World Health Organization (n.d.). *Health workforce for ageing populations*. Retrieved from www.who.int/ageing/publications/health-workforce-ageing-populations.pdf.

World Health Organization (2011). *Global health and aging*. Geneva, SZ: World Health Organization. Retrieved from www.who.int/ageing/publications/global_health.pdf.

World Health Organization (2012). *Global health observatory*. Retrieved from www.who.int/gho/en/.

Yeung, D., & Zhou, X. (2017). Panning for retirement: Longitudinal effect on retirement resources and post-retirement well-being. *Frontiers in Organizational Psychology, 8*, 1300. doi:10.3389/fpsyg.2017.01300.

Zacher, H., & Frese, M. (2009). Remaining time and opportunities at work: Relationships between age, work characteristics, and occupational future time perspective. *Psychology and Aging, 24*, 487–493. doi:10.1037/a0015425.

Zacher, H., Hacker, W., & Frese, M. (2016). Action regulation across the adult lifespan (ARAL): A meta-theory of work and aging. *Work, Aging and Retirement, 2*, 286–306. doi:10.1093/workar/waw015.

Zacher, H., Rudolph, C. W., & Reinicke, C. (2017). Caregiving, organizational support, and employee strain and well-being. In R. Burke & L. Calvano (Eds.), *The sandwich generation: Caring for oneself and others at home and at work* (pp. 129–151). Cheltenham, UK: Edward Elgar.

Zaidi, A. (2010). *Poverty risks for older people in EU countries – An update. Policy brief January (11) 2010*. Austria, Vienna: European Centre for Social Policy and Research.

NAME INDEX

Abrams, D. 306
Ackerman, P.L. 127, 160
Adams, G.A. 23, 26, 160
Akkermans, J. 163
Alcover, C. 304
Alfonso-Benlliure, V. 180
Allen, T.D. 257
Annick, L. 76
Armstrong-Stassen, M. 136
Artistico, D. 126
Arvey, R.D. 68–69, 74
Avolio, B.J. 126, 130

Bal, P.M. 76, 136, 176
Baltes, B.B. 138, 264, 266, 299
Baltes, P.B. 294, 304–305
Banaji, R.B. 77
Banks, G.C. 126, 137
Barnes-Farrell, J.L. 134, 146
Barratt, C.L. 129
Barron, L. 72
Baruch, Y. 308
Becker, G.S. 172
Beehr, T.A. 18, 20–21, 28, 201
Bégat, I. 157
Beier, M.D. 124, 132, 173
Bennett, M.M. 21
Berg, S.A. 177
Berry, C.M. 129
Binneweis, C. 181
Birdi, K. 130
Blum, T. 104

Boehm, S.A. 218–219
Bohlmann, C. 124
Bolino, M.C. 205
Borman, W.C. 137
Bostwick, W.B. 45
Bourhis, A.C. 65, 70
Bowling, N.A. 201
Boyd, C.J. 45
Brandtstadter, J. 173
Bronfenbrenner, U. 293
Bruch, H. 218–219
Bruyère, S. 138
Bull, R.A. 68

Cadiz, D.M. 125
Cahill, K.E. 19
Caldwell, S.D. 158
Callahan, C.M. 126
Campion, M.A. 68
Caplan, L. 126
Carpenter, N.C. 129
Carstensen, L.L. 262
Cascio, W.F. 126
Cavanagh, T. 132
Cervone, D. 126
Chao, G.T. 305
Charmarkeh, H. 76
Charness, N. 201, 235
Chasteen, A.L. 42, 65
Cheung, C.K. 62
Chiu, W.C.K. 71
Chung-Herrera, B.G. 42

Church, A.H. 14, 16
Chyung, S.Y. 177
Clark, A. 149
Clemons, T. 68, 75
Cleveland, J.N. 70, 162, 301, 303
Cohen, D.A. 202
Costa, G. 134
Cox, C.B. 72, 132, 173
Crenshaw, K. 36
Cross, C. 303
Czaja, S.J. 130, 201, 234, 244

De Cuyper, N. 133–134
De Lange, A.H. 163
De Vos, A. 139
Deaux, K. 44
Demerouti, E. 179
Dencker, J.C. 183
Dendinger, V.M. 160
DeViney, S. 150
Dikkers, J.S.E. 163
Dimaggio, P. 204
Doorewaard, H. 160
Dugan, A.G. 258
Duguid, M.M. 62
Dujardin, J.-M 139
Dumke, H.A. 127
Duncan, C. 79
Dutton, J.E. 201
Duval, E.M. 256
Duxbury, L. 257

Ekerdt, D.J. 150
Elder, G.H. 294
Ellefsen, B. 157
Erber, J.T. 70

Fa-Kaji, N. 70
Fedor, D.B. 158
Feinberg, B. 196
Feldman, D.C. 38, 129, 151, 182, 193, 205, 255
Ferris, G.R. 149
Fields, D. 104
Finegold, D. 152
Finkelstein, L.M. 37, 64, 68–70, 76–77, 103, 106, 115, 125, 174, 257
Fisher, G.G. 134
Fisk, A.D. 239
Fiske, S.T. 61–63, 78, 303
Foreman, M. 110
Forrier, A. 133
Franz, G. 183

Frese, M. 178
Fritzche, B. 63
Fusilier, M.R. 75

García-Ballesteros, M. 180
Gegenfurtner, A. 176
George, G. 137, 139
Geyer, P.D. 149
Gielens, T. 139
Ginther, N.M. 17
Goffman, E. 34–35
Goldberg, C.B. 70, 104, 115
Golom, F.D. 44
Goodkind, D.E. 2
Goodman, J. 104
Gordon, R.A. 68–69, 74
Grant, A.M. 221
Green, S.G. 162
Greller, M.M. 124, 158–159
Griffin, B. 17
Grosch, J.W. 134
Guerrero, L. 38

Haefner, J.E. 75
Hagestad, G.O. 77, 79
Hamann, D.J. 103
Hammer, L.B. 125
Hanke, K. 306
Hanrahan, E.A. 103, 125
Hanscom, M.E. 301
Harper, S. 137, 139
Hassell, B.L. 74
Hastings, S.B. 129
He, W. 2, 296–300
Hebl, M.R. 70
Hedge, J.W. 137
Helson, R. 131
Hendrick, J. 160
Heraty, N. 303
Herold, D.M. 158
Hertel, G. 124
Herzberg, F.I. 149
Hesketh, B. 17
Higgins, C. 257
Hill, R.L. 256
Hitt, M.A. 75
Ho, J.H. 276
Hollensbe, E.C. 182
Huang, L.-L. 306
Hughes, T.L. 45

Ilmarinen, J. & V. 134
Innocenti, L. 128, 149

Jacobson, J.D. 160
James, J.B. 154
Jansen, P.G.W. 163, 176
Jerdee, T.H. 64, 106
Jex, S.M. 241
Jiménez, I. 304
Jones, C. 131
Joshi, A. 183
Junco, E. 116
Jung, Y. 203

Kacmar, K.M. 149, 152
Kanfer, R. 103, 127, 160
Kang, S.K. 42
Katz, I.M. 179
Kautonen, T. 207
Keenan, T.A. 174
Kerman, S.C. 174
Kibler, E. 207
Kinnunen, U. 134
Kinsella, K.G. 296
Kirves, K. 134
Kite, M.E. 44, 68, 74
Kooij, D.T.A.M. 135, 149–150, 163, 263
Kowal, P. 2
Kraiger, K. 132
Krampe, R.T. 235
Krapp, A. 175
Kulik, C.T. 65, 137, 139
Kunze, F. 218–219
Kwan, V.S.Y. 131
Kyndt, E. 184

Lagacé, M. 76
Lakhdari, M. 158
Lanivich, S.E. 116
Lankau, M.J. 42
Lavigne, K.N. 179, 203
Lawrence, B.S. 69, 71
Lee, C. 257
Lee, J.A. 68, 75
Lee, M.D. 281
Lee, S.Y. 75
Lepisto, L.R. 21
Leviatan, U. 159
Levine, R. 17
Levy, B.R. 77
Liberman, B.E. 44
Liker, J.K. 294
Loh, V. 17
Long, B.A. 70
Lorence, J. 152
Lyons, S.T. 182

Man-hung Ngan, R.M.H. 62
Marcus, J. 63
Mariappanadar, S. 20
Martin, G. 23
Masterson, S.S. 182
Mäkikangas, A. 134
Matthews, R. 146
Maurer, T.J. 64, 153, 158
Mayes, B.T. 218
McCabe, S.E. 45
McCarthy, J. 303
McDaniel, M.A. 126, 137
McEvoy, G.M. 126
McGonagle, A.K. 134
McKechnie, S. 154
Meléndez, J.C. 180
Meyers, C. 139
Miene, P.K. 62
Minniti, M. 207
Mitchell, T.R. 196–198
Mohrman, S. 152
Moon, H. 305
Mor-Barak, M. 159–160
Morgeson, F.P. 68
Morin, L. 158
Müller, A. 266

Nauta, A. 134
Nesselroade, J.R. 294
Ng, T.W.H. 38, 126, 129, 151, 182, 255
Niessen, C. 181
North, M.S. 63, 78, 303
Nussbaum, J.F. 77

Oates, G. 126
Ohly, S. 181
Olson, D.A. 194
Ones, D.S. 129
Ostroff, C. 196
Oswald, A. 149
Ovejero, A. 304

Park, D.C. 65, 126
Parlamis, J.D. 70
Paullin, C. 24, 26
Peeters, M. 179
Peng, X. 241
Perrewe, P.L. 74
Perry, E.L. 65, 69–70, 77, 115
Pesta, B.J. 126, 137
Pettigrew, T.F. 48
Pezzuti, L. 126
Phelps, J.A. 259

Phillips, D.R. 296
Pond, S.B. 149
Posthuma, R.A. 38
Profili, S. 128, 149

Quinn, J.F. 19

Rau, B.L. 23, 26
Raymo, J.M. 276
Reider, M.H. 68
Reis, C. 308
Renaud, S. 158
Rhodes, S.R. 126, 147–148, 151, 159
Richardson, M. 309
Roberts, B.W. 131
Rosen, B. 64, 106
Roth, P.L. 116
Rothermund, K. 40, 173
Rotolo, C.T. 17
Rudolph, C.W. 37, 124, 179–180, 183, 203, 266
Ruggs, E.N. 70
Ryan, S. 137, 139

Sackett, P.R. 129
Salthouse, T.A. 126, 235
Sammarra, A. 128, 149
Sartori, S. 134
Sawyer, K.B. 125
Schaie, K.W. 130
Schein, E.A. 205
Schooler, C. 126
Schwarz, N. 65
Semeijn, J.H. 134
Severinsson, E. 157
Sewell, C. 74
Sharit, J. 130, 244
Shin, Y. 196
Shoptaugh, C.F. 259
Shore, L.M. 70, 104, 162
Shull, A. 115
Shultz, K.S. 194
Silzer, R. 16
Simonton, D.K. 249
Simpson, P. 158–159
Singer, M.S. 74
Siu, O. 296
Smola, K.W. 164
Snyder, M. 62
Sonnenfeld, J.A. 203
Spindler, K. 104
Spreitzer, G.M. 152
Sterns, H.L. 300

Stroh, L.K. 124, 158–159
Sturman, M.C. 126
Sturn, A. 129
Sukhapure, M. 202
Sutton, C.D. 164
Swanberg, J. 154

Takeuchi, N. 203
Tanguay, J. 76
Taylor, O.A. 129
Teachout, M.S. 132
Thomas, C.L. 103, 125
Thomas-Hunt, M.C. 62
Thornton, W.J. 127
Thoroughgood, C.N. 125
Thrasher, G.R. 299
Tims, M. 163
Tishman, F. 137
Toossi, M. 236
Topa, G. 304
Tornau, K. 178
Treadway, D.C. 262
Triandis, H.C. 75
Truxillo, D.M. 137–138

Uhlenberg, P. 77, 79
Unson, C. 309
Urick, M.J. 182–183
Ursel, N.D. 136

Valero, E. 304
van den Heuvel, M. 179
Van der Heijden, B.I.J.M. 80
Van Iddekinge, C.H. 116
van Kleef, M. 176
Van Looy, S. 137
Van Selm, M. 80
van Vuuren, T. 134
Van Yperen, N.W. 154
Vauclair, C.-M. 306
Vauras, M. 176
Veld, M. 134
Verbruggen, M. 133
Verschuren, P. 160
Viechtbauer, W. 131
Visio, M.E. 259
Vogelsang, E.M. 194
Vygotsky, L.S. 293

Waldman, D.A. 126, 130
Walker, A. 79
Walker, S.S. 70
Walton, K.E. 131

Wanberg, C.R. 17, 103–104
Wang, M. 17, 241
Warr, P. 130, 149, 154
Webster, J.R. 125
Weigelt, O. 129
Weiss, E.M. 64
West, B.T. 45
Widiss, D.A. 110
Wolfson, N. 132
Wrzesniewski, A. 201

Wynne, K.T. 299

Yang, J. 219
Yeung, D.Y. 304

Zabel, K.L. 138, 299
Zacher, H. 37, 124, 179, 203, 219
Zhang, Z. 103
Zhou, X. 304
Zukin, S. 204

SUBJECT INDEX

Page numbers in *italics* denote figures.

AARP, age of eligibility for membership 124
adaptive performance 129–131
age, negative perceptions/social stigma 34
age and work attitudes, context-sensitive research 165
age bias in the workplace: components and meaning 60–61; consequences 75–76; context of occurrence 67–72; cultural context 71–72; cultural/national solutions 79–80; decision-making context 67–69; example of *59, 81*; expanded view 59–82; influence of information on the target 74–75; influence of rater demographics 74; influence of rater's age 72–74; influence of rater's employment type 74; job context 69–70; motivating factors 61–63; organizational context 70–71; the process 63–66; recruitment/retention considerations 22–23; research recommendations 80–81; role of attribution and self-fulfilling prophecies 66–67; role of negative affect in discrimination 65–66; role of rater accountability 69; role of stereotypes in discrimination 64–65; solutions for bias holders 76–77; solutions for bias targets 77–78; solutions for organizations 78–79; value of age discrimination laws 79

age discrimination: cost-based defence 104; damages provisions 105–106; disparate treatment based on stereotypes 106–107; EEOC cases 102–103; as focus of workplace age bias research 60; impact on older workers 103–104; implications of technology 116; as motivation for career change 195–196; as obstacle to career change 200–201; organizational policy options 311–312; as outcome of Western perceptions of old age 283; perceived organizational climate 222–223; removal of protections against 110; role of stereotyping 64–65; value of legislation 79
Age Discrimination in Employment Act (ADEA) of 1967: amendments 113; comparison with Title VII of the Civil Rights Act 105–106; definition of older worker 81; income protections 112–113; treatment of younger workers 105
age stereotypes: dimensions of variation 38; examples of 106; legal protections 106–107; literature review 38; positive 38, 60, 66, 69–70, 73–75; role of at societal level for age-based outcomes 306; role of in discrimination 125
ageism: cultural perspective 306; institutionalization of in humour 79;

Subject Index

legislative perspective 72; prevalence 308; in recruitment language 106–107; role of in discrimination 65; role of in performance assessment 172; and selection practices 311; *see also* age discrimination
age-job satisfaction relationship: developmental explanations 156–157; explanations for 154–157; facet satisfaction 148; form of the relationship 149–150; functional explanations 155–156; implications of retirement 150–151; job change hypothesis 156; overall satisfaction 147–148; U-shaped hypothesis 149
aging: changing perceptions 301–304; cognitive effects 216; cultural influence 305; global rates and trends 1–4; physical effects 215; social-emotional effects 216–217
aging and job performance 125–131; adaptive performance 129–131; broader organizational context 133–135; citizenship performance 127–128; conceptions of age 123–125; counterproductive work behaviour 128–129; employability 133–134; HR perspective 135–137; influence of changes in personality traits 131–137; practical implications 138–139; research recommendations 137–138; sustainability perspective 135; task performance 126–127; technology-based performance 132–133, 240–242; work ability 134–135
aging workforce 4–6; cross-cultural issues 306–308; cross-national issues 308–309; employment law 102–117 (*see also* employment law); HR perspective 135–137; national policy options 309–311; organizational policy options 311–312; role of non-governmental organizations 312; *see also* workforce participation rate
allocation of resources: lifespan perspective 304; for training and development 172–173
anonymity, role of in talent management 27
artificial intelligence 248
attitudes to work *see* work attitudes
attitudes towards aging, cultural variations 303–304

attribution theory 172–173
average life expectancy, global trends 2

baby boom cohort: progressive aging 4; *see also* boomers
behaviour, counterproductive work behaviour 128–129
boomers: age of eligibility for social security benefits 13, 16; and the effects of demographic transition 4; importance of knowledge sharing opportunities 24; marketing research 29; organizational impact of mass retirement 281; and potential retirement funding crisis 273; research recommendations 287–288; social and financial impact 273–274
boredom, as push factor in late career change 194
boundaryless careers 191, 308–309
bridge employment: affective reactions as predictor of interest 20–22; career embeddedness and 204–205; definition and examples 5, 160, 192–193, 281–282; desirable aspects 23; economic considerations 19; implications for organizations 282; motivations for engaging in 20, 160–161, 276–278; organizational vs occupational commitment 21; research recommendations 227, 287; role of society in enabling 285; role of stress in preferences for or against 21

career adaptability: levels of among older workers 203; relationship with job satisfaction 151
career anchors, research recommendations 205–206
career change: the concept 192–193; constraints 200–201; individual-level motivations 193–194; job-level motivations 194–195; occupation-level motivations 195–196; older workers' motivations 193–196; potential costs 194, 199; role of networks 205
career counselling, continuing 18
career crafting 201–203; *see also* career embeddedness
career embeddedness 191–207; career crafting and 201–203; career stability and 196–203; of CEOs 203–204; the concept 196–200; and the concept of career change 192–193; constraints on

332 Subject Index

career embeddedness *continued*
entry into alternative careers 200–201; and motivation to change career 193–196; practical implications 206–207; research recommendations 203–206
career mobility, research limitations 191
career self-management 203
careers, definition 192
caregiving: caring for grandchildren 259–260, 288; consequences for well-being and work outcomes 299; economic value of informal care 299; employment opportunities 299–300; the sandwich generation 260; and work-family conflict 258–260; *see also* eldercare
chronological age: alternative measures of aging 162–164; problems with exclusive use in definitions of aging 124; treatment of in studies of work attitudes and behaviour 164
citizenship performance 127–128
Civil Rights Act, comparison of ADEA with Title VII 105–106
cognitive and affective attitudes: age-related reactions to organizational treatment 154; job involvement and organizational commitment 151–152; towards change and development 152–154
cognitive effects of aging: compensation strategies for older workers 126–127; and work 216
community, role of in career embeddedness 198–199
continuous learning 158, 171, 177, 183, 202
counterproductive work behaviour (CWB) 128–129
creativity, and innovation 180–182
cross-cultural issues: practical implications 316–317; research recommendations 309, 314

decline in demand for labour, as push factor in late career change 195
delayed retirement: affective reactions as determinants of 21; choice factors 16; financial considerations 19; gendered perspective 277–278; increasing interest 18
dementia, global projections 298

demographic deficit, options for addressing 310
demographic transition 1–2, 4
demographic trends: considerations for an aging workforce 305–312; institutional considerations 309–312; practical implications 315; research recommendations 313; and workforce aging/age diversity 295–301; work-relevant consequences 301–305
dependency ratios, expected increase 297
designing for an aging workforce *see* job design
development: core tenets of human development 37; lifespan perspective 37, 293–295
development and training 171–184; *see also* training and development
disability, definition 225
discrimination: impact on life chances 35; impact on physical and mental health 45; intergroup contact theory 48–49; intersection of race and sexual identity at older ages 45; perceived 47, 51, 76, 80, 196; transgender employees' experience of at work 43; *see also* age bias in the workplace; age discrimination; ageism
diversity: diversity issues for an aging workforce 34–51; and intersectionality 36–46; need for in research 236–237; and stigma theory 35–36

economic perspectives: boomers' social and financial impact 273–274; delayed retirement 19; recruitment/retention programs 19–20, 24; retirement and income variability 285–286
eldercare: definition and responsibilities 258–259; health impact on older workers 259; and the life stages model 260; national policy options 310–311; support for carers 265–267
employability: the concept 133–134; job crafting and 183; strategies to enhance messages of 79–80
employee benefits, role of in career embeddedness 199
Employee Retirement Income Security Act (ERISA) of 1974 112–113
employment: changing trends 114–115; new forms of 196

employment law: anti-discrimination legislation 104–106 (*see also* Age Discrimination in Employment Act (ADEA) of 1967); barriers to pursuing cases 109–110; disparate impact theory of liability 108–109; disparate treatment based on stereotypes 106–107; Employee Retirement Income Security Act (ERISA) of 1974 112–113; and the gig economy 115; limits to resources 110–112; occupational health and 225–226; research recommendations 114–117; role of state and local legislatures 113–114
entity theory 173–174
entrepreneurship, and quality of life 207
environment, working *see* workplace environment
experience, as positive stereotype of old age 70, 75
expertise: as compensation for functional decline 126–127; role of in job crafting 179, 184

Fair Labor Standards Act (FLSA) of 1938 105
family: age and work-family conflict 255–265; categories of family size 257; effects of retirement decisions 276; practical implications 266–267; research recommendations 265–266, 277; role of in career embeddedness 200; *see also* work-family conflict
fertility rates: cause and impact of decline 295; global trends 2
fit, role of in career embeddedness 198–199
flexibility of work: and attraction to bridge employment 20; and occupational health 224–225; options for building 20, 24; and remote work opportunities 267; and work-family conflict 266–267
freelance workers, legal protection 115
Frost, Robert 207
future time perspective (FTP): metastereotypes and 76; relationship with motivation to work 163, 216, 263; relationship with work-family conflict 262–263

gender: gendered perspective of workforce participation rate 6, 39; intersectionality of gender identity with sexual orientation and age 43–46; intersectionality with age 39–40; and retirement 277–278
General Aptitude Test Battery 130
generational differences, in work values 156, 163–164, 182–183
generations, contextualised lifespan perspective 37
generativity: definition 221; as motive for bridge employment 161
geriatricians, ageism-related decrease in numbers 300
gerontechnology 237
gig economy: attractions for older workers 236; challenges for older workers 115; the concept 114; legislative perspective 115
global perspectives: lifespan perspective 293–295; population and workforce aging trends 292; in work, aging and retirement 292–317; *see also* demographic trends
Gorsuch, Neil 110
government retirement savings plans 285

health: economic impact of chronic conditions 299; global perspectives on health care 298–300; health promotion 224; healthier lifestyles and human lifespan 34; impact of discrimination 45; implications of retirement and national health care systems 284–285; as motivation to change career 194; practical implications 315–316; as predictor of post-retirement adjustment 18; research recommendations 313–314; wellness model 214; and the workplace environment 214, 217–219; *see also* occupational health
hearing changes, technology and 246–247
human capital theory 158, 172, 179
human development, core tenets 37
humour, institutionalization of ageism in 79

immigration: influence on age distribution of populations 2; options for addressing demographic deficit 310
implicit person theories 172–173
incremental theory 173
informal caregiving, economic value 299
informal learning: and job crafting 177–180; participation of older workers 177–178

innovation, creativity and 180–182
inter-generational interaction, importance of 183
intergroup contact theory 48–49
internet, use of by age group 238
internet-based recruiting, research on 26
intersectionality: definition 36; diversity and 36–46; of gender with age 39–40; intersection of race and sexual identity at older ages 45; lifespan theories 36–37; practical recommendations for individuals 50–51; practical recommendations for organizations 47–49; race/ethnicity and social experiences 36; of race/ethnicity with age 41–43; recommendations for practice 47; research approaches 46; research recommendations 46–47; of sexual orientation and gender identity with age 43–46; social classifications included in new definitions 36; stereotypes of older workers 37–38 (*see also* age stereotypes; stereotypes; stereotypes of older workers)

job change: vs career change 192; hypothesis 156
job control, definition 181
job crafting: definition 179, 221; informal learning and 177–180; occupational health and 221–222; primary behaviours 201–202; research recommendations 287; role of expertise 179, 184; *see also* career crafting
job design: designing supportive environments 245–247; importance of scheduling flexibility 225; lifespan perspective 227; occupational health and 219–221
job embeddedness 196–197; *see also* career embeddedness
job insecurity, health impacts for older workers 218
job involvement, and organizational commitment 151–152
job performance, aging and *see* aging and job performance
job satisfaction: relationship with career adaptability 151; *see also* age-job satisfaction relationship
job security, generational differences in attitudes to 156

lack of appreciation, as push factor in late career change 194–195
lack of fit, as predictor of occupational change 196
learning motivation, and performance predictors of older workers 174–177
learning rates: impact of age on 235; *see also* training and development
life expectancy: expected increase 295–296; global projections 298; increases in 297; WHO healthy life expectancy index 298
Life Reimagined for Work Program 26
lifespan perspectives: of development 37, 293–295; intersectionality 36–37; and work attitudes 159, 163
links, role of in career embeddedness 197–198

marketing, as promising area for research 29
media, portrayal of older workers 70
mental health, impact of intersectional discrimination 45
mentoring 24–25, 27, 221, 250
mortality rates 2, 298, 313

national policy options: for age bias in the workplace 79–80; for an aging workforce 309–311; for eldercare 310–311; for health care 284–285
negative affect, role of in discrimination 65–66
negative perceptions, of age 34
negative stereotypes: of older workers 38; self-efficacy impact 173–174
networks, role of in career mobility 205

occupational health: aging and 213–228; cognitive effects of aging 216; the concept of employee health 213–214; and employee assistance programs 226; and employment legislation 225–226; environmental considerations 217–219 (*see also* workplace environment); and flexibility in scheduling 224–225; health promotion 224; impact of aging processes 215–217; improvement interventions 219–226; and job crafting 221–222; and job design 219–221; and organizational climate/culture 222–223; physical effects of aging 215; practical implications 227–228; research recommendations 227; social-emotional effects of aging 216–217; and training methods 223–224; *see also* health

Occupational Safety and Health (OSH) Act of 1970 225

old age: age discrimination as outcome of Western perceptions 283; cultural variations 302–303; experience as positive stereotype 70, 75; extension of 2

Older Americans Act 124

older employees, recruitment and retention 13–30 (*see also* recruitment/retention of older employees)

older female workers, motivation for return to work 160

older worker, ADEA definition 81

older workers: aging and job performance 125–131 (*see also* aging and job performance); attitudes to career development 150; career adaptability levels 203; childcare responsibilities 259–260, 288; cognitive deficit compensation strategies 126–127; contribution of age-related advantages in emotion regulation to health and well-being of 217; defining 123–125, 235–237, 303–304; effect of workplace environment on 217–219; effects of job characteristics and stressors on health 217–218; effects of organizational climate on health 218–219, 222–223; evolution of the concept 125; impact of discrimination on 103–104; increased opportunities for 104; learning motivation and performance predictors 174–177; levels of career adaptability 203; media portrayals 70; motivations for career change 193–196; organizational support desired by 311; participation in informal learning activities 177–178; permissibility of discrimination in favour of 105; and positive age stereotypes 38, 60, 66, 69–70, 73–75; self-efficacy impact of negative stereotypes 173–174; stereotypes 37–38, 60, 62, 64; training considerations 242–245

Older Workers Benefit Protection Act (OWBPA) 113

organization change, definition 192

organizations: age discrimination policy options 311–312; aging and job performance in the context of 133–135 (*see also* aging and job performance); and citizenship performance 127–128; discrimination climate research 218–219; health effects of organizational climate 218–219, 222–223; modern characteristics of change 152; organizational support desired by older workers 311; policy options for an aging workforce 311–312; and retirement 278–282

part-time work 5, 19, 234, 236, 250, 299

pension systems, large-scale change 279

perceived discrimination 47, 51, 76, 80, 196

performance: adaptive 129–131; citizenship performance 127–128; *see also* aging and job performance

personal finances, as moderator of recruitment/retention programs 19–20

personality: influence of changes on performance 131–137; role of in motivation to change career 193–194

person-job fit 135, 180

phased retirement 19, 24–25, 258

population age, projections 34, *296*

population aging: the concept 2; declining fertility levels as catalyst for 297; key driver of 1; rate of increase 1

population growth, global perspectives 297

population size, global trends 2

population stability, required birth rate 2

post-World War II baby boom 4; *see also* boomers

poverty 161, 286, 305; global variation in risk rate for older people 305

predictors, of individual retirement choices 275

productivity, improvement framework 241

promotion opportunities, role of in career embeddedness 200

race/ethnicity: intersectionality with age 41–43; and managerial stereotypes 42; and social experiences 36

recruitment/retention of older employees: performance assessment 17; practical implications 29–30; research recommendations 27–29; social media and age-targeted recruitment 117;

336 Subject Index

recruitment/retention of older employees *continued*
 steps 14; talent management approach to workforce planning 14–17; *see also* recruitment/retention programs
recruitment/retention programs: affective reactions 20–22; age bias considerations 22–23; communication modality 26; design 17–22; enrichment considerations 24–25; evaluation 27; financial incentive considerations 24; flexibility considerations 20, 24; implementation 22–26; implications for design and implementation 30; implications for planning 29–30; personal finances as moderator of 19–20; recommendations for design and implementation research 28–29; recommendations for planning 27; social considerations 25–26
remote working 267
replacement rate 2
research recommendations: age bias in the workplace 80–81; aging and job performance 137–138; boomer generation 287–288; bridge employment 227, 287; career anchors 205–206; career embeddedness 203–206; caring for grandchildren 288; cross-cultural issues 309, 314; demographic trends 313; employment law 114–117; family issues 265–266, 277; health 313–314; intersectionality 46–47; job crafting 287; occupational health 227; recruitment/retention of older employees 27–29; retirement 277, 286–288; retirement age 313; successful aging at work 138; technology 249–250; training and development 182–183; work attitudes 164–165; worker mobility 314; work–family conflict 299; workforce aging 313
resources: allocation of *see* allocation of resources; loss of in retirement 284
retirement: boomers and potential funding crisis 273; as career development stage 17; career embeddedness and 204–205; changing perceptions 304–305; implications for national health care systems 284–285; and income variability 285–286; individual level 275–278; and loss of resources 284; organization level 278–282; pension systems 279;

as personal decision 274; phased 19, 24–25, 258; research recommendations 277, 286–288; role of government savings plans 285; societal level 282–286; status comparison with unemployment 283–284; types of 276; *see also* delayed retirement
retirement age: governing factors 16; increase as solution to demographic deficit 310; research recommendations 313

sacrifices, role of in career embeddedness 199–200
sandwich generation 260
selection, optimization, and compensation (SOC) training 265–266
self-efficacy: career-relevant development and 153; impact of stereotyping 181; resilience creation role 50; role of job crafting 180
self-employment, as post-retirement option 22
senior executives, career challenges 203–204
seniority pay systems, impact 280
sexual identity: implicit inversion hypothesis 44; and managerial stereotypes 44–45; transgender employees' experience of discrimination at work 43
sexual orientation, and experience of discrimination at work 43
similarity-attraction theory 69
skills, as push factor in late career change 195
social approval, as predictor of post-retirement career intentions 20
social bias, core motives 62
social considerations, in the work environment 25–26
social experiences, race/ethnicity and 36
social identity theory, and work attitudes 163
social judgeability theory 68
social media: and age-targeted recruitment 117; use of in the applicant screening process 116–117
social security benefits, age of eligibility for boomer cohort 13, 16
socioeconomic status, relationship with work-family conflict 258
socioemotional selectivity theory 262–263

Subject Index

stereotypes: age-based 37–38, 60, 62, 64; common stereotypes of older workers 38 (*see also* stereotypes of older workers); consequences of co-occurrence 42–43, 45; drivers of stereotyping 63; of LGBT people 44–45; managerial stereotypes 42, 44–45; *see also* age stereotypes; stereotypes of older workers

stereotypes of older workers: disability stereotypes 46; gender stereotypes 39–40; individual-level solutions 50–51; negative 38; organizational-level solutions 47–49; positive 38, 60, 66, 69–70, 73–75; racial and ethnic minority stereotypes 41–43; role in discrimination 64; role of in age discrimination 64–65; sexual or gender minority identity stereotypes 45–46; *see also* age stereotypes

stigma: contact hypothesis 48–49; definition and impact 34; examples of pre-existing stigmas 34; Goffman's theory 35–36; workplace impact of intersection of pre-existing stigmas with age 35 (*see also* intersectionality)

stress: effects of job characteristics and stressors on health of older workers 217–218; as predictor of post retirement work/career intentions 21; as push factor in late career change 194; role of in preferences for or against bridge employment 21

successful aging at work: the concept 124; HR perspective 137; psychological and organizational climate for 219; research recommendations 138; role of organizational climate 219, 223; sustainability perspective 135

sustainability perspective, of aging and job performance 135

talent management 14–17; four-stage model 16; role of anonymity 27; socially oriented systems approach 16

task interdependence, role of in career embeddedness 197–198

technology 234–251; adoption and use framework *239*; age-related use 237–239; artificial intelligence 248; definition 237; and the future of work 248–249; and hearing changes 246–247; implications for age-based discrimination 116; input/output devices 245, 247–248; internet use by age group 238; lack of skills as barrier to employment 242; as obstacle to career change 201; older workers' interaction 239–240; performance-related perspectives 133, 240–242; practical implications 250–251; productivity improvement framework 241; research recommendations 249–250; retraining issues 240–241; supportive work environments 245–247; training considerations for older adults 242–245; and vision changes 245–246

telework 267

Title VII of the Civil Rights Act, comparison of ADEA with 105–106

training: age discrimination in access to 200–201; definition 223; pace and timing considerations for older adults 244

training and development: allocation of resources 172–173; creativity and innovation 180–182; HR perspectives 183–184; impact of perceived support 176–177, 180; informal learning and job crafting 177–180; learning motivation and performance predictors of older workers 174–177; occupational health perspective 223–224; practical implications 183–184; research recommendations 182–183; role of self-efficacy beliefs 153; on SOC strategies 265–266; technology considerations for older adults 242–245; theoretical frameworks 171–174

transgender employees, experience of discrimination at work 43

unemployment: relationship of duration with age 103–104; status comparison with retirement 283–284

upcoming retirements, typology of organizations' reactions 29

vision changes, technology and 245–246
volunteering, as post-retirement option 22

wealth, and motivation to change career 194
wellness model, of health 214
women, workforce participation rates 39
work ability, the concept 134–135

work and retirement, global perspectives 300–301
work attitudes: age and job satisfaction 147–151 (*see also* age-job satisfaction relationship); career development 150; cognitive and affective attitudes 151–154; the concept 147; and emerging measures of aging 162–164; explanations for positive attitudes among older workers 154–157; organizational changes and 153–154; research recommendations 164–165; role of intersectionality and multiple discrimination 161–162; self-efficacy beliefs for development 153; work motivation and motives 157–161
work motivation: motives in understudied populations 160–161; varying motives and values 158–160
worker mobility: practical implications 316; research recommendations 314
work-family conflict: care supports for dependants 265; caregiving responsibilities 258–260; coping strategies 260–261; and flexible scheduling 266–267; and identification with work 264–265; impact of lower socioeconomic status 258; life and career stages 256–258; lifespan approaches 261–262; relationship with age 255–265; and remote work opportunities 267; research recommendations 299; socioemotional selectivity theory 262–263; training on SOC strategies 265–266; and work motivation 263–264

workforce aging: practical implications 315; research recommendations 313
workforce participation rate: changes over time 4–6; definition 4; future expectations 4; gendered perspective 6, 39; low-income countries 300; racial and ethnic diversity perspective 6
workforce planning: range of techniques 14; talent management approach 14–17
work–life balance: attitudes to 256; changing perceptions 182–183; correlation with organizational commitment 152; flexibility fit and 139, 267
workload, health impacts for older workers 218
workplace environment: increasing unpredictability 133; as influencing factor in employment considerations 22; and job satisfaction 149; person-environment fit 214; relationship with age 146; relationship with stereotyping 43; role of in research 235, 251; social considerations 25–26; supportive 245–247; technology perspective 242, 246–247
World Health Organization's (WHO), healthy life expectancy (HALE) index 298
worldwide population, rate of aging 1

younger workers, lack of protection from age discrimination under the ADEA 105